Inequality in American Communities

This is a volume of

Quantitative Studies in Social Relations

Consulting Editor: Peter H. Rossi, University of Massachusetts, Amherst, Massachusetts

A complete list of titles in this series appears at the end of this volume.

Inequality in American Communities

RICHARD F. CURTIS *arnsworth*
Department of Sociology
University of Arizona
Tucson, Arizona

ELTON F. JACKSON
Department of Sociology
Indiana University
Bloomington, Indiana

ACADEMIC PRESS **New York** **San Francisco** **London**
A Subsidiary of Harcourt Brace Jovanovich, Publishers

To
Mitzi
and
Janet

ACADEMIC PRESS, INC.
111 Fifth Avenue, New York, New York 10003

United Kingdom Edition published by
ACADEMIC PRESS, INC. (LONDON) LTD.
24/28 Oval Road, London NW1

Library of Congress Cataloging in Publication Data

Curtis, Richard Farnsworth,   Date
      Inequality in American communities.

      (Quantitative studies in social relations)
      Bibliography: p.
      1.   Social classes—United States.   2.   Social
status.   3.   Equality.   4.   Cities and towns—
United States.   I.   Jackson, Elton F., joint
author.   II.   Title.
HN90.S6C87   301.44'0973   76-19485
ISBN 0—12—200250—4

PRINTED IN THE UNITED STATES OF AMERICA

CONTENTS

Part II Consequences of Social Rank

PREFACE

This is an empirical study of stratification in American communities and its influences on individual Americans. Many difficulties in reading (or writing) such a research report stem from the fact that the problems of large-scale empirical research are complicated enough in their own right to distract the reader's (or writer's) attention from the sociological interests that led to the study in the first place. Let us consider some of these difficulties.

Our goals in reporting this investigation were (a) to present our findings and conclusions clearly within the framework of substantive sociological interests in stratification and (b) to provide the level of detail required for readers to judge the adequacy of the data and the research logic, and to make independent judgments of the relevance and implications of the findings. To some extent, these goals are mutually opposed, and that opposition has led to some potential ambiguities in the language of this book.

Our language, for example, could be taken to imply proof of the nature and direction of causal relations where no such interpretation is intended. The reader is warned of our causal language habits at appropriate points in Chapter 1 and Chapter 3. We have attempted to write in English as well as statistical terminology, but may well have been carried away at times by the relative simplicity of statistical styles of problem formulation.

We have made no attempt to review systematically the enormous literature on the various topics covered in the data, but have used ideas from that literature freely. We assume general familiarity with the appropriate stratification literature on the part of the reader.

The most severe language problem is probably a matter of apparent overgeneralization of the data. We intend to distinguish clearly between strict statements of findings, referring to adult male family heads in six specified communities as of a given date on the one hand, and remarks on American communities, stratification in general, or the human condition on the other. Since such larger concerns were the motivation for the study, the language we use to discuss findings may occasionally imply greater literal generalization than we intended.

The nature of our data results in an overuse of the word "men." For reasons discussed in Chapter 1, the sample was limited to adult male family heads. To refer to respondents as "people" would be correct (as far as it goes), but might be understood to imply that we think adult women or young boys necessarily react to their social statuses in the same way that our respondents do. In the long run, of course, we are more interested in the human condition than in the specific plight of unemployed agricultural workers in Safford, Arizona, so that we often use the word "people" in broader discussions of social stratification. In some contexts, however, it is not altogether clear which term is appropriate because we do not know the outer limits of the universe of social relations to which our findings may, in fact, apply.

Built-in attempts at replication are an important feature of this research. Scientific generalizations are more firmly based on replicability than on rigid sampling. That a given relationship appears in all six of our communities, of course, does not prove that (therefore) the relationship necessarily exists in all American communities. Yet we are interested in exploring the relative replicability of different relationships, and our results indicate that some propositions apply more widely than others. The language we use in drawing conclusions may be misleading in implying firm evidence of the applicability of results to all U.S. communities when in fact we have only given propositions a few chances to fail in generality.

We have tried to keep technical details, tables, data descriptions, and discussions of research procedures to the minimum required for the reader's full understanding. Nevertheless, some readers will want more information, whereas others will feel that the major points of the project have been lost in a mass of detail. We sympathize with both points of view.

Our approach to the relationship between the data and broader theoretical interests is neither an attempt to state and test a unified, general theory of stratification nor is it simple induction. This issue is discussed in Chapter 1 and in Chapter 5. Some of our apparent vacillation regarding hypothesis-testing can be explained by our conviction that what we did *not* find has as much significance and importance as what we *did* find.

We could not have done this research, of course, without vast assistance of various kinds. The basic funding for this project was provided by a series of research grants from the National Institute of Mental Health (MH 08157, MH 12263, MH 10991, and MH 21261). The project was also supported by the National Science Foundation (GS 1020), and additional support was forthcoming from Indiana University Faculty Research Grants-in-Aid, and the Center for Applied Manpower and Occupational Studies (Indiana University). Computer time and consultation were made available by the University of Arizona Computer Center and the Marshal H. Wrubel Computing Center of Indiana University.

Data were collected by Elmo Roper Associates (Carolyn Crusius, study director) and by the Indianapolis Area Project of Indiana University. Administrative support was provided by the Institute of Social Research of the Sociology Department, Indiana University, directed by Sheldon Stryker and later by Marvin Olsen. Additional interviews in Indianapolis were collected by a group of professional interviewers organized and supervised by Patricia Selmanoff. Special credit is due Adah Thomas and Opal Barnard of this group.

For useful and penetrating comments on early drafts of the manuscript, we wish to thank Lawrence Hazelrigg, Richard L. Simpson, Angela V. Lane, and several anonymous reviewers. We are indebted to Ralph Turner for his far-sighted suggestions as a site visitor, early in the course of the project.

Whatever merit this project may have is in large part due to the efforts and talents of the many research assistants who have been associated with it over the years. In particular, we owe special debts to Dianne Timbers Fairbank and Michael Cabat. Others who can be singled out include Reta Artz, Penny Rosel, and Judy (Tully) Corder–Bolz, but we also wish to express our appreciation for the work of Charles Starnes, Albert Stephen Gates, Barbara Ibrahim, Patrick Horan, Robert Wait, and Barbara Lettes.

We would like to thank the participants of the Indianapolis Area Project, as well as John T. Liell, who taught the associated methods training course. Research supervisors included Marlene Simon, Robert Cushing, and Robert Stirling. The students were Prudence Amos, Bernadette Barry, Ann Boone, Gerald Bronitsky, George Crum, Vilis Donis, Veronica Elias, Mary Ann Brezina, William Fox, Phyllis Greenfield, Kathryn Grzelkowski, Suzanne Hubbard, Bill Kenworthy, Nancy Malone, Theodore Sawyer, Sheldon Sklare, Lowell Spencer, James Teevan, Douglas Vice, Robert Wait, Philip Weinberger, and Karen Yinger.

For secretarial assistance, we would like to thank Nancy Edwards, Martha Taysom, and Karen Edwards. The final manuscript was typed by Al Hite, Debbie Adams, Sandy Goers, and Dorothy Weise.

Acknowledgment is made to reprint material from the following:

p. 223: From Lipset, Seymour Martin, "Social Stratification and right-wing extremism," *The British Journal of Sociology* 1959, *10*, 346–382.

p. 285: From Lipset, Seymour Martin, *Political man: The social bases of*

1

INEQUALITY IN THE COMMUNITY

Two universals, community and inequality, form the theme of this study. Almost all Americans now live in cities or towns. In their daily round among their fellow townsfolk, they are constantly presented with evidence that they are superior to some in the community and inferior to others. Although the city is not the only arena for ranking and comparison, it is a most immediate and tangible one. Our problem in this book is to understand how inequality is patterned in American communities and how those patterns influence the attitudes and behavior of the community residents.

The data for this study come from sample surveys in six American communities, chosen to differ in size and region. In each survey, male heads of households were questioned about attributes that ranked them in the system of inequality and about a variety of attitudes and behaviors that might be affected by their ranks. Our basic analyses ask how social rank affects various attitudes and behaviors and compare these effects from community to community.

The major questions of the study are

- 1. How (and how much) do the patterns and processes of inequality differ in the different communities?
2. How are individuals affected by their ranks within the community system of inequality?
3. How (and how much) do the communities differ in the ways in which social rank affects individuals; that is, are the communities different *contexts* for rank effects on individual behavior?

The basic focus of our study, then, is how a person's life is shaped by his position in a local structure of inequality.

THEORETICAL ORIENTATIONS ON COMMUNITY STRATIFICATION

To introduce and provide a theoretical basis for the rest of the study, we need here to raise and discuss three topics:

1. What concepts and assumptions are most fruitful in thinking about social inequality?
2. How might high or low social rank affect attitudes and behavior?
3. How might systems of inequality differ from community to community?

Our answers to these questions do not form a fully specified, tightly organized body of unified theory; they are tentative orientations only. But these orientations help to explain why we did this study, why we did it the way we did, and in what ways the findings have significance for sociological theory.

Concepts and Assumptions in Thinking about Inequality

What is the best way to conceptualize social inequality? One popular vision of inequality in American communities describes a set of prestige groups, established by a common sense of social worth and identified by the recognizable and distinctive styles of life of group members, particularly those aspects of life having to do with intimate association: marriage, visiting, neighboring, social club membership, etc. (see, for example, Warner 1949: Chapter 9, 1960: Chapter 1 or Coleman and Neugarten 1971:5–6). The basic feature of this view is that a single dimension of superiority–inferiority is produced in American communities by the fact that prestige tends to organize social life.

Other well-known approaches to inequality have also posited single dimensions of superiority–inferiority, but differ basically in what it is that tends to organize social life, producing such a dimension. Karl Marx felt that no matter what else might go on in a society, the ultimate organizing principle was the division of a population into two classes: those who own the means of production and those who do not. Others have felt that the basic issue was the exercise of authority and influence (e.g., see Mills 1956). A multitude of variants on these theoretical themes can be distinguished by answers to other questions, for example, is behavior influenced by deprivation or by identification with others at the same level of deprivation (Centers 1949)? What status distinctions are clearly enough shared by all members of a society to constitute aspects of culture (Davis, Gardner, and Gardner 1941)? How are understandings of social status passed on between generations (Hollingshead 1949)? What all these approaches have in common, however, is their insistence that there is one dimension of superiority–inferiority in social organization.

Our approach is the contrary: It assumes that there are many different ways in which one person can be superior or inferior to another. Some of these are income, education, and occupation. In this study, our term for such variables will be *rank dimension* and our theoretical orientation thus begins with the observation that inequality may be *multidimensional*.[1] This formulation does not prohibit one from thinking about a unidimensional set of classes; such a situation would arise whenever one rank dimension were paramount or whenever the correlations between all pairs of important rank dimensions were extremely high. But a multidimensional view also allows for other possibilities, since it leaves the saliency of the rank dimensions and the degree of correlation between them open for theoretical speculation or empirical verification. The multidimensional view also raises questions obscured by an a priori, unidimensional view, such as which form of social rank has the most effect on a given attitude or behavior, or whether holding high position on one rank dimension and low on another might have special effects on the individual in that anomalous position.

The distinction between uni- and multidimensional theories of stratification has many important logical implications that may not meet the eye immediately. For example, consider an auto mechanic and an assistant professor of sociology, both of whom earn $12,000 a year. How do their ranks differ? A multidimensional theorist would insist that their income ranks are identical, though the individuals might differ in other respects. A unidimensional theorist, on the other hand, would say that the social status of the mechanic was lower, though not so much lower as that of a $10,000 a year mechanic. Unidimensional theory necessarily implies some kind of averaging procedure, so that high income and low education add up to medium status, while multidimensional theory implies that high income is high income, no matter what may be experienced along with it.

A second fundamental element in our orientation is that these rank dimensions are related in a *causal process*. This point of view has been developed most convincingly in empirical form by Blau and Duncan in *The American Occupational Structure* (1967). Rank dimensions form a process in two senses. First, a person growing into maturity begins with one or more origin ranks (for example, father's occupation) and successively attains a given level of education, followed by occupational and income attainment, which themselves may well change in the course of a career. Second, and more fundamentally, the rank dimensions are combined in a process because a

---

[1]The multidimensional position is hardly an odd one in sociology, having been presented early by both Weber (1925) and Sorokin (1927:11–12). Our position here draws heavily from the theoretical orientations of Werner Landecker and Gerhard Lenski (see Freedman *et al.* 1956:Chapter 7; Landecker 1960a, 1960b; and Lenski 1966:Chapters 10–12).

person's position on one dimension influences his chances of attaining a given level on another (see Blau and Duncan 1967:163–241; Sewell *et al.* 1970; Sewell and Hauser 1975).

To this point, our conceptual apparatus includes a number of more or less specific rank dimensions, plus the notion that the causal relations between them form a process. The next step is the assumption that one general feature of this process is *equilibration*. We have borrowed this somewhat unwieldy term from Benoit–Smullyan, who defines it as follows:

> As a result of status conversion processes which are normally at work in every society, there exists a real tendency for the different types of status to reach a common level, i.e., for a man's position in the economic hierarchy to match his position in the political hierarchy and for the latter to accord with his position in the hierarchy of prestige, etc. This tendency may conveniently be called "status equilibration" . . . [1944:160].

In the present context, of course, we are concerned with more specific dimensions than overall political or prestige hierarchies, but the same line of argument applies.

Several kinds of "conversion processes" seem to produce equilibration. Parents attempt to insure that their children will enjoy at least the same level of advantages that they themselves do. Advantages thus tend to persist from generation to generation, producing a positive correlation between origin and current ranks. Rank on some dimensions, such as education, provide access or leverage to attain rank on other dimensions, such as occupation or income. People tend to associate with people somewhat like themselves in terms of rank, thus promoting equilibration between such dimensions as the education of a woman and the occupation of her husband.

We think it most helpful to conceptualize equilibration as varying in degree, rather than as an all-or-none state. The tendency toward equilibration is never absent—unless some very unusual manipulations are going on, rank dimensions will always be correlated positively. But a very high degree of equilibration also seems very unlikely: "In a dynamic and mobile society status equilibrium is always being disturbed since pronounced changes in status occur ordinarily in only one type of status at first, and are only gradually 'converted' into equivalent statuses in the other hierarchies (Benoit–Smullyan, 1944:160)." Hence, the strength of the positive correlations, reflecting the strength of the various tendencies toward equilibration, is thus left as a variable. In this way, the conceptual apparatus can embrace both weakly organized and tightly organized systems of stratification. If the tendencies toward equilibration are very strong, the rank dimensions will be closely related and the system can then be thought of as a single dimension. But this simplification is not justified in describing other situations.

Inequality becomes most vivid when embodied in social groups, that is, in situations in which most of the people in the community or society collect themselves into two or more superior and subordinate groups. One important element in the formation of these groups is the development of boundaries to social interaction, so that relationships of, for example, marriage and friendship tend to be found mainly within such groups rather than between them. Such a set of ranked groups may also develop, out of their shared interaction, different styles of life or subcultures, including shared symbols and possibly attitudes of hostility toward other such groups.

Our tentative orientation is to consider the formation of such groups very unlikely unless the several rank dimensions are so highly related as to approximate a grand overall dimension. Such groups might also form if one rank dimension became so salient in the society as to override other forms of superiority and inferiority. Even this, however, is but a necessary condition, for a single overall or specific rank dimension could exist as a more or less unbroken continuum, without boundaries in terms of social relationships or differences in life styles existing at any point. Hence, we consider the formation of groups (or "organized classes," which may or may not have distinctive subcultures) based on inequality as a matter of degree and a subject for theoretical explanation and empirical exploration.

An additional comment is necessary to deal with racial–ethnic rank. In some past work (e.g., Hollingshead and Redlich 1958:64–65), this variable has been treated as a system of categories which divides a community into racial–ethnic (and religious) subcommunities, each such subcommunity having a somewhat different system of stratification. Although this view is not spelled out in detail, it seems to imply either that racial and ethnic subcommunities are not ranked in comparison with each other or if they are, they are separated by clear social boundaries from one another. We again regard such a view as binding the investigator to a priori assumptions about matters that are better settled by looking and seeing.

We begin by treating racial–ethnic rank simply as a rank dimension, such as occupation and education. We only assume a priori that racial and ethnic categories are subject to ranking, hence denying the assumption that they must necessarily be equal and independent. In most settings, racial–ethnic rank is an attribute which powerfully affects the prestige one is accorded and the chances one has of attaining high rank on other dimensions. In these respects, it is like any other rank variable, differing mainly in that mobility along it is less possible. As with other dimensions, we leave open the question of the salience of the ranking and the existence of boundaries in terms of social interaction. If clear social boundaries empirically appear on the racial–ethnic dimension and, further, this dimension were found to be more or less unrelated to other rank dimensions, then the view would be supported of independent subcommunities, each with its own system of inequality. But we do not wish to adopt this possible (and rather unlikely, we think) outcome as an a priori assumption about how communities are organized.

How Social Rank Affects Behavior

We now turn to the second question: How might high or low position on a dimension of social rank affect a person's attitudes and behavior? Here again we want to outline a general framework of possible processes which can fit many different situations.

Our basic assumption, which follows almost automatically from any definition of social rank, is that high rank is rewarding and low rank depriving. Low rank deprives, first of all, because the comparison with others better off is inherently galling. Low rank also, in general, means fewer resources for achieving goals (money is the most obvious example, but not the only one); hence, low rank means experiencing failure and frustration more often. The lack of resources also means that life is more fragile, people of low rank are less protected from sudden, perhaps chance, episodes of trouble. A banker on crutches, for example, has only to endure a few smiles-behind-hands; a construction laborer in the same situation will lose pay he may desperately need.[2] Individuals' reactions to their low (or high) rank may depend upon the extent to which the associated deprivations (or rewards) are perceived or felt. In some conditions, deprivations may be keenly and immediately felt and hence directly translated to reactions. Perhaps more commonly, however, adults adapt and come to terms with their relative rank so that the routines of their lives are built on a more or less ungracious acceptance of prevailing inequalities (in Auden's ironic line, ". . . the poor have the sufferings to which they are fairly accustomed . . ."). In such instances, the differences in attitude and behavior of persons of high and low rank may not be great.

In other words, the degree of felt deprivation may be an important intervening variable between objective rank and behavior. If felt deprivation plays a central intervening role, then the spread in *satisfaction* between the top and the bottom of a ranked group remaining after people have made their adjustments would be more crucial in predicting behavior than the spread in income or other forms of objective rank. We shall investigate some of these issues in Chapter 6 and following chapters.

The spread in felt deprivation depends on several features of the social context. First, and obviously, there tend to be greater differences in felt deprivation where differences in objective deprivation are greater. However, the actual amount of deprivation may have little effect on felt deprivation if true inequality is either hidden from view or muffled about by cultural myths. If the poor are hidden away, the rich need not confront them, but neither need the poor confront the rich. Conversely, one of the results of

[2] It is true that high rank may often bring with it a variety of disadvantages such as the envy of others, and difficulty in establishing relationships with "inferiors." However, it is difficult to believe that this order of problems is sufficient to make high rank as depriving as low rank. This matter will receive further discussion in Chapter 6.

urban concentration is that poor inhabitants of the central city are exposed to great wealth whenever they go downtown. Mass transit and mass media both keep inequality in view.

Myths or ideologies that can affect felt deprivation come in several forms. A general ideology which ascribes the worth of a person to individual efforts at one's own level—executive or janitor—and not to the level itself helps people to come to terms with low status. Cultural definitions of legitimacy or fairness may do the same; higher incomes may be cheerfully granted to physicians if they are thought to be on call at all hours. These ideologies run in the direction of justifying inequalities. Myths of the opposite type may also be current, ideologies that sensitize people to their disadvantages and emphasize that high rank may not be, indeed probably cannot be, legitimately justified. If these ideologies are current, then the spread in felt dissatisfaction may be greater than the spread in objective deprivation.

So far, we have argued that low rank, or objective deprivation, may be translated into felt deprivation that in turn may lead to attitudes such as anomia or behavior such as voting for a given political party. This process could reflect decision-making entirely at the individual level, but it may also be substantially guided or modified by the cultural and social context.

A cultural process that might account for the relationships between rank and behavior is institutionalization, that is, a process in which the behaviors appropriate to the several ranks are culturally prescribed, embodied in formal norms, and enforced by a variety of sanctions. More realistically, culture may set forth rank-related expectations which serve to orient behavior while not dictating its details. Potentially, much of the behavior and attitudes of people of different rank could be explained by culture *about* social rank. People of low income would vote Democratic because they were expected to do so. In the extreme case, this model could explain rank-related behavior without resorting at all to any notions of deprivation or dissatisfaction at the level of the individual.

Such a degree of institutionalization is largely unfamiliar to most contemporary Americans. Nevertheless, a few illustrations can be found. For example, some cultural prescriptions affect the behavior of a real estate agent in advising a "good area" for an executive on the one hand or a craftsman or laborer on the other. The proper behavior of blacks to whites and vice versa is partly institutionalized also. Like the institutionalized relations between the sexes, these are being disestablished rapidly enough to cause conflict and lack of consensus, but not rapidly enough to satisfy the group disadvantaged by the cultural prescriptions. Some of the analyses in Chapter 4, Perceptions of Inequality, bear on the issue of cultural institutionalization of rank behavior.

The pattern of social relations between individuals may also affect the way in which differences in rank are translated into differences in behavior. The extent to which a person associates with others, and the social rank of those others, should affect his reactions to his own rank. Suppose that in a given setting people usually associate with others of the same rank, so that most groups were more or less homogeneous by rank. These groups would exercise some control over their members' behaviors through the normal mechanisms of commitment and reinforcement. If so, individual behavior could be as strongly related to social rank *as if* status behavior were in-stitutionalized in the general culture of the society. The classic formulation of these effects is Marx's, in which a growing awareness of common class interests bring workers together to a mutual definition of their situation and common action in support of their aims.

However, the results of social interaction between individuals of the same rank may not necessarily be behavior focused on their class or rank interests, but may well include many elements simply growing out of the common culture of the groups they belong to. For example, such a pattern of group membership might well yield differences between ranks in voting and party identification beyond that due to differences in the parties' stands on class-related controversies. In other words, if the network of interactions is con-gruent with the structure of inequality, rank may be related to behavior in ways that neither society-wide institutionalization nor "class interests" could explain. This model of behavior resembles the descriptions of classes advanced by Warner and Lunt (1941:378–450) and Hollingshead (1949:83–120) in the communities they studied.

The extent to which social networks are built within rank levels, then, is an important contextual condition affecting the relationship between rank and individual behavior. If people tend to associate with others freely across rank levels, the relationship between social rank and behavior should to that extent be weakened. The analyses in Chapter 7, on informal social participa-tion, will treat the issue of homogamy by rank to some extent.

The family and the school are two contexts for interaction that may have special importance in affecting the way in which rank is related to individual behavior. First, people at a given level in occupation or income may tend to act alike and differently from people at other levels because they may have been brought up in the same way by their parents. This means that some patterns of behavior might be located in a given rank "stratum" because a given culture is transmitted from generation to generation rather than due to the current interests of people at that rank level (for example, see Hodge and Treiman's argument that participation in formal organizations depends sub-stantially on patterns of joining inherited from parents, 1968b).

Education may have the same effect; people who have had the same educational experiences may tend to develop somewhat similar patterns of attitude and behavior. If they also tend to enter similar jobs and make similar incomes, people at a given occupation–income level may resemble each other in life style partly because of similar educational experiences. We might furthermore expect these effects to be stronger on attitudes than on behavior, since behavior is more constrained by a variety of current circumstances, such as income, stage in the family life cycle, etc.

Similarities among persons of a given level of rank are not, of course, necessarily explained by culture or social interaction. Other things being equal, individuals in similar social environments should be expected to behave similarly, in that they are responding to the same stimulus. Individuals with high incomes might all disapprove a more progressive tax proposal, not because of some form of collective decision, but simply because each individual stands to lose by the proposal.

We look on social stratification as part of the social conditions which limit and guide the individual's behavior. The system of stratification is part of the objective reality in terms of which individuals strive to meet their goals. Hence, social stratification provides part of the environment within which the person is located; his behavior is affected by the nature of the environment and by his location within it because they set conditions for his behavior.

To pose an analogy (which we would ask the reader not to take overseriously), consider the rat in a Skinner box. Knowing the construction of the box, we know that unless the rat presses the bar it will have to do without food pellets. The rat may press the bar with its right paw, its left paw or its nose; it may be too stupid or too inactive to find the bar or it may simply prefer to starve. Given simple assumptions about rats, it is possible to roughly predict behavior from the way in which the box is constructed, simply because the strategies for survival are limited. More important, it would not be possible to predict behavior at all adequately without knowing the construction of the box.

In our study, the box is the structure of stratification which affects individuals by limiting their behavior in some respects and by making some strategies for responses dominant. It is equally clear that the analogy is useful only to a point. In particular, people are able to understand the boxes they are in and under some conditions respond by reshaping the box.

As sociologists, we are primarily concerned with the nature of the social environment and how it channels the responses of individuals. Knowledge of social conditions will not allow us a perfect prediction of individual action, nor is this our goal. We do not attempt to account for all the factors which make individuals respond to their setting in one possible way rather than in another. We will be prepared, therefore, to explain only a moderate amount of the variation in any behaviors we will study.

The unit of analysis in this study is the individual male head of household, studied partly as an individual and partly as a representative of his household. We study individuals first because we are concerned with the effects of the social environment on individual behavior, but, second, because social environment *consists of* organized individual behavior in the aggregate. The aggregated social characteristics of individuals and the relationships between individual characteristics *are* the social environment. For example, the stratification system includes such things as the average income and the dispersion of income and the extent to which social origin, education and income are related.

The effect of the stratification system can only be seen by averaging behavior over numbers of individuals, the behavior of none of whom is completely determined by the environment. For example, a man's feeling of euphoria or despair on a given evening depends not only on his rank in society, but also on the events of the day at home and at work, the evening news, the state of his health, the tranquility of his wife, and so on. Only by averaging the responses of many different individuals is it possible to estimate the implications of a given social position.

To return briefly to our analogy, it is as if the Skinner box were invisible and the nature of its workings had to be inferred from the average behavior of a series of animals run through it. In this sense, our ideas about the influence of the stratification system are given to us by predictions we make about the average behavior of people in given rank positions. These influences may be accurately estimated even if they only account for a small part of the total variation in behavior.

We study the effects of the social environment with the assumption that most such effects do not act directly upon the individual in a simple stimulus–response fashion, but are mediated by the person's symbolic apparatus and the patterns of social interaction in which he is involved. To understand the effects of the social structure, these mediating influences must also be considered.

The approach we are using, then, leads us to think of relationships between social rank and behavior as arising from several sources: from individual responses to deprivation, including rational action directed at improving one's rank level; from society-wide or community-wide norms stating how people at various rank levels should act; and from shared experiences in groups that are made up of people at the same rank, including both actions relevant to class interests and behaviors and beliefs that do not arise from such common concerns. These groups include ones the person currently belongs to, but also past groups such as, particularly, the family of origin and the school.

The above processes could take place whether the structure of inequality were unidimensional or multidimensional. However, if we think of a population arranged on several dimensions of superiority and inferiority, additional questions are raised that would not emerge in a unidimensional theory (with the corresponding disadvantage that the theory becomes more complex and thickety issues arise about disentangling effects).

As we said above, one major question raised by a multidimensional approach is whether the several forms of rank might have different kinds of effects on different dependent variables. In much past work, rank dimensions have sometimes been treated as essentially interchangeable: Occupation is used as an overall indicator of rank or status in one study, education in the next, and a combination of education and occupation in a third (see Lazarsfeld 1959:60–67). Such a procedure seems to be based on an implicit assumption that any rank dimension is but a given aspect of "upness" and so has about the same kind of effect as any other on a given dependent variable. The procedure of using a single index or indicator of overall rank makes it impossible to examine this assumption.

But it is quite plausible that several rank dimensions might affect a given dependent variable in different ways. Certainly, low income reflects a different kind of deprivation than low education or low origin status. Institutionalized norms might specify that persons of different occupations must act in different ways, but might be silent with respect to educational or income differences. Finally, social interaction could be much more affected by, let us say, income or racial–ethnic differences than by occupation or education. For these reasons, a given dependent variable might well be differently influenced by different rank dimensions. Prejudice (among whites), for example, might vary much more strongly with education than with income. Or attitudes toward the "welfare state" might be more affected by occupation than by education.

Such net effects might even appear in different directions: more income increasing fertility, while more education decreases it. Of course, if rank dimensions were very highly correlated, so that anyone high on income was almost always high on education also, such differences in effects would be both theoretically unimportant and difficult to isolate. But where rank dimensions are moderately or poorly correlated, it is essential not to define all rank effects a priori as being similar. In other words, a potentially multidimensional view is called for, not only in understanding the rank system, but also in understanding its effects on individuals.

It may be necessary to introduce still a further complication in order to accurately understand some kinds of rank effects. Not only might different rank dimensions have different net effects; it may also be that a given specific rank dimension might have in and of itself a number of different kinds of net effects. That is, a given rank dimension might operate on a given dependent variable through a number of different intervening mechanisms. Let us use education as an example. If education turns out to have an outstandingly important effect on, let us say, anomia (we shall encounter this problem in Chapter 10), the question arises: How do two people who differ on education really differ—how does an additional year of education really reduce anomia? A number of answers come to mind. Educational differences probably reflect differences in prestige and also differences in competence or certification and hence more security in earning a livelihood. But differences in education also possibly mean, as we suggested above, that the two people have been socialized in different sets of norms and standards. A more educated person may also tend to hold a broader, more flexible view of the world (see Kohn and Schooler 1969). For all these reasons and more, education may affect a given dependent variable.

It is important to note that some of these effects are connected to superiority and inferiority and the deprivation which arises thereby, while others are essentially *nonstatus* effects (Blalock 1975). People high and low on a given rank dimension differ in the extent of their reward and deprivation and also in the nature of their interests which arise from their rank positions. But they may also differ in a number of respects that are essentially irrelevant to superiority and inferiority. We pointed out above that subcultures that develop at a given rank level might well involve attitudes, beliefs, and shared behaviors which are not all connected to the interests of people at that rank level. In addition, high (or low) position may carry with it various other nonstatus factors, such as the additional information or the potentially more complex view of the world obtained in the course of additional education.

The net effect of a given rank dimension should therefore be thought of as the sum of its effects through a variety of intervening variables, some of them involving inferiority and deprivation and some of them not. This is another reason, in addition to those given above, why we could well expect various rank dimensions to have different effects on a given dependent variable and why the pattern of these effects should shift from dependent variable to dependent variable. If rank dimensions exercise their effects through somewhat different sets of mediating or intervening variables, the effect of a given rank dimension on a given dependent variable depends on whether the intervening variables associated with that rank dimension have important effects on that particular dependent variable. The analyses in Chapters 10 and 11 are two examples of how this reasoning works out in assessing the effects of various rank dimensions on the dependent variables of anomia and intolerance respectively. The specific and various effects of a single rank dimension present issues too complex to be settled definitively in this study. However, this possibility has considerable value both in interpreting our findings and in thinking about new directions for research.

Communities as Contexts for Rank Effects

As a final orienting question we now ask: Do patterns and processes of inequality differ across communities, and if so, do these differences in the community context influence the ways in which people are affected by their rank positions? In a sense, the question that faces us here is whether it is necessary to take community-level events into account when studying social inequality.

It may help initially to contrast two views of stratification, as a society-level versus a community-level phenomenon. The first view represents rank as totally a product of the nation–society. In this situation, inequality is derived entirely from one's ranking in the general society and hence a person keeps the same rank positions as he moves from community to community. If all forms of rank behave in this fashion, each community would simply be a geographically restricted reflection of a dominant societal system of inequality.

If social rank were totally a product of the local community, on the other hand, there would be no general societal rank dimensions and a person's standing would depend entirely on how he is ranked in his own community. The process of transferring rank from one community to another would therefore be quite problematic. In the most extreme form, the mechanisms of rank might be quite different or differently defined in one community while morality would be the essential quality in another; Norwegian ancestry might be prized in St. Louis and despised in Minneapolis. Even if the same sorts of rank dimensions existed in all communities, community-level rank would provide the basic definitions if rank depended exclusively upon one's relative order *within* his community, rather than upon his rank-order in wealth, education, morality, etc., relative to the society at large.

Between these two hypothetical extremes there exist a large number of more plausible possibilities, in which the patterns and processes of inequality derive in some respects from the national society and in others from the local community. Let us explore these briefly by listing a number of aspects of stratification which could vary from community to community, that is, ways in which ecological and other local factors might to some extent produce, or modify the societal system into, a unique local configuration.

First of all, some important kinds of inequality might be "manufactured" only at the community level. The most obvious possibility is local reputation. In general, we would expect this dimension to be more important in small towns than large cities, and to become less important as one moves farther away from home base.

A second way in which communities may play an independent role in shaping the system of stratification concerns the *salience* of certain rank dimensions. For example, in communities in which there are frequent bitter conflicts between labor and management the rank dimensions of occupation and income may come to be more important than, say, education. In other communities these interests based on current rank might be more or less submerged or eclipsed by other forms of inequality (or possibly by conflicts based on age or sex differences, etc.). In such communities, the behavior of people at different ranks may differ primarily because of differences in socialization and current subcultures, rather than differences in pursuing particular "class" interests. However, differences in interests remain a potential force. If an issue arises which raises the salience of income or occupational differences (for example, a proposal to shift the prior more or less accepted distribution of goods), then the effects of these rank dimensions may quickly increase. In such a situation, the past effects of educational and family socialization may prove important; if they have made people now similar in class interests also similar in culture, such people can more easily mobilize in defense of their interests.

The salience of racial–ethnic rank may also vary considerably from community to community. Conflict in this area, involving school or housing integration, for example, may make racial and/or ethnic differences highly salient and more influential in behavior. Regional differences may also affect racial salience: One would expect, for example, that the distinction between black and white would be at least somewhat more salient in the South, and that Orientals and Mexican–Americans would be more set apart in the West and Southwest, respectively. Finally, the salience of lineage and/or neighborhood may also vary from community to community.

Another obvious difference between communities (and one that may affect the salience of certain rank dimensions) is the amount of inequality, the degree of dispersion along a given rank dimension. If the range of inequality in a given community were wide and unconcealed, we would expect that persons low in the scale would feel more relative deprivation and dissatisfaction, compared to people equally poorly off in communities in which there was little, or little obvious, inequality. In the case of racial–ethnic rank, high dispersion means that the community houses a variety of racial–ethnic groups of rather different rank, as opposed to communities which are more or less homogeneous with respect to race and/or ethnicity. We will see below that this is one of the major differences between the six communities studied in this research.

The way in which rank dimensions are related to one another may also differ from community to community. For example, the extent to which family background affects later success, or the importance of education in getting a good job possibly might be much greater in some cities than in others.

Homogamy, the extent to which friendship, marriage, neighboring, and so forth bring together people of similar rank, is another important respect in which communities may differ. We would expect from our earlier discussion that the effects of rank on behavior should be especially striking in the context of a community in which these social ties are mainly contracted within, rather than between, rank levels. High levels of homogamy may produce in time a high level of "class" consciousness. This too could be an important contextual variable: In communities where people are sharply aware of their rank standing, and of their "kinship" with others of similar rank, we should expect the effects of rank on attitudes and behavior to be more profound than in cities where rank differences are not accompanied by such attitudes of fellow-feeling.

A final, and potentially fundamental, aspect of the community context is whether the several rank dimensions are tightly or loosely interrelated. In the U.S. individuals are often vertically mobile both as compared to their fathers and to their early careers; they are also inconsistent in the ranks they occupy at a given time. If a community has high rates of mobility and/or status inconsistency (that is, if the rank dimensions in that community are loosely related) how will the effects of social rank on individual behavior be influenced?

In a mobile, status-inconsistent community none of the mechanisms described in the previous section for translating rank into behavior will work as cleanly. For example, the deprivation one feels is plausibly reduced if he has hopes for upward mobility, just as the satisfaction one of high rank feels is perhaps reduced by contemplating the possibility of falling in rank. Similarly, one low in rank may feel less deprived if he is compensated by high rank on another dimension (see Wilensky 1966a:132–133).

Nor could well-established institutional norms governing rank behavior be expected in communities with high rates of vertical mobility and status inconsistency. It is unlikely that a set of norms could develop to govern appropriate behavior for each possible combination of ranks (say, a poorly paid Anglo clerk with a college degree whose father was a cobbler).

Further, lines of conflicting interest cannot be so clearly drawn if mobility and/or inconsistency are present. Suppose an issue, say a proposal for a steeply progressive income tax, tends to make income differences quite salient, while another issue, school integration, tends to make racial rank salient. Even if each issue is vital enough to set at opposition the groups threatened and benefited by the proposals, each proposal will be specific to one particular rank dimension. If income and racial rank are not highly related, there is no basis for a community-wide polarization of conflicting groups: Many people divided by the income issue would find themselves on the same side in racial conflict and vice versa.

Finally, we would expect that the mediating effect of patterns of social interaction would be weakened. In communities with high rates of status inconsistency, groups homogeneous on occupation would be likely to include a variety of incomes, social backgrounds, etc. Some groups might be homogeneous with respect to income, while others were homogeneous in education (yacht clubs versus amateur symphonies, for example). If such groups did succeed in thoroughly schooling their members in similar attitudes of a particular kind, the distribution of those attitudes in the community might then be related to income, for example, but not especially related to education. In the same way, the socializing effect of the family or the school system would not generalize to other categories of people. For example, a group with a given income or occupation might have quite disparate educational experiences, so education could serve only weakly to give them a common cultural heritage.

For these reasons, then, we suspect as rates of mobility and inconsistency rise, the effect of social rank on behavior and attitudes is likely to be weakened, since the various intervening mechanisms will tend to transmit the effects of rank into behavior only while introducing considerable random "noise" in the process.

We should also note here that mobility and inconsistency have been held by some writers to have effects at the individual level. That is, if a person moves up or down on some rank dimension, or holds at one time high rank on some dimensions and low rank on others, he will, *by virtue of those experiences,* feel, believe, or act differently from others. Examples of these propositions are: Downwardly mobile men will scapegoat and thus be prejudiced (Bettelheim and Janowitz 1964:25–48); people who have high occupation or income and low racial–ethnic rank will back liberal or left-wing causes (Lenski 1954). The reasoning behind these propositions suggests a variety of intervening variables such as frustration, individual isolation, cognitive and social uncertainty, and conflicts of expectations. The accuracy of some of these propositions will be examined in our analyses in Chapter 5.

To return to the contextual level, it may be that any individual-level effect of mobility or inconsistency may well depend on the status arrangements in the surrounding community. For example, a mobile person might have great difficulty maintaining ties with old friends and making new friends in a community in which mobility was rare, but in a setting in which mobility was the rule rather than the exception, the experience of moving up (or conceivably moving down) might cause much less strain. In the same way, an individual's status inconsistency might have few if any effects on his behavior in a community in which most other people also had jagged status profiles.

These, then, are a series of ways in which social stratification may differ across communities, differences that are important for their own sake but also important as contexts which may affect the ways in which individual social rank influences individual behavior. How likely are marked differences in these respects to appear between communities? There are several reasons to expect that communities will indeed differ significantly in their arrangements of inequality. The first and most obvious factor that comes to mind is size: For a variety of reasons stratification in small towns could be expected to differ substantially from that in large cities. Other factors which might have the same result are differences between communities in basic economic activities, in rates of in- and out-migration, and in region. Regions differ, of course, in economic patterns and in migration rates. Regional subcultures may also include variations in the emphasis placed in daily life on rank and status. We have chosen cities in this study to vary systematically by size and region, but we shall see that our communities are also rather different on the other factors mentioned.

On the other hand, several others factors would argue that social stratification is essentially a characteristic of the entire society and should not vary significantly from one city to another. These include such factors as similarities in culture throughout the U.S., the pervasiveness of the mass media, the availability of transportation and communication even over long distances, and the ease with which people can pick up stakes and migrate to another locality. All these factors will be discussed further in the final chapter after we have gained a more precise notion of the ways in which the six studied communities actually differ.

Although it may help our thinking to contrast society-wide with local-community processes, we assume that any actual situation is likely to form a somewhat complicated mixture. Let us suggest some possible elements in such a mixture. First, some rank dimensions (such as occupational prestige) might be "manufactured" nationally while others (such as reputation) could derive mainly from the local community. Or some segment of the population (such as persons of high education) could be more influenced by national standards of evaluation, while others' view of their rank depends heavily on their relationship to the local setting. The relationships between rank dimensions could also be partly affected by national and partly by local processes. It is plausible to think, for example, that the relationships between income and occupation and between occupation and education might be standard everywhere in a society, since these relationships may depend mainly upon nationwide technology and labor markets. But the relationships between origin rank and degree of education could well vary from community to community, since the policy and practices of education are under substantial local control in the U.S. Also, regional variations in the degrees and types of discrimination against minority groups should produce strong relationships between racial–ethnic rank and education or income in some localities and weak relationships in others (however, even here there are tendencies for national organizations such as corporations, the Congress, and the courts, as well as the mass media to provide uniform cultural definitions narrowing the limits within which the relationships of racial–ethnic and other ranks may vary). Finally, the structure of relationships between the various objective rank dimensions could be basically similar in every community, while the forms of consciousness by which rank is understood exhibit peculiar permutations and vivid changes in form from city to city.

OBJECTIVES OF THE STUDY

The following sections in this chapter discuss our basic research methods and describe the six cities which we chose to survey. In succeeding chapters, we take up the major questions of the study:

1. Do the systems of stratification differ in different communities, and if so, how? These questions are analyzed in Chapters 2, 3, and 4.

2. How are individuals affected by their positions within the community system of stratification? This involves several inquiries,

   a. How do the various dimensions of rank combine to affect individual behavior? For example, are effects additive, or do mobility and inconsistency effects appear? Chapter 5 examines these questions.

   b. If effects are additive, which dimensions of rank seem to influence each dependent behavior most strongly? Chapter 6 considers rank effects on feelings of deprivation and dissatisfaction and Chapters 7 and 8 deal with rank effects on informal and formal patterns of social contact. These forms of behavior are interesting both on their own account and as possible intervening variables which may translate objective rank positions into further individual responses. Chapters 9, 10, and 11 deal with rank effects on three important kinds of individual responses: political orientations, anomia, and attitudes of intolerance. The ways in which rank affects these variables are, of course, interesting for their own sake, but we also regard these dependent variables as central illustrations of potential personal responses or adaptations to social rank. Hence, any pattern of effects found with respect to these variables at least suggests hypotheses about how rank may affect a variety of other sorts of attitudes and behavior.

3. Are the stratification systems of the communities different *contexts* for individual behavior? More specifically, do the communities differ in the ways in which social rank affects individuals? For example, is education the prime determinant of political party identification in one community and income the prime influence in another? Does the entire set of rank dimensions influence behavior strongly in one community and only weakly in another? If these community contextual effects do not occur in our data, it will suggest that societal structures of inequality dominate community systems, at least at this time in this country. These matters will be examined in Chapters 5 through 11 and summarized in Chapter 12.

DATA AND METHODS

In the following chapters, we will present evidence and draw conclusions on the basic questions of the study. To help readers judge how strong the evidence is for a given conclusion and how widely it might apply, we now briefly describe the methods which we used in collecting and analyzing our data.

To study social inequality at the community level, we required both a sample of communities and, within each of these, a sample of individuals. We wanted to choose communities that were similar enough to make comparisons meaningful; for this reason we omitted such special sorts of cities as one-industry towns. We also wanted the cities to all be more or less independent entities, so we did not consider suburban and satellite communities. At the same time, we wanted the communities we studied to be different enough so that if the stratification systems of American communities *are* different and/or if they *do* present different contexts for the effects of rank, then such differences should show up in the set of cities we selected. Put the other way, if the communities we choose turn out to be quite similar in stratification or rank effects it should *not* be because we chose a completely homogeneous set of cities to start with.

We argued above that population size and region might well affect the stratification system of a community. We therefore chose six communities to differ systematically in these two respects, as follows:

	Region (State)	
Size	Midwest (Indiana)	Southwest (Arizona)
About 5000	Linton	Safford
About 25,000	Columbus	Yuma
About 700,000	Indianapolis	Phoenix

We will give a short sketch of each community below. The cities were chosen to be markedly different in size (the medium-sized towns 5 times as large as the small, the large cities over 25 times the size of the medium) on the grounds that differences of this order might well be required to produce differences in systems of inequality. Varying region by choosing Indiana and Arizona cities was, of course, natural, given our university locations, but these two states also provide a considerable contrast in regional history, tradition, economy and culture (although not as great as if we had chosen a New England versus a Southwestern or Southern setting). We chose cities matched in size from each of the regions so that we could look at size differences separately within each region and regional differences separately with size controlled. Even so, our leverage on the problem is limited, since the sample size for examining city effects is only six.

This sample of cities will not permit us to study all of the possible effects which city-type could have on stratification since certain important kinds of cities are omitted. We have, obviously, no Southern or New England cities. Such cities are popularly believed to have more rigid systems of inequality, but our data cannot examine this assertion. We also (as Chapter 2 will show) have no cities with large populations of southeast-European ethnic groups.

Finally, our largest cities, while they do serve as metropolitan centers, certainly are different from such supermetropolises as New York or Los Angeles. Therefore, we can present some evidence on some community effects, but our conclusions in this area will necessarily be br   tentative and incomplete.

In choosing individuals within each of our six cities, we wanted to place some limits on the scope of the sample, since our sample sizes were not large enough to analyze a large number of rather different types of people. In particular, we decided to limit the age range, the sex and the household status of our respondents. At the same time, we wanted to interview a group that represented most of the households in the stratification system. Our attempt to reconcile these two somewhat conflicting demands was to select a sample of adult (21 and over), male heads of households (including men living alone).[3]

There is no completely satisfactory unit of analysis in social stratification. The household is a fortunate unit in being a structure that specifically relates the organization of production to the organization of consumption. It is an unfortunate unit in that households are not all alike in demographic composition or in the way incomes are pooled for the purposes of consumption.

We represent households with male household heads in order to keep the relationships that different units bear to the occupational role system as comparable as possible. This decision carried the cost of not representing 15% to 20% of the households, but also the benefit of avoiding the kinds of analytic problems that beset us in the case of ethnicity. Basically, those are that another variable must be considered in all analyses, and that it is a variable one must suspect of interactions with social ranks in relation to dependent variables. This complicates linear analyses. To have included female household heads, or males and females who are not household heads, that is, would have greatly increased the amount of information provided by this study, but would also have increased the size, cost and complexity of the project by an even greater amount.

The households to be contacted for an interview were selected randomly from the address sections of the most recent city directories for the cities in question (including, in Indianapolis and Phoenix, the suburban directories).[4] Our respondents, therefore, represent nonclustered probability samples. We assume that the geographical area sampled resembles roughly the urbanized

---

[3]In 1970, the percentage of the total number of households (including individuals living alone) headed by a male was 78% in the Indianapolis urbanized area, 79% in Columbus, 80% in the Phoenix urbanized area, and 83% in Yuma. Census figures were not available for Linton and Safford. Our samples therefore cover most of the households in each city, but are not fully representative of all households.

[4]These samples were drawn by the Roper firm without supplement. For a discussion of the advantages and disadvantages of this procedure, see Kish (1965:352–353).

area of each community. In Linton, no city directory was available, so the utilities lists were used as the sampling list for households.

The collection of the data was done in several stages. A small pilot survey was conducted in the summer of 1964 in New Haven, Connecticut. A further pretest was done in Bloomington, Indiana in the winter of 1965, followed by the survey of the Indianapolis sample from January to April of 1966. These interviews were collected partly by professional interviewers and partly by members of the Indianapolis Area Project, an M.A. training program conducted annually by the Indiana University Department of Sociology. Preliminary results from the Indianapolis survey were used to modify the schedule for use in the other five cities, although most questions were carried over intact. The data collection in the other two Indiana cities and in the three Arizona cities was done by the Roper Research Associates research firm, who pretested the revised schedule and then carried out the final interviewing between December, 1966, and April, 1967. The interviewers were generally residents of the sampled communities, hired and trained by the Roper firm.

Over 700 cases were collected in Indianapolis, but since the population sampled in this survey was defined simply as adult residents, all females, and males that were not heads of households, were dropped in the analyses reported in this study, leaving 322 cases. About 700 male heads of households were interviewed in Phoenix and between 300 and 400 in the other four cities. The completion rate for the interviewing was above 80% in four cities, but dropped to 66% in Phoenix and 69% in Linton.[5]

The specific ways in which questions were asked, coded and scored to measure specific variables will be discussed as each variable is introduced in the analyses that follow. Here we merely want to describe our general approach to measurement. First, we attempted to measure as many variables as possible as interval scales or as ordinal scales with enough positions that we could use them to approximate interval scales. As the discussion below will make clear, our method of analysis demanded this. Second, we followed as much as possible the same procedures in all of the cities. For example, we did not attempt to define scale weights for most indexes separately for each city. (Of course, our procedures sometimes had to be different in handling the Indianapolis data, when different questions were asked in that schedule.) Consistent procedures across cities means the results are comparable from city to city in at least the obvious sense that the same questions are scored and combined in the same way in all communities. Whether comparability of a more subtle sort might have been gained by

---

[5]The number of men interviewed and the completion rate for each city are: Indianapolis, 322 (82%); Columbus, 376 (86%); Linton, 298 (69%); Phoenix, 686 (66%); Yuma, 375 (87%); Safford, 306 (81%).

choosing a procedure which gave up this obvious comparability is a moot point. We chose the more straightforward procedure.

Finally, it was necessary to decide how to handle cases in which the respondent had failed to answer one or more questions. Our usual procedure was to drop from any analysis those cases which had missing data on any of the variables involved in that analysis. However, we had moderate amounts of missing data for some of the rank variables (such as father's occupation or father's education, and respondent's income) that were entered in most of the analyses. Dropping cases with missing data on such variables would have biased the sample upon which the analysis was done; also, the sample used in an analysis which included father's education, for example, would differ markedly from the sample in an analysis not involving this variable. For these reasons, for such rank variables we substituted the mean of the city for any missing values, thereby keeping those cases (with their data on all or most of the other variables) in the analysis. More detail is given on this matter in Chapter 3, when relationships between the rank variables are analyzed.

We now want to introduce the reader to the general mode of analysis we shall use in the following chapters. Our choice of analysis methods depended on the objectives of the study, questions about the nature of the stratification system and the effects of stratification on the individual, within community contexts. These questions involve us in several kinds of complexities. In the first place, our view of stratification as multidimensional means that we need to look at how a number of rank dimensions are related at the same time to a given dependent variable. Controls must also be added to clarify these relationships. Finally, we wish to see if relationships between variables have the same form and strength in each of our communities.

Thus, our typical analysis questions are: How do various dimensions of class origin and early achievement affect a man's eventual occupation and income, and are these causal patterns the same in all communities? How do education, occupation and other rank dimensions affect, for example, political party identification (net of the effects of other variables), and do these patterns vary across cities? Hence, the orientation of the study requires us to analyze data in ways that allow us, even with moderate N's, to handle a number of variables simultaneously, to assess the effects of each of these, and to compare patterns of effects across communities.

To handle these demands, we chose multivariate parametric statistics—in particular, multivariate regression analysis and the analysis of covariance—as the major methods. In presenting the results, we will try to present enough of the detailed evidence to allow statistically sophisticated readers to judge whether our interpretations and conclusions from the data are justified and reasonable. At the same time, we will try to state our problems and conclusions as clearly as possible in English, so that our line of argument is clear to readers who have little interest in or even, possibly, stomach for the supporting technical manipulations. Since explanations of our techniques are not necessary for statistical readers and would have to be too brief to help non-statistical readers we shall merely mention below available expositions of these methods. We will, however, indicate briefly why we think these methods are natural choices in manipulating the data to answer the questions we pose in this study.

Beginning in Chapter 3 (where the method is discussed more fully), we turn to path analysis in order to present causal models of status phenomena: systems of equations based on causal assumptions. Path analysis allows us to formulate and analyze the systems of causal relationships between a sizable number of variables. It provides an explicit join between such a theoretical system and the data. Since our systems are all recursive (the assumptions do not allow simultaneous or reciprocal causation) the actual analysis will be done by obtaining estimates of paths using multiple regression. Nominal-scale variables and some nonlinear (especially nonmonotonic) relationships will be handled by introducing dummy variables. At the same time, path analysis is much more helpful than multiple regression by itself. Complex regression analyses can be set up and interpreted in so many different ways that it is hard to make sense of the findings. But using a path analysis forces the researcher to make at least some prior assumptions about what kinds of relationships do not make theoretical sense and may lead him to spell out in some detail the various remaining sensible theoretical alternatives. Although these spelled-out models often do not express with total fidelity theory at the most abstract level, they can express in some detail the various ways in which one or more abstract theories might be working in a concrete empirical situation. That is, we expect that such models will especially help us to state the sorts of empirically-grounded generalizations which we hope will be the staple product of this study.

When we can compare actual results with the results we would expect from explicit models based on prior theory, we will. However, prior theory will often either be absent or inadequate or clearly not applicable. That is, often our goal will not be hypothesis testing, but exploration. In this case, our problem is not being able to predict the results in advance, but being able to recognize them in the data. Path analysis will allow us to find, in the data, one or (in some cases) several alternative empirical models which can be tested in future studies.

Causal analysis also steers us away from some kinds of mistakes in the interpretation of data. For example, in constructing path models it becomes clear that a variable can have most of its effects through other, mediating variables: But in such a case the influential independent variable may show up with a small regression coefficient (representing the direct path). By thinking in terms of causal models we are encouraged not to dismiss such variables as trivial. This is one specific instance of a more general benefit—this type of analysis directs our attention to the way in which variables affect each other, and away from an obsession with increasing R-squares. Unrestrained, complex regression analysis, like Mephistopheles, tempts the tired scholar with visions of explained variance, distracting him from salvation in the realm of theoretical significance.

The major cost of path analysis is that it requires demanding assumptions; to the extent that our data fail to fit them, our results are open to question. Among these assumptions are that the relationships being investigated are both linear and additive, that the variables are measured as interval scales, and that variables not included in the analysis are not confounding the estimates of effects. We will present analyses in Chapter 5 to show that it is reasonable to consider our major relationships to be linear and additive. Our data obviously do not meet the measurement assumption—many of our variables are clearly ordinal scales. We use them here as interval scales in the hope that the extra understanding we can get about the behavior of systems of variables outweighs the possible distortion of the relationships which we risk by assuming that ordered categories form an interval scale.

In one sense, these demands for linearity, additivity, and interval scaling provide, perversely, an argument for the use of path analysis. Multivariate parametric statistics are usually conservative, in that the usual result of not meeting an assumption is to weaken the relationships revealed by the technique. Hence, failing to meet one of these assumptions may cause us to miss some effects, but we are unlikely to overstate a relationship or proclaim a nonexistent effect.

This conservatism does not hold with respect to the assumption of uncorrelated errors, that is, that potentially confounding variables have all been included in the analysis. Leaving out important variables may either obscure true effects or present spurious ones as true. On the other hand, this assumption is implicit in all forms of analysis which attempt, however roughly, to gauge causal relationships. Hence the only effective response is to try to include all important variables in the analysis rather than retreat from a method which explicitly assumes uncorrelated errors to methods for which the assumption, while no less real, is only implicit.

The analysis of covariance is a natural companion to path analysis in this study, since one of our basic goals is to see if rank variables have the same effects in different community contexts.[6] In this kind of analysis, we first compute the relationship between various rank dimensions and, for example, anomia, separately within each community. Then we can test to see if the form of this relationship seems to be similar in the six cities, that is, whether the differences in effects could reasonably be due only to chance. If so, we have a strong replication, since a constant result appears in rather

[6]Basic descriptions of the analysis of covariance can be found in Blalock (1972: Chapter 20) and Schuessler (1971: Chapter 5). Cohen (1968) discusses how the analysis of covariance is related to multiple regression.

disparate settings. Where relationships differ, we will ask why those particular effects change as they do across the six community contexts.

Our choice of analysis methods is designed to help us to study social structure through aggregating individual attitudes and acts. Our primary theoretical interest is in the social structure of the community (though we are not without interest in individual behavior). Summaries of individual characteristics and the relations between individual characteristics are important aspects of social structure. Hence, when we compute mean incomes, or the proportion of a community which is black, or the correlation coefficient between education and income, we interpret them as aspects of social structure, even though they are aggregated from individual attributes.

This being true, our readers should not be disturbed to notice in the following chapters that the proportion of variation which we are able to explain in various individual-level variables is not large. In the nature of the case, our R^2's must necessarily be low.

There are a number of reasons for low explained variance, some of which argue for rejection of the theoretical model, and some of which do not. But since there are so many reasons for unexplained variance to be high, one is well advised to regard predictability as a relative matter. A model should be evaluated, that is, not by the absolute proportion of the variance it explains, but by a comparison to the variance explained by some other model. If no other basis for comparison is available, one may use a random model, which is one of the values of tests of statistical significance. If, for example, an independent variable explains no more of the variance in a dependent variable than a random variable would be expected to (given the same distribution and the same population), it is hardly a useful model.

Random measurement error (including error in coding, punching, etc.) is a very likely explanation for a high proportion of unexplained variance. Random error does not pose any particular theoretical problem; it is simply a low signal-to-noise ratio, which is irritating (and confusing) in practice.

The theoretically most important explanation for low explained variance is the set of characteristics which were not measured, but which do, in fact, influence the dependent variable. Insofar as such omitted variables are uncorrelated with included rank measures, of course, they simply increase the error term, indicating that our models are not so much wrong as incomplete. In this situation, rank could have strong effects, yet the R^2 would be low, indicating considerable ignorance about potent nonrank effects. But whether those omitted variables are relevant to the model or not is a theoretical, rather than a methodological or technical, issue.

One such category of variables is a long list of personal characteristics of the individual, omitted from the present study as irrelevant to our central purposes. How recently did the respondent have a fight with his wife? How does he express himself? How accurate is his memory? On the face of it, one should not expect to predict individual behavior perfectly without somehow

taking account of such variables. It may be assumed that many such characteristics are uncorrelated with rank, which makes them simply another
source of random "error" in this study.

Other methodological decisions we have made, such as concentrating
upon linear models and substituting means also tend to reduce the levels of
explanation possible in the study. Finally, our measures are at the level of the
individual. But our analysis at the individual level does not average out these
influences by aggregating our respondents into larger units. Theil (1970) puts
the point eloquently:

> It is well known that, by and large, multiple correlation coefficients tend to be smaller
> when the regression is computed on data which are characterized by a lower degree
> of aggregation. It is not too difficult to obtain an R^2 larger than .9 when running a time
> series regression of total per capita consumption on per capita income. The R^2 is
> usually smaller when the dependent variable is consumption of a particular commod-
> ity group, such as meat. It is lower still when we use cross-section rather than
> time-series data in such a meat regression, because there is then no aggregation over
> consumers. The R^2 will typically be further reduced when the cross-section data refer
> to consumption during a month instead of a year, because there is then less aggrega-
> tion over time. Disaggregation typically raises the importance of accidental factors
> and thus lowers R^2 [p.133].

Almost all past studies of social class at the individual level also yielded
fairly weak relationships. But this is often not apparent, since they usually
present no explicit figures on the strength of relationships, but concentrate
mainly on whether a relationship exists and whether or not it disappears
when controls are introduced. Many of these studies also present data in the
form of percentage tables, which can make even sickly relationships seem
muscular.

Therefore, too much importance should not be granted to the proportion
of the variation explained (see the discussion in Duncan 1975:65–66).
Our interest in this study is in groping for scientific laws, stating how much
change in one variable results from change in another. As long as the
disturbances due to other variables are random, good estimates of such
effects can be made even when the proportion of variation explained by the
variables introduced is low.

The data to be presented in later chapters do not themselves provide final
proof for either the existence or direction of causation (for a statement of the
ways in which we take our causal models to be causal, see Chapter 3). We
are interested in causal theory, and with what causal propositions are most
compatible with the data we assemble and arrange. Nevertheless, we have
not assigned values of any independent variables, we gathered data at one
point in time, and our "controls" are all statistical. The very strongest sense
in which any of these data are even evidentially relevant to causation is in
the nonrejection of an hypothesis. For example, we think sons' occupations

are causally related to fathers' occupations. If, however, we found no statistical association between the two, we would reject that hypothetical assertion. Since we do find such an association, we do not reject it.

The language we use in reporting findings, however, has a thoroughly causal flavor, for two reasons. First, we inherited much of the language used here from the statistics of analysis of variance (or covariance). These were originally designed for the analysis of experimental findings, though they are often applied to nonexperimental data. Second, the theoretical propositions in which we are interested are causal, and we find it convenient to discuss findings in that kind of language. Nevertheless, we should not want readers to be misled by linguistic convenience.

A DESCRIPTION OF THE COMMUNITIES

In the next two chapters, we will describe the distributions of various rank variables—income, education, etc.—in the six communities and the ways in which they are related to form systems of inequality. To provide a context for these comparisons, we now describe other basic aspects of the com- munities.

The large cities, Indianapolis and Phoenix, are the capitals of their respec- tive states. Indianapolis is centrally placed in Indiana, Phoenix is located in south–central Arizona. Columbus lies about 40 miles south of Indianapolis, on the main Louisville–Indianapolis highway. The small town of Linton is located about 70 miles to the south and west of Indianapolis. In Arizona, our middle-sized city, Yuma, is located in the far southwest corner of the state, close to the Mexican border and the California state line. Safford is located about 140 miles to the east of Phoenix and about 90 miles northeast from Tucson.

The first panel of Table 1.1 gives details on size and growth in population over the past three decades. The differences in size are, of course, built-in, since we selected matched pairs of cities by size. The cities also differ markedly in their patterns of recent growth. The Arizona cities grew rapidly between 1950 and 1960 and more slowly in the next 10 years. Phoenix and Yuma, in particular, exploded in size in the former decade. The growth in Indianapolis was steady at about 25% per decade over the twenty years. Columbus is the only city to have grown substantially faster in 1960–1970 than in the previous decade. Linton is unique in losing population in both decades (and, indeed, in the 1940–1950 decade also). Our sample of cities, then, includes those growing steadily, those having extremely fast growth, and one declining in size.

We have relied upon census figures to describe the size of the com- munities. The remainder of the data in this and other tables in this chapter

Table 1.1 *Community Size and Characteristics of Migrants*

	Indianapolis	Columbus	Linton	Phoenix	Yuma	Safford
Size and growth[a]						
1960 population (000s)	639.3	20.8	5.7	552.1	24.0	4.6
1970 population (000s)	820.2	27.1	5.4	863.4	29.0	5.3
Estimated population at survey (000s)[b]	729.8	24.0	5.6	707.8	26.5	5.0
1950-1960 change (%)	+ 27.3	+13.1	- 4.0	+155.6	+162.2	+23.7
1960-1970 change (%)	+ 28.3	+30.6	- 5.0	+ 56.4	+ 21.0	+14.7
Length of residence in community (%)						
Under 5 years	11.1	20.1	9.4	16.7	26.1	17.6
5 - 10 years	7.5	11.4	6.4	21.6	17.9	10.1
10 - 19 years	15.6	19.7	12.7	25.8	21.6	15.4
20 years or more	65.9	48.7	71.4	35.9	34.4	56.9
N (100%)	322	375	297	686	375	306
Where respondents were brought up (%)						
In community area						
In community itself	c	18.7	20.6	9.0	8.7	10.4
Outside community itself						
Nonfarm	c	2.5	6.9	1.9	3.9	10.4
Farm	1.7	4.4	7.5	.8	1.3	14.0
Total	41.2	25.6	35.0	11.7	13.9	34.4
Not in community area (size of community)						
Farm	33.1 (39.4)[d]	30.0 (40.3)	23.2 (35.7)	21.3 (24.0)	29.8 (34.5)	26.6 (40.4)
Rural nonfarm	1.3 (2.3)	4.8 (6.5)	8.2 (12.7)	4.8 (5.5)	6.8 (7.9)	3.9 (6.0)
Town	19.4 (33.1)	17.9 (24.1)	26.0 (39.9)	28.2 (31.9)	25.2 (29.2)	23.3 (35.4)
Medium city	8.8 (14.9)	12.8 (17.3)	5.1 (8.0)	14.9 (16.9)	12.7 (14.8)	7.2 (11.0)
Large city	6.1 (10.3)	8.8 (11.9)	2.4 (3.7)	19.2 (21.7)	11.7 (13.5)	4.6 (7.1)
N (100%)	301	376	294	685	373	305
Major migration sources (%)[e]						
Same state	25.3	46.3	55.4	8.7	10.7	23.3
Illinois, Ohio	6.3			13.9		
Kentucky, Tennessee	13.3	12.8				
Old South	f			9.0	13.1	8.8
Texas					8.8	
Northeast				10.5		

Table 1.1 *Continued*

	Indianapolis	Columbus	Linton	Phoenix	Yuma	Safford
Northern plains				15.6	14.2	
Foreign	2.3	1.3	0	4.5	3.8	4.3

[a]Sources: United States Bureau of the Census. Census of Population: 1970. Volume 1, *Characteristics of the Population*. Part A, Number of Inhabitants. Section 1, United States, Alabama-Mississippi. United States Government Printing Office, Washington, D. C., 1972.

United States Bureau of the Census. Census of Population: 1960. Volume 1, *Characteristics of the Population*. Part A, Number of Inhabitants. United States Government Printing Office, Washington, D. C., 1961.

Figures for Indianapolis and Phoenix are for the urbanized area; figures for other cities are for the central city.

[b]Mean of 1960 and 1970 populations.

[c]These data are not available, owing to the wording used in the Indianapolis survey.

[d]Percentages in parentheses are expressed to the base of respondents not reared in the community.

[e]Percentages are expressed to the base of all respondents.

[f]Blank cells indicate minor sources (i.e., furnished fewer than 10% of the *migrants* from the United States).

are drawn from our samples, however, and so refer only to male heads of households. The attempt is to compare our samples (and thereby the sampled populations) to provide a context for later findings from these samples.

The comparisons of size and growth leads to questions about migration patterns. Migration is important to social stratification and the structure of opportunities—in this country, moving on has historically been one way of improving one's lot. We would have liked to be able to get information on both the people that moved into and out of our communities, but obviously the out-migrants were gone at the time of the survey, so we only have data on the in-migrants.

In-migrants were very numerous—in *no* city had a majority of the men interviewed been brought up there. As the growth figures would suggest, the cities with most in-migrants were Phoenix and Yuma. Less than 15% of the respondents in these cities had been brought up there and about 40% had lived there less than 10 years. On both these counts, the cities with least in-migration are Indianapolis and Linton. Two kinds of consistent differences emerge. First, the in-migration rates are higher for each Arizona city than for the matching city in Indiana. Second, within each state, in-migration is higher for the middle-sized city than for either the large city or the small town.

The cities also differ in the hinterlands from which they have drawn their migrants. The Indiana communities and the small towns pulled more heavily from their home state, while migration into Phoenix and Yuma was especially likely to have been from out-of-state. When Indianapolis and Columbus did draw from outside Indiana, they drew mainly from Kentucky and Tennessee. Phoenix and Yuma, however, drew from a variety of regions in the country. All three of the Arizona cities received a sizable contingent of migrants from the Old South, possibly indicating differences in regional culture between the two states. The Arizona cities also have relatively large proportions (4–5%) of men who were reared abroad; these are about 60% Mexican in the two smaller communities, but the foreign migrants into Phoenix come from a variety of countries.

Our respondents were also asked to describe in general terms the size of the community in which they were raised.[7] The proportion of migrants from a farm was large for all our cities, between 25% and 40%. Over 60% of the migrants into each of our cities came from a small town or a rural area. This is especially true of men currently living in the small towns. The only community which drew many migrants from other large cities is Phoenix. The major moves seem to be from a farm or from a small urban place to a place of the same or larger size.

The major differences in the cities' industrial composition are with respect to two situses, manufacturing and extraction (see Table 1.2). Indianapolis and especially Columbus have much higher proportions of employment in manufacturing than the other cities. This is not to say that the other cities are altogether pastoral—Phoenix, for example, has a good deal of manufacturing in absolute terms, even though only a sixth of our sample from that city were so employed. Large industries have been located in Columbus since the 1880s. The city now houses several large factories, including the main plant of the Cummins Engine Company, a major manufacturer of diesel engines. Indianapolis has a mix of manufacturing, including automotive parts, heavy machinery, food processing, and electronics. Eli Lilly, Inc., a major manufacturer of pharmaceuticals, has always been based in Indianapolis.

The two small towns both have high proportions of men employed in extraction, but far different industries are involved. Linton is located in an area of coal fields which extends through southwest Indiana and southern Illinois. Three-quarters of the men employed in extraction are miners. This

---

[7]To measure this variable we asked: "Which of these best describes where you were raised?" The interviewer then asked the respondent to choose from the following list:

On a farm
In the country, but not on a farm
A small town
A medium sized city
A suburb of a large city
A large city

Table 1.2 *Employment Status*

	Indianapolis	Columbus	Linton	Phoenix	Yuma	Safford
Selected situses (%)						
Manufacturing	30.6	43.6	13.7	16.0	14.2	6.8
Extraction	0	2.0	15.8	3.9	6.7	21.0
N (100%)	304	344	284	643	345	295
Labor force status (%)						
Full-time employed	84.2	85.1	74.5	79.3	81.4	75.5
Part-time employed	1.6	2.7	5.7	2.8	2.4	2.9
Unemployed	2.2	1.9	2.7	2.9	5.3	3.6
Retired	11.8	10.4	17.1	14.4	10.9	17.0
Student	.3	0	0	.6	0	1.0
N (100%)	322	375	298	686	374	306

industry has persisted in the area, although mining here has experienced cycles of prosperity since the early part of this century. Extraction in Safford means farming—five-sixths of the extractors in that city are so employed; Safford is the most heavily committed to agriculture of the six cities.

With respect to labor force status, the two small towns have higher proportions of retired people and lower proportions of men fully employed than the medium and large cities. For the men interviewed, unemployment was higher at the time of the survey in the Arizona cities than in the Indiana cities. However, the unemployment rates in Linton and surrounding communities have at times been high, due partly to the cycles in coal production.

Patterns with respect to age and family life cycle (Table 1.3) partly reflect the industrial and labor force distributions. The manufacturing cities of Indianapolis and Columbus have relatively more young men and fewer men over 65 than the other cities. The two small towns, on the other hand, both have about a fifth of their sample over 65 years of age. Similarly, Indianapolis and Columbus have the largest proportions of families with very young children, while the largest proportions of older families with grown children (or no children) are found in the small towns.

Finally, the cities are substantially different in religion. The proportion expressing a Catholic religious preference is higher in Arizona than in Indiana; 30% of the men in Yuma were Catholics. Linton and Columbus are overwhelmingly Protestant. One other important difference is not revealed by the figures. Mormons settled in Safford in 1879 and 43% of our Safford respondents indicated a preference for that faith. Hence the "Protestants" in Safford are a different composite from those in the other cities.

It may be useful to briefly review the unique features of each of our cities, as a capsule summary of the main differences between them. Indianapolis

Table 1.3 *Family Status, Religion, and Age*

	Indianapolis	Columbus	Linton	Phoenix	Yuma	Safford
Family life cycle (%)						
Single	4.4	2.3	6.1	8.6	9.1	3.9
Age 20-39, no children	5.7	4.9	2.0	4.9	5.3	1.0
Children under age 6	32.4	33.1	22.2	25.2	25.9	26.2
Children age 6-21	33.0	31.5	33.1	36.4	36.5	38.6
Age 40 or older, no children or children grown	24.5	28.2	36.5	24.7	23.1	30.2
N (100%)	318	365	293	674	363	301
Religion (%)						
Protestant	76.7	82.7	91.0	67.8	61.0	71.5
Catholic	15.4	9.3	4.7	23.8	30.2	21.2
Jewish	1.6	0	.3	1.7	0	.6
Other	2.6	4.8	.3	1.3	.5	.3
No preference, atheist, or agnostic	3.6	3.2	3.7	5.2	8.3	6.2
N (100%)	305	376	298	685	374	305
Age (%)						
20 - 34	30.2	30.0	22.8	21.5	25.8	16.4
35 - 49	34.2	34.2	28.1	35.7	34.6	32.7
50 - 64	23.4	24.0	27.2	29.5	28.1	32.7
65 or older	12.1	11.9	21.8	13.4	11.5	18.3
N (100%)	321	374	298	686	375	306
Mean	44.8	44.6	49.6	47.3	45.9	50.0

and Phoenix are both large cities of over a half-million residents and are the capital cities of their respective states. Factors which set off Indianapolis from the other cities are its heavy employment level in diversified manufacturing and its relatively young population. Indianapolis is also unusual as one of the cities which attracted few new immigrants.

Phoenix in contrast experienced explosive growth, especially during the 1950's, much of it from immigration. Phoenix draws from many areas of the country for immigrants, including the South and other large urban areas. A final difference is the relatively high proportion of Catholics in our Phoenix sample.

The two medium-sized cities, Columbus in Indiana and Yuma in Arizona, are alike in experiencing strong population growth; Yuma grew rapidly in the 1950s and somewhat more slowly since 1960; Columbus, by contrast, grew more rapidly during the later decade. Columbus has the highest level of employment in manufacturing of any of our cities, drawing migrants from other parts of Indiana and from the Border states to fill these positions. Its population is relatively young. Religiously, the city is heavily Protestant.

Yuma, in contrast, has drawn migrants from all parts of the country, including the South, although the city does not have high levels of manufacturing. In religion, Yuma also contrasts with Columbus, having the highest proportion of Catholics.

Our two small towns, Linton in Indiana and Safford in Arizona, are alike in having relatively high proportions of older and retired men. In other ways they are sharply different. Linton has lost population for the past several decades, partly because employment in the area has depended somewhat on coal-mining. The town has attracted relatively little migration from out of state. Religiously, Linton is our most Protestant community.

Safford, on the other hand, has grown moderately in the last 2 decades. It is the only one of our communities with substantial employment in farming. Safford's Mormon population also gives it a unique religious position.

In the next chapter, we begin to examine the stratification structures of the communities. It is clear from the discussion above that our cities are highly disparate in many respects. One of our major concerns is to see whether these differences are translated into differences in patterns of inequality.

Part I

Inequality in Six Communities

2

PATTERNS OF INEQUALITY

Social stratification may serve as a context for individual behavior in at least two ways. One is the existence of a pattern of inequality at a given time, as exemplified by a particular occupational distribution, or by the joint distribution of occupation and education. The latter pattern would describe an individual's social surroundings by indicating, for example, how reasonable it would be to expect an acquaintance to hold a college degree, knowing only that the acquaintance worked as a minor executive in a local auto parts plant. The other way stratification provides a social context is through its causal processes, exemplified by the process of status attainment. Is it more reasonable, in a given community or society, to plan for a child's career in the military by buying a commission as soon as possible, or by providing special encouragement for work in mathematics and English while the child is in elementary school?

How do the stratification systems of American communities differ (if, indeed, they *do* differ)? Does the basic process of status attainment vary from one community to another? Even if the process is the same, does it always result in the same patterns of inequality?

The patterns of inequality *could* differ among communities, even if the present residents had all been subject to a single process of rank attainment. A copper mine near one town, and a university with a medical center in another, for example, might well attract migrants with contrasting occupations. In this chapter we shall describe the patterns of inequality in the six communities, and in the next chapter we shall attempt to infer the underlying processes which yielded the patterns described here.

The communities were selected to differ in region and size; as the last chapter showed, they are markedly different in other respects as well. We want to see if these differences in history and current circumstances affect patterns of stratification of several types. A first question is whether some communities are generally higher in rank than others and whether some exhibit greater amounts of inequality in income, education, etc. than others. Next, is the connection between all forms of rank so close in any community that, in effect, there *is* only one dimension of general rank? Is the extent to which rank variables are correlated a pattern that varies among communities? Finally, our analysis will ask if various forms of rigidity such as social immobility or status consistency tend to occur together, so that some communities can be regarded as generally more restrictive in stratification than others, or if the communities display different forms of status rigidity.

The picture of each community we are about to develop, a picture of the status arena within which the residents carry out their lives, will be useful when, in Parts II and III, we come to questions of how rank affects individual behavior. As an example: if one of our communities has relatively low rates of mobility and inconsistency (i.e., is more rigid in its stratification), it will be interesting to see if rank affects behavior more powerfully in that city.

The greatest differences by far among these communities have to do with racial–ethnic rank. In order even to describe the communities, it is necessary to report the specific nature of the data collected. Furthermore, in order to explain decisions we made in analysis, it is necessary to allude to research findings reported in greater detail in later chapters. Throughout this discussion, it should be remembered that our intent is not to describe ethnic subcultures or their origins with great precision, but to portray the place of ethnicity in systems of social stratification.

The basic data are of two kinds. First, the interviewer was asked to classify each respondent in one of the following categories by direct observation: White, Negro, Oriental, American Indian, Spanish or Mexican–American, or Other. Since this was done after the interview, all the information elicited in responses to the entire schedule was available to the interviewer.

Second, among other questions on place of birth and where the respondent's father was raised, we asked, "What was the original nationality of his family?" In order to quantify the rank aspect of nationality, we turned to the system of social distance scores developed by Emory S. Bogardus (1959). The numbers on this scale reflect the responses of large samples from various parts of the nation on questions about the degree of social intimacy they would accept with members of various racial–ethnic groups. Lower numbers reflect less distance, and hence higher rank. We assigned the social distance score from the appropriate region to each respondent on the basis of his reported nationality (blacks were also assigned Bogardus scores, though they were not asked the nationality question).

The aspect of race or ethnicity that is relevant in social stratification could be either the gradations of social distance accorded to the many different groups and nationalities, or it could be simply that certain minority groups are singled out for special treatment in given social contexts (or both). The latter possibility argues for a dichotomous classification of community members, majority and minority, instead of a continuous scale. In Chapter 3 and elsewhere, we find the dichotomous description to be the one that portrays the operation of the racial–ethnic rank system in the stratification of these six communities most appropriately.

As a useful theoretical definition of *minority,* we adopt the elements of Williams' (1964:304) statement: (a) cultural or physical distinctiveness, (b) self-consciousness, (c) hereditary membership combined with endogamy, and (d) the existence of political, economic discrimination on the part of some segment of the majority group. Clearly it is a matter of degree whether one should consider a particular group part of the minority in a given locale, so that the exact placement of the line between majority and minority members is partly arbitrary (see Chapter 3). We found that defining minority status as a Bogardus score of 240 or less identified the same individuals in our samples as the combination of all categories except white in the interviewer's observation described above.

The importance of this dichotomous variable in stratification, varying in specific definition among communities (e.g., the minority is mainly black in Indianapolis but Mexican–American in Safford) will be seen in later chapters. There is good reason to believe, however, that we missed classifying one ethnic group as a minority, though it meets Williams' criteria to a substantial degree. This group is referred to by the name "hillbillies" by local residents in such midwestern industrial cities as Cincinnati, Cleveland, Detroit and Chicago, and its existence serves as a qualification to our conclusions regarding ethnic variability, particularly in Columbus and Linton. The qualification is that, although Columbus and Linton appear in the data to be reported as ethnically homogeneous communities without minorities (varying only in terms of the social distance among European nationalities), there probably is a small group in those communities that resembles the minorities in other communities in many respects.

Appalachian highlanders from eastern Kentucky and eastern Tennessee have family ties, traditions, linguistic similarities, regional loyalties, educational and religious characteristics, and patterns of social participation (Giffin 1962) that distinguish them from other residents of lowland communities to which they migrate in search of work. The original nationalities they report are Scotch–Irish, English, German and "American." In our data, however, they cannot be distinguished from other southern rural migrants who report the same original nationalities, and many of whom bear quite similar cultural characteristics, but who participate more fully in the organized social life of the community and probably assimilate more readily. In fact, we should have defined this particular minority by membership in the specific extended families that account for the solidarity and exclusiveness of the group. Since we did not, the possibly relevant ethnic minority for Columbus and Linton cannot be identified for comparison to minorities in other communities.

The six communities differ markedly in the distribution of racial–ethnic rank (see Table 2.1). With the qualification just noted, the samples from Columbus and Linton include almost no representatives from the minority

Table 2.1   *Cities Compared on Rank Characteristics*

Rank dimension	Indianapolis	Columbus	Linton	Phoenix	Yuma	Safford
Race and ethnicity						
Distribution (%)						
"American"	8.7	19.8	15.8	3.1	2.7	3.3
Northwest European	70.0	73.5	80.5	74.4	70.1	72.8
Southeast European	6.2	4.3	3.0	11.0	6.7	4.6
Mexican-American	.3	.3	0	7.9	14.1	18.0
Black	14.0	1.1	0	2.6	5.1	.3
Other	.8	1.1	.7	1.1	1.3	1.0
N (100%)	322	373	297	684	375	305
Bogardus social distance scores						
Mean	159.0	138.2	135.7	153.0	163.3	157.5
Median	142.3	141.9	141.6	133.1	133.3	132.9
Standard deviation	54.2	29.2	21.3	50.5	60.1	59.0
Education						
Distribution (%)						
Less than 6 years	6.9	5.3	4.0	3.4	6.4	9.8
6 - 8 years	15.9	16.8	25.3	16.1	16.0	19.6
9 - 11 years	20.2	14.4	15.8	13.3	21.1	22.2
12 years	28.0	31.7	37.7	30.7	32.3	20.9
13 - 15 years	12.8	13.9	10.8	17.9	12.5	13.7
16 years	6.9	11.5	3.0	9.3	7.7	6.2
Over 16 years	9.3	6.4	3.4	9.2	4.0	7.5
N (100%)	321	375	297	685	375	306
Years completed						
Mean	11.5	11.6	10.8	12.0	11.1	10.7
Median	11.8	11.9	11.6	12.1	11.7	11.2
Standard deviation	3.9	3.5	3.0	3.6	3.5	4.2
Current occupation						
Distribution (%)						
Professional, technical, and kindred	16.3	16.1	10.4	18.8	11.9	12.0
Farmers and farm managers	.3	1.4	2.8	1.0	3.0	10.0
Managers, proprietors, and officials	18.1	24.2	18.7	22.5	21.9	25.4
Clerical and kindred	4.7	6.7	4.8	6.7	5.9	3.3
Sales workers	8.1	3.9	5.5	8.0	4.6	2.0
Craftsmen, foremen, and kindred	19.1	19.4	24.6	23.5	25.7	20.1
Operatives and kindred	24.1	20.6	26.0	8.3	12.4	12.7

Table 2.1 *Continued*

Rank dimension	Indianapolis	Columbus	Linton	Phoenix	Yuma	Safford
Service workers	4.7	4.4	4.8	5.6	7.3	4.3
Farm laborers and foremen	0	.3	0	1.6	2.2	6.4
Laborers	4.7	3.1	2.4	4.0	5.1	3.7
N (100%)	320	360	289	676	370	299
Occupational prestige (Duncan SEI) scores						
Mean	44.4	45.7	37.5	46.1	40.3	37.7
Median	44.0	44.4	37.2	44.9	39.8	35.8
Standard deviation	25.9	25.5	24.8	24.0	23.0	23.8
Personal income						
Distribution (%)						
Less than $ 3,000	8.3	4.8	21.2	14.8	11.0	15.7
$ 3,000 - $ 4,999	10.9	11.5	14.3	11.0	11.9	16.8
$ 5,000 - $ 7,999	38.1	34.0	33.2	31.3	36.4	32.9
$ 8,000 - $ 9,999	18.2	19.3	14.0	17.5	16.9	12.9
$10,000 - $11,999	9.3	10.3	6.6	11.6	12.9	11.2
$12,000 - $14,999	7.0	9.0	4.8	4.5	4.8	2.3
$15,000 or more	8.3	11.2	5.9	9.3	6.2	8.1
N (100%)	302	312	273	654	362	293
Dollars (000s)						
Mean	8.35	9.24	7.07	8.36	7.94	7.70
Median	7.48	7.55	6.46	7.49	7.47	6.50
Standard deviation	5.51	5.63	5.52	6.27	5.15	6.08

groups defined above. Over 90% of the residents of these two communities are either of Northwest European background or else were whites not able to identify their ancestry on either side, in which case they were scored as "American."

The other four cities have substantial populations from minority groups and somewhat fewer "Americans." The Indianapolis sample is 14% black and the Safford sample is 18% Mexican–American. Minority groups in Phoenix and Yuma are divided, about one-quarter being black and three-quarters of Mexican–American ancestry. None of the cities has a substantial group of men of Southeast European background.

There is (all things considered) far less inequality in ethnicity in Columbus and Linton than in the other four communities. The Bogardus means are lower (indicating greater prestige) in these two communities, and the standard deviations (indicating amount of inequality) are much lower than in the other four communities.[1] Indianapolis and Phoenix, by the same token, show somewhat less ethnic inequality than Yuma and Safford.

We turn now to three major achieved dimensions: education, occupation, and income. The measurement on education is straightforward, being the number of years of school completed in the regular educational system. Income is scored in dollars. In this part of the book, when we are investigating stratification systems per se, we shall generally use the personal income of the head of the household. However, when in Parts II and III we use various rank dimensions, income among them, to explain attitudes and behaviors of our sample, we will generally use total family income, since this reflects the resources which the family has available to consume. Occupation is shown in Table 2.1 in terms of the usual census categories, but when using it as an interval scale we score each person's occupation using Duncan's *Socioeconomic index of occupations* (Duncan 1961).

When the cities are compared on these achievement rank dimensions, a consistent pattern appears: within each region, the larger the city, the higher the average rank, except for Columbus, which on all three dimensions ranks higher than Indianapolis. On the achieved ranks, then, Columbus ranks with the two large cities in a generally high group, followed by Yuma, and then by the two small towns.

The cities can be compared on the dispersion of achieved ranks as well as average rank. Dispersion is as important for a comparison of community stratification systems as means or medians because it reflects the *degree* of inequality; two communities with the same mean on income or education would nevertheless be quite different social settings if the people in one were homogeneous on these attributes while in the other great differences existed between the highest and lowest citizens. The standard deviations in Table 2.1 can be taken as rough measures of the inequality with which each of the achieved values is distributed. Inequality on the three achieved dimensions tends to be smallest in Yuma, but no city is consistently high in dispersion.

The differences among these communities in terms of rank distributions can be summarized as follows. There are major differences among communities in both the average racial–ethnic social distance score and the amount of ethnic inequality. These differences seem to reflect region and history, but not necessarily the size or industrial type of the community.

_____
[1]The medians on this scale behave differently from the means because the median is more sensitive to differences in the middle of a scale and less to differences at the ends. This produces anomalies such as Columbus having a higher (less prestigious) median than Yuma because the Northwest Europeans in Yuma belong to somewhat higher-status nationalities than in Columbus (about 30% of the Columbus sample is of German ancestry). The Arizona communities also have somewhat lower (more prestigious) medians because people in the West are somewhat less inclined to maintain distance from Northwest European groups (see Bogardus 1959).

There are much smaller differences among the communities in the averages of education, income and the socioeconomic status of occupations, and those seem to be patterned by size and industrial types. All six communities are relatively similar, on the other hand, in terms of the amount of inequality in these three achieved ranks. Such minor differences in amounts of inequality as do exist seem not to be patterned by anything.

One might pick out Yuma as the equalitarian community, on the basis of its low standard deviation in income and occupation (though not in education). However, the differences are truly minute, and, as noted above, balanced by the high standard deviation in ethnicity. Thus the emerging picture is one of similarity among communities in the amount of inequality along achieved dimensions, in spite of some difference in average community prosperity.

THE INTERRELATEDNESS OF RANKS

Consider a second aspect of patterned inequality: the extent to which the many measures of rank upon which our respondents can be ordered are related to one another. To put the question in extreme fashion: To what extent are all the different measures of rank simply redundant (though error-prone) measures of the same thing? More importantly, do the communities vary in the extent to which this is true? Is it possible, for example, that certain small towns have such tightly interrelated rank systems that a single status order is an adequate description of rank differentiation, while large cities show more complex systems of stratification by virtue of less simplicity in rank differentiation (see Wirth, 1938)?

We approached these questions in a principal axis factor analysis of seventeen rank variables for men aged 40–64 in the six communities (reported in detail in Artz et al. 1971). Five factors were extracted in each city, and the loadings for the first factor (before rotation) in each city are presented in Table 2.2.

Our questions about the extent of rank interrelatedness can be partially answered by observing the extent to which the factors explain variance in the rank measures. The proportion of the total variance explained by all five factors varied from 66% in Indianapolis to 55% in Linton. In all cities the first factor accounted for much more variance than the second and succeeding factors. Thus the ranks are substantially interrelated. However, these interrelationships only imperfectly reflect a single status order, since relations between the rank dimensions are described by four factors in addition to the first.

The cities were remarkably similar in the patterns of interrelationships. The proportion of total variance accounted for by all five factors did not vary much from city to city, nor were these variations patterned by region or

Table 2.2 *Factor Loadings (Unrotated First Factor) Men, Ages 40-64*

Variable	Loadings of rank dimensions on first principal factor					
	Indianapolis	Columbus	Linton	Phoenix	Yuma	Safford
1. Area rating by interviewer	.75	.88	.76	.78	.78	.63
2. House rating by interviewer	.77	.87	.73	.78	.77	.66
3. Rating of respondent (R) by interviewer	.84	.88	.81	.80	.84	.73
4. Class self-placement	.70	.63	.62	.66	.63	.60
5. R's education	.77	.73	.72	.75	.77	.79
6. Father's education	.60	.50	.40	.55	.48	.58
7. Mother's education	.54	.50	.41	.54	.52	.59
8. Wife's education	.62	.72	.62	.58	.61	.69
9. Family income	.71	.61	.60	.64	.52	.60
10. R's job[a]	.82	.71	.64	.69	.68	.68
11. Father's job	.65	.33	.44	.53	.47	.40
12. Father-in-law's job	.49	.47	.40	.38	.28	.39
13. First friend's job	.60	.68	.56	.55	.54	.59
14. Second friend's job	.71	.48	.41	.54	.49	.52
15. R's first job	.74	.56	.67	.60	.60	.60
16. Neighborhood rating by R	.48	.63	.35	.53	.42	.33
17. Majority racial-ethnic rank	.38	b	b	.51	.60	.57
Common variance	67%	70%	63%	63%	62%	56%
Total variance	45%	43%	35%	39%	37%	36%

[a]Jobs are scored by Duncan's Socioeconomic Index for Occupations.

[b]Majority racial-ethnic rank omitted in these cities since these samples have few or no minority members.

community size. The extent to which one single factor tended to exhaust the matrix was also basically similar among the six cities, but varied slightly by region and city size within region. In Table 2.2, the proportions of common variance (or, even more clearly, proportions of total variance) explained by one factor are smaller in Arizona than in Indiana, and tend to decline with city size within state. These differences are probably too small to bear much interpretation, but it is worth noting that the ranks in small towns are *not* more readily reducible to a single dimension. If anything, the variance accounted for by a first factor is greater in larger communities.

Third, the profile of variable loadings on this first factor is quite similar (though not identical) from one community to the next. In an analysis of such similarities among factors in different cities and age groups (Artz *et al.* 1971) we found this to be the most common feature of different community stratification systems. Similarity of factor loadings between men aged 40–64 and those of men aged 20–39 in the same city was the next most common feature. Oblique rotation of factors for the purpose of interpretability resulted in somewhat *less* similarity of factors among communities.

The rotated factors (see Artz *et al.* 1971) are probably the most useful static descriptions of the individual communities, and they do show some (partly idiosyncratic) variability. The possibility that detailed descriptive differences between joint distributions stem, nonetheless, from common processes (see Chapter 3), is foreshadowed in the greater replicability of the unrotated first factor than that of interpretable rotated factors. We shall return to these factor loadings in Part II, where they will be used for the purpose of constructing a single index of rank in general, for comparison to a multidimensional conception of rank.

RIGIDITY IN COMMUNITY STRATIFICATION SYSTEMS

By the flexibility (opposite of rigidity) of a system of stratification, we mean the extent to which an individual within that system is not constrained by any one order of rank: for example, that his position within some other order of rank in that system of stratification may be quite different. Note that this is a property of the system of stratification, not of the individual, and that it does not depend on the consequences of rank. If rank had no consequences in individual behavior, then the flexibility of stratifications might be irrelevant, but it still could vary. If all ranks had the same effects on individual behavior, then individuals within a rigid system would be simply and inescapably subject to that effect, based upon their positions within the (effectively) single order, but individuals within a flexible system would experience that effect from the position of high rank in some respects and low rank in others.

Rates of social mobility and status inconsistency are specific instances of flexibility in systems of stratification that have received considerable attention from sociologists. In that good repute among other persons is a value distributed in a population, the associations among *subjective, objective* and *reputational* ranks (see Chapter 4) are also measures of rigidity. The extent to which a whole set of different kinds of rank can be summarized by a single measure (as in a single factor) can be taken as a global indicator of rigidity. Our interest in this section is in the amount of rigidity–flexibility in American communities. We shall first consider a global measure of rigidity and then rates of vertical mobility and inconsistency.

This analysis will serve as a prelude and context for later findings. In a later chapter we shall investigate the general hypothesis that experiences of mobility or inconsistency appreciably affect individuals—the findings in this chapter may help to put those results in context. More generally, our results here will complete our picture of the status patterns of these cities. If we understand how people are stratified, we can better understand how they are affected by stratification in our communities. To the extent that one city has materially higher rates of mobility and/or inconsistency it should be a different kind of place to live in.

In addition, the general question of whether American communities have different rates of mobility and inconsistency has some theoretical interest in and of itself. In Chapter 1, we suggested some theoretical reasons why communities might possibly differ in rigidity. Having only six cases, we can hardly prove any of these hypotheses, but on such topics, which have been more discussed than studied, any additional data should be welcome.

However, a caution is necessary before we begin. In Chapter 1 we found that in each of our communities, less (and sometimes much less) than half of the members of the sample had been raised there. The majority had migrated in, some long ago, some recently. This means that the characteristics we discuss below (and elsewhere, particularly in Chapter 3) can most accurately be taken as describing the current male population of the community, but not necessarily as providing, in some fundamental sense, a description of processes that have occurred within the community itself.[2] For example, if we find below that one of our communities has a high rate of vertical mobility, it should be taken to mean that a relatively high proportion of the male household heads in that city have experienced mobility, i.e., that those males were not severely restricted by their father's occupation in attaining their own occupation. But since much of this mobility occurred in other cities, or in the course of moving from one city to another, the high rate of mobility should be taken as describing the contemporary population of the town, but not necessarily as meaning that the community is one in which all mobility is easy or encouraged. For it could be that the boys currently being raised in the town are comparatively restricted in their choices of occupations, especially if they stay in town. Describing the men currently living in a city is, of course, important as a description of context.

A Global Indicator of Rigidity

We reported above that in all six communities a first principal factor explained much more of the variance in 17 rank dimensions than the second and succeeding factors. Therefore we treated this first factor as a rough approximation to a basic status dimension in each of these communities. As an initial and global measure of the extent to which the rank dimensions in a given community are closely woven together, we can ask how much of the

---

[2]See Blalock (1967b) and Blalock (1968:192–196) for discussion of the problems involved in studying populations that are not "closed."

common and/or total variance is explained by this first principal factor (see Table 2.2).

The Arizona cities are generally a little less rigid than those in Indiana, and within states the towns are less rigid than the two larger cities. On this criterion, then, the small towns do not appear to have tightly woven status systems. Columbus and Indianapolis appear to have the most rigidly structured stratification systems. The differences are not dramatic, however.

These data indicate that none of these six stratification systems is close to being completely organized or rigid. Actual stratification systems can depart from perfect rigidity in a number of ways. Two general departures are that ranks at origin can become independent of later attained rank (vertical mobility) and that the several ranks currently held by an adult can come to be less than perfectly matched (status inconsistency). We now turn to an analysis of these more specific forms of flexibility.

Vertical Mobility

Although the measurement of vertical mobility (and of status inconsistency) has been subject to considerable elaboration and some controversy in the literature (e.g., Duncan 1966a; Wilensky 1966a; Jackson and Curtis 1968; Goodman 1969; Tully et al. 1970), we shall confine our measures here to relatively straightforward techniques. We will also deal only with occupational mobility.[3] We shall first treat occupation as a categorical variable, and mobility as movement from one category to another. Then we shall move to a more quantitative analysis in which origin and destination occupations are scored on the Duncan interval scale of prestige. This will permit us to use the correlation coefficient between these two ranks as an indicator of mobility.

We begin by cutting our occupational scales into five categories (upper white collar, lower white collar, upper blue collar, lower blue collar, and farmer) and cross-tabulating the respondent's current occupation with his father's occupation and with his first job (tables not shown). These yield data on intergenerational and career mobility, respectively. Measures which summarize various aspects of the mobility process from each table are given in Table 2.3.

About two-thirds to three-fourths of the men have moved out of the category of their father's job; the figure for career mobility is lower: about 60% in all cities. A context for interpreting the observed proportion of movers is given by the next figure (Full-equality mobility), the proportion

---

[3]Our questions on origin occupations were: "What was your father's usual occupation while you were growing up?" and "What was your first full-time job after you finished school?" We assume that the phrase "while you were growing up" led the respondent to give an answer reflecting the rank position of his family at the time he was being educated and otherwise being prepared for his own future achievement.

Table 2.3 *Summary Statistics for Father-Son and Career Mobility*

	Indianapolis	Columbus	Linton	Phoenix	Yuma	Safford
Father-son mobility						
Observed mobility (%)	70.3	75.5	72.0	70.6	70.5	67.0
Full-equality mobility (%)	80.2	81.7	77.0	80.1	81.5	80.3
Goodman & Kruskal's tau[a]	.071	.062	.044	.039	.031	.064
Cramer's V	.231	.197	.200	.179	.177	.232
Sharply up-mobile (%)[b]	18.3	24.8	19.8	25.3	19.5	23.9
Moderately up-mobile (%)	17.9	18.3	25.8	16.9	14.1	14.2
Stable (%)	40.6	35.3	35.7	38.7	40.9	46.9
Moderately down-mobile (%)	17.0	8.7	11.5	12.1	12.7	7.1
Sharply down-mobile (%)	6.1	12.8	7.1	7.0	12.7	8.0
Career mobility						
Observed mobility (%)	57.6	60.6	59.8	65.3	60.1	61.6
Full-equality mobility (%)	74.5	78.3	75.3	80.7	80.0	80.4
Goodman & Kruskal's tau[a]	.121	.124	.110	.103	.112	.121
Cramer's V	.276	.294	.289	.282	.324	.326
Sharply up-mobile (%)[b]	16.3	22.9	19.6	22.4	19.4	23.7
Moderately up-mobile (%)	23.3	19.4	23.8	28.1	25.2	23.1
Stable (%)	46.7	46.9	45.3	38.9	45.0	43.2
Moderately down-mobile (%)	6.7	6.6	7.5	7.1	5.4	5.3
Sharply down-mobile (%)	7.0	4.3	3.7	3.5	5.0	4.7

[a] Predicting respondent's occupation.

[b] These percentages and those below are computed for urban sons of urban fathers only.

which would have moved if father's (or first) occupation had no influence at all on son's occupation. The proportion of actual father–son movers comes close in all cities to the full-equality proportion. The same is true, but to a less marked degree, for career mobility.

For both forms of mobility, upward movement is more common than downward movement. This is true in all cities, for sharp movement, and for movement of only one "step."[4] The same finding is seen when we calculate rates of mobility treating occupation as an interval scale. The jobs currently held by our respondents exceed in mean prestige both those of their fathers and their own first jobs (see Table 2.4). The average change in occupational prestige is thus positive, generally between 10 and 15 points on the Duncan scale. This is, of course, to be expected in a society in which the number of high-prestige jobs is increasing faster than the number of low-prestige jobs.

[4] In calculating these figures, only urban sons of urban fathers are included. The "farmer," category includes a potentially high range of ranks, so that movement, for example, from "farm," to "lower blue collar," cannot unambiguously be considered upward mobility.

Table 2.4 *Means and Correlations Reflecting Occupational Mobility*

	Indianapolis	Columbus	Linton	Phoenix	Yuma	Safford
Means						
Father's occupation	30.8	30.9	19.0	31.6	30.7	22.4
First occupation	31.7	31.4	23.5	31.9	28.0	27.1
Differences between means						
Father's occupation minus respondent's occupation	+13.6	+14.8	+18.5	+14.5	+ 9.6	+15.3
First occupation minus respondent's occupation	+12.7	+14.3	+14.0	+14.2	+12.3	+10.6
Correlation coefficients						
R's occupation × father's occupation	.45	.32	.33	.33	.23	.34
R's occupation × first occupation	.63	.51	.57	.52	.46	.57
R's occupation × first occupation and father's occupation[a]	.67	.54	.56	.55	.47	.58

[a]Multiple correlation coefficients.

In addition, our sample, being from urban areas, includes relatively few farmers, but many sons of farmers. Since farming is given a low prestige score, the usual move for such people would contribute to the positive mean.[5]

Another aspect of mobility, perhaps more important than sheer change, is the extent to which the occupation of the respondent is dependent upon his first or his father's job. In this case a high mobility rate is indicated, not by a large number of people actually moving or the distance of their moves, but by final occupations that are largely independent of origin rank. Measures of this independence are given in Table 2.3 (Tau and V, based on the

[5]One problem in our interval-scale occupational scoring should be pointed out. The Duncan scale was developed to predict occupational prestige scores from figures on the general educational and income attainment of members of each occupation. Although the prediction is very good on the whole, it is poor in the case of farmers. The 1947 NORC study of occupational prestige yielded a prestige score for a farm owner and operator which is much higher than the score which the Duncan procedure assigns to such people (Duncan 1961:126). That is, the prestige of farming as an occupation far exceeds the prestige that would be expected from general education and income levels of its practitioners.

Despite this problem, we chose to use the Duncan score of 14 for farmers on the grounds that the lower score, while understating the prestige of, for example, the father's occupation, better reflects the resources of the respondent's home of origin, resources which to some extent affected his own quest for status. Since most of the farms owned by the fathers in question were probably modest in scale, such a decision seems justified.

cross-tabulations) and in Table 2.4 (r, based on the Duncan scores). High correlations reflect low mobility rates.

Both sets of correlations indicate that father–son mobility rates are higher (show lower correlations) than career mobility rates. This is entirely consistent with the view that relatively recent ranks have more influence on current rank than do ranks in the more distant past. However, even when father's and first job are used simultaneously to predict current job, the highest correlation in six cities is .67, indicating that current occupation is influenced, but by no means determined, by past ranks. In that respect, all of the communities here exhibit reasonably high mobility rates.

To what extent do these cities resemble each other in rates of mobility? As in the analysis of global rigidity, the communities differ on the various summary measures of mobility, but the differences are not huge. For example, the cities exhibit a range of only 8.5 percentage points in observed father–son mobility, and of 7.4 percentage points in sharp upward career mobility. However, the differences in correlation coefficients are somewhat more substantial, the range being about .20 for both father–son and career mobility. Although some of this variation is due to sampling fluctuation, it is clear that our communities represent moderate variations in mobility rates, although around the same central theme.

The data in tables 2.3 and 2.4 should remind the reader that there is no single answer to the question "How much mobility is there?" because there is no single question (for an illustration of this point, see Coleman 1964:77–84). The best answer to the question "How permeable have occupational boundaries been, in the collective experience of these men?" is probably given in Chapter 3. Our present interest is in the joint distributions of occupational variables, but even so, the question can be posed enough different ways to afford ample opportunity for ambiguity, and that is just what the data provide in comparisons among communities.

The lowest proportions of men who have not moved out of their fathers' broad occupational categories (percentage stable, Table 2.3) occur in Columbus and Linton, while the highest proportions appear in Safford, Yuma and Indianapolis. At the same time, however, the measures of association among these broad categories for occupations of fathers and sons (tau and V) are lowest in Yuma. In other words, city comparisons of direction and degree of occupational movement yield different results than city comparisons of the existence of movement (downward mobility of any kind is relatively more frequent in Yuma, Indianapolis and Columbus, though these cities differ in the amount of stability). The same set of comparisons in terms of career mobility yields yet another ordering of communities.

Considering the socioeconomic status of occupations, rather than broad categories, yields a somewhat different picture (Table 2.4). Intergenerational mobility (as measured by correlations) is highest in Yuma and lowest in Indianapolis, while the (almost identical) rates for the other cities are intermediate. Career mobility orders the cities the same way (though the intermediate rates are not identical).

With only six cases, it is not possible to demonstrate an explanation for these city differences. In the first place, the order of the cities varies somewhat from measure to measure. This should raise doubts about studies which order cities (or societies) with respect to only one or two measures, since quite different conclusions might have been reached with other kinds of rates. In the second place, no simple explanation in terms of community size or region will explain the ordering on most measures. In particular, small towns do not necessarily appear to have lower rates of mobility than large cities.

Status Inconsistency

Besides vertical mobility, communities depart from a rigid stratification system when income, occupation and other ranks held by adults are not highly related, that is, when rates of status inconsistency are high. We will examine these rates in our communities by computing correlations between each paired combination of the rank variables of income, occupation, education and racial–ethnic status (expressed as a dichotomous majority–minority variable). Small correlations, naturally, reflect high rates of inconsistency (see Table 2.5).

Certain types of inconsistency are more common than others. The most frequent type of inconsistency (i.e., the lowest correlations) involves the comparison of an achieved rank with racial–ethnic rank. The correlations between majority and any one of the achieved ranks range from about .15 to about .35. The rates of inconsistency are especially high between racial–ethnic rank and income. The next most common type of inconsistency is that involving a comparison of income with occupation or education. The r's for this type range from about .25 to about .45. This type of inconsistency, then, is about as common as father–son mobility. Finally, the least common type of inconsistency is that between education and occupation. The r's here range between .55 and .65, about the same range seen for career mobility. However, none of the correlations explain as much as half of the variation, so overall, rates of inconsistency, like rates of mobility, can be considered to be fairly high, compared to an absolute standard.

Do the cities differ, on the whole, in their rates of status inconsistency? Here again there is a basic similarity, although some of the differences in correlations between cities are substantial. The range across cities is especially wide for income–occupation and education–majority inconsistency. For the three types of inconsistency involving pairs of *achieved* ranks, Indianapolis seems to be generally rigid and Yuma seems to be generally flexible, though even this ordering is most tenuous. Little consensus emerges, however, for the inconsistencies between achieved and ascribed

Table 2.5   *Correlations Reflecting Degree of Status Inconsistency*

Zero-order correlations	Indianapolis	Columbus	Linton	Phoenix	Yuma	Safford
R's income × R's occupation	.44	.33	.38	.43	.31	.26
R's income × R's education	.44	.35	.46	.39	.38	.36
R's occupation × R's education	.62	.58	.54	.56	.56	.59
R's income × majority[a]	.18	-.04	.00	.20	.20	.18
R's occupation × majority[a]	.34	-.04	-.09	.31	.28	.32
R's education × majority[a]	.14	-.07	-.19	.34	.36	.35

[a] In Columbus and Linton scores on the Bogardus scale were used in place of the majority variable. The negative correlations mean that high achieved rank accompanies low distance (i.e., high racial-ethnic prestige).

ranks. For example, of the four cities with minority populations, Indianapolis has the most inconsistency between majority and education, but the least majority–occupation inconsistency.

SUMMARY AND CONCLUSIONS

The major aim of this chapter was to describe and compare our six cities with respect to several patterns of rank stratification. The major results can be summarized as follows:

1.   Our cities differ considerably in racial–ethnic composition. Columbus and Linton have few members of minority groups; in Indianapolis, the minority group is primarily black and in Safford, Mexican–American; Phoenix and Yuma have substantial proportions of both blacks and Mexican–Americans.

2. In average position on the achievement rank dimensions of education, occupation and income, Indianapolis, Phoenix and Columbus are all relatively high, Yuma has a middle position, and Linton and Safford are low.

3. In a factor analysis of a number of rank dimensions, the first principal factor explains a substantial amount of the variance and much more than succeeding factors. Loadings of the rank dimensions on this factor were all positive and relatively high, and the pattern of loadings was similar across cities.

4. Compared to any absolute standard, the stratification systems of our cities are not very rigid. In particular, rates of mobility and inconsistency are high in all cities.

5. In general, for all cities, some pairs of ranks are more closely tied to

each other than other pairs; that is not all types of mobility or inconsistency are equally common. The ordering is, from most to least common:

Inconsistency between majority and an achieved rank.
Inconsistency between income and occupation or education; father–son mobility.
Education–occupation inconsistency; career mobility.

The reasons why some types of mobility or inconsistency are more common than others are explored in the next chapter on causal relations between the rank dimensions.

6. The cities are fundamentally the same with respect to rigidity, including rates of mobility and inconsistency. That is, the differences seem to mainly be variations within a restricted range; they are never so great as to suggest that one community is *qualitatively* different from another.

7. Within the limited variation in rigidity which does exist, the several aspects of rigidity do not order the six communities in the same way. The cities can be ordered by a general measure of rigidity (variance explained by a principal factor) from relatively rigid systems such as Columbus and Indianapolis to less rigid systems such as Linton, Safford and Yuma. But different orders emerge when the cities are compared with respect to mobility rates and inconsistency rates. That is, it is perfectly possible for city A to be more rigid than city B with respect to one type of rigidity and for the order to be reversed, perhaps radically, with respect to another kind. Evidently rigidity may be useful as an umbrella concept, but not as a unidimensional variable capable of ordering cities.

The most that can be said in the way of summary on city differences in rigidity is that Indianapolis seems on most of our measures to be more rigid than our other communities. The data also suggest that Yuma, although seldom ranking first, consistently shows relatively high rates of mobility and inconsistency.

The first, very general, impression to be drawn from the data is one of basic similarity between our communities. With the exception of racial–ethnic composition, the differences between our cities seem more like variations on a central theme than fundamental qualitative differences.

One of the most *variable* features of American community status systems is the existence, social definition and treatment of deprived minority groups. Because this study heightened such variability, it illustrates the manifold nature of castelike relations. Communities differ in what minority groups are present, and in what proportions.

Thus far, then, the data suggest that communities show some different patterns of stratification, but that within contemporary U.S. society, at least, they are also alike in fundamental respects. In the next chapter we shall examine the processes from which these patterns emerge and see to what extent they vary from city to city.

When differences between the cities did emerge they were often hard to understand because the ordering of the cities on related aspects of stratification was often markedly different. The major stable differences between the cities are three: the differences in the existence and composition of minority groups; the ordering of the cities with respect to average values on income, occupation and education; and the finding that on most measures of rigidity Indianapolis scored relatively high and Yuma low.

Only highly speculative interpretations can be given to such differences. In the first place, we have only six cases, so of necessity a very great number of community-level variables must remain uncontrolled. Second, we should remind the reader again that comparisons between cities tell us only that the group of male household heads *currently residing* in one community have undergone, for example, more (or the same) mobility than that group in another community. Since in- and out-migration substantially affect our results, they should not be taken as representing the patterns we would find if each community were closed for a long period of time so that children growing up could be allocated only those roles and rewards available in that community.

In general, our findings suggest that the larger the city, the higher its average on various dimensions of achieved rank. The high means for Columbus, however, suggest that highly industrialized smaller communities can equal or exceed larger communities in these respects.

The differences with respect to rigidity, on the other hand, are not open to any simple interpretation in terms of size or region effects. It is clear, however, that our data present severe counterexamples for any theory that increases in city size lead to more fluid rank systems. Our small town do not appear to exhibit especially rigid or calcified stratification systems.[6] Evidently much of the reasoning in the previous chapter which predicted rigid stratification systems in small towns is open to question.

---

[6]These remarks refer specifically to relations among rank variables (e.g., compare these results to those of Hochbaum *et al.* 1955). Whether small town folk erect reputational status systems that are rigid in some different sense is a different question.

3

PROCESSES OF INEQUALITY

Patterns of inequality are the conditions to which community members are subject at a given time. Having described the similarities and differences in patterns of inequality among the six communities, we now examine the processes which produce those patterns. The processes of inequality are conditions to which present members of the community have been subject throughout their lives, and, insofar as experience is a basis for expectations, represent the ways in which community members may expect the system of stratification to operate in the future.

We know already, from the results in the last chapter, that the influences linking the rank dimensions are not so strong as to produce a rigid structure in which most men are ranked in the same way on all dimensions. This finding naturally raises other questions, in particular questions about the detailed skein of influences which exist, questions of which causal links appear to be powerful and which tenuous. We will be especially interested in how ascribed ranks, such as racial–ethnic rank and social origin, affect achieved ranks such as occupation and income, and whether such effects are direct or mediated through such ranks as education. These analyses will show how strongly social barriers handicap men's attempts to attain high rank and the ways in which such handicaps may operate.

As before, a major emphasis will be upon differences between the cities. Our cities do not span the entire range of variation of American communities, but the differences between them are very substantial. We found in the last chapter that none of them has a highly rigid social stratification system, although some differences on this score existed. We will present more evidence on this question here, but more importantly we want to ask whether the processes of status attainment look the same in the different city samples. This again bears on the issue of whether communities can develop unique status structures or whether they are basically reflections of a societal system of rank.

Two sets of findings will be presented in this chapter: first, a basic model of rank achievement, including rank origins and early and late achievement; and second, estimates of the effects of racial–ethnic rank.

A BASIC MODEL OF THE STRATIFICATION PROCESS

For the sake of simplicity in presentation, we consider first a basic, single model of the processes of stratification to which members of all six communities appear to have been subject. Then we consider possible variations from this model according to age and community of residence. The research itself, of course, proceeded in the reverse order. Thus the order of presentation is based on an important finding: As far as status attainment is concerned, the six communities could have been random samples from a single universe. With very minor exceptions, that is, we found that (apart from ethnic differences) the members of different communities were all subject to the same process of status attainment.

This basic model is illustrated in a path diagram (Figure 3.1). Since excellent descriptions of path analysis and associated techniques are available elsewhere for readers of all levels of sophistication (Duncan 1966b; Blalock 1972; Hauser and Goldberger 1971; Land 1969; Duncan 1975), we make no attempt to explain the methods here. However, for readers interested in stratification but not statistics, we shall attempt to make clear at every point the substantive intent of our analysis and to state interpretations and conclusions in English rather than algebra.

The values of paths in Figure 3.1 are provided by the standardized regression coefficients of the average within-city regression equations in the leftmost column of Table 3.1[1] Thus after a series of analyses of covariance (discussed later) predicting education, first occupation, present occupation and income in turn, we concluded that the common slopes were an adequate summary of the slopes within each community. The population reported in this analysis is restricted to majority men, aged 20 to 64.

In this basic model, background ranks generally affect later ranks only through education. Father's occupation, however, has small but nonnegligible independent effects on both first occupation and current occupation, even after the effect of education has been removed. Education, pivotal in that it carries the other effects of background, has independent effects on first occupation, present occupation and income, though the magnitude of the direct effects declines in that same order. First occupation not only

[1]The correlation coefficients given in Figure 3.1 (among mother's education, father's education and father's occupation), are for the total sample described here, not for within-city averages.

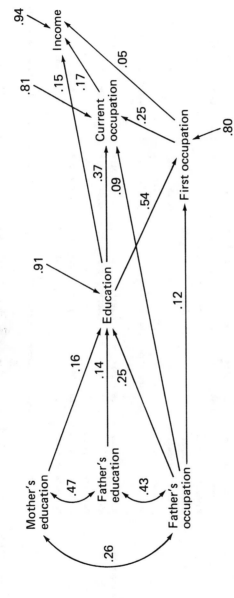

Figure 3.1. A basic model of the stratification process, for male household heads, 20–64, of majority racial–ethnic rank (numerals are average within-city path coefficients; those below .05 are omitted).

Table 3.1 A Basic Model of the Stratification Process, for Men, 20–64, of Majority Racial-Ethnic Rank

Dependent variable	Independent variable	Regression coefficients: Unstandardized and standardized (in parentheses)[a]						
		Average within-city	Indianapolis	Columbus	Linton	Phoenix	Yuma	Safford
Income (00s)	Occupation	.41 (.17)*	.37 (.17)*	.41 (.20)*	.12 (.06)	.77 (.28)*	.15 (.07)	.17 (.06)
	First occupation	.13 (.05)*	b	.27 (.12)*	.50 (.20)*	.19 (.07)	.15 (.06)	-.51 (.18)*
	Education	2.64 (.15)*	2.94 (.20)*	1.26 (.08)	3.97 (.22)*	2.06 (.10)*	2.44 (.13)	5.43 (.29)*
	Father's education	b		.81 (.05)			.97 (.07)	-1.52 (.08)
	Father's occupation			-.13 (.05)	-1.15 (.05)			
	Mother's education		.45 (.20)*				2.44 (.14)*	2.83 (.12)
	City R²		.21	.12	.17	.16	.11	.08
	Total R²c	Imposing common slopes: .12				Allowing individual city slopes: .15[d]		
Occupation	First occupation	.26 (.25)*	.28 (.28)*	.18 (.17)*	.36 (.31)*	.25 (.25)*	.22 (.22)*	.34 (.34)*
	Education	2.74 (.37)*	2.75 (.40)*	3.14 (.43)*	2.67 (.32)*	2.38 (.33)*	3.28 (.40)*	2.14 (.32)*
	Father's education		.32 (.05)		-.42 (.05)		-.54 (.09)	
	Father's occupation	.10 (.09)*	.11 (.10)*	.09 (.07)	.13 (.10)*	.14 (.14)*	.40 (.05)	.09 (.07)
	Mother's education			.67 (.07)				
	City R²		.47	.37	.35	.31	.30	.40
	Total R²c	Imposing common slopes: .37				Allowing individual city slopes: .37		
First occupation	Education	3.80 (.54)*	4.33 (.64)*	3.19 (.48)*	3.92 (.55)*	3.65 (.50)*	4.31 (.54)*	3.85 (.57)*
	Father's education	.13 (.12)*	.07 (.06)	.69 (.09)	.62 (.09)	.13 (.13)*	.08 (.09)*	.43 (.06)
	Father's occupation			.17 (.15)*	.16 (.15)*		.36 (.05)	.18 (.14)*
	Mother's education							
	City R²		.46	.36	.41	.31	.34	.41
	Total R²c	Imposing common slopes: .38				Allowing individual city slopes: .38		

Education							
Father's education	.13 (.14)*	.08 (.08)	.17 (.15)*	.10 (.10)	.12 (.14)*	.05 (.08)	.29 (.27)*
Father's occupation	.04 (.25)*	.06 (.36)*	.04 (.26)*	.04 (.23)*	.03 (.22)*	.04 (.32)*	.02 (.11)
Mother's education	.19 (.16)*	.31 (.22)*	.32 (.23)*	.16 (.14)*	.12 (.11)*	.13 (.14)*	.28 (.21)*
City R^2	.28	.28	.24	.13	.14	.17	.20
Total R^{2c}	Imposing common slopes: .20			Allowing individual city slopes: .21[d]			.20
Approximate N	239	306	223	511	257	192	

[a] Asterisked coefficients are those with associated t-values of 1.65 or higher; hence, significant at about the .10 level (two-tailed test).

[b] Coefficients are not shown when the standardized path coefficient is less than .05; i.e., for relatively weak effects. None of these omitted coefficients were significantly different from zero.

[c] Percentage explained by city differences and independent variables together.

[d] Interaction significant at the .05 level.

influences present occupation, but also has a very small direct effect on income. Current occupation, caused primarily by education and first occupation, but with a little additional help from father's occupation, goes together with education to have the major effects on income.

In order to explore the meaning of the path coefficients in Figure 3.1 in greater detail, we must first explain the sense in which this and subsequent models are causal. To begin with, it is *not* that these data prove either the direction or the strength of any causal relation. It is easy to forget that ". . . one can *never* infer the causal ordering of two or more variables knowing only the values of the correlations (or even the partial correlations!) [Duncan 1975:20]." Even though we make causal assumptions, below, for the sake of logical power, the reader must not forget that the data are monochronic. It is reasonable to assume that sons' occupations are unlikely to have caused their fathers', but there is no true substitute for overtime data in testing causal propositions. (Suppose, for example, that low status fathers in 1935 really did produce sons who became successful, but that the successful sons all died or moved to Europe by the time our study was conducted.)

The causal aspects of the models are all provided by assumptions, rather than by empirical evidence, but they are very special assumptions. First of all, we do not assume that fathers' occupations are causally related to sons' occupations. Rather, we assume that it might be, and let the data decide whether that assumption is still plausible. Second, the crucial assumptions are statements of what relations are *not* causal. The diagram in Figure 3.1, for example, assumed that income was not the cause of occupation, first occupation, education or background ranks, that occupation was not the cause of any variable listed to its left, and so on, except that a causally agnostic pose was struck with respect to the mutual relations among father's education, mother's education, and father's occupation. The fact that a coefficient of .15 appears on the path from education to income means that the hypothesis that education is one cause of income was not rejected. The fact that no such coefficient for a path from mother's education to income was afforded by the data means that we do reject that possible causal hypothesis.

All the models explored here are simple recursive models, meaning that our causal assumptions are as follows: (a) There is a list of exogenous variables about which we make no assumption; (b) for a list of endogenous variables, we assume that each variable *cannot* have caused any variable preceding it on the list; (c) all the remaining possible relationships might be causal, but this possibility will be rejected by partial regression coefficients close to zero. Causal order is symbolized by the directions of arrows.

The causal processes we are thinking about are a step or two removed from the data we present. For example, individuals are the statistical units in what follows, but we doubt that the causal nature of the relationship between education, say, and occupation, lies at the individual level. On the contrary, an individual has to contend with a social environment in which employers in general might not grant him a job unless he can produce a diploma. What causes the relationship between occupation and income is not the actions of the people who receive the incomes, so much as it is the decisions of corporate employers.

In asserting that X is a cause of Y, we mean simply that (other things being equal) if you were to change the value of X, the value of Y would change also, and that this result would obtain under a (possibly unknown) variety of conditions. Neither entertaining a causal hypothesis, nor failing to reject it, tells us anything at all about the *nature* of the causation. Finding that a causal relationship may exist, that is, is not the same as specifying *how* two variables come to be causally related.

Finally, it might be said that the sense in which these models are causal is that they are empirical models in search of a causal theory. When someone states a causal theory, that is, and from it deduces a model of status attainment of this sort, the figures shown here are what he will have to deduce in order to fit the data. It is our hope, of course, that theorists can do their job more effectively if they know what models their theories will have to generate. Thus, when we investigate "causal models of status attainment," what we are doing is assembling empirical data in a form that we hope will be useful in theory construction, not "finding the causes of occupational status."

The most general conclusion that can be drawn from the network of relationships in Figure 3.1 is that (with the exception of the placement of first occupation, to be discussed in detail later), each variable is affected most heavily by the variable immediately prior to it in the assumed causal sequence. The direct effects of a given variable on other ranks tends to decline as the "distance" in the causal sequence increases.

The effects of education seem to be especially crucial. Like other ranks, the effects of education decline with causal order. Its effect is greatest on first job, less on current occupation and least on income. But these effects are relatively strong, and sometimes are greater than those of "later" variables. For example, education has more effect on current occupation and on income than does first occupation.

Most of all, education seems to be crucial in the sense that it mediates most of the effects of origin rank upon later achievement. Father's occupation has a direct effect on later attainment, but this is no larger than its indirect effect through education. The other origin variables affect later attainment *only* through education. This suggests, for example, that the scion of an upper class house has little advantage over a less well-bred boy with equal education. It follows, then, that one source of downward mobility are sons of upper class families who both fail to achieve an education of their own efforts and thwart their fathers' efforts to attain for them the appearance of one.

The effects of social origin, however, would nevertheless be quite power-ful if such sons were few, that is, if origin variables more or less completely controlled educational attainment. In such a case, even if such variables as father's occupation had very little *direct* effect on later attainment, the indirect effect of origin would be immense. In our data, however, education is controlled by social background only to a modest extent. As the residual arrow headed ".91" indicates, about 80% of the variance in education seems to be independent of the three origin variables we included. Social origin variables, then, do not have substantial direct effects, nor do they operate powerfully through their influence on education.

Next we must examine the opposite interpretation: that each man's even-tual attainment is heavily controlled by his earlier achievements in educa-tion and occupation. Such a model calls forth, for example, a picture of powerful educational gatekeepers sifting the "unfit" from the "fit" and sending forth the latter to assured success in the form of high-prestige jobs and good incomes.

The data do not support this view. While the effects of early achievement are clearly more important than those of origin, even achieving high rank on education or in a first job far from guarantees high rank on subsequent rank dimensions. About two-thirds of the variance in first or current occupation is unexplained by prior variables in the model and about 85% of the variance in income is unexplained. That is, many early successes fail to maintain their rank; and many early failures eventually do well.

The overall impression, then, is that a man's rank on any given dimension is only moderately influenced by his ranks on other dimensions.[2] The system is loose rather than rigid, permissive rather than coercive. This, of course, only restates one of the major conclusions of the last chapter. These results are also generally consistent with those reported by Blau and Duncan (1967:165–177; also Duncan, Featherman, and Duncan 1972:37–45) for the nation as a whole.

There is no single career sequence in the order assumed here: education, first occupation, current occupation, income. What these figures represent is an average that combines several sequences. A not inconsiderable group of men interrupt their educations, for example, to get a first full time job, and then either become students again or obtain more education while employed, after which they may or may not change occupational levels (Duncan, Featherman, and Duncan 1972:210–224). Disproportionately,

---

[2]The influences described here are of variables *as they are measured*. This may be narrower than the name of the variable implies. The most important examples of this problem are with respect to occupation and racial–ethnic status. We are using scores for these variables which represent only their prestige aspects. If certain occupational groups have industrial,subcultural or other characteristics which might affect other ranks, but these characteristics are not reflected in the prestige scores, we shall not capture these influences. We discuss the problem further with respect to racial–ethnic rank below.

such men come from disadvantaged backgrounds. The problem is not simply that respondents failed to answer our question correctly (" . . . first full-time job after you had finished your education . . ."), but that the timing of education and entry into the job market is more complicated than the basic model indicates.

Furthermore, there are ups and downs to occupational status as well as to income that are not shown in the basic model. Once again, we are averaging a general trend over a career to the present. A detailed picture of careers in general would be even more complicated, since there are small lagged effects of prior occupations (and even of father's occupation): One's occupational level this year is not simply a function of his level 10 years ago (Featherman 1971b).

We now describe the particular pattern of average effects on each rank dimension, so as to fill in the picture upon which the above general comments are based.[3] Beginning with income, we see that its major determinants are occupation and education, plus a small independent effect of first job. The proportion of the variance explained in income is the smallest of any of the rank dimensions, even though the greatest number of predictors are

[3]We did additional analyses to see if the effects we have described might be at least in part spuriously due to the influence of age. For example, if young men tend both to be better educated and to have higher prestige jobs than older men, then combining them into the same analysis, as we did above, will tend to inflate the education–occupation relationship and hence overstate the actual effect which education has on occupation in the life of each man.

Such a problem could arise, for age is systematically related to all of the rank dimensions in all of the cities. These relationships in general take one of two forms. First, the means of the three origin variables, of respondent's education, and (with some exceptions) of first occupation, decrease with age. This monotonic decline is presumably due to a consistent secular trend in upgrading the average level of both education and occupation in the society—only the secular trend explanation is appropriate here since the above variables all occur at roughly the same point in each man's life. Second, the distributions by age of current job and income are usually curvilinear. The general pattern is that the mean increases as one moves from the youngest to the 35–49 group, and then declines for the older cohorts. These differences are presumably due to a combination of career and secular trend effects.

To what extent does our description of the basic model remain accurate *after* controls for age? Very few of the effects in the basic model appear to have been spuriously affected by age differences in the sample. To gauge the extent of the problem we compared the average within-age-group path coefficients within each city to the path coefficients for that city calculated with age ignored. The former figures are not affected by age differences, and the latter are. Differences only appeared in two areas. First, the effect of mother's education upon the education of the respondent was reduced by about .08 in three of the six cities. Second, in four of the six cities, there was a drop averaging about .06 in the path coefficient reflecting the effect of education on income. In some cities, then, some of the direct effect of mother's education on respondent's education and some of the direct effect of education on income appears to be due to the uncontrolled effects of age. In both cases, however, substantial effects remain after age is controlled.

On the whole, then, we can reject the notion that the basic model is spuriously shaped in any important way by age differences. It reflects the processes occurring within each age cohort to a much greater extent than it does differences between age cohorts.

available to explain it. Since income represents generalized access to a very great range of rewards provided by the society, its relative independence of other rank dimensions is an important fact, calling into question, among other things, the extent to which it effectively serves to reward and reinforce educational and occupational efforts.

The major influences on current occupation are education and, of course, first job. Education naturally also exercises a major effect on the man's first job, although a moderate direct path also exists from father's occupation.

The education attained by the respondent is affected about equally by the educations of each of his parents (but see one qualification in Footnote 3), but stronger than either of these paths is the influence of father's occupation.

We now pass from a consideration of the average process over the six cities to the question of how the stratification systems in the six cities differ from one another. The cities were deliberately chosen to differ greatly in size and region; the data in Chapter 2 also indicated several other marked differences between them. We now ask whether these differences are accompanied by differences in the process relating the rank dimensions.

One general hypothesis that might serve to guide the analysis is that the web of rank relationships should be more rigid, especially with respect to the effects of social origin upon attainment, in small as compared to large communities. This general prediction proceeds from the arguments advanced in Chapter 1. The data to examine their truth is supplied in Table 3.1. Here we present the (unstandardized) regression coefficients and the (standardized) path coefficients for the determination of income, occupation, first occupation, and education separately for each of the six cities. We also performed a test for statistical interaction, to see whether the differences in effects (slopes) across the six cities were greater than might have been expected due to random fluctuation.

The processes within the cities are basically similar. This is congruent with Lane's conclusion after studying a set of large cities:

> Residence in a particular city modifies the *degree* of the influence contributed by a man's background to his subsequent status, but does not alter the basic relation between these background variables and achieved status [1968:749].

Mueller (1974) reached a similar conclusion. Our data seem generally to support such a conclusion, not only about the relations between origin and achieved variables, but also about influences between achieved variables.

We can look to two kinds of data for support of this conclusion. In the first place, only in the processes determining education and income are there differences between cities that cannot reasonably be attributed to sampling or other random error. That is, interaction—differences of slope—is not statistically significant for the determination of occupation or first occupation. Secondly, we can get some idea of the extent and importance of the differences between cities in their stratification processes by asking how much better we can explain variation in a given rank variable by employing the best-fitting slopes within each city versus using a single set of average slopes for all the cities. As the rows entitled "Total R^2" indicate, practically no improvement at all occurs when predicting either current or first occupation using individual city slopes. But even for the predictions of income and education, where the differences between cities in slopes are statistically significant, very little improvement is gained. By predicting from the particular processes in each city we can explain only an additional 2.7 percentage points of variation in income and an additional 1.6 points in education. An initial, broadbrush conclusion, then, is that the stratification processes in these six cities show considerable similarity.

For two reasons, we must go beyond this first general conclusion and examine Table 3.1 in detail for city differences. First, we need to find out what differences seem to be producing the significant interactions with respect to income and education. In addition, a detailed search is motivated by some distrust of the criterion we used above, the additional amount of variation contributed. If one or two of the independent variables did have markedly different effects in one or two cities, no great improvement in variation explained would be obtained by taking such differences into account; yet, such differences might signal theoretically interesting differences between the cities.

Of course, the detailed set of slopes will undoubtedly contain some differences due to chance, all the more so because of measurement error (see Blalock 1968:173) and because our independent variables are at least moderately intercorrelated. Such multicollinearity will tend to produce differences in the coefficients from city to city, even if the true coefficients do not differ.

We will discuss each dependent variable in turn. In comparing the cities, we will focus on differences in the unstandardized coefficients, since these represent the amount of change in the dependent variable (dollars or *Duncan points* etc.) expected from a change of one unit (e.g., a year of education) in the independent variable. Such comparisons are not affected by differences between the cities in variances on the various rank variables, as comparisons of standardized coefficients would be (see Blalock 1968: 189–191).

For the process influencing education, the main differences between the cities concern the effects of parents' education. Mother's education has a somewhat greater effect in Columbus, Indianapolis, and Safford than in the other three cities. Safford also shows a relatively strong effect of father's education, so that in this city father's occupation has less effect than either the education of the mother or the father, as shown by the standardized coefficients. We have no ready explanation for these varying effects of parents' education. The somewhat small effect of father's occupation in Safford, however, possibly happens because over half the respondents in

Safford are sons of farmers, a much greater percentage than in the other cities. Such fathers would receive rather low Duncan scores, even those that were relatively prosperous and able and inclined to support longer educations for their children. Hence, in the Safford sample, the father's occupational prestige score would have less effect on the son's education. Once again, we remind the reader that such differences found between the cities should not be automatically taken to mean that the current status attainment process in a given city differs from that in another. Because of the high migration rates into these cities, much of the early status attainment of these men took place elsewhere. The data describe the male heads of households in the cities, but not necessarily the current patterns of effects on, for example, educational attainment.

In the process by which a man's first job is influenced, the cities are practically identical. In all of them, education has a massive effect and father's occupation a much smaller influence, with minimal influences exercised by the parents' education.

The cities are also rather similar in effects on current occupation, but some differences appear. In both of the small towns, the effect of first job on current occupation is slightly higher than in the other cities in the same region, indicating slightly more career continuity. In both middle-sized cities, the effect of education is slightly greater. Finally in one city, Yuma, father's occupation has no direct effect on current occupation. Since interaction was not significant in this regression, these differences may be due to random fluctuations.

The cities are most different in the ways in which prior ranks are converted into income. A basic similarity is that, with a few exceptions, the more proximate achievement dimensions of education, first occupation, and current occupation exercise the main effects, with only small effects from the three origin ranks. However, the main effects are not consistent from community to community. First, the influence of occupation on income is higher in Phoenix and is relatively muted in Linton, Yuma and Safford. A partial explanation is that these three cities have smaller proportions of professionals than the other cities (see Table 2.1). If professional occupations represent one strong link between high occupational prestige and high income, their scarcity might produce a smaller effect of occupation on income. Also, professionals in small communities may be less able to procure large incomes for themselves.

The effects of education on income exhibit a further interaction, being low in Columbus and greatest in the small towns. The most bizarre difference in slopes across cities is the effect of first job on income. On the average, this was a small positive effect. But this was the outcome of averaging together small–to–moderate positive effects in four cities, a major positive effect in Linton, and a major *negative* effect in Safford. Our first hunch was that perhaps this effect was somehow due to the high concentration of farmers and sons of farmers in Safford. But this negative effect of first job on income also appears for the subsample who were neither raised on nor ever worked on a farm. Barring an explanation in terms of random error, we must simply present this as one limited, clear, and currently unexplicable example of a city serving as an idiosyncratic context for rank attainment.[4]

In all this welter of detail, is there any clear picture of either general city–size or regional effects? For example, is there any evidence that ascriptive factors play a stronger role in smaller communities or cities located in the Midwest? The general answer to these questions must be "no." We have pointed out above a few scattered cases where certain kinds of influences have varied with city size, but the variations are not general enough to conclude that the processes in small towns are systematically different from those in the larger communities. With respect to region, even fewer effects are found.

The ascriptive origin variables do not consistently vary in effect in cities of different sizes or in different regions. For example, consider the extent to which the three origin variables explain the variance in educational achievement. This R^2 increases with city size in Indiana and decreases with city size in Arizona. Ascriptive effects on education seems highest in Indianapolis and Safford and lowest in Linton and Phoenix, but the explanation of these differences obviously can turn on neither simple effects of size or of region. Similarly, no clear region or size differences appear in the direct effects of origin variables on later achievement variables. Six cases, of course, can hardly disconfirm a theory, but we at least find little or no support for general notions that social background becomes more crucial in smaller towns or older regions.

The city R^2's, reflecting the extent to which the prior variables determine placement on each of the four attainment dimensions, can be used to compare the cities in terms of rigidity of their status processes. The data reveal (as did the analysis in Chapter 2) that Indianapolis is consistently the most rigid city and Yuma is consistently toward the fluid end of the continuum. The other four cities show little consistency and often wide swings in order from variable to variable.

Two more general conclusions can be drawn from the detailed comparisons of cities. First, departures from the average patterns of effects are more frequent in medium-sized than in large cities and most frequent in the small towns. That is, as city size decreases, within each of our regions, idiosyncratic patterns of effect appear more often. A second conclusion, however, is that in general the extent of the departures from average effects was modest, that is, even the most idiosyncratic communities resembled the others in most respects. With one or two exceptions, the differences between cities are those of degree rather than kind. The detailed comparisons support

---

[4]A control for age-group (see footnote 3) did not alter any of these interaction effects.

rather than question our previous conclusion, that the processes of inequality in our cities seem to represent variations on a common theme rather than qualitatively different systems.

THE ROLE OF RACIAL–ETHNIC RANK

We now turn to the question of how racial–ethnic rank fits into and affects the processes of inequalility we have outlined above. The analyses so far have omitted blacks, Mexican–Americans and other minority groups and have ignored differences in ethnic background. The results are therefore seriously incomplete, for the racial–ethnic variable may play several important roles in a community stratification system. We shall ask whether the processes of inequality have different forms in different racial–ethnic groups, how racial–ethnic rank affects other dimensions of rank, and how these effects vary from city to city.

The first conclusion we reach is that in its influences on other rank dimensions, racial–ethnic rank is not equally effective over its whole range. It seems to make a difference whether a man belongs to the majority or to a minority group, but within the majority, the particular rank level has little influence. In other words, the relationship between racial–ethnic rank and other rank dimensions seems to be curvilinear, having an essentially flat slope to the point where the scale shifts to minority positions, and then dipping downward.

The main minority groups in this analysis are blacks and Mexican–Americans, although very small numbers of American Indians, Chinese, and Japanese also appear in our samples.[5]

Two kinds of analyses led us to conclude that the only effective racial–ethnic differences were between majority and minority men. In the first, we continued to restrict the sample to men aged 20–64 of majority racial–ethnic standing, and re-ran the basic stratification model, adding Bogardus scores as a variable. Given the nature of this sample, the Bogardus scores essentially measured ethnic standing within the majority range.

The ethnic variable, in this situation, had practically no effects on the other rank variables. In 24 regressions (predicting education, first occupation, current occupation and income, in each of six cities), the path coefficient associated with the Bogardus score (that is, the *direct* effect of this variable on the dependent variable, with other background variables and intervening variables controlled) was significant (at the .10 level, two-tailed

[5]Majority rank was operationally defined as a Bogardus score of 240 or less. On the Bogardus scale 2.40 represents a degree of avoidance between "would have as close friends" (2) and "would have as next door neighbor" (3). This criterion excluded blacks, Mexican–Americans, American Indians (in Arizona) and Orientals from the majority. Jews, however, were not defined as minority members by this criterion, for their Bogardus scores in the two regions were 2.02 and 2.12.

test) in only three instances. The additional variance explained by adding the Bogardus score was miniscule in one of these instances and about three percentage points in the other two; the dependent variable in these two cases was education. Further, in both cases the effect was *negative;* that is, groups with lower ethnic rank achieved higher education. This is almost surely attributable to the Appalachian highlanders discussed in Chapter 2. Appalachian migrants have high ethnic rank, but their education achievement lags behind that of other members of the community (see also Blau and Duncan 1967:213–219). Whether this group should theoretically be considered a minority by the definition in Chapter 2 is a fascinating question, but one which we cannot pursue in this study, since our measures of membership in this group are not likely to be very accurate.

Our second attempt to gauge the effect of ethnicity within the majority group produced equally bland results. We omitted both minority members and men who did not know their ancestry or who identified their ancestors as "American." For this group of men with known European or other ancestries, we computed zero order *r*'s within each city between the Bogardus social–distance scores and a wide variety of other rank variables ranging from mother's education to the interviewer's rating of the area in which the respondent lived. Only seven of these correlations were above .10 and only one was above .20.

Within the majority group, then, the nationality or ethnicity dimension seems to be unrelated to other rank dimensions, in the two regions which we have studied. (For national sample evidence leading to similar conclusions, see Duncan and Duncan 1968.) One interpretation of this result is that ethnic rank is simply not a rank dimension. However, the results by Bogardus (1956, 1959) make it clear that people do impute different degrees of prestige to different majority ethnic groups.

If ethnicity is a true rank dimension, why is it not related to others? One explanation is that the prestige of an ethnic group may not be the only reason why that group stands high or low on occupation, income, etc. Prestige may determine patterns of discrimination, which in turn affect achievement, but the subculture of the ethnic group may have equally strong or stronger effects. For example, some ethnic groups may stress achievement for their children more than others or place more emphasis on education (see Rosen 1959). Our scale would not tap these differences unless these subcultural traits were highly correlated with prestige. Therefore, if some groups (Jews might well be an example) both rank relatively low as an ethnic group and socialize their children toward achievement, then the two effects are in opposing directions. Such a group might achieve well despite its low prestige, thus weakening any ethnicity–achievement relationship. In other words, our scale does not represent all aspects of ethnicity which might be relevant to achievement; it reflects only vertical standing.

Another, simpler explanation is that the prestige aspect of ethnicity, although forming a scale, does not form an impressively salient or effective one, at least in the regions we studied. One reason for this is that the connection of most of these men with their ethnic heritage is probably rather tenuous. Among majority men, aged 20–64, less than 10% had foreign-born fathers. One can speculate that most of the effect of ethnicity in the status attainment process has been dissipated by the third generation.

Whatever the explanation, ethnic differences among majority men do seem to have little effect on other rank dimensions. Hence, we will conduct our analyses of racial–ethnic effects measuring that scale only as a dichotomy: majority versus minority. The reader will remember from Chapter 2 that practically no minority-group members appeared in the samples for Columbus and Linton; those cities therefore do not appear in this analysis. In the other cities, the composition of the minority sample varied, being almost wholly black in Indianapolis, almost wholly Mexican–American in Safford, and a combination of these two groups in Phoenix and Yuma. We would have liked to study, in these last two cities, the differential effects of being black versus being Mexican–American, but we did not have a large enough minority sample to allow this. Hence we use a single dichotomy, majority–minority, the meaning of which varies from city to city.

The numbers of minority men interviewed are too small, given the complexity of the analysis contemplated here, to serve as a very reliable basis for statistical generalization. Better estimates of minority disadvantage in the U.S. in general can be obtained from other sources (e.g., B. Duncan 1967; Blau and Duncan 1967:209–213; Duncan 1968). The data presented below are intended to illustrate the fact that, in spite of the general similarity of the process of rank achievement to which current residents of different communities were subject, communities can differ substantially in the processes experienced by small subpopulations of residents.

The processes of stratification do not appear to be identical for majority-group and minority-group members, but the differences only appear for certain rank variables in certain cities and often are more differences of degree than of kind.[6] Beginning with the earliest achievement dimension, education, we see from Table 3.2 that majority-minority differences in the effects of the origin ranks on education differ by community. Most importantly, the slope on mother's education is steeper for minority men in Phoenix, Yuma and Safford, but steeper for majority men in Indianapolis. Presumably, this difference reflects the life conditions of Mexican–

---

[6]In the analyses in this chapter, means (for each city) were substituted for missing data on father's occupation, father's education, mother's education, first occupation and income. In order to provide slightly better estimates for the missing values, means calculated for the majority men were substituted for missing data for majority cases. Similarly, means calculated from the minority samples were substituted when minority men had missing data on the above variables. Hence, in Table 3.1 only majority means were substituted, but in Tables 3.2 and 3.3 the means substituted depended upon the racial–ethnic rank of the case with the missing data.

Americans, as opposed to blacks. These differences are substantial, but not enormous: The slopes imply that in Safford the difference between a son whose mother completed high school and one whose mother did not attend would be about 2.7 years of education if he were Mexican–American, but only about 1.1 years if he were Anglo. In Indianapolis, the same difference would be about six-tenths of a year among blacks, but about 1.2 years among whites.

In the determination of the first job, the data show that the yield from an extra year of education is consistently greater for majority men than for minority men. The minority disadvantage would seem to be somewhat less for Mexican–Americans in Phoenix and Yuma, but those in Safford suffer as great a disadvantage as blacks do in Indianapolis, so that this cannot be a simple matter of which ethnic group is concerned.

By the time of attainment of present occupation, differences between majority and minority men in the extent to which a prior rank "pays off" have largely disappeared in our communities (all four interactions by race are non-significant). Once a man has been educated and employed, that is, the process of further rank attainment is similar for majority and minority men. A minor exception to this is the fact that in the two large cities, Indianapolis and Phoenix, first occupation does not appear to help minority men in the attainment of present occupation, even to the (small) degree it does among majority men.

However, one difference in slopes did appear in all four cities: an advantage for majority men in converting education directly into income (over and above any effects through occupation). This ranged from an advantage of $40 per year of education in Phoenix to an extra $460 in Safford. In Indianapolis, the difference was one of kind rather than degree: For majority men, the direct effect of education on income was $290 per year; but for minority men this effect was essentially zero.

One other, completely unanticipated, finding appeared in our analysis of income: The extent to which income is determined by prior rank variables (as measured by R^2) is higher for the minority sample than for majority men in all four cities. The differences are considerable, extending to an extra 33 percentage points of explained variance in Safford for the minority sample. These sorts of majority–minority differences did not consistently appear over the cities for the determination of the other rank variables. It seems that even though the process which determines income is more or less similar for majority and minority men (differing only in that education has less direct influence for minority men), minority incomes are more tightly controlled by their other rank positions. Majority incomes are evidently affected by a number of additional factors, making it more difficult to predict their income from their rank positions. These additional factors, whatever they are, clearly do not affect minority incomes as much.

Our next analysis deals with minority handicaps in the total attainment of

Table 3.2 A Basic Model of the Stratification Process, for Males 20-64, by Majority versus Minority Racial-Ethnic Rank

Dependent variable	Independent variable	Unstandardized regression coefficients[a]							
		Indianapolis		Phoenix		Yuma		Safford	
		Majority	Minority	Majority	Minority	Majority	Minority	Majority	Minority
Income (OOs)	Occupation	.37*	.91*	.77*	.37*	.15	.53	.17	.32
	First occupation	b	.80*	.19	.08	.15	.63	-.51*	.38
	Education	2.93*	-.58	2.06*	1.63*	2.44	1.35	5.43*	.82
	Father's education		3.38*		-.73	.97	.96	-1.53	4.80*
	Father's occupation	.45*	-.32		-.30				.14
	Mother's education		-1.22		1.93*	2.44*	-2.47	2.83	-5.43*
	R^2	.21	.47	.16	.33	.11	.21	.08	.41
Occupation	First occupation	.28*	.10	.25*		.22*	.29*	.34*	.30
	Education	2.75*	3.09*	2.38*	1.97*	3.28*	2.98*	2.14*	2.63*
	Father's education	.32	.85		1.07	-.54	-.51		-.73
	Father's occupation	.11*	.21	.14*	.16		-.10	.09	.41*
	Mother's education				.62	.41	-.53		-.99
	R^2	.47	.59	.31	.33	.30	.39	.40	.40
First occupation	Education	4.33*	1.75*	3.65*	2.03*	4.31*	2.03*	3.85*	1.12*
	Father's education	.07	.23	.13*	.05	.08	1.10	.43	.43
	Father's occupation		.09		.53		.24*	.18*	.27*
	Mother's education		.26			.36			2.29*
	R^2	.46		.31	.34	.34	.33	.41	.55
Education	Father's education	.07	.18	.12*	.16	.05	.13	.29*	.29
	Father's occupation	.06*	.05	.03*	.09*	.04*	.04	.02	-.02

72

Standardized coefficients

Predictor								
Mother's education	.68*	.27*	.43*	.13*	.37*	.12*	.15	.31*
R^2	.33	.20	.19	.17	.30	.14	.19	.28
Approximate N	50	195	69	260	73	516	40	241
Income								
Occupation	.22	.06	.23	.07	.31*	.28*	.45*	.17*
First occupation	.19	-.18*	.23	.06	.05	.07	.29*	.28
Education	.10	.29*	.11	.13	.25*	.10*	-.05	.20*
Father's education	.47*	-.07	.05	.07	-.09		.31*	
Father's occupation	.07				-.16		-.13	
Mother's education	-.48*	.11	-.14	.14*	.23*		-.09	
Occupation								
First occupation	.22	.34*	.24*	.21*	.37*	.25*	.08	.28*
Education	.49*	.32*	.53*	.40*	.37*	.33*	.57*	.40*
Father's education	-.11		-.07	-.09	.17		.16	.05
Father's occupation	.28*	.07	-.06		.11	.14*	.17	.10*
Mother's education	-.13		-.07	.05	.09		.17	
First occupation								
Education	.28*	.57*	.43*	.54*	.52*	.50*	.44*	.63*
Father's education	.08	.06	.17		.05		.06	
Father's occupation	.06	.10	.19*	.09	.05	.13*	.10	.06
Mother's education				.05	.11		.17	
Education								
Father's education	.08	.27*	.09	.06	.16	.14*	.18	.08
Father's occupation	.36*	.11	.15	.33*	.09*	.22*	.22	.36*
Mother's education	.22*	.21*	.32*	.14*	.37*	.11*	.12	.22*

[a] Asterisked coefficients are those with associated t-values of 1.65 or more; hence, significant at about the .10 level (two-tailed test).

[b] Coefficients are not shown when the standardized path coefficient is less than .05; i.e., for relatively weak effects. None of these omitted coefficients were significantly different from zero.

rank, rather than with the "conversion" of one rank into another. For example, it deals with the incomes of men, not the rate of pay-off for a year of education. Perhaps this analysis, and its relation to the previous one, can best be described by using the diagram in Figure 3.2. We show here the relationship between a given rank variable, occupation, and a prior rank variable, education, for majority and for minority men. (This is a simplification of the analysis to follow, since we will always have several prior rank dimensions acting as independent variables, but the analysis can be illustrated using only education as an example of the set of independent variables.

What our analysis to this point has suggested is that the *slopes* of two such regression lines are not markedly different for majority and for minority men, especially with respect to predicting current occupation and income. That is, the yield in current occupation from an extra year of education is about the same for minority and majority men.

This is not to say, however, that their occupations will in fact be equal even if their educational (and other prior) ranks are equal. This is because the racial–ethnic variable may well have an effect on achievement in and of itself; such an effect is shown in Figure 3.2 by the different levels of the

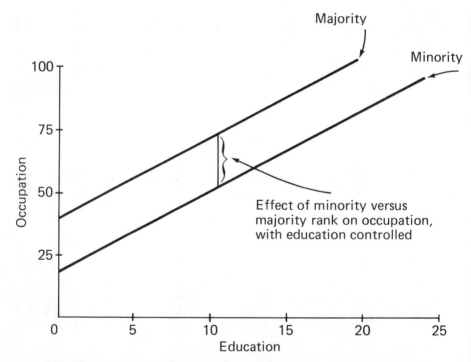

Figure 3.2.   A representation of the relationship between occupation and education, for majority and minority men, assuming no difference in slopes.

majority and minority regression lines. These different levels show that of two men who are alike in prior rank dimensions, the majority man will attain a higher level of occupational standing than the minority man, on the average.

The next stage in the analysis, then, is to investigate the presence and size of such racial–ethnic handicaps, and the points at which they appear in the achievement process. The question is: if a minority man has the same background as a majority man, will he do as well in achieving an education, an occupation and an income? If not, how sizable are the handicaps he faces, do they vary from city to city, and are they present at every point or are they concentrated only at certain stages in the achievement process? The data to answer these questions are presented in Table 3.3.

Our basic conclusion is that minority rank can be a substantial handicap, but the handicap varies both with city and with the achievement variable being considered. It appears that racial–ethnic rank affects achievement in different ways in different communities.

Let us look at the detailed results. Although our prior analysis showed it to be not quite accurate, we are assuming here that the attainment process has the same form (equal slopes) for both majority and minority, that is, we assume additivity. This allows us to compare the uncontrolled differences between majority and minority means in education, occupation, etc. (labelled "Unadjusted R–E Difference" in Table 3.3) with the differences between adjusted means. Such differences (labelled "Majority (Adjusted)" in Table 3.3) are equivalent to the differences in levels in the two regression lines in Figure 3.2. Adjusted differences are obtained in Table 3.3 by repeating the same regressions which yielded us the estimates of the basic model in Table 3.1, but adding majority–minority as an additonal (dichotomous) predictor. The regression coefficients for the majority variable are equivalent to adjusted differences between racial–ethnic means in an analysis of covariance. They essentially tell us how different is the attainment of hypothetical majority and minority men who have the same positions on all prior rank variables.

Beginning at the earliest point in the achievement process, we see that racial–ethnic rank directly affects education in only two cities. In all four cities, minority men have attained less education than majority men. These unadjusted differences range from 3 or 4 years in Arizona cities to a year and a half in Indianapolis. When the three background variables are controlled, however, we see that the differences become inconsequential in Safford and Indianapolis; that is, in these cities minority men attain less education only because they come from homes of lower rank. An additional handicap due to minority rank remains in Yuma and Phoenix.

A direct racial–ethnic effect on first occupation appears only in Indianapolis. Although in all of the cities the mean prestige of the first jobs held by minority men is well below that for majority men, the differences are

Table 3.3 Effects of Racial-Ethnic Rank, in a Basic Model of the Stratification Process, for Males 20-64, in Four Communities

Dependent variable	Independent variable	Regression coefficients: Unstandardized and standardized (in parentheses)[a]			
		Indianapolis	Phoenix	Yuma	Safford
Income (00s)	Unadjusted R-E difference	30.13	41.92	28.63	33.82
	Majority (adjusted)	10.68 (.07)	11.23 (.06)	2.23 (.02)	12.22 (.08)
	Occupation	.41 (.20)*	.73 (.29)*	.24 (.11)*	.22 (.08)
	First occupation	.14 (.06)	.21 (.08)*	.22 (.09)	-.43 (.16)*
	Education	2.54 (.17)*	1.76 (.10)*	1.98 (.12)*	4.15 (.26)*
	Father's education	b		1.06 (.08)	
	Father's occupation	.38 (.16)*			
	Mother's education	-.90 (.05)		1.46 (.10)	1.70 (.10)
	R^2	.25	.20	.16	.11
Occupation	Unadjusted R-E difference	24.54	23.97	15.84	20.22
	Majority (adjusted)	13.29 (.18)*	9.35 (.13)*	4.29 (.08)	4.63 (.08)
	First occupation	.26 (.25)*	.23 (.22)*	.23 (.22)*	.33 (.32)*
	Education	2.83 (.40)*	2.31 (.34)*	3.10 (.44)*	2.17 (.35)*
	Father's education	.39 (.06)		-.51 (.08)	
	Father's occupation	.12 (.10)*	.13 (.13)*		.12 (.09)*
	Mother's education				
	R^2	.54	.38	.37	.46
First occupation	Unadjusted R-E difference	19.55	14.92	11.90	17.45
	Majority (adjusted)	12.47 (.18)*	-1.40 (.02)	-2.45 (.05)	-.53 (.01)
	Education	3.90 (.58)*	3.33 (.52)*	3.52 (.53)*	3.53 (.55)*
	Father's education				.45 (.08)

Father's occupation	.08 (.08)	.13 (.13)*	.11 (.12)*	.20 (.16)*
Mother's education				
R^2	.47	.34	.35	.46
Education				
Unadjusted R-E difference	1.48	3.99	3.14	3.74
Majority (adjusted)	.04 (.00)	2.16 (.20)*	1.21 (.15)*	-.21 (.02)
Father's education	.09 (.10)	.13 (.15)*	.06 (.07)	.29 (.29)*
Father's occupation	.06 (.34)*	.03 (.20)*	.04 (.26)*	.02 (.08)
Mother's education	.28 (.21)*	.15 (.15)*	.20 (.22)*	.34 (.34)*
R^2	.28	.27	.29	.34
Approximate N	281	589	329	245

a Asterisked coefficients are those with associated t-values of 1.65 or more; hence, significant at about the .10 level (two-tailed test).

b Except for majority effects, coefficients are not shown when the standardized path coefficient is less than .05; i.e., for relatively weak effects. None of these omitted coefficients were significantly different from zero.

entirely due to the lower origins and educations of the minority men except in Indianapolis, where an additional handicap of 12 points on the Duncan scale still remains.

A minority handicap in current occupation appears in all of the cities, but the only large and statistically significant adjusted differences are in Phoenix and Indianapolis. In Yuma and Safford, the initial differences of about 20 points reduce to disadvantages of only 4 or 5 points after background (including first job) is controlled.

For income, the unadjusted differences between majority and minority range from $4200 to $2900, but these diminish considerably, to about $1200 or less, after controlling for prior variables. Nor are any of these remaining differences statistically significant, although all of them are in the same direction—a handicap for the minority man. If the estimates of the disadvantage are not simple due to sampling error (which seems unlikely, since they are all in the same, plausible direction), then the minority handicap is not inconsiderable, being over $1000 per year in three of the cities (see Duncan 1968:108, for a similar estimate from national data).[7]

We therefore end with a picture of considerable variation in our sixteen racial–ethnic effects (four cities and four attainment variables). Five of the effects seem to be effectively zero, since the adjusted coefficient for the majority–minority variable is either extremely small or negative. These are for the attainment of education in two cities and of first job in three cities. In these situations, the difference between majority and minority men can be wholly attributed to prior variables. Such minority disadvantages are not due to effects at that stage of attainment, but to the persistence of handicaps carried from earlier stages. In three other cases, in the determination of occupation in Yuma and Safford and of income in Yuma, we seen relatively minor statistically insignificant effects. Half of the effects of racial–ethnic rank, therefore, are rather small and/or likely to be chance fluctuations. Most of these effects appear in Yuma and Safford.

The other eight effects represent sizable handicaps. Racial–ethnic rank is directly responsible for handicaps of 1 or 2 years of education in two cities, of 9 to 13 points of prestige for first and/or current occupation in two cities,

[7]The reader will notice the R^2's in Table 3.3 are somewhat higher than those in Table 3.1 and may then conclude that the additional explanation that was obtained is solely due to the predictive power of the majority–minority variable, which was added in Table 3.3. This is not correct. When the minority subsample was added to the analysis in Table 3.3, extra variation was also introduced in other variables, since the added subsample had lower means on the origin ranks, education, etc. We can obtain the added explanation due to majority–minority rank *per se* by running the basic model on the sample used in Table 3.3 and comparing the R^2's so obtained with the R^2's reported in Table 3.3, which reflect the explanation obtained by the basic model *plus* the majority–minority variable. In those eight instances in which small and/or insignificant majority effects appeared, the additional explanation was negligible. In the other eight regressions, in which the majority variable had substantial effects, the additional proportion of the variance explained was about 3 or 4 percentage points.

and over $1000 in income in three cities (although these latter differences did not attain statistical significance). Although these effects are large in absolute terms, the standardized regression coefficients indicate that the effect of majority rank is usually substantially less than the effects of the prior achieved ranks. In the determination of occupation in Phoenix, for example, the beta (standardized coefficient) for majority is .13, as compared to betas of .22 and .34 for first job and education. However, in its effects on education in Phoenix and Yuma, racial–ethnic rank is about as powerful as each of the three origin variables.

Most of the racial–ethnic effects appeared in the two large cities. In these communities, the minority man is faced by an additional handicap at nearly every stage of attainment; the impact of these handicaps is cumulative (for a similar result, using national data, see Duncan 1968).

SUMMARY AND CONCLUSIONS

In this chapter, we compared our six communities with respect to a basic model of the stratification process involving three origin variables, two intervening variables (education and first occupation) and two *outcome* variables (current occupation and income). We then attempted to gauge the role of racial–ethnic rank in this process. Our major results are:

1. In the basic model, the direct effects of a given rank variable on others generally grows weaker as the "distance" (in terms of the causal ordering) increases between the two variables.

2. Education seems to be an especially crucial variable, partly because its effects are stronger than those of most other variables, and partly because most of the effects of social origin on later achievements are carried through education.

3. The stratification system is not tightly woven. A man's rank on each dimension is only moderately determined by his ranks on prior variables. This is especially true of the determination of education and of income.

4. The processes of inequality described by the basic model are approximately similar in all of our cities. The variations which do appear seem to be minor or moderate deviations from a common pattern rather than implying that certain cities or sets of cities have unique systems of stratification. The main variations that do appear concern the effects of education, first occupation and current occupation on income. The sorts of variations are not clearly patterned by either region or city size; for example, the effect of origin on attainment is *not* generally stronger in the small towns. However, the smaller the community the more often deviations of one sort or another appear; smaller cities seem to be somewhat more idiosyncratic in their stratification processes.

5. The effects of racial–ethnic rank on other rank dimensions seem mainly due to differences between blacks and Mexican–Americans on the one hand and majority racial–ethnic groups on the other. Ethnic differences within the majority group seem to have little effect.

6. The workings of the basic model of stratification appear to be similar in many respects within the majority and the minority groups, but several differences do appear. These are that (a) mother's education usually (in the Arizona cities) has a greater effect on educational attainment in minority groups than in majority groups; and (b) education has stronger effects on first occupation on income for majority men than for minority men. These results must be received with caution, given the small numbers of minority men in our analysis.

7. Under the assumption that the basic stratification processes were identical for majority and minority groups, we assessed the direct effect of minority versus majority membership on the other rank dimensions. Substantial minority handicaps are found only rarely in the medium and small cities, but appear at nearly every stage of achievement in the two large cities.

From these findings, we can draw several general impressions about inequality in American communities. First, our attempts to find marked differences in the processes of inequality between communities came up with similarities instead. Although some variations appear, it seems in general that roughly the same process operates in the various subpopulations we examined. This supports the argument in the first chapter that migration and market forces make communities and subcommunities relatively permeable and place limits on the uniqueness of a local stratification system (compare Mueller 1974).

One striking feature of this roughly universal stratification process is its looseness. The last chapter told us that rigidity is low; the same result is expressed here in the finding that the effects of one rank variable on another are far from coercive. Tendencies toward equilibration are undeniably present, but they are not strong enough to produce a tightly woven system of stratification, a single continuum of inferiority and superiority which describes accurately the placement of individuals. At each state of the attainment process the position one might expect based on past attainment is disturbed by variables not included in our model and/or by chance factors.

Some comment is required about the interpretation of the effects we have described. What meaning should be given to the coefficients linking education and occupation, or racial–ethnic rank and income? Here we can mainly raise issues but not provide answers.

For example, racial–ethnic handicaps appearing in the results can be interpreted as indicators of discrimination. That is, those persons enpowered to allocate years of schooling, good jobs, and higher incomes systematically decide in favor of majority candidates, even when equally well-qualified minority candidates (in terms of prior achievement or background) are available.

This explanation is probably correct to a considerable degree, but it is not the only possible one. If it were, one could explain, for example, the relative educational overachievement of Jews (see Featherman 1971a) only by assuming that teachers systematically bias their decisions in favor of Jews. Instead, in this case, an argument in terms of subculture can be advanced: that the racial–ethnic group in question has advantages in terms of socialization into achievement values, productive work styles, information about opportunities, etc. These subcultural advantages improve their chances of success over and above the effects of whatever prior rank attainments they may have. Turning the argument about in this case, we might argue that blacks or Mexican–Americans in our cities were heir to partially disabling subcultures that would lead to less attainment, even in the complete absence of discrimination. These are not opposing explanations; it is perfectly possible, even probable, that discrimination and subcultures which help or hinder achievement both affect the success of a minority group. Further, a subculture hindering achievement may well be a product of current discrimination or a residue of past discrimination.

We cannot disentangle these two factors with our data, since we lack the necessary range of accurate measures on subcultural styles and on experiences of discrimination. All our results establish is that the net effect of discrimination and minority subcultures is a set of handicaps for minority men. These handicaps may be entirely due to discrimination, entirely due to nonproductive subcultures, or due to some combination of the two factors, such as widespread discrimination, partially but not entirely compensated for by subcultures that *assist* achievement.

Similar ambiguities overtake us when asking about the meaning of the links between various achieved ranks. A functionalist perspective, for example, would interpret the relatively strong effects of education on occupation and of occupation on income as showing that high prestige jobs are those which are functionally important and require scarce talent. Hence, more years of education are typically required to train a person for them, and to motivate persons to enter them and to perform well, higher incomes are likewise required. Presumably, these relationships are more or less the same throughout the society, which would account for the similarities in rank processes we observed. However, from other perspectives, it can be argued that, for example, the link between education and occupation arises from sources besides the necessity to attain technical competence; that education is used by some occupational groups to restrict entry and increase their security and prestige and by some employers to guarantee docile middle-class employees (see Collins 1971).

This chapter and the last have presented data on the relationships between several more or less objective measures of rank attainment. We turn, in the next chapter, to questions about how our respondents subjectively interpret their community's system of inequality and their own position within it.

4

PERCEPTIONS OF INEQUALITY

This chapter completes our analysis of the rank systems of the six communities by asking how the men in our sample *perceive* those systems and their places within them. Conceivably, each man could perceive his own rank and that of others according to his own unique perceptual apparatus and perspective. But for individuals to communicate with each other about systems of inequality or act in common regarding them, some agreement between individual perspectives is necessary. Our interest here, then, will be on shared symbolic understandings of social class, even though our data will consist of aggregated individual responses.

It may be profitable to briefly contrast "social class" with other sorts of differences about which social perceptions could exist. Sex, for example, is an attribute which plays a central social role because (a) everyone is *aware* of the distinction and can use it to classify other people; (b) *consensus* on the nature of the attribute and (to some extent) on its social meaning is widespread; and (c) the attribute is *salient* in many social situations, that is, it affects behavior. Other kinds of differentiation can also be rated on these dimensions. For example, at the other pole from sex on the awareness and salience dimensions is such an attribute as "blood type." Although individuals differ with respect to this attribute, some people do not know that different blood types exist; and those that are aware of the variable do not usually know the blood types of the people they interact with. Since blood type rarely affects social interaction, it ranks as low on salience as it does on awareness. For these reasons, the consensus of perceptions on blood type is presumably socially irrelevant.

People can answer the question, What sexes are there? with confidence and authority; can they also answer confidently with respect to categories of rank superiority and inferiority? Are there perceptions of differences with respect to social rank, especially perceptions of global categories such as "social classes," upon which awareness, salience, and consensus are as high as for sexual differences?

Presumably racial differences occupy such a place in American culture. Educational, occupational, and income differences probably rank somewhat lower in awareness (almost everyone knows about these attributes, but cannot as easily place all of his acquaintances on them as with respect to race or sex). However, consensus has been shown to be high for perceptions of occupational prestige (see Reiss et al. 1961:194–195); consensus is also presumably high for educational and income differences. But are these perceptions of individual rank differences bound together and organized by perceptions of ordered global categories, "classes," which perhaps are also salient in organizing competitive or conflict relationships?

Further, is there a high degree of consensus on such global perceptions? Such consensus could be of two kinds. First, as with sex, there could be perspectives which are shared almost uniformly throughout the society. Secondly, shared perspectives may develop a particular form in certain communities or within certain sectors of society (among "lower class" people, for example), whereas in other sectors either no consensus develops or a different, perhaps opposing perspective is widely accepted.

It can be argued (see Hodge and Treiman 1968a) that clear, agreed-upon perceptions of social class categories are unlikely to develop in the United States because the correlations between education, occupation, income, etc. are only moderate. For this reason, many people (and many people they know) are, for example, "middle class," in some respects and "lower class" in others. Such people are unlikely to develop a clear notion of "classness" to categorize themselves and other people.

Another argument to the same end is that even if most people did have consistent rank positions, the relationships between rank and other experiences (friendships, ethnic subcultures, regional affiliations, etc.) are so low that these cross-cutting allegiances will prevent the formation of clear class identities or consciousness. This argument may be valid for consciousness, but it seems weak with respect to simple conceptual identity. Sex, once again, is a variable subject to many cross-cutting allegiances, yet a clear social definition has emerged. Cross-cutting allegiances between class and other kinds of ties should not prevent notions of class categories from arising, but they may well (as they have done with respect to sex) hinder the formation of solidary groups based on class similarity.

It can also be argued that not even low correlations between rank variables necessarily prevent clear notions of class from developing. For example, if income differences were central and crucial enough, they would form an overriding basis for social perceptions of differences (for example, "rich," "well-off," "doing all right," "poor"), regardless of the educations and occupations of the people involved.

Of course, people's behavior in their communities with respect to stratification (their attempts to attain higher rank, their responses to frustration in attainment, etc.) may be carried on *without* a clear and common perspective. That is, the stratification system of the community may affect behavior and represent the conditions for individual effort without being clearly conceptualized by the participants. However, if such common perspectives develop, their form should be crucial in understanding how people individually and in concert react to inequality.

The analyses below fall into three parts. First we shall investigate perceptions of the system of classes. Second, we shall analyze how people place themselves in a predetermined list of classes and how this is affected by objective rank. Third, we shall return to the individual's view of the stratification system as a whole and investigate perspectives of class dissensus and legitimate success. Each issue involves studying individual responses (by methodological necessity), but we shall be especially interested in the description of communities, the nature and extent of agreement within each community, and possible differences between the communities.

DO AMERICANS PERCEIVE A CLASS STRUCTURE IN THEIR COMMUNITIES?

Our initial attempt to find out how clearly the people in our communities perceive a class structure involved only the first survey, that of Indianapolis. Following Neal Gross's procedure (1953), we asked the open–ended question: "There has been a lot of talk recently about social classes in the United States. I wonder what you think about this. What social classes do you think there are in Indianapolis?" We hoped this question would pick up any structured orientation toward class which might be held by the population in general.

The results suggest that consensus in this area is incomplete, partial and exists only on a very general level. To begin with, about a third of the respondents replied that they didn't know, or were otherwise unable to answer the question.[1] Often the term "social class" was unfamiliar to them. This kind of result is probably not peculiar to Indianapolis. Gross (1953) obtained very similar findings in his study of Minneapolis.

Our interviewers could not clarify the term, "social class," for the respondents because the intent of the question was to find out what the respondent meant (if anything) by the term. Thus the questioning process itself raises a paradox. In order to ask a question, one must orient the respondent to the thing asked about. The clearer the orientation, the more clearly the answer can be interpreted. Where the question is about the respondent's orientation

---

[1]The Indianapolis responses to this question reported here refer to the entire Indianapolis sample, including women and men who were not household heads.

in the first place, however, the more an investigator orients the respondent, the more he predetermines the nature of the answer. In the extreme case, a clear orientation means that the answer is given in the question and is therefore the sociologist's, not the respondent's.

Evidently for a third of the Indianapolis sample the phrase "social class" did not carry a clear meaning, as the terms "race" or "sex" would have; objects named "social classes" were not present in their system of social perception. Perhaps these respondents possess only a set of fuzzy notions about the various forms of social inequality or perhaps they have very sharp, clear perceptions which simply aren't connected to the words "social class." It does seem unlikely, however, that they would perceive a stack of clearly delineated and unequal social groups and not reflect this view in their answers.

Two-thirds of the sample, then, did give an answer to the question. Of these, only a very small fraction (1.7% of the sample) maintained the extreme egalitarian position that "there are no classes" (or words to that effect). Most of the rest of the sample responded with a list of the groups they perceived as "social classes." The number of groups listed varied from one to eleven, but three was the modal response, given by 51.4% of the responding sample. Two (13.1%) and four (14.7%) were the next most popular numbers. In short, about a third of the total population said "don't know," about a third listed three classes (of one sort or another), and the rest listed a variety of other numbers of classes.

What kinds of differentiation were reflected in the lists of classes given? Respondents did not limit themselves to any one continuum in listing classes, so that many sorts of differentiation were referred to, sometimes even by the same respondent. General class categories (e.g., upper, middle, below average, etc.) were mentioned most frequently, followed by economic classes (e.g., high income group, the poor). About 5% mentioned "high society" sorts of classes and about 5% mentioned "working class." Other classes, based on power, education, race, morals, etc., were mentioned very infrequently.

In Indianapolis, then, the people that did furnish a list of classes did not agree on their number or nature. Further, when asked (as an open-end question) "What social class do you think you are in?" a fifth of the respondents who had listed classes placed themselves in a class that had not previously appeared on their list.

These results strongly suggest that no clear, widely accepted view of classes is part of the perceptual culture of Indianapolis residents. The findings suggest instead that many of the respondents were struggling manfully to answer a question which had little natural meaning to them. Some consensus evidently exists (witness the frequency of responding with three classes and the use of general class terms such as "middle"), but evidently the residents are not clearly aware of "social classes" in the typical sociological sense.

CLASS PLACEMENT BY SELF AND OTHERS

Returning to the full sample of adult male family heads in six communities, we want to examine, in this section, how the respondents placed themselves in a list of classes and how they were placed by an outside rater (the interviewer). To measure self-placement, we adapted a question that was devised by Richard Centers (1949) and used in many studies since (Hodge and Treiman 1968a; Jackman and Jackman 1973). The specific form of the question we asked was: "If you were asked to use one of these names for your social class, which would you say you belonged to?" The interviewer then handed the respondent a card with class titles (in this order): lower class, working class, upper class, poor class, middle class. If the respondent chose the latter term, the interviewer then asked him: "Would you say you were in the upper-middle class or the lower-middle class?"[2] Men who refused to make this final choice were listed as "middle-middle." In some of the analyses that follow, we use the titles listed above as categories; in others we score the titles from 0 (for lower class) to 6 (for upper class) and use the scores as an interval scale for correlations, regressions and the like.

Using this question involves us in a severe problem: Since we concluded in the previous section that most people do not think in terms of a clear, agreed-upon set of social classes, how are we to interpret their choices when placing themselves in a list of classes presented by the interviewer? Do their answers mean anything?

We believe that the way people answer this question roughly indicates perceptions of general standing in the community, but does not indicate very much about the development of class consciousness or about identification with a social class. (Hence, our title for this variable is "class self-placement," not "class identification.") People undoubtedly think at times about matters of superiority and inferiority and despite the lack of clear concepts about class, develop some notion of their relative standing in the community. Our argument, then, is that the concepts of most people are accurately summed up by some such statement as: "I don't know much about social class, but I do know where I am." By the same token, a person might know that he lives near the Loop without being able to draw an accurate map of metropolitan Chicago.

[2]The form of the question given above was used in the five-city survey. In Indianapolis, after the open-end question on class, we asked the self-placement question as above, except that in the list of classes the positions of middle class and poor class were reversed.

Self-placement is not difficult, evidently; in every city over 98% of the men were willing and able to answer the question. We shall also see, below, that their replies are not capricious, but are related in plausible ways to various objective measures of rank. However, the respondent's ability to perform this chore when asked does not show that he normally thinks of inequality in terms of a set of classes in the community, or that he identifies himself with any such class. In the same way, a man 6 feet in height could select the term "moderately tall" to describe himself; this indicates that he knows men differ in height and where he places in that particular ordering, but it does not necessarily mean that he sees 6-footers as a separate solidary group or feels any identification or emotional tie with the other 6-footers. We will use these responses, therefore, simply to reflect subjective perceptions of general standing. We shall not force this question to carry the extra freight of measuring class consciousness or identification in the sense of a bond with men who share a common fate.

We were also interested in how people rank each other in terms of superiority and inferiority. It is difficult to get at this directly even in the small towns and nearly impossible in the larger cities, since most people do not know each other well. We therefore tried to get at the matter indirectly, by asking our interviewers after each interview to classify the respondent as "upper class, upper-middle class, lower-middle class, working class, or lower class." In this way, we used the interviewer, who usually was a member of the community, to obtain a rough and imperfect measure of how each man would be rated by other people in his city. Since our interviewers were typically middle-class, middle-aged women, and since they were (as a result of the interview) privy to much information about the respondent, including his present ranks, his origin and his own self-rating, it is apparent that the measure is indeed "rough and imperfect."

In this section, we want to treat three aspects of subjective rank: (a) how self-ratings and interviewer-ratings are distributed in the cities and related to each other; (b) how self- and interviewer-ratings of the neighborhood are related; and (c) the ways in which a man's self-placement is affected by his objective ranks.

The distribution of self-placement in each community (see Table 4.1) is unavailable to direct observers of the community, but represents a kind of aggregated, collective self-image. These distributions were fairly similar in our cities (the relationship between the variables of "city" and "self-placement" yielded a Goodman and Kruskal's tau of only .01). The categories of upper class, lower class, and poor class were avoided by all but a few respondents in all the cities. The working-class label was chosen by between a third and a half of the men in each city; most of the remaining men rated themselves as upper-middle or lower-middle class. That is, when provided with a list of labels ranging from the megalomaniac to an open admission of failure, our men generally divided themselves into a sizable

Table 4.1 *Cities Compared on Self-Placement*

Self-placement	Indianapolis	Columbus	Linton	Phoenix	Yuma	Safford
Upper	5.0%	3.5%	2.1%	2.8%	2.7%	2.6%
Upper-middle	25.9%	28.5%	21.9%	29.4%	27.4%	28.5%
Middle-middle	9.1%	27.2%	21.2%	22.6%	12.2%	14.8%
Lower-middle	18.9%	6.4%	4.1%	9.0%	11.1%	11.1%
Working	37.9%	33.1%	49.3%	33.2%	44.4%	41.3%
Lower or poor	3.2%	1.3%	1.4%	3.1%	2.2%	1.6%
N (100%)	317	375	292	681	369	305

working class group and a somewhat larger group choosing one of the three middle-class labels.

The proportion who see themselves as working class or below is lowest in Phoenix and Columbus and highest in Safford and Linton. The proportion of upper-middle or upper class identifiers seems to be fairly constant from city to city, so that the clue to psychological class differences between the cities would seem to be the proportion identifying with the working or a lower class.[3]

In an analysis below we will try to determine to what extent the cities differ in patterns of self-placement because they differ in patterns of objective rank. For example, the two cities with least working-class placement have high means on income, education, etc. We would not expect a one-to-one correspondence, however. The level of working-class identification in a community probably results not only from the level of education and poverty and the distribution of occupations, but also from the treatment of workers—on and off the job—and from feelings about that treatment as well. Self-placement is affected by social conditions, that is, as well as by objective life circumstances.

Central among these social conditions is placement by others. Theoretically, self-placement should be a social-psychological consequence of, among other things, rankings by various significant others. Our data show that others' ratings (indexed here by interviewer's rating) are strongly related to self-placement (scoring them both numerically). The zero-order r's range from .46 in Safford to .60 in Columbus (see Table 4.2).

The pattern of the relationship between self- and interviewer-ratings

[3]Another large difference between the cities is the proportion who choose the "lower-middle class" label rather than insist on remaining simply "middle class." We hesitate to interpret these shifts across cities, however, since the largest difference (between Indianapolis and the other cities) is due at least in part to differences in the format of the interview schedule that made it harder for an Indianapolis interviewer to allow the respondent to give "middle" as a final answer.

Table 4.2 *Correlations between Self-Ratings and Interviewer-Ratings*

Pairs of ratings correlated	Indianapolis	Columbus	Linton	Phoenix	Yuma	Safford
Self-placement and interviewer's rating of R	.52	.60	.49	.52	.51	.46
R's neighborhood rating and interviewer's area rating	.49	.67	.46	.55	.55	.39
Self-placement and R's neighborhood rating	.32	.43	.19	.34	.31	.25
Approximate N	312	373	291	674	362	303

shows that self-placements are not whimsical (or they would not agree so well with interviewer ratings) but are biased, and the pattern of the bias is not uniform throughout the class structure (see Table 4.3). People hesitate to place themselves at the top or the bottom, and yet the extremes of a status continuum are easiest to judge reliably. In consequence, upper- and lower-class persons as rated by the interviewer tend to rate themselves, quite predictably, more toward the center: 57% of the former placed themselves as upper-middle, and 58% of the latter rated themselves as working. Literal agreement was highest, however, for the working class; 64% of those classed as working by the interviewer classified themselves the same way. Agreement between self and other was lowest in the middle categories.

We are also able to compare self- and other-placement with respect to another form of rank, the prestige of the respondent's neighborhood. A person's choice of neighborhood is an important aspect of social consumption. It provides a central and visible arena within which he may express and

Table 4.3 *Self-Placement by Interviewer-Rating, for the Six Cities Combined*

Interviewer's rating of respondent	Social class in which the respondent placed himself						
	Upper	Upper-middle	Middle-middle	Lower-middle	Working	Lower or poor	N (100%)
Upper	21.1	56.9	16.5	1.8	3.7	0.0	109
Upper-middle	3.8	46.5	24.8	10.4	14.1	.3	737
Lower-middle[a]	1.8	22.5	21.9	14.6	38.1	1.1	570
Working	1.3	11.9	12.8	7.6	63.8	2.5	788
Lower	.9	5.4	6.3	7.2	57.5	22.5	111

[a]Includes 18 cases in Indianapolis for which the interviewer could not decide between "upper-middle" and "lower-middle."

enjoy (or regret) the extent of his success. If general social standing depends as much or more on consumption, or style of life, as on one's role in the system of production, neighborhood should be especially important in organizing the subjective aspects of social rank.

It may even be that, in the U.S., neighborhood labels come closer than any other collective notions to establishing group boundaries which most people in a community agree on and use to organize their ideas of superiority and inferiority. That is, to the extent that class consciousness exists for most people in the U.S., it may involve people categorizing and ordering other people with respect to neighborhoods rather than, for example, with respect to production or income groups. Sometimes neighborhoods have even acted as conscious solidary groups, taking collective action to support their current privileges or improve their share of privilege.

To measure perceptions in this area, respondents were asked: "How would you say this neighborhood rates compared to other neighborhoods in (community)?" They were then offered a card with the list: one of the best; one of the better neighborhoods; a little above average; a little below average; below average. We also asked the interviewer to rate the "residential area" in which the respondent lived, with the same categories used to rate the respondent.

The interviewer's rating of the neighborhood agreed quite well with the respondent's rating (scored numerically), though somewhat less so in the two small towns (see Table 4.2). In short, there was roughly the same self-other agreement about the area or neighborhood that there was about the person, with the partial exception of the small towns. This exception was also reflected in the factor analysis findings (Artz et al. 1971) in which a residence factor was much more apparent in the large and medium-sized cities than in the towns.

The respondent's placement of himself is also related to his rating of his neighborhood (Table 4.2). His residential consumption is at least congruent with, if not an influence on, his conception of his standing in the community. Once again, this correlation is lower in the two small towns. Perhaps the systems of reputation in such towns do not have to rely on residential consumption as a sign of success, because much more is generally known about each person by a substantial portion of the population. Moreover, these towns may be too small to maintain the extensive residential differentiation possible in a much larger population, so neighborhoods may be less distinctive. In sum, we must qualify our earlier suggestion that many subjective concepts of inequality might be organized around neighborhood labels: This may be an accurate description for even medium-sized cities, but in towns as small as Linton and Safford concepts of rank do not appear to be as congruent with concepts of neighborhood, if, indeed, clear concepts of neighborhoods even exist there.

We now turn to an analysis of the ways in which the dimensions of rank affect class self-placement. The analysis is guided by a model that states that one's self-placement is determined (but not completely, as we shall see) by his current and earlier rank positions. That is, we shall treat self-placement as an *outcome* of the process analyzed in Chapter 3. This may well be an over-simplification, however. A more adequate picture of the process would be to think of the person as having a subjective rank, or self-placement, at each point in his career (during his education, entering his first job, etc.). Presumably, the person's subjective rank at any given time is affected by his subjective rank at earlier times, as well as by his current rank standing. That is, in path analysis terms, there should probably be a strong direct path from self-placement at each time period to self-placement at the next, and so on.

Further, the effects may be reciprocal: Self-placement may affect, as well as be influenced by, objective rank. Some studies (Sewell *et al.* 1970; Woelfel and Haller 1971) suggest that a person's image of himself and his standing in the eyes of others may affect motivations, decisions and actions that contribute to objective success. It may well be, for example, that a person declined to take a permanent job just after high school, continuing to college instead, because he thought of himself as upper-middle, or because he perceived that others thought of him as upper-middle and expected this behavior of him. Given the design of our study, we could not collect the data (measures of self-placement and other-placement at earlier times) to test such a model. In the interpretation of the data below, however, the reader should keep in mind that the effects presented may be summaries or simplifications of more complicated processes involving effects of earlier self-placement both on objective ranks and on later self-placements.

The rank dimensions that have the greatest effects on class self-placement appear to be income and occupation (see Table 4.4). These effects are consistently strong across all the communities, although the data suggest that the effect of occupation is somewhat weaker in Arizona and in the small towns. The next most influential variable is education, which again exhibits a regional difference: Educational effects are greater in Arizona than in Indiana.

In general, then, the major effects are carried by variables reflecting current, achieved rank. The effects of background and ascribed variables are smaller and less consistent. Class of origin, as reflected in father's occupation and mother's education, has some positive influence in all of the cities except Safford, but the effects are relatively weak and scattered in patterns from city to city.

The effects of the racial–ethnic majority variable are especially unstable and weak. Although we expected that belonging to a minority group would depress (or majority membership inflate) class self-placement, in only two cities, Yuma and Safford, did even a moderate effect of this kind seem to be

Table 4.4 Self-Placement Regressed on Rank Variables

	Regression coefficients: Unstandardized and standardized (in parentheses)[a]						
Rank variables	Average within-city	Indianapolis	Columbus	Linton	Phoenix	Yuma	Safford
Family income	.004 (.19)*	.003 (.12)*	.006 (.23)*	.005 (.19)*	.004 (.19)*	.004 (.16)*	.005 (.22)*
Occupation	.016 (.28)*	.025 (.47)*	.017 (.32)*	.013 (.24)*	.014 (.24)*	.016 (.27)*	.009 (.15)*
Education	.044 (.12)*	b	.036 (.10)*		.058 (.15)*	.044 (.11)*	.075 (.23)*
Father's occupation	.005 (.08)*		.005 (.09)*	.008 (.11)*	.009 (.14)*		
Mother's education	.019 (.04)*	.031 (.06)	.031 (.06)			.023 (.06)	-.034 (.09)
Majority[c]						.251 (.08)	.366 (.10)*
R^2		.35	.31	.17	.32	.23	.23
Mean		3.3	3.6	3.2	3.5	3.3	3.3
Adjusted mean[d]		3.3	3.5	3.4	3.4	3.3	3.5
N		322	373	297	686	375	306

[a]Asterisked coefficients are those with associated t-values of 1.65 or higher; hence, significant at about the .10 level (two-tailed test).

[b]Coefficients are not shown when the standardized path coefficient is both nonsignificant and less than .05, i.e., for relatively weak effects.

[c]In Columbus and Linton, the Bogardus (social distance) racial-ethnic scale was used instead of the dichotomous racial-ethnic majority variable, since these two samples contained practically no men of minority rank.

[d]Means of self-placement calculated after statistically making the cities equal with respect to the independent variables (see Blalock, 1972:491-497).

present, and these effects were reduced to insignificance when a control for age was introduced.

Our analysis is based on the assumption of additivity, that is, that such variables as education and occupation affect self-placement in about the same way for majority and minority men. Jackman and Jackman (1973) present data to dispute this assumption: They conclude that current achieved ranks affect self-placement among whites, but not among blacks. To investigate this possibility, we first tested for non-additivity in the prediction of self-placement from ethnicity and occupation (Jackson and Curtis 1972), according to procedures described in Chapter 5. Rejecting that hypothesis, we next regressed class self-placement in the total sample on education, occupation and income separately for white Anglo–Americans, Mexican–Americans and blacks. The regression slopes were similar for the Anglo–Americans and Mexican–Americans. For blacks, self-placement was not affected by education or income, but was substantially influenced by occupation. Jackman and Jackman's conclusion that no achieved rank affects self-placement among blacks does not hold up in our data. Since all groups showed some effects of current rank on self-placement we concluded that an assumption of additivity was justified, if only as a first approximation.

Table 4.4 also suggests that self-placement is less affected by objective rank dimensions in the smaller towns (the R^2's drop to .17 and .23 in Linton and Safford). This is consistent with the notion that in a small town a person's status is affected more by unique local reputations perhaps revolving around such factors as ancestry or moral repute. People in small towns have, presumably, more information about their fellow townsfolk than those in a large city, hence, they have a greater number of characteristics upon which to base their relative standing, over and beyond the more or less objective and visible standards of income and occupation.

The final step in our analysis of self-placement was to introduce several new variables, both to see if any of the above findings were spurious and to search for variables which intervene between objective rank and subjective self-placement. We therefore added the occupation of the respondent's best friend (scored on the Duncan scale) and a dichotomous variable representing union membership (members scored as 1, nonmembers as 0) to check our prediction (partly based on findings by Hodge and Treiman 1968a) that self-placement is influenced by the rank of the people a person associates with informally or formally. We also added the variables of age, because of its relationship with the various rank variables, and first occupation. The racial–ethnic majority variable was omitted, since we had found that its effect was restricted to two cities and quite small when age was controlled. The results are presented in Table 4.5.

We first see that the introduction of the new variables only slightly changes our prior conclusions about the effects of the rank variables upon

Table 4.5 Self-Placement Regressed on Rank Variables and Control Variables

	Regression coefficients: Unstandardized and standardized (in parentheses)[a]						
Rank variables	Average within-city	Indianapolis	Columbus	Linton	Phoenix	Yuma	Safford
Family income	.004 (.18)*	.002 (.07)	.005 (.20)*	.004 (.19)*	.004 (.18)*	.005 (.18)*	.006 (.24)*
Occupation	.011 (.20)*	.021 (.39)*	.015 (.29)*	.009 (.17)*	.008 (.14)*	.009 (.15)*	.009 (.15)*
First occupation	b	.004 (.08)		.006 (.09)		.006 (.10)	-.006 (.09)
Education	.056 (.15)*		.057 (.14)*	.036 (.08)	.065 (.16)*	.061 (.15)*	.087 (.26)*
Father's occupation	.005 (.07)*	.005 (.09)	.006 (.09)*	.006 (.08)	.009 (.14)*		
Mother's education	.021 (.04)*	.036 (.07)	.029 (.06)	.028 (.05)		.031 (.07)	-.023 (.06)
First friend's job	.004 (.07)*	.003 (.06)	.006 (.10)*		.006 (.10)*	.005 (.09)*	.004 (.07)
Union membership	-.192 (.05)*			-.204 (.07)	-.191 (.05)	-.223 (.07)	
Age	.012 (.13)*	.009 (.09)*	.011 (.12)*	.020 (.24)*	.012 (.13)*	.017 (.17)*	
R²		.36	.37	.24	.32	.28	.23
Mean		3.4	3.7	3.2	3.5	3.3	3.4
Adjusted mean[c]		3.4	3.6	3.4	3.4	3.4	3.6
N		278	296	237	608	336	274

[a] Asterisked coefficients are those with associated t-values of 1.65 or higher; hence, significant at about the .10 level (two-tailed test).

[b] Coefficients are not shown when the standardized path coefficient is both nonsignificant and less than .05, i.e., for relatively weak effects.

[c] Means of self-placement calculated after statistically making the cities equal with respect to the independent variables (see Bialock, 1972:491-497).

self-placement. Income and occupation still have the major effects, although the direct effect of the latter is smaller. The effect of education is *increased* somewhat, compared to Table 4.4. This is probably due to the effects of age. The data show that older people consistently rank themselves more highly, net of the effects of their current and past status ranks. This positive effect of age on self-placement coupled with the fact that the older men are less well educated served to slightly depress the true effects of education in Table 4.4, where age was not controlled.

The social participation variables also influence self-placement, but the effects are neither as strong nor as consistent as the effect of age. If a man has a best friend in a prestigious job his self-placement tends to go up; belonging to a union tends to decrease self-placement (although the effect is minimal in 3 cities). These social participation variables, then, have mild direct effects, net of a man's rank, but they do not seem to be major mediators between achievement and self-placement. That is, introducing these variables did not cause the direct effects of the rank variables to markedly diminish. Interaction pattern is not a major reason why income and occupation affect self-placement.

Does the relation of self-placement to the rank variables throw any more light on the hypothesis of a unique community versus a uniform national system of social rank? A unique system of community subjective rank could arise in a number of ways, two of which will be mentioned here. The first is that, in a given community or set of communities, the objective ranks are translated into subjective placements in unique ways. In general, this did not happen in our sample of six cities—the processes converting objective to subjective rank were more or less similar. However, as we said above, the conversion processes were less determinate in the two small towns. And in one of the small towns, Safford, moderate departures from the common pattern can be seen (for example, smaller or negative effects of rank origins, larger effects of education, smaller effects of age).

Even if the processes (that is, the regression slopes) in the communities were identical, unique community systems of subjective rank could arise if the men in each community determined their self-placement only with respect to the other men in the community and not with respect to an overall national ranking system. If this were true, for example, a poor man in a poor town would give himself a higher subjective rank than an equally poor man in a richer town. The question is: With respect to whom is deprivation relative? If each man ranks himself relative to national scales of occupation, income, etc., the result is a pattern in which the raw score means on self-placement in the two communities are different, but the adjusted means are the same (see Blalock 1972:491–497). But if the men in each community compare themselves only to other men in that community, we should expect equal raw score self-placement means and different adjusted means.

Which scheme do our data seem to resemble? The data in Tables 4.4 and 4.5 show that the raw score means on self-placement differ more from city to city than do the adjusted means. This suggests that the actual process, although probably a mixture of the two, is closer to that of men ranking themselves mainly with an eye to national dispersions on income, occupation, etc., rather than strictly relative to local distributions. Such an effect is plausible in light of the effects of mass media and migration, both of which tend to broaden the horizon of a man's reference group beyond his own community.

PERCEPTIONS OF CLASS DISSENSUS ON PUBLIC ISSUES

We now turn our attention back to the way in which the respondent perceives the status system in general, as opposed to his own place in it. Our interview schedule included questions on two additional perceptions of the system: whether "classes" agree on public issues and whether people attain success by legitimate means.

An orientation of special interest is the view that workers are opposed to owners and managers on important issues in the community. If businessmen and workers take opposite sides on important public issues, and if this is generally realized, then consciousness of class and class interests in the community is not completely latent. In fact, this kind of polarization may be one important step in converting people similar in rank into a solidary group.

To measure the extent to which our respondents saw people in different parts of the class structure as having different political stands, we asked, after a series of questions tapping opinions on domestic political issues, the questions: "Do you think that most businessmen in (community) would agree with your opinions on Medicare and on the Poverty Program?" and "Do you think that most workingmen in (community) would agree with your opinions on Medicare and on the Poverty Program?" If the respondent answered that businessmen agreed with him while workingmen did not, or vice versa, we scored him below as "perceiving dissensus." If he felt that both groups agreed with him or that neither group agreed (this last an infrequent response), he is classified below as "perceiving consensus."

In general, more men perceived agreement than dissensus. To begin with, about 30% of the respondents said "don't know" to one or both questions, suggesting that they lacked the information needed to judge consensus or dissensus. For the men who answered both questions, 37.5% (about a quarter of the whole sample) perceived dissensus (as scored by the above procedure). Most other men felt that *both* workers and businessmen agreed with them. This response suggests a perception of widespread community consensus and certainly not of strong class consciousness. Such people may well see various cleavages in their community (as between "good people" and "bad people"), but not between the "haves" and the "have nots."

Perceiving dissensus on public issues does not seem to be uniformly related to a man's perception of his own class standing, but does show some changes from community to community. The data are shown in Table 4.6. We should emphasize that the number of cities is small and the pattern is not clear–cut, so our conclusions are highly tentative.

In Indiana communities, perceptions of dissensus decline with city size both for the total sample and within each self-placement group. This change with city size shows up in Arizona only among men who place themselves in the working or lower classes. Small-town men, then, and especially small-town workers, are less likely to see disagreement than men in larger cities.

We can restate the result by saying that in small towns working class men perceive dissensus less than middle-class men, but this difference disappears in the larger cities. Perceiving dissensus should lead to some sense of collective identity as a result of perceiving disagreement or conflict with another group. If so, then our findings can (tentatively) be read to suggest that in small towns middle and upper-middle class men tend to see some collective interests, while the workingmen do not. In the large cities, all three groups seem to be more or less equally conscious of a collective identity. However, if the strong relationship *among workers* between city size and seeing dissensus holds for the entire range of city sizes, then we would expect that working men in metropolitan cities would be more conscious of collective interests than middle-class men. We should add, though, that these are variations within a general context of consensus (and by implication, of a low sense of common identity). In almost every group in every city, more men perceived consensus between businessmen and workers than saw them as disagreeing on public issues.

PERCEPTIONS OF LEGITIMATE SUCCESS

Another crucial aspect of perceptions about the status system is whether individuals are seen as being rewarded fairly, that is, whether successful persons are seen as attaining their success in ways generally regarded as legitimate in American society. We shall here be interested in the general extent to which men see success as legitimate, and whether this varies from city to city, but our main question in this final analysis is whether the judgment about legitimacy is affected by rank. If success is regarded by the successful as fairly gotten, but by the unsuccessful as unfairly gotten, the system of stratification cannot be regarded as resting on a basis of legitimacy.

Table 4.6 *Perceptions of Class Dissensus by Self-Placement*

	Indianapolis		*Columbus*		*Linton*		*Phoenix*		*Yuma*		*Safford*	
						Percentage perceiving dissensus[a]						
Self-placement	%	N	%	N	%	N	%	N	%	N	%	N
Upper and upper-middle	41.8	(79)	34.8	(92)	29.1	(55)	41.7	(163)	41.7	(72)	39.7	(68)
Middle-middle and lower-middle	50.7	(71)	32.5	(77)	24.0	(50)	42.9	(147)	36.2	(47)	50.0	(52)
Working and lower	44.3	(106)	43.0	(65)	14.5	(76)	42.0	(176)	27.7	(119)	26.7	(86)
Total	45.3	(256)	36.3	(234)	21.5	(181)	42.2	(486)	33.6	(238)	36.9	(206)

[a]Percentages are based on the number of men answering both the "businessmen" question and the "workingmen" question.

99

Such a basis requires agreement by all that success is (usually) fairly come by.

To gauge each respondent's perceptions on this matter, the interviewer handed him a card with the following list:

Opportunities his family gave him
Hard work
Knowing the right people and pull
Ability
Good luck
Drive and initiative

and asked: "Which of these do you think are the main reasons behind a man's success in America today? Any others?" We assume in what follows that "hard work," "ability," and "drive and initiative" are legitimate reasons for success in terms of American values and that the others are not (although "knowing the right people and pull" is perhaps somewhat less legitimate than "opportunities . . ." or "good luck").[4]

In all six communities, the legitimate reasons were clearly and consistently chosen more often than the illegitimate reasons. Generally, each legitimate reason was chosen by 60% or 70% of the men, while the illegitimate reasons were chosen by between 15% and 35%. Although a considerable amount of illegitimate success is perceived, then, it is outweighed by perceptions of legitimate success.

However, as we said above, a preponderance of legitimate perceptions is not sufficient to support morally a system of inequality if the perceived illegitimacy is heavily concentrated among the deprived groups in the community. To find out if this were so, we first regressed each of the six choices upon seven rank variables (family income, occupation, education, father's occupation, mother's education, majority, and self-placement). If most of the perceived illegitimacy were concentrated among people of low rank, these rank variables should correlate highly with each of the six reasons. Further, the rank variables should have *positive* regression coefficients when predicting the legitimate choice items and *negative* coefficients for the illegitimate items.[5]

[4]By the same token, these legitimate items are also more socially desirable responses. Choosing one or several of the "illegitimate" items is tantamount to criticizing "our American system" (for this reason we wish now we had asked the question in terms of the particular community instead of "America") and some respondents may have suppressed their true feelings about the illegitimacy of success on that account.

[5]A possible artifact of verbosity had to be ruled out. Allowing multiple choices had the advantage of getting a more accurate description of what each respondent really thinks is at the root of success, but it is subject to the difficulty that some subjects simply provide more responses than others. Since these verbose respondents tend (generally) to be of somewhat higher rank, our question produces an artifactual positive relationship between rank and each of the six choices. To eliminate this, we added the number of reasons chosen as a control to

This analysis (not shown) indicated that the relationships between rank and choosing a given legitimate or illegitimate reason are rather weak. For each of the first five reasons, the seven rank variables together explain only 2% to 4% of the variance in each city. The R^2 reaches .06 only once and .05 only three times in these 30 regressions. The item, "drive and initiative" is related to rank a little more strongly, with R^2's ranging from .06 to .12.

However, the relationship, though weak, is present. Lower-rank people do perceive illegitimacy more and legitimacy less than higher ranked people. Regardless of the *strength* of the relationship, the *form* is that the lower the rank, the higher the likelihood of choosing an illegitimate item as an important reason for success in America today. The ordering of the reasons in terms of propensity to be chosen by lower-ranked people is clear. "Opportunities his family gave him " is first, followed by "knowing the right people . . ." and then by "good luck." "Hard work" seems to be a reason evenly chosen throughout the rank structure. It was chosen by over half the sample in each city, and is poorly related to the rank variables (R^2's range from .01 to .04). The choice of "ability" is positively related to rank, but the item most likely to be chosen by higher-ranked people is "drive and initiative." While all classes see simple effort as leading to success, the objectively successful men are somewhat more likely to also see that self-assertiveness and independence are useful and profitable qualities.

To give us a summary of these rank effects, we formed an overall index of legitimacy. This took the value of $+1$ for men who mentioned more legitimate than illegitimate items, 0 for men who chose equal numbers and -1 for men who chose fewer legitimate than illegitimate items. Regressions of this index of legitimacy on the seven rank variables used above are presented in Table 4.7. Since the interaction term across cities was not significant, the pattern of effects can be considered to be reasonably similar from city to city, although we shall indicate a few suggestive differences.

The great majority of effects worth attending to are positive, indicating again that men of lower rank do indeed tend more to see success as illegitimate. But also, as the R^2's indicate, this is only a weak tendency. Only in Yuma do the seven rank variables together account for as much as 10% in the variance in the legitimacy index. In the two small towns the explained variance does not exceed chance levels. On the whole, then, perceptions of legitimacy both predominate over perceptions of illegitimacy and are spread rather evenly, being only slightly more likely to be found in the upper reaches of the rank structure.

---

each of the six regressions. The effects described in the text are in addition to (net of) any effects due to verbosity.

Note that the index of legitimacy presented in Table 4.7 is not affected by this artifact, since it balances legitimate items against illegitimate items and so is not biased by the total number of reasons chosen.

Table 4.7 Index of Legitimacy Regressed on Rank Variables

Rank variables	Regression coefficients: Unstandardized and standardized (in parentheses)[a]						
	Average within-city	Indianapolis	Columbus	Linton	Phoenix	Yuma	Safford
Family income	.001 (.07)*	b	.001 (.10)*	.001 (.10)	.001 (.07)*	.001 (.10)*	.001 (.10)*
Occupation	.002 (.07)*	.003 (.13)	.004 (.15)*	.003 (.10)	.002 (.07)	.002 (.05)	-.003 (.10)
Education	.027 (.15)*	.020 (.12)	.029 (.15)*		.031 (.17)*	.052 (.26)*	.024 (.15)*
Father's occupation		-.002 (.07)		-.003 (.08)			
Mother's education						-.020 (.10)*	.011 (.06)
Majority[c]		.236 (.12)*				.147 (.09)	.078 (.05)
Self-placement			-.037 (.07)				
R^2		.07[d]	.06[d]	.03	.05[d]	.12[d]	.03
Mean		.59	.55	.62	.60	.56	.54
Adjusted Mean		.57	.56	.67	.56	.58	.56
N		320	376	298	684	375	304

[a] Asterisked coefficients are those with associated t-values of 1.65 or higher; hence, significant at about the .10 level (two-tailed test).

[b] Coefficients are not shown when the standardized path coefficient is both nonsignificant and less than .05, i.e., for relatively weak effects.

[c] In Columbus and Linton, a random variable was used instead of the majority variable, since these samples contained almost no minority men.

[d] Statistically significant (p<.05).

Of the rank variables affecting (to a mild degree) perceptions of legitimacy, education and occupation are the most important, with education
tending to be relatively more important in the Arizona cities, and occupation
more important in the Indiana cities. Income also generally has a positive
effect. The effects of self-placement and of the two origin ranks were small.
In three of the four cities with minorities, majority men were somewhat more
likely to perceive legitimacy than minority men; this effect was strongest in
Indianapolis, where blacks form the minority group. It appears that the
relatively small influence of rank on legitimacy is primarily due to the
achieved dimensions, especially education and occupation. The successful
do see success as fairly gained, but so do the unsuccessful, by and large. This
is true in all of our communities, but especially in the small towns.

The last two rows of Table 4.7 indicate how the communities differ in the
average level of perceived legitimacy. The adjusted means indicate that,
after being equalized on the rank variables, the cities show rather similar and
high levels of perceived legitimacy, with a somewhat higher level present in
Linton.

SUMMARY AND CONCLUSIONS

The major conclusions which can be drawn from the analyses in this chapter
are:

1. We found no evidence that classes exist in the form of clear cut, widely
shared and salient cultural categories.

2. Nonetheless, the men were willing to place themselves in a list of
classes presented to them; presumably this roughly indicated their notion of
their general standing in an overall social ranking. In all communities, a
sizeable group placed themselves in the working class and a somewhat
larger group chose one of three middle-class labels.

3. A man's self-placement agrees reasonably well with the class in which
the interviewer placed him (but less well in the two small towns). Neighborhood ratings of interviewer and respondent agree about as well (less well,
again, in small towns) and neighborhood rating is related to self-placement
(though quite weakly in the small towns).

4. The achieved rank variables of income, occupation and education are
the major influence on a man's class self-placement. Background variables
had minor and less consistent effects. Racial–ethnic effects were weak or
absent. The social rank of associates also had a minor effect on self-
placement; this is not a major mediating variable between rank and
self-placement. These variables all together fell far short of determining
self-placement; the variance explained was always less than 40%.

5. The cities were generally similar in the ways in which objective rank was translated into subjective class self-placement, but self-placement was less strongly determined in the small towns. Self-placement seems to respond to national (not merely local) standards of reference.

6. Most men do not see disagreement between economic groups (businessmen and workingmen) on domestic political matters. The proportion of men perceiving dissensus tends to decline with city size. This is especially true of working class men, so in small towns, the middle-class men are somewhat more likely to see dissensus than working-class men, whereas in the large cities the two groups are equally likely to see dissensus.

7. Most men attribute legitimacy to the system of stratification; they see success as being obtained by legitimate means. Men of lower rank are only slightly more likely to think that illegitimate means lead to success. The relationship between rank and perceiving legitimacy practically disappears in the small towns.

Our results illustrate the maxim that men's ideas about inequality and their own standing are affected by, but do not match one-to-one, the objective system of inequality. The very existence of rank hierarchies is of course a potential basis for people subjectively to divide themselves into solidary and conflicting groups, but this potential is not always fulfilled. It would probably be easiest for people to develop clear notions of solidary class groups when some of the population held high ranks on all of the important dimensions, others held all medium ranks and the rest held all low ranks. In such a situation, information about another's income, occupation, education, etc., would all be reinforcing, allowing most people to be unambiguously placed as upper or middle or lower.

But in the last chapter we found that the various rank dimensions are not highly related, so others typically present conflicting information about their place in society. The character of the objective system, then, is plausibly responsible for our result in this chapter, that men are only minimally aware of class groupings. Most of the men in our communities do not see clear-cut economic or status groups in conflict or competition with one another. They tend to see success as legitimately attained and agreement rather than dissensus between groups of high and low standing.

Our respondents are not blind or indifferent to the existence of inequality, however; when provided with class labels for general ranking they were willing and able to use them. Perhaps the pervasive influence of achievement values in the U.S. is shown by the fact that men place themselves more strongly according to their current achieved ranks rather than according to their origin or even their racial–ethnic rank. Each achieved rank, however, affects self-ranking independently; no one rank (income, for example) dominates the process. This suggests that even when a man is trying to make sense of his own position in a broad social hierarchy, his ranks, which are likely to be inconsistent, present him with contradictory stimuli, all of which are taken into account and averaged in his choice of a class category. The evidence indicates that men who employ terms such as "working class" as natural social categories, and who identify with the category or have clear perceptions of a shared fate, are a minority in these populations.

Contrary to the interpretations of Jackman and Jackman (1973), we take these findings as evidence for a *pluralist* rather than an *interest-group* model of American communities (but see our discussion in Chapter 9). We find in Part II that these same men behave as if they had interests—defined by occupation, income, ethnic status, and education, *not* by broad groupings such as "working-class." Having an interest in common with others of the same income level means that that interest is held in common with people of *different* levels of occupation and education. The interests of occupational levels unite a different group of people than the interests of educational levels.

We also find in Part II that self-placement is generally much weaker in affecting dependent variables than the present rank variables are. Moreover, self-placement is not the mechanism through which the objective characteristics have effects; in the few cases of real self-placement effects, those effects are in addition to objective effects. Part of the reason (but only part, we think) for this fact is the unidimensional tradition in thought about subjective rank. Perhaps we should have asked different questions about consumption self-placement, cultural self-placement and specifically occupational self-placement, though such questions were not called for by our initial open-end investigation.

Significantly, self-placement was less related to objective rank in the small towns, where perceptions of disagreement with business- or working-men were most infrequent, and where legitimacy was not only most widespread but also least concentrated among high-ranking residents. Perhaps our conclusions about pluralism and self-placement would have been different if we had included two cities with over a million residents.

Mann (1970) argues that social cohesion in the liberal democracies is not based on consensus, or at least not among the unpowerful. He maintains that only leaders are (or need to be) united by consensus on the legitimacy of the system of distribution, and that the posture of lower-class people is one of *pragmatic role acceptance*. What we find in these communities is a fairly vast *perception* of consensus, (although one may still suspect that the perception is in fact incorrect). Along with the perceived consensus, we find only a weak relationship between rank and felt legitimacy, and this relationship is specifically based on the objective measures, not class self-placement.

In general, subjective class did not seem to be strongly conditioned by the community context. Men appeared to refer more to national than to community comparisons in judging their general social rank. Our cities were at least roughly similar in distributions on subjective class-placement and in the process by which objective ranks converted to subjective placement. However, they did differ more from one another in these respects than they did with respect to the system of objective rank.

In particular, the small towns differed from the other cities in a number of ways: Neighborhoods were not as closely related to self-placement, small town men perceived less dissensus on public issues, the relationships between rank and self-placement and between rank and perceptions of legitimacy were lower in small towns.

One interpretation of these findings of lower R^2's is that objective rank affects subjective class less in a small town. But this is true only in a certain sense. A look at the regression coefficients in our tables shows that the effects of income, occupation, etc., are generally not smaller in the small towns; in this sense, differences in objective rank have no less influence. However, the lower R^2's indicate there is more scatter around the scores predicted from objective rank. What this may mean is that in the small town a number of factors besides objective achieved rank can come into play, while in larger cities, these factors can have only a small role. For example, in a small town a person's family history (but not the rank of his family, evidently) or his moral stature, can have some bearing on his sense of standing or his opinions on legitimacy, whereas in larger cities, perhaps because anyone knows only a small proportion of the others in the city, such factors play a much smaller role (see Form and Stone 1957).

But these local factors affect subjective rank *in addition* to the achieved ranks, not *in place* of them. The fact that objective rank *does* make a difference fits even the small town resident into the culture of American society. For example, being the heir-apparent of a farm-owning Mormon pioneer family in Safford, Arizona is a community status the importance of which is only hinted at vaguely in our data. Yet even in Safford, such a person is affected, in his self-placement and placement by others, by his income and occupation. In this sense, all of our communities exhibit basically similar systems of subjective class.

Part II

Consequences of
Social Rank

5

Models of Rank Effects

The problem of the rest of this study is how social rank affects individual behavior, why these effects occur, and how they are altered by the community context. In the chapters to come, we shall examine personal deprivation and adjustment to it as correlates of rank and as a possible channel through which rank affects other variables. Next we shall consider the correlates of rank in formal and informal social participation, which are also often thought to mediate other personal consequences of social rank. Finally we shall take up the implications of rank for such diverse areas of individual attitudes and behavior as political ideology, anomia and intolerance. In all of these areas, we shall look for evidence that the community affects the impact of social rank on the different dependent variables: either evidence that different rank effects (i.e., different slopes) occur in different communities or evidence that the same relationships are stronger in some communities than in others (i.e., different R^2's).

To guide these analyses to come, this chapter inquires about types of rank effects in general. What general type of model of rank effects, that is, turns out to be adequate in relation to a great range of dependent variables? Is there, in fact, a general form in which the various ranks affect most or almost all of the relevant individual attitudes and behaviors? This leads us to questions about the linearity and additivity of rank effects; the appropriateness of unidimensional or multidimensional conceptions of social rank; whether a given, small set of rank variables provide effective predictions of a range of dependent variables; the variations (if any) in patterns of rank effects from community to community; and possible patterns of rank effects, including the possibility that two rank variables might affect a dependent variable in opposite directions.

Our theoretic goal, which is beyond the immediate reach of these data, is a set of connected causal propositions at what Merton (1957:5–10) has called the "middle range." We doubt that it is profitable to try to formulate theories of great generality at high levels of abstraction until solid generalizations have accumulated from work at a lower level. Moreover, we make no attempt to provide the logical connective structure of which strong theory consists. Thus the reader will find no grand, overarching theory to be tested in this and subsequent chapters. On the other hand, our interest in empirically defensible generalizations in the first place lies in the possibility that those generalizations have important logical implications, and we intend to speculate about the implications, guided by the extant bits and pieces of sociological theorizing. In reporting findings and our thoughts about their implications, then, we shall be fluctuating between the "upper-lower" and "lower-middle" ranges of theory.

Therefore this chapter reports a systematic inductive search for a type of model that is most appropriate to the representation of effects of rank in general. We begin with an exploration of the 17 rank variables mentioned in Chapter 2 as they relate to 43 dependent variables listed below. After all, a general social position such as rank might well be of greater importance in the number of different behaviors and attitudes it affects, than in the strength of its effect on any one. Rank may have many different correlates, that is, though each correlate may be affected more strongly by other variables than rank. Subsequent chapters take up classes of dependent variables one at a time for more detailed analysis; this chapter reports the range of correlates.

The search narrows down to the models we carry on to later chapters: additive, linear, multidimensional models with overlapping but different variable lists for different dependent variables. Nonadditive models and their theoretical significance are considered and rejected first. Next, nonlinear models are found to be unnecessary. Several different types of unidimensional models are then examined and dismissed. Next, various multidimensional linear additive models are described and applied in a preliminary broad analysis of the data. Beginning with 17 rank variables, we carry out zero-order and multiple correlations with a shortened list of 30 dependent variables. Retaining only effective rank variables for each dependent variable, and limiting the sample to majority men, we ask whether multidimensional models differ significantly among communities in an analysis of covariance. Finally, we enquire into the theoretical significance and actual occurrence of rank predictions in opposite directions, that is, of rank regression coefficients with opposite signs.

ARE RANK EFFECTS ADDITIVE?

We show in this section that additive theories of the personal consequences of social rank are quite adequate: Nonadditive models are, in general, not necessary. This conclusion has several substantive implications for a theory of social stratification.

An additive relationship is one in which several variables combine *independently* of each other to affect a dependent variable. In an additive equation predicting, for example, anomia (A) from education (E) and income (I), the effect attributed to education does not depend upon the value of income, and vice versa. The additive model looks like this:

$$\hat{A} = a - b_1E - b_2I \tag{5.1}$$

A single value, namely b_1, tells how much A is expected to change due to a year's increase in education, and the form of the equation is such that this change will be the same, regardless of what value income happens to have. The coefficient b_2, likewise, gives the effect of I independently of the value of E. In other words, additive models state that the effect of a given rank variable on the dependent variable does not depend on the values of the other rank variables.

To show what our rejection of nonadditive models as unnecessary implies, we shall present some examples of specific nonadditive models. In the empirical search described later, however, we looked for *any* kind of departure from additivity which could have been useful as a general model. By finding *none,* of course, we in effect reject any specific nonadditive model.

As a first example, consider equation 5.2:

$$\hat{A} = a - b_1(E)(I) \tag{5.2}$$

This model asserts that anomia depends upon the product of education and income; hence, the effect of an extra year of education is not independent of income, but increases as income increases (and vice versa). Also a raise in income would have no (or little) effect on anomia if the man had no (or only a little) education. Substantively, the model implies that one must be high on *both* education and income to be free from anomia and that all who are very low on *either* education or on income (or on both) are highly anomic. (A nonadditive model that asserts the reverse might also be plausible: that a high rank on any single dimension is sufficient to produce low anomia, or high satisfaction, etc.)

Another nonadditive model might state that the dependent variable responds to the quotient of the rank variables:

$$A = a - b_1 \frac{E}{I} \tag{5.3}$$

This equation suggests that the effect of education decreases as the value of income increases (among the poor, extra education reduces anomia, but among the rich additional years of school affect anomia only a little). Conversely, a rise in income has the most effect (a positive effect, by the way) among the well educated, but among individuals with no education, changes in income have no effect at all. Equations 5.2 and 5.3, of course, only hint at the great range of possible nonadditive functions, but they may be sufficient to suggest that such models are interesting and could intuitively be more reasonable than additive models in some situations. For example, a multiplicative model could suggest that one characteristic can be thought of as assisting the effect of another: Grades in college are not earned by either ability or hard work alone, but only by both combined.

Despite their appeal, however, such models may not fit the data well; the intuitive interest of the model does not guarantee its truth. We will even ask that nonadditive models fit the data better than additive models. If the fit is equally good, we will, in general, prefer the additive models because of their parsimony.

Another important substantive application of nonadditive models has been to describe the effects of vertical mobility and/or status inconsistency upon the individual. In the past 25 years, many sociologists have maintained that these types of status discrepancies affect the individual in addition to any effects of rank per se. As a simplified example, consider the theory that upward mobility interferes with the ability to make friends. This effect presumably occurs in addition to a possible general rank effect: that people of higher rank generally make more friends. If the hypothesis about mobility effects is true, then an additive model would not be adequate. For example equation 5.4, an additive model,

$$\hat{F} = a + b_1 FO + b_2 SO \tag{5.4}$$

states that increases in the occupation of a son increase his number of friends, regardless of the occupation of his father. However, if the father's occupation were low, a higher occupation for the son (meaning, for him, upward mobility) might also result in difficulties in making friends. In this case the additive model would overestimate the number of friends of upward mobiles. If so, a nonadditive model such as Equation 5.5 might be more adequate, since it includes a term representing the experience of upward mobility:

$$\hat{F} = a + b_1 FO + b_2 SO - b_3 \frac{SO}{FO} \tag{5.5}$$

Similarly, many notions of the effects of status inconsistency translate into nonadditive models. If people who are poorly educated but highly paid are especially prejudiced, or minority members in high-prestige jobs are especially politically liberal, it means that certain *combinations* of ranks have an effect over and above that which an additive model would predict from their separate effects on the dependent variable. Such inadequacies of an additive model would show up as a significant interaction term; that is, the null hypothesis of additivity would be rejected.

Two rank variables might, however, produce statistical interaction which could not be reasonably interpreted as a mobility or inconsistency effect. For example, the way in which the effects of son's occupation varies at different levels of father's occupation could be entirely meaningless or the pattern might suggest some entirely different kind of effect from that predicted by mobility theory. That is, not all interactions (that is, nonadditivities) reflect mobility or inconsistency effects. Also, as Blalock (1966) has noted, not all mobility or inconsistency effects show up as statistical interaction. (We shall examine additive models of mobility and inconsistency effects—so-called *difference models*—in the section below on multidimensional models). However, if additive models are usually adequate to represent rank effects, nonadditive models of mobility and inconsistency effects can be ruled out as either inadequate or unnecessary.

We analyzed the adequacy of additive models by looking for statistical interaction in a large number of two-way analyses of variance, each one involving two independent rank variables and a particular individual-level dependent variable. Nonadditive (and nonlinear) models appeal to many sociologists because they do not impose assumptions upon the data regarding the way in which rank effects combine or the form of the rank effects. On the other hand, the charm of the additive (and linear) model is its classic simplicity and disdain for showy ornamentation. We would prefer to state our theories in such parsimonious terms, unless the data show us that some nonadditive (and/or nonlinear) model pays solid dividends in theoretically reasonable explained variance. In searching through the set of possible nonadditive models, then, we did not ask whether relaxing assumptions allows more accurate description of some particular event—of course it always does—but rather whether some specific nonadditive model is general enough and/or explains enough additional variance to justify including it, rather than a more parsimonious form, in our theory.

Our criterion for rejecting the additive model, therefore, was an interaction term (a) unlikely to occur by chance, (b) exhibiting some meaningful pattern, and (c) with *some* kind of regularity across communities or across dependent variables. In the case of mobility or inconsistency, there is a body of theory to identify which patterns of nonadditivity are meaningful, but in the case of other possible nonadditive effects, some of which may never have been formalized, we must rely mainly on regularity. If there is no regularity for some set of cities or dependent variables, then we are reluctant to elevate the interaction term to the status of a nonadditive law.

The mode of analysis employed in our search is worth describing, since it contrasts so clearly with the type of analysis presented in later chapters. We ran 2064 two-way analyses of variance. In each, two rank variables were trichotomized and cross-classified, yielding nine cells. For career mobility, for example, respondent's occupation was divided into high, medium and low within the high, the medium and the low categories of first occupation. Means of the dependent variable were calculated for each of the nine cells, showing the basic pattern of the joint rank effects on that dependent variable. Differences between these means form the between subcells sum-of-squares, measuring the variation in the dependent variable that could be explained by the two rank variables without assuming additivity (or linearity). In a good many instances, this sum-of-squares was not significantly different from zero, indicating that the two rank variables had no effect of any kind on the dependent variables.

An equation was then calculated which yielded the additive (but not necessarily linear) model which best fit the pattern of the nine means. If the nine means exhibited an additive pattern, this equation fit them well, so that the scores predicted by the equation closely reproduced the actual means. If the fit was not good (if the deviations of the predicted from the observed means were significantly larger than zero), then we entertained the possibility that a nonadditive model might be preferable.

The two-way analyses of variance were carried out for eight pairs of rank variables (father's occupation versus occupation, first occupation versus occupation, racial–ethnic versus education, racial–ethnic versus occupation, racial–ethnic versus income, education versus occupation, education versus income, and occupation versus income), reflecting intergenerational and career mobility and six forms of status inconsistency. Each pair of rank variables was run against the 43 dependent variables listed in the next section, separately within each of the cities, yielding the 2064 tests. The results, along with details on the analysis, are given in Jackson and Curtis (1972) and are not repeated here.

The additive model was usually retained. In about 89% of the analyses in which rank was found to have some sort of effect, an additive model was adequate. The other instances were examined for our criteria of regularity and interpretability. In terms of regularity, the instances of nonadditivity did not seem to especially recur for any dependent variable, for any pair of rank variables, or within any city.[1] For each instance of nonadditivity we also looked at the ways in which the values predicted by the additive equation differed from the actual means, to get an idea of the kinds of nonadditive effects which may exist. Thus, if the deviations in the analysis of, say, father's occupation and respondent's occupation against organizational memberships showed positive deviations in the high–high, medium–medium and low–low cells and a large negative deviation in the low–high cell, it would suggest that upward mobility does indeed make membership more difficult, over and above the effects of origin and destination, per se.

Neat interpretable patterns, however, were not what we found among those instances where a statistically significant interaction effect did occur. What we found were positive and negative deviations of varying magnitudes

---

[1]For the eight pairs of rank variables, the percentages of significant interactions range from 9.2 to 15.3; for the six cities, the percentages of significant interactions range from 5.8 to 14.7. Hence, nonadditive effects do not seem to appear especially often for any form of mobility or inconsistency or within any community.

scattered around like colored pebbles on a beach. And in the few instances in which interpretable patterns did appear they failed to replicate from city to city.

The result of this omnibus analysis, then, is that the proper strategy in building general theories of rank effects is to adopt additive models. Such a conclusion, though of course tentative, implies that the effects of social rank are generally independent of one another. This pill is theoretically hard to swallow, though the amount of empirical evidence for it (here and elsewhere) is substantial. Much sociological theory on the personal consequences of social mobility and status inconsistency, for example, is specifically based on the premise that the effect of one rank depends upon the level of another rank. Mobility theory holds that one cannot accurately predict the effect of present status unless one knows whether the individual has moved up to that status, down to it, or has remained at the same level, which is to say that *the effect of present status depends on past status*. Our data indicate that such propositions about mobility effects are wrong. If mobility theory means only that present and past rank are both relevant to behavior (though independently), then the mobility position is theoretically identical to an additive, multidimensional theory of the effects of social rank.

The dynamics of most theories of personal effects of status inconsistency hold that the effect of one rank depends on the level of some other rank held by the same individual, that is, that the simultaneous effects of social rank are nonadditive.[2] Our data indicate this is false. If status inconsistency theory merely means that behavior is affected (independently) by more than one social rank, then it is not different from an additive, multidimensional theory of the personal consequences of social rank (but see the discussion of difference models below).

ARE RANK EFFECTS LINEAR?

We show in this section that there is no reason to abandon linear models of rank effects. In general, the rank effects found in these data do not seem to be nonlinear in any regular lawful or theoretically useful way.

---

[2]Notice the distinction between possible multidimensional definitions of rank, on the one hand, and, on the other, hypotheses about the effects of rank that depend on the different ranks held by individuals in specific forms of social interaction. Hope (1975) points out that interpersonal difficulties arising from status inconsistency (e.g., the traditional black physician and his equally traditional white patient) are properties of that interaction, not of the individuals concerned. Presumably the inconsistency would not even be relevant in the interaction between the same black physician and black patient. Since our units are persons, not social interactions, those specific status inconsistency hypotheses are not tested here. If, on the other hand, repeated life experiences in such interaction leave their mark on the individual (e.g., see Borhek 1965), then holding an inconsistent status may be correlated with specific orientations, attitudes or behaviors, and individuals are appropriate units of analysis.

To say that some rank variable has a linear effect on some dependent variable means, in theoretical terms, that an increase of one unit in the rank variable has the same amount and kind of effect on the dependent variable regardless of the original value of the rank variable from which the increase begins. For example, if education affects anomia linearly, an extra year of education would reduce anomia by the same amount whether the increase in education were from 2 to 3 years, 9 to 10 years, or 26 to 27 years. When graphed, this kind of effect shows up as a straight line, reflecting its simplicity.

Following the principle of parsimony, we prefer to retain this simple form of rank effects in our theoretical generalizations unless the data convince us that more complicated forms will yield better explanations. Nonlinear effects almost always explain a little more variation than linear effects, since they can take advantage of random fluctuations; we would not want to abandon linear models just on these grounds. Hence we ask that a nonlinear effect explain significantly more variance than a linear effect, and show up with some kind of interpretable regularity across cities and/or dependent variables, before it is accepted into a theoretical generalization.

Rejection of nonlinear models implies the rejection (for the moment at least) of a whole series of interesting methodological and theoretical possibilities in social stratification. Many interesting explanations are unnecessary, that is to say, because they do not yield empirical improvements over simpler formulations. To give point to our conclusion, we shall briefly describe some of these explanations.

Nonlinear effects might be expected, first, on grounds of method. The units of measurement (years of education, thousands of dollars of income, occupational prestige scores, etc.) might be a curvilinear transform of the "true" interval-scale metric according to which the rank variable is linearly related to other variables. For example, the prestige differences between occupations scored in the 30's might be much larger than the prestige differences between occupations scored in the 60's. Second, the basic law relating two "truly" measured variables might not be linear in form.

For either or both of these reasons, data relating rank variables to dependent variables may exhibit various departures from linearity. Three of these are: (a) smooth monotonic curves, (b) step functions, and (c) nonmonotonic curves. Each type of departure suggests a class of substantive or methodological interpretations.

A smooth monotonic curve, for example, could be produced by the measurement problem in our example above. If political conservatism, for example, were really a linear function of occupational prestige, then the biased measure of occupation described above would produce a rapid rise in conservatism as occupation rose from 30 to 40, but a gentler rise in the region from 60 to 70. A theoretical basis for the same kind of curve would be that each additional ("true") unit of occupational prestige has less and less effect on conservatism, so (given accurate measurement) the curve of prestige although always positive, would increase at a decreasing rate with increases in occupation.

A step function, on the other hand, suggests that a rank variable has no effect until a given level is reached, when an abrupt effect occurs. This brings to mind images of barriers which cannot be burst until sufficient pressure has been collected. Another, more prosaic interpretation is that societal norms set conventional cut-points for permitting certain forms of behavior: Most 15-year-olds don't drive while most 16-year-olds do. Our analyses below will indicate whether a high-school diploma or an income of, say, $15,000 has similarly abrupt effects.

It is also conceivable that the effect of a rank variable might not even be monotonic, but have a positive effect within some range and a negative effect within another. If, for example, the very rich have no need to worry about the good opinion of others, while the very poor will not get the good opinion of others no matter what they do, immorality may be high for low values of income, decline as income goes up to middle-class levels, and the increase again as income continues to rise. Yet we should like to suggest that such curves should be few and far between in a valid theory of stratification.

In our search for nonlinear effects we analyzed the relationships between each of the 43 dependent variables listed below and the rank variables of education, occupational prestige and income (separately). (We will continue to treat racial–ethnic rank as essentially a dichotomous variable.) Each of these relationships was examined within each of the six communities, making 771 tests.[3]

In the following list of dependent variables, the numbers in parentheses indicate the number of cities in which there were significant departures from linearity in relation to education, occupation and income, respectively. Dichotomous variables are starred.

1. Formal social participation.
   a. Number of associational memberships (3,2,5).
   b. Infrequency of attending most important association (0,0,0).
 * c. Held office in most important association (0,1,2).
 * d. Church membership (0,0,2).
   e. Political activity index (0,1,3).
2. Informal social participation.
 * a. Relatives in the community area (3,0,1).
   b. Infrequency of visiting with relatives (0,1,1).
   c. Infrequency of visiting with friends (0,0,1).
   d. Rather visit relatives than friends (0,0,1).

[3]Tests were performed in only five cities for the dependent variable called Dogmatism because of a technical error in the results for Indianapolis. The analysis of covariance in Table 5.1 omits Dogmatism for the same reason.

    * e. Became friends with co-members of association (0,0,2).
      f. Infrequency of visiting with association co-members (2,1,3).
      g. Doesn't get along with work associates (0,0,0).
    * h. Have someone to turn to in need (1,0,2).
  3. Political liberalism.
    * a. Changes are needed (2,0,2).
      b. Domestic liberalism index (3,1,3).
      c. Considers himself a conservative (1,0,0).
      d. Democratic party identification (2,0,1).
  4. Satisfaction and symptoms of stress.
      a. Satisfaction with job (0,0,2).
      b. Satisfaction with income (1,0,0).
      c. Satisfaction with success (2,0,0).
    * d. Satisfaction with enjoyment in life (0,0,0).
      e. Psychophysiological symptoms index (1,0,3).
  5. Intolerance.
    * a. Mentions Negroes as undesirable neighbors (1,1,0).
      b. Disapproval of Negroes as neighbors (0,0,1).
      c. Index of punitiveness against deviants (2,0,2).
      d. Index of adherence to conventional norms (1,1,3).
      e. Dogmatism index (3,0,4) (five cities).
  6. Anomia.
      a. Anomia index (0,2,1).
      b. Political potency index (1,0,1).
  7. Aspirations for son.
      a. Disappointed if son were machine operative (0,0,2).
    * b. Wants son to have a better job than R does (0,0,3).
    * c. Wants son to be more successful than R is (1,0,2).
  8. Leisure activities.
    * a. Engages in active sports (1,1,3).
    * b. Engages in passive activities (0,0,2).
  9. Self-Perceptions.
      a. Powerless in the community (2,0,1).
      b. (High) social class self-placement (3,1,2).
 10. Salience of rank.
    * a. Only join an association backed by important people (0,0,1).
      b. Family should sacrifice to get a man ahead (0,1,1).
    * c. Important to live in the best area (0,0,1).
 11. Perceptions of responsibility and legitimacy (0,0,0).
    * a. Perception of being treated unfairly (0,0,0).
    * b. Perception of blocked opportunity (0,0,0).
      c. Responsible for own success or failure (0,0,0).
    * d. Drive and initiative are a main reason for success in America (2,0,0).

For each test we divided the rank variable into several (usually between seven and nine) successive categories and computed the means on the dependent variable for the men within each category. The way in which the means rose or fell from low to high categories of the rank variable provided a picture of the linearity of the relationship. Since chance variation would produce some fluctuation around linearity we checked first to see how many of the 771 relationships were more nonlinear than might be expected from random error. To do this, we tested for the significance of the difference between r (indicating the strength of the linear relationship) and eta (indicating the strength of the relationship imposing no assumption on form). The results are given above.

Statistically significant improvements based on nonlinearity were least frequent for occupation (5% of the tests) and next least frequent for education (15%). They appeared most often for income (25%). At the very worst, then, one could say that the linear model was adequate 75% of the time, while for occupation nonlinearities appeared only as often as one would expect on a purely random basis.[4]

The pattern in the findings may give us clues not only about the frequency of nonlinearity, but also about which of the two possible sources is responsible. If improper measurement units were a source of difficulty, then we should find similar kinds of curvilinearity appearing when a given rank dimension is related to a number of different dependent variables. This should not necessarily be true of a curvilinear law, but if there were any generality to a curvilinear law, it should appear the same way in different communities. Thus replication across some set of dependent variables is required to establish the former kind of generalization, while replication across a set of communities is required for the latter generalization. To search for such regularities we examined the plots of the dependent variable means for the 116 statistically significant nonlinearities.

As far as the issue of measurement is concerned, the overall results would lead us to suspect that our rank measures most closely resembled accurate interval scales in the case of occupation and least well in the case of income. However, the graphs of income (and education) means show little regularity across dependent variables. Nor have we been able to find any single transformation for education or for income that generally or substantially increases the amount of variance explained over that provided by the linear function.

---

[4]The reader may object that many of the dependent variables are dichotomous and that such variables cannot have linear relationships with a rank variable. In a strict sense, this is true. What we are asking here, however, is whether the *proportion* of men in one category of the dependent variable (which is its mean, under a zero–one scoring) rises linearly as one looks from the low to high categories on the rank variable. If so, a linear equation describes accurately the relationship between the rank variable and that dependent variable.

The failure of any single transform to substantially improve the measurement of income or education could have occurred for either of two reasons. First, the apparent nonlinearities may have been only apparent. The plots of means did not show any consistent pattern, and nonlinearities were not concentrated by city, suggesting that the fluctuations were random. The additional variance explained by departures from linearity was low where it did occur (for examples, see below). Second, other sources of measurement error may have introduced enough randomness so that the "true" size of units is a bootless issue. Perhaps the *real* measurement problem with a man who reports an income between $9000 and 10,000 is not whether dollars are an appropriate unit, but whether he actually had an income of $7459 or perhaps $12,000.

With respect to curvilinear laws, it is already clear, of course, that no *general* curvilinear law for rank effects is called for by the data. However specific rank variables may curvilinearly affect specific dependent variables. Hence we must consider the dependent variables one at a time, paying special attention to replication between communities. We find that nonlinearity was significant in as many as four cities for only two dependent variables (associational memberships and dogmatism) in relation to income, and for none at all in relation to education and occupation. And here again, an examination of patterns yields little in the way of regularities.

We shall illustrate the general failure of the search for consistent curvilinear rank effects by presenting results for the "extreme successes." The knowledge that all the other relationships were less curvilinear than those presented should convince the reader of the general utility of linear models for use with data of this sort. Included in the presentation, however, are some trace findings which point the way to future research, but do not make enough difference to warrant special attention in the present study.

Each dependent variable received 18 tests: according to three independent variables within six cities. Only one dependent variable (number of associational memberships) indicated nonlinearity even a majority of the 18 times. For even the variables with a relatively large number of significant tests the incidence of nonlinearity was usually misleading. A nonlinear relation between education and presence of relatives in the community area, for example, was significantly better than a linear relation three times: The explanation increased from 12% to 16% in Columbus, from 1% to 5% in Yuma and from less than 1% to 4% in Safford. But there was no pattern whatever in the plotted means: The departures from linearity seemed to call for a random law. The prediction of reporting active sports as a leisure activity on the basis of income (its best predictor) showed significant improvements by allowing nonlinearity in three cities: from 4% to 8% in Linton, from 4% to 5% in Phoenix and from less than 1% to 2% in Indianapolis. But the type of nonlinearity indicated was grossly different in each of those three cities. The domestic liberalism index also showed different departures from linearity in different cities.

A few dependent variables produced traces of nonlinearity that might be worth following up in an investigation where measurement error in the dependent variables was much lower. For example, the effect of social rank on whether the respondent answers a question on "What changes are needed in this country today?" by insisting that no changes are needed, appears to be a step-function in Columbus and Phoenix, and possibly Yuma. The very lowest levels of social rank—4 years of education or less, or an income under $4000—tended to express no need for change, as opposed to the rest of the population, which had lots of changes in mind. This could be of theoretical interest: Perhaps personal concerns are so pressing at that level of rank that one cannot think about wider changes, or persons of that level of rank may be fearful of discussing such matters with an interviewer. In this study, however, there is evidence for such a position in only three of the six communities, and in relation to the size of the error term, nonlinearity simply doesn't make that much difference.

The nonlinear relations of dogmatism and income are not regular, but some consistency appears in its relation to education. The form roughly resembles a smooth monotonic decrease at a decreasing rate. The first few years of education cause sharp drops in dogmatism, while more education produces smaller effects. Even in this instance, where the case for curvilinearity is close to maximal, the patterns within cities are not clear, and the results are somewhat equivocal. The improvement was significant only in Linton, Phoenix, and Safford, where the respective improvements were from 9% to 11%, from 18% to 19% and from 20% to 23%. Thus, the departures from linearity are not great.

The variable showing most nonlinearity is the number of associational memberships. Income, for example, would predict memberships better in five cities if transformed; however, the greatest gain in percentage of variance explained is from 12% to 15% (in Safford). The gain is one percentage point in the other four cities. Improvements, though real, seem to be minor. Further, the appropriate nonlinear slope was slightly convex in some cities and slightly concave in others, suggesting that a full-scale research project would be required in order to properly explain the departures from linearity.

Our conclusion, then, is that it is rarely necessary or profitable to posit nonlinear effects; the effect of social rank does not seem to depend regularly on the level of social rank itself. However, this conclusion calls for several qualifications or cautions, given the nature of the data gathered here.

To begin with, the amount of unexplained variation is usually large, so that our conclusion could be restated, "there is so much scatter around the category means that it is hard to tell whether the true relationship is linear or not." Therefore, when we accept a linear form as a general model, we only mean to adopt a conservative position concerning the burden of proof: We assume a simple linear formulation to be adequate until it can be shown that some specific curvilinear prediction is empirically more adequate. Certainly for our data nonlinear models are both unparsimonious and spuriously precise.

Second, we should remind the reader that our conclusion holds only for the three achieved rank dimensions of education, occupation and income. Nonlinear, racial–ethnic effects are not investigated, nor are departures from linearity in the effects of origin rank dimensions, such as father's occupation.

Another important feature of these data is that they are confined to certain normal ranges of social rank, and the number of respondents at the extreme values is small. Our statements of the form of an association are therefore most accurate within a standard deviation or two of the mean of each rank distribution. The most frequent theoretical reason for a curvilinear law is some type of approach to a limit, such as no education whatever, or a Ph.D. An increment of 1 year's education might be expected to have an especially high or low effect on some dependent variable as either limit was approached. Laws are often quite linear within a specified range of values for the independent variable, but curve up or down for values outside that range. Estimation of the precise changing value of a slope outside two standard deviations from the mean, where the number of cases is sharply reduced, is probably the last thing our data should be expected to do. The slopes we discuss are probably reasonably linear only within a central range of values; beyond that range, the curves must be estimated from some other body of data.

Finally, we should remind the reader that our assertion of linearity does *not* necessarily mean that if the mean values of a dependent variable are plotted for 10 categories of an independent variable, the means fall neatly into a straight line like beads on a stick of spaghetti. Often they do not. In fact, they often vary wildly and randomly. Asserting linearity means that we regard the wild fluctuation as error, and only attempt to generalize about the linear trend in the data.

Our main result, then, even with these qualifications, is that linear models are adequate to represent rank effects. Even where there is maximal evidence in favor of curvilinear laws, the evidence is neither clear nor strong, and the improvement gained in prediction over a linear approximation of the effect is quite small.

This is not an automatic conclusion that would have been universally expected in advance. Linear models of rank effects leave large portions of variance unexplained. It is a plausible suspicion that this happens because the linear form masks strong curvilinear effects. For example, satiation effects might have been expected, meaning that additional increments of rank would have smaller and smaller effects. Or, conversely, each additional increment of rank might, in some circumstances, only fuel higher expectations, producing accelerating curves. If so, relaxing the assumption of linearity should have led to substantial improvements in our ability to explain. But this did not happen. Our data suggest, therefore, that strong curvilinear effects do not exist and that any line of theoretical reasoning predicting their occurrence is dubious.

IS A UNIDIMENSIONAL MODEL ADEQUATE?

In this section we will compare unidimensional and multidimensional models and present our grounds for concluding that unidimensional models are not usually adequate to represent the effects of rank upon individual attitudes and behavior.

We begin by trying to clarify the distinction between unidimensional and multidimensional models. In many studies that which have related social class or socioeconomic status (SES) to various dependent variables it has been common to use a single measure of social class or SES. Sometimes a single rank dimension, often occupation, has been taken as the best single measure. Often, however, an index of SES has been constructed. For example, Hollingshead's *index of social position* (Hollingshead and Redlich 1958:387–397) first assigns scores to a person's occupation, education and residential address and then weights and adds the scores, yielding a single index score which is then cut into categories to yield a system of five classes. In the sort of research we are describing the single rank dimension or the index is then taken as the major (often the only) measure in relating class or SES to a variety of dependent variables. Using such procedures assumes theoretically that a unidimensional model of rank effects is adequate.

A unidimensional model is one stating that rank is properly thought of as a single variable or dimension which affects various dependent variables. A multidimensional model states that there are several types of rank and the effects of these must be studied separately, since the pattern of effects may differ from one dependent variable to another (for example, income may be the principal influence upon political identification, while education is the principal influence upon anomia).

What sorts of reasoning would lead one to think that rank is essentially one variable, so that rank effects are unidimensional? We can distinguish at least three theoretical models, each of which yields a somewhat different picture of unidimensional effects.[5] The simplest of these states that one

[5]The single dimension of general social rank discussed by Hope (1975) is not included in this list because it is part of a multidimensional model of rank effects. It represents, in fact, a contrasting conceptualization of the multidimensional models introduced later. For other discussions of this alternative type of orientation, see also Ploch (1968) and Jackson and Curtis (1968).

particular rank dimension is the only one which affects individual attitudes and behavior. For example, one might posit that income, as the crucial outcome of the status attainment system, is the only rank which has direct effects upon any dependent variable. We can represent this theoretical situation as follows:

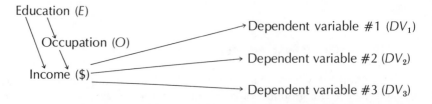

A second type of unidimensional thinking asserts that observed rank dimensions determine a person's position on a single basic, crucial dimension of inequality which in turn affects a variety of individual attitudes and behavior. This basic dimension (power or prestige, for example, or general possession of socially desirable attributes and/or possessions) can be a continuum or a set of ordered and bounded classes; it may or may not be institutionalized in the culture of the community or society. To present one concrete possibility, let us suppose that the various rank dimensions are tied together in the causal net presented in Chapter 3, and that each dimension influences a person's prestige, which in turn influences various dependent variables. This amounts to saying that there is a standard pattern of evaluation in the community by which a peron's positions on the various rank dimensions are toted up and averaged out into a general prestige standing, and that this prestige standing mediates all rank effects on the various dependent variables. In picture form:

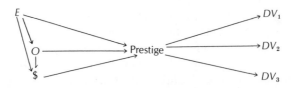

A third kind of unidimensional reasoning posits that a person's position on the various rank dimensions *are caused by* his position on a single basic underlying dimension of superiority and inferiority, and this basic dimension affects his attitudes and behavior in various ways. This is similar to the model underlying notions of IQ: An underlying dimension (intrapersonal, in this case) causes responses on various paper and pencil questions and affects the person's life in various ways. A possible sociological version would be a theory of estates: Belonging to an institutionalized ordered category enshrined in custom and law defines a person's place in the basic hierarchy of the society. Membership in an estate on the one hand affects one's various rank attainments (education, occupation, etc.) and on the other determines his political attitudes, visiting patterns, etc. However, the estate model is only one version of this theory. Another is that the position of a family on a basic social continuum of prestige or power affects the rank positions of the sons of that family and also affects the various ways they act and think. The graph of this form of thinking is:

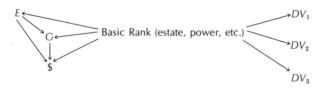

We will discuss varieties of multidimensional models below, but presenting a graph of one such model now will allow us to illustrate some conclusions about what these models imply empirically. Let us suppose, for example, that education controls one dependent variable, occupation another, and occupation and income together a third. Then we would have:

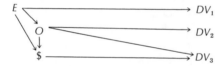

We should note that the three unidimensional models and the illustrative multidimensional model are all linear and additive in form. That is, they all can be written as a set of linear, additive equations; no curvilinearity or interaction effects are implied by these models. Having decided above that linear additive models are generally acceptable, we are now distinguishing between two basic forms of such models and asking whether unidimensional or multidimensional models are generally preferable.

The essential characteristic of these unidimensional models is that only one dimension directly affects the dependent variables. This clearly has the advantage of parsimony—multidimensional patterns of effects could change radically from dependent variable to dependent variable, making the explanatory theory potentially much more complex. The last two unidimensional models also direct our research toward defining the basic dimension and explaining the nature of its influences on the dependent variables.

If such a basic dimension (e.g., social prestige) were the crucial variable, it might also allow us to generalize our theory over a greater variety of social settings—an important theoretical advantage. That is, even if rank variables were empirically related to a given dependent variable in different ways in two settings, it could be that the same *social prestige* theory applies in both cases, but that the ways rank positions combine to define social prestige differs in the two settings. Note, however, that this model would be rejected by varying effects of different rank variables *in the same setting,* across different dependent variables (Hodge 1970; Hope 1975).

This very advantage affords a clear empirical criterion for choosing between unidimensional and multidimensional models. In all the unidimensional models, only one dimension (either observed or underlying) affects the various dependent variables. In a given setting, the effects linking the observed ranks to each other and to an underlying dimension are the same, regardless of the dependent variable. Therefore, if several dependent variables were regressed one at a time on several observed rank dimensions, the results should differ only because the single arrow to the dependent variable is stronger in some cases and weaker in others.

Hence, *if unidimensional models are correct, the rank variables should have the same order of relative importance in predicting any dependent variable,* as long as the dependent variable responds to rank at all (see Hodge 1970). As a concrete illustration, suppose we regress anomia on several rank dimensions and find that education has the strongest effect, income a moderate effect, and occupation and the other dimensions little or no effect. If one of the above unidimensional models is operating, these rank variables should have this same order of importance when predicting any other dependent variable. The form or direction of the relationship could vary, of course, but constancy (in a given setting) of the definition of status is what is meant by a unidimensional approach.

It will become apparent in the following chapters that the various rank variables do *not* maintain the same relative order in their effects on various dependent variables within communities. This alone shows that rank variables do not affect attitudes and behavior in a unidimensional form. Hence, it will not be necessary to present any extensive data analysis on the relative explanatory power of unidimensional versus multidimensional models.

However, to give the reader some estimate of how well a unidimensional model might explain some dependent variables, we have calculated one possible unidimensional scale and will report its explanatory power in the following chapters along with that of our multidimensional analyses. This scale, which we will call the *general rank index,* is based on the relationships between the 17 rank dimensions, as measured by the loadings (for men aged 40–64) of those variables on the first unrotated principal factor (see Chapter 2). The reader will recall that these loadings are reasonably consistent from city to city. The scale was constructed by converting each man's 17 rank scores into standard scores, using the means and standard deviations of the total sample, and taking a weighted average of the resulting scores, using as weights the average of each rank dimension's loadings on the first principal factor across the six cities.

Unlike additivity or linearity, we found multidimensionality regularly yields improvements in explained variance. To enquire "how much more" with too much precision would be wasteful and beside the point, since the answer is not "little or none." There being some additional explained variance, that is, we prefer multidimensional models on different theoretical grounds.

The general rank index is a measure of overall "upness" on a general continuum formed by virtue of the fact that rank dimensions are positively correlated, presumably because of a status conversion process in the social system itself. We could have constructed this measure in other ways; for example, a multiple indicator approach might be more appropriate for the second unidimensional model presented above (see Hauser and Goldberger 1971). However, the general rank index provides one possible unidimensional index and in all probability any alternate index would correlate highly with it. Education and occupation generally turn out to be our best predictors, after all, and they receive the highest weights on the general rank index.

One feature of unidimensional models is that they usually mask, rather than reflect, the true form of rank effects. An index essentially fixes the relative order of the regression coefficients in explaining a dependent variable (that, indeed, is the value of a unidimensional model), rather than letting them vary and take those values which maximize explanation and clarify interpretation. Hence, the use of a unidimensional index may prevent interesting theoretical questions from coming to light. If occupation and income turn out to be the main influences on one dependent variable and education and father's occupation the main influences on another, the researcher is led to think about theoretical reasons why these particular ranks should affect these particular dependent variables. Looking for such answers should lead to a better understanding of rank effects, yet the findings that provoked the question would never have emerged if a unidimensional index had been used. In this way, multidimensional models are essentially preferable because they reflect reality more closely and hence push the sociologist to develop more adequate theory.

AN EXPLORATION OF MULTIDIMENSIONAL MODELS

Multidimensional models can have many different forms. Here we want to set out some possible multidimensional models, explore their implications, and present some initial data to suggest which possibilities actually show up in our cities.

The guiding heuristic model for rank effects to be used in subsequent chapters is illustrated in *Figure 5.1*. Simplified as it is (e.g., origin ranks include majority, father's occupation, father's education, mother's education, and others, such as wife's education, occupations of first friend and

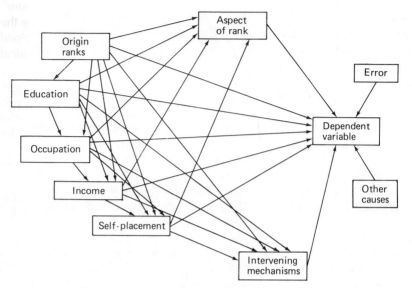

Figure 5.1. *A multidimensional model of rank effects.*

second friend, respondent's first occupation and his rating of his neighbor-hood, are omitted), the illustration is clearly becoming quite complex. Still, it can be used to highlight the various issues we shall be addressing below.

First, we shall examine the effects of each rank with other ranks "held constant." Now we actually think that the various ranks are causally related in a process, as described in previous chapters, and as indicated in Figure 5.1. To reduce the complexity, however, we shall treat the rank variables as if they were correlated but causally unordered in subsequent analyses, that is, we will report direct effects only. Thus when we report an effect of mother's education, for example, it is that portion of the total effect of mother's education not carried through son's education, occupation, and so on. But by the same token, a reported son's education effect will be that not accounted for by the ranks of his parents. This latter reporting strategy would seem to contradict our view of the causal ordering of ranks, but it works out well in practice. Our typical finding is one of direct effects for certain present ranks, with or without direct effects of origin ranks. Direct effects of origin ranks without direct effects of present ranks are quite rare. Thus the findings generally fit our theoretical orientation regarding causal relations among the rank variables themselves, though those relations are considered in our interpretations of findings, rather than in the statistical presentations.

For example, our statistical analysis might suggest equal independent effects of occupation and father's occupation on some dependent variable. In our interpretation, we will be aware of the fact that occupation has only a direct effect, while father's occupation has both a direct effect and an indirect effect, through its connection to present occupation. By the same token, reporting a direct effect of occupation but not father's occupation does *not* mean that father's occupation is uncorrelated with the dependent variable: the occupation effect shows that it is.

Second, we will speculate on what it is about rank that has a given effect. In Figure 5.1, one possibility is represented by "aspect of rank," an unmeasured intervening variable. If power, for example, is the way income and occupation both influence some dependent variable, then there may be both direct effects of income and occupation and indirect effects, based on the influence of occupation and income on power and the effect of power on the dependent variable. Stated differently, not all effects of the observable rank dimensions (for example, income) are mediated; some are direct. In their off hours, as it were, these rank variables affect various dependent variables for reasons other than their translation into power, status, or class interest, etc. In fact, such effects may have little to do with rank or standing of any kind. For example, education presumably provides people with information and this extra knowledge about the world in and of itself may reduce anomia. In the same way, the work characteristics of certain occupations may inculcate attitudes independently of the prestige or power of the occupation (for example, see Kohn and Schooler 1969).

The unmeasured aspects of rank and other unmeasured non-rank intervening variables will, of course, not appear in the statistical analysis. We can only speculate on their nature on the basis of the pattern of direct rank effects. We assume, for example, that parental ranks and respondent's education have more to do with socialization, and total family income has more to do with financial resources, though this supposition is in no way *tested* by these data.

Third, we have measured and included certain possible intervening variables (e.g., general satisfaction, informal and formal social participation, etc.) as possible explanations for the effects of rank variables. Do rank variables affect some dependent variable by affecting an intervening mechanism, which in turn affects the dependent variable? Are there both direct and indirect effects? Is the effect of some rank variables mediated by intervening mechanisms while that of others is not?

Fourth, Figure 5.1 shows an effect of "other causes" of the dependent variable. To be relevant, this set of variables would have to have potential arrows to all the rank variables (and to the intervening mechanisms), but we have omitted them from the figure to make it look less like a spider web. The issue here is whether rank effects are spurious or not: Can they be explained by common antecedents of rank and the dependent variable?

Fifth, (remembering that aspects of rank are unmeasured), what are the relative strengths of the direct paths from the rank variables to the dependent variable? How large is the error term? These are the basic statistics from which we shall make interpretations of patterns of rank effects.

We pointed out, in rejecting unidimensional models, that the patterns of rank effects change somewhat as different dependent variables are considered. Let us point out briefly some possible models, or patterns of effects.

First, some dependent variables are affected primarily by only one rank dimension. This shows up in the regression analyses when the regression coefficient for one rank dimension is sizable while the coefficients for other rank dimensions are all close to zero. This pattern did occur, for example, in analyzing answers to the question: "Do you think you could be just as happy living somewhere else other than the (community) area?" Education affects this response (well-educated people are more cosmopolitan), but other rank effects are generally negligible. However, in other instances of this pattern the single active rank dimension is income, or interviewer's rating of the respondent. Such findings are the clearest instances of evidence against a unidimensional model. This pattern suggests that specific properties of education may affect one dependent variable, while the peculiar properties of income produce effects on another.

Second, at the opposite extreme is a model in which all rank dimensions affect a dependent variable and all effects are positive (or negative). Such results suggest that the dependent variable is responding to the common property of the rank variables, namely superiority versus inferiority. That is, holding a high rank affects the attitude or behavior, no matter which kind of high rank it is. In such a case, high education produces an increase in, say, satisfaction, while high income produces an additional increase, and likewise high position on any other dimension.

A third type of multidimensional model would be an instance in which several rank variables affected the dependent variable, but some of the effects are positive and others negative. We shall consider the theoretical reasons for such a pattern below and examine our data to see how often it appears.

Finally, we will want to see how often a fourth pattern of rank effects appears, the pattern in which the effects differ by city. This would suggest important differences in the city contexts, so that certain ranks are perhaps more salient in one city than in another. One interesting example is the model in which being high on any one of several dimensions is sufficient to boost the person up to a high level on the dependent variable within a given city, but the effective variable changes from city to city. Our most realistic example of this case of substitutable rank variables of the same general type concerns the effects of either education or wife's education on informal visiting. (Of course, if within a given community sample high rank on *any one* of several dimensions yielded a high dependent variable score which was then not increased by high rank on other dimensions, the effects would be nonadditive). Another possible variation is that in some city or set of cities all of the rank effects might be muted suggesting that social rank in general affects life less in those communities. Such findings lead in turn to questions about what differences in economic structure, value systems, etc., could be responsible for the cross-community differences in rank effects. We return to this question in Chapter 12.

Explanatory Power of Multidimensional Models

To provide a broad, systematic and inductive search for models of rank effects, we began with a set of regression analyses within each city and then used the information from these to structure a set of analyses of covariance between cities. For the regression runs the 17 rank dimensions employed in Chapter 2[6] were used as independent variables. Of a large number of dependent variables, representing a variety of attitudes and behavior, 30 showed enough relationship with rank to warrant further analysis (our criterion was that at least one of the six city regressions yield an R^2 of .10 or more). These dependent variables are listed in Table 5.1, along with the proportion of variance in each dependent variable explained by the 17 rank variables within each city.

The proportions of explained variance in Table 5.1 suggest that social rank is far from a coercive or compelling influence in the affairs of individuals. Only about one-fifth of the regressions yield R^2's as high as .20 and none of them an R^2 as large as .40. Further, we can take these results as representing the upper limit on the amount explainable by rank (at least with this quality of measurement), since 17 rank variables were used and the form of the regression was allowed to vary so as to explain as much as possible within each city. Nor are any variables controlled which might be spuriously increasing the apparent predictive power of rank. However, in reaching a final judgment on the importance of rank in American life we shall also have to consider the size of the regression coefficients in the analyses in the following chapters.

Differences Among Cities

To find out how often the pattern of rank effects differs from community to community we next constructed a series of analyses of covariance, with city as the nominal scale. Differences between the cities in rank effects show up in the interaction terms in such analyses.

The analyses of covariance were simplified in several ways, compared to the above regression analyses. In the first place, we were certain in advance that the differences between the cities in racial–ethnic composition would yield differences in any racial–ethnic effect. To allow differences in the

---

[6]In Columbus and Linton, Bogardus social-distance scores were used in place of the dichotomous majority variable. Community means were substituted for missing data on the rank dimensions.

Table 5.1 Variance Explained by Multidimensional Models of Rank Effects

Dependent variables	Proportion of variance explained by 17 rank variables (R^2)						Analysis of covariance: proportion explained		
	Indianapolis	Columbus	Linton	Phoenix	Yuma	Safford	Within-city regression[a]	Interaction	k[b]
Formal social participation									
Number of associational memberships	.29[c]	.30*	.36*	.25*	.30*	.39*	.24	.04*	10
Infrequency of attending most important association	.09	.09	.21*	.07*	.05	.16*	.03	.02[c]	4
d*Held office in most important association	.14*	.10	.17*	.11*	.10	.16*	.06	.03+	7
*Church membership	.13*	.16*	.14*	.06*	.08*	.12*	.05	.03*	7
Infrequency of church attendance	.15*	.18*	.07	.06*	.11*	.12*	.05	.03*	7
Informal social participation									
*Relatives in the community area	.13*	.20*	.07	.05*	.08*	.14*	.04	.03*	9
Infrequency of visiting relatives	.08	.09	.11	.10*	.06	.11	.02	.06*	9
Infrequency of visiting friends	.12*	.10*	.05	.04	.07	.07	.02	.02+	5
Rather visit relatives than friends	.12*	.18*	.24*	.11*	.10	.14*	.07	.03+	7
Infrequency of visiting comembers of association	.08	.08	.11	.06	.09	.10	.02	.02	5
Does not get along with work associates	.07	.19*	.06	.04*	.09	.13*	.02	.03*	6
Political variables									
*Changes are needed	.07	.12*	.17*	.07*	.13*	.15*	.03	.04*	10
Domestic liberalism index	.21*	.14*	.12*	.12*	.20*	.22*	.06	.02+	7
Democratic party identification	.16*	.14*	.06	.11*	.12*	.10*	.04	.02+	3

								N[b]
*Voted locally	.14*	.12*	.08	.03	.11*	.11*	.03	.02*	5
Public officials care what you think	.09*	.21*	.15*	.12*	.08*	.14*	.09	.02+	6
Intolerance									
Disapproval of Negroes as neighbors	.09	.10*	.09	.06*	.11*	.20*	.02	.02+	6
Civil rights movement gone too far	.31*	.06	.07	.09*	.14*	.11*	.02	.03*	9
Index of punitiveness toward deviants	.22*	.27*	.16*	.22*	.32*	.27*	.17	.02+	9
Index of adherence to conventional norms	.15*	.18*	.07	.18*	.16*	.20*	.09	.03*	10
Dogmatism index	e	.24*	.13*	.24*	.22*	.30*	e		10
Other									
General satisfaction index	.17*	.17*	.07	.11*	.05	.10*	.07	.03*	9
Psychophysical symptoms index	.14*	.08*	.10*	.08*	.09*	.10*	.04	.04*	10
Anomia	.25*	.20*	.20*	.20*	.24*	.27*	.15	.02	10
*Wants son to have a better job than R	.16*	.06	.09	.10*	.10*	.09*	.04	.01	5
*Equally happy living somewhere else	.13*	.10*	.11*	.05*	.12*	.10*	.03	.02*	5
Responsible for own success or failure	.10*	.09*	.11*	.12*	.13*	.09	.04	.03*	8
*Drive and initiative main reasons for success	.21*	.17*	.13*	.10*	.19*	.18*	.10	.02+	7
Religiosity	.11*	.18*	.08	.03	.07	.05	.03	.02+	6

[a] All 29 average within-city regressions were significant at the .05 level.

[b] Number of rank variables in prediction equation.

[c] An asterisk indicates significance at the .05 level or less; a plus sign indicates significance (of interaction) between the .05 level and the .25 level.

[d] Asterisked variables are dichotomous.

[e] The analysis of covariance was not performed for dogmatism; Indianapolis data were in error on this variable.

effects of other rank variables to be seen more clearly, we restricted the samples to majority men. Second, we wanted to drop rank variables which exhibited no effects in the regression runs on the dependent variable in question. Therefore a different set of rank predictors was chosen for each dependent variable; a rank dimension was included if it had a standardized regression coefficient of .10 or more and an associated t-value of 1.65 or higher *in any one city* in the 17-variable regression analysis. Since a variable was included if it had affected the dependent variable even in only one city, the procedure maximizes the chances of contrasting models in different cities.

We had expected that this procedure would dispense with many variables on the 17 variable list, that is, that some short list of five or six rank variables would be generally adequate. This proved not to be true (see discussion of this point in Chapter 12). While only five to ten variables were typically retained for each dependent variable (Table 5.1), according to this decision rule, different variables appeared on different lists.

A high degree of correlation between the set of independent variables (i.e., multicollinearity) in a regression analysis will tend to make the regression coefficients somewhat unstable over samples from similar populations or over repeated samples from the same population. We expected, therefore, that the cities would differ somewhat in their rank effects due to this instability. We will use a test of significance to gauge the extent to which the differences we pick up can be totally assigned to this source. In a further attempt to reduce this problem, we also omitted the trio of interviewer ratings from the set of independent variables because they were by all odds the most tightly interrelated set of predictors and because we were less interested in their direct effects.[7]

The results (in Table 5.1) suggest that multidimensional models of rank effects generally vary somewhat from community to community. Our measure of the extent to which the same model is applicable in all six communities is statistical interaction: the extent to which the set of slopes within communities depart, in the aggregate, from the slopes of the average within-city regression equation. Unfortunately, the statistical decision rule draws inferences by leaning over backwards, and it is not possible to lean backwards in both directions: Interaction significant at the .05 level means that differences among the cities are probably not due to chance, but insignificance at that level does not mean that the cities are the same. Moreover, noting that the differences among cities are not due to chance

---

[7]Multicollinearity is at least moderate in our 17-variable analyses, as evidenced by the results of the factor analyses reported in Chapter 2. To provide a rough estimate of the extent of the problem in the analysis of covariance runs, and also in the multiple regression analyses reported in later chapters, we selected ten typical rank variables and calculated the proportion of the variance explained in each rank variable by all of the other 9 together. The highest predictability in such a list is typically 60% to 70%.

does not make them large enough to notice. Therefore, Table 5.1 presents three possible decision rules, in the effort to lean both directions, and it also presents proportions of the variance in the dependent variable attributable to interaction and to the average within-city regression. The interaction term was significant at the .05 level 14 times, and significance fell in the indeterminate .06 to .25 range 12 of the remaining times. Interaction was clearly insignificant (p greater than .25) only 3 times out of 29.[8] Multidimensional models differ among communities.

For the 15 dependent variables for which interaction failed significance at the .05 level, we are inclined to see general merit in the average within-city regression model in its own right. There may be special community details which vary, and perhaps importantly so, but the model does have an across-community generality. Further, for these variables, allowing the models to vary across cities only explains an additional 2% (or, infrequently, 3%) of the variance.

For the 14 variables with interaction terms significant at the .05 level, the within model may be useful or it may not, but it is clear that there are city-specific models, and that the only argument revolves around *how* different they are.

The extent to which city-specific models differ can again be seen in the magnitude of the interaction term, that is, the proportion of variance it explained. For these 14 variables, allowing separate city models added an additional 3% or 4% of explained variance in most instances. It is also instructive to look at the added proportion in relation to the variance explained by the average regression equation. Cities may differ in minor details concerning a very useful general model; it may be that the general model applies to two or three cities, but simply does not apply in the others; or it may be that the models contrast sharply between communities. For example: interaction accounted for 3.6% of the variance in number of associational memberships, but that becomes a minor detail in relation to the 24% of the variance accounted for by the average regression equation. At the other extreme, 6.1% of the variance in visiting relatives was accounted for by interaction, and only 1.6% by the average within-city regression, which suggests that one throw away the average regression equation and examine multiple regressions individually within cities (see Chapter 7).

City differences can also be found in the lists of partial regression coefficients. Interpretation will render some of the differences between city-specific models trivial. An effect of occupation in six cities, for example, combined with an effect of father's occupation in two, father's education in two, wife's father's occupation in one and mother's education in one, could appear to call for very different models in the eyes of an unthinking analysis of

---

[8]The analysis of covariance was not performed for the dogmatism variable, since the Indianapolis data for this variable were incorrect.

covariance, but is a suggestively similar pattern to the student of social stratification.

More frequently, though, the force of the analysis is to show clearly that an effect exists in (say) two communities, but that nothing more than a negligible descriptive effect is to be found in the other four. A comparatively frequent kind of city-specific effect, that is, is simply the fact that rank *has* an effect in some communities, but not in others.

As in the linearity analysis, a frequent cause of apparently important interaction is simply a minute rank effect. A typical pattern (*disapproval of Negro neighbors* is an example) is one in which the interaction and the within-city regression explain about the same amount, but both figures are low enough to stimulate disinterest. Many city differences seem to involve relatively weak rank effects.

We return, then, to the analogy of a theme with variations: Most rank effects of any size take a consistent form, from which each community deviates to a greater or lesser extent. The theme-with-variations perspective affords an explanation for an apparent anomaly. National surveys often indicate very little community effect, but comparative community studies often suggest great differences between communities. This is because comparatively extreme communities taken from a large sample characterized by a basic pattern with deviations will contrast greatly from one another, though they will not differ too dramatically from the national average. Vast numbers of other communities, at the same time, will represent intermediate patterns between the extremes selected.

Rank Effects of Opposite Sign

There is a series of theoretical issues in sociology and social psychology which call for a dependent variable to vary with the *difference* between two independent variables.[9] It has been claimed, for example, that actual reward or achievement is less important (or no more important) in affecting attitudes and behavior than the gap between investment and reward or between aspirations and achievement (see, for example, Kleiner and Parker 1963). Incongruity between actual and perceived status has been treated similarly. We are especially interested here in further examples of difference theories: hypotheses of mobility and status inconsistency effects.

As we said above, some forms of these hypotheses predict statistical interaction between two independent variables. Some theories of mobility effects, for example, suggest that the experience of movement produces effects on the person over and above the independent effects of growing up

[9]Such theories pose problems in statistical analysis that we take some pains to avoid. For discussions of these problems, see Blau and Duncan (1967:194 ff) and Fuguitt and Lieberson (1974:135–141).

in stratum A and of living now in stratum B. Such interaction theories have been substantially rejected above in our analysis of additivity, on grounds of parsimony: Since relationships are generally additive, then models of more complicated processes (which might also predict the data well) can be rejected in favor of the simpler model of independent effects of the rank dimensions.

However, if the additive model turns out to be one in which some rank dimensions are related positively to the dependent variable and others are related negatively, an interpretation in terms of a *difference effect* can still contend with hypotheses of independent effects of rank dimensions. For example, let us suppose that in truth political liberalism (P) is increased by intergenerational downward mobility and decreased by upward mobility, but is not otherwise affected by either father's occupation (FO) or current occupation (CO). This verbal truth can be modeled:

$$\hat{P} = a_1 + b_1(FO - b_2 CO) \tag{5.6}$$

where all coefficients are positive. But equation 5.6 is algebraically equivalent to equation 5.7:

$$\hat{P} = a_1 + b_1 FO - b_1 b_2 CO \tag{5.7}$$

Unfortunately, Equation 5.7 looks like a multivariate regression equation in which father's occupation and current occupation both affect liberalism, but in opposite directions.

Suppose we find, in regressing a measure of liberalism on rank variables, that the significant betas include occupation ($-.10$) and father's occupation ($+.10$). This could be interpreted by the above theory of mobility effects. On the other hand, it could be interpreted to mean that socialization at a high level of social rank gives a man the kind of psychoeconomic security made famous by wealthy families such as the Roosevelts and the Kennedys, which allows him to encourage the economic underdog, while at the same time, *being* of high occupational rank throws a man into competition with those underdogs and makes him unwilling to give them an unfair (or fair) advantage. *The data do not discriminate between these hypotheses.*

Hence, mobility and inconsistency effects (and other difference effects) can produce rank effects of opposite signs (for an empirical example, see Hodge 1970). If the analysis of rank effects yields such results, it is hard to know whether independent, opposite rank effects or a difference effect is responsible. We will discuss the interpretative problems posed by such results below, but we first wish to present at least a rough count of how often such effects appeared in our data.

As a preliminary step, the regression coefficients were examined from each of the 180 17-variable regressions listed in Table 5.1. A notable feature of partial coefficients of opposite sign (even when both are significant) is that they tend not to replicate across communities as readily as single rank effects do. For example, the regressions for the *index of punitiveness against deviants* shows a significant negative beta for education in all six communities, and hints at a perceptual incongruity (difference) effect with positive betas for class self-placement in five cities, but the clear pattern of significant partial coefficients, opposed in sign, appears only in Columbus (see Chapter 11). The results for Anomia show three significant reversals, but the pattern is different in each city: The variables of opposite sign are education and self-placement in Columbus, education and first occupation in Yuma, and education and father's occupation in Safford (see Chapter 10).

There is little point in constructing a theoretical explanation for every instance of opposite signs, since the conditions of our study guarantee that some instances will appear just by chance. Regression coefficients become less and less stable as the independent variables in a regression equation are correlated with one another (i.e., as multicollinearity increases). Yet if there is anything to the multidimensional theory of stratification, it is that models of rank effects *must* consist of precisely that: predictions from a set of correlated independent variables.

This instability, produced by the multicollinearity between our rank variables, means that some of the opposite-sign regression coefficients should not be theoretically interpreted but rather regarded as random deviations from coefficients of the same sign. If (for some dependent variable) the beta for father's occupation is $+.10$ while the beta for respondent's occupation is $-.12$, the first coefficient might be a sampling fluctuation from a true value of $-.07$, or both might be random fluctuations from true values of zero. Random fluctuations are not particularly upsetting, except when they cross the arbitrary line which separates $+$ from $-$, thereby altering the theoretical implications of the model drastically. As one guard against random fluctuation we shall use the decision rule afforded by the test of statistical significance.

Along with tests of statistical significance, another proper response to excessive random fluctuation is to increase the size of the sample. We do this by using the series of analyses of covariance presented above to test community contextual effects. By using the *average within-city* regression coefficients in these analyses, we can look for instances of opposite-sign effects in the entire sample of over 2000 (adjusting for the effects of living in a particular city). If an instance of opposite signs appears in these coefficients, we are much more confident that they represent genuine effects which require a theoretical explanation. This allows only an estimate, however, since the frequent interaction we found in the analyses of covariance means that the separate city regressions are somewhat different and the average figures only roughly represent them.

Rank effects of opposite sign appear in about one-third of the analyses. All of the significant regression coefficients had the same sign in 19 of the 29 average within-city regressions. The significant standardized regression coefficients for the other 11 runs are shown in Table 5.2.

The table has no instance of powerful opposed effects, for example, a positive beta of .20 or greater combined with a negative beta of the same or greater size. The largest reversed beta(s) are .10 and .11 (in two instances); for seven of the eleven regressions the reversed betas are no larger than .05 or .06. When opposite effects appear, then, the opposition is usually between a general and/or strong effect in one direction combined with one or two weak effects in the opposite direction. The findings suggest that one-third would seem to be the highest estimate of the overall existence of opposite signs that could be defended and that dramatic oppositions are extremely rare.

This result does not tell us about opposite effects involving the racial–ethnic dimension, since this variable was not included in the analyses of covariance, but the 17-variable regressions do not suggest that the above estimate would increase much if the racial–ethnic dimension were considered. We shall see some instances of such racial–ethnic reversals in the chapters below on formal social participation and on intolerance.

How can we interpret these results showing opposed rank effects? We are presented with the empirical result of a regression analysis, and we would like to know the linear law which produced those results. But we have seen that a single result could be interpreted as supporting either a hypothesis of some kind of difference effect or a hypothesis of opposed independent effects (or a great many combinations of these). In other words, we are again confronted by a problem of statistical identification.

Without additional data that might possibly distinguish between these hypotheses, we must content ourselves with pointing out alternate explanations and perhaps making a tentative choice on grounds of theoretical plausibility or taste. Parsimony may also be some help, but difference theories, as a class, are not clearly less parsimonious than opposite-effect theories and hence we cannot dismiss them as easily as we did nonadditive theories above.

We have suggested several alternate kinds of difference theories. Theories of the effects of mobility and inconsistency are only two examples, although they are the ones which especially interest us here.

Interpretations in terms of independent opposite effects lead us to think about how rank dimensions differ in the experiences they represent and in the interests they reflect. For example, one can readily see that achieved rank dimensions might have net effects quite different from that of racial–ethnic rank. Low racial–ethnic rank means exposure to different kinds of experiences than holding low educational rank, for example; it may mean that ties are established or felt with other blacks or Mexican–Americans and/or that one participates in a distinctive subculture. It also represents a

Table 5.2 *Average within-City Regressions Yielding Rank Effects of Opposite Direction*

| | Significant average within-city standardized | | | | |
Dependent variables	Class self-placement	R's education	Father's education	Mother's education	Wife's education
Infrequency of church attendance		-.15		.05	
Relatives in the community area	.05				-.05
Infrequency of visiting relatives			-.07		
Infrequency of visiting comembers of association			.09		
Changes are needed		.18			
Disapproval of Blacks as neighbors		-.09			
Civil rights movement gone too far		-.12			
Index of punitiveness toward deviants	.09	-.33			
Index of adherence to conventional norms		-.17		-.06	
General satisfaction index	.11				
Psychophysiological symptoms index	.06	-.12		-.05	

[a]The list of independent variables is different from dependent variable to dependent variable (as explained in the text). For included independent variables, coefficients are shown that are significant at the .10 level (two-tailed test).

different kind of deprivation. Hence, low racial–ethnic rank could have quite different effects on, say, certain political attitudes than low education has.

It is clear, however, that the results in Table 5.2 do not represent any single type of difference or opposite-effect phenomenon. The results for *adherence to conventional norms,* for example, suggest that income, occupation (present and past) and education all independently reduce conventionality, but that at any so defined level of rank, having a high-status friend increases conventionality. Alternatively (a difference model), having a good friend whose rank is lower than is warranted by one's own rank produces (or at least is associated with) unconventionality. The results for punitiveness and for symptoms suggest the kind of perceptual incongruity mentioned above. General satisfaction (as detailed in the next chapter) is a dependent variable expected to vary positively with rewards, such as income, neighborhood rank and their embodiment in self-placement, but negatively with expectations, as engendered by father's occupation. The church atten-

Table 5.2 *Continued.*

regression coefficients of independent variables[a]

Family income	R's job	Father's job	Father-in-law's job	First friend's job	Second friend's job	R's first job	R's neighborhood rating
							-.14
.05	-.09				-.07	-.06	
.08	.06						
		-.11		.12			
						-.06	
.08					-.05		
.06	.10					-.06	
	-.06		-.05				
-.07	-.10		-.06	.05			
.16		-.05					.11
-.08							-.07

dance results suggest an educational mobility effect. Coefficients for disapproval of Negro neighbors suggests effects of quite different aspects of social rank: Rewards, measured in income, increase disapproval, while greater experience with the normative system taught through public education decreases it. These examples suggest that the observed patterns of reversals call for a variety of explanations.

Such results only add conviction to our conclusion that mobility and inconsistency, as opposed to social rank, are not pervasive influences upon personal attitudes and behavior. Such effects, in some theoretical formulations, should produce regression coefficients of different sign, but these opposed effects occur only in a minority of our analyses. Further, the instances of opposed effects come to a great variety of patterns, so no specific type of mobility of inconsistency can account for a significant portion of them.

It should be noted that, in addition to the scattered mobility or inconsistency effects just mentioned, there may be many more (which do *not* replicate across communities, because they would affect the average within-city regression if they did), the effect of which is quite small in magnitude in relation to the net effects of single rank variables. Some of these will appear in the following chapters.

SUMMARY AND CONCLUSIONS

Our inquiries about which models of rank effects are adequate and general have yielded the following major conclusions:

1. Rank effects combine additively to affect various individual attitudes and behaviors. That is, the effect of one rank variable does not seem to depend upon the value of another. The few nonadditive (interaction) effects we found were usually not interpretable nor did they replicate across cities. Nonadditive models are, in general, rejected because the complexities they introduce are not required to explain the data.

2. The effects of current achieved rank dimensions on various individual attitudes and behaviors can usually be adequately reflected by a linear model. The nonlinearities we observed usually did not take an interpretable form, or replicate across dependent variables of communities, or add much as all to the explained variance. It would appear to be rarely necessary of profitable to posit nonlinear effects in data such as these.

3. A unidimensional model, one that states that dependent variables are affected by only one observable rank dimension or by one basic underlying rank dimension, implies that the observable rank variables should maintain the same relative order in their effects over various dependent variables. Since the data show that the relative order of effects is different for different dependent variables, unidimensional models do not adequately represent rank effects.

4. Although the above conclusions mean that linear additive multidimensional models reflect rank effects most adequately, the explanatory power of such models, over a range of dependent variables, is not overwhelming. They usually explained less than 20% and never as much as 40% of the variance in our dependent variables.

5. The exact form of multidimensional effects varied somewhat from community to community for about half of the dependent variables we considered. However, allowing the effects to vary from community to community rarely added more than an extra 3% or 4% to the explained variance. In other words, most rank effects of any size take a consistent form, from which communities often deviate to some extent.

6. We did not find a single short list of rank variables adequate to represent all rank effects in all cities. Education and occupation are generally important rank variables, but others add valuable information, depending on the community and the dependent variable.

7. Usually, all of the rank variables which affect a given dependent

variable exercise their effects in the same direction (positive or negative). We found no instance of powerful opposed effects which replicated across communities. Those opposed effects that do replicate do not involve strong oppositions, and do not reflect a single sort of phenomenon (that is, different sets of rank variables are opposed in affecting different dependent variables).

In this chapter we have considered various possible models of rank effects and selected linear, additive, multidimensional models as most adequate. We regard such a model as a tentative first approximation, but as the best concrete and specific model to guide further work. Any contending models should be similarly concrete and specific. That is, the lack of an assumption is not in itself a model. A claim that rank effects are nonlinear and nonadditive, without specifying a particular form for the effect, is to assert that "the dependent variable might vary in some direction, according to some form, with the independent variable." It would indeed be difficult to deduce specific testable propositions from such a position.

We would claim further that selecting a specific type of model at this point is a conservative procedure, rather than the opposite. Failure to specify the form of an association is not the conservative procedure it is often thought to be, and usually results in the *over*statement of findings. For example, reporting the variance in some dependent variable explained by 10 discrete income categories would take advantage of a big jump in the mean value of the dependent variable from the third to the fourth category, though the placement of that big jump might be quite random. A linear model would only report variance explained by a proportionate increase in the dependent variable between all adjacent categories. If the big jump could be shown *not* to be random (by replication in different communities, for example), then it might be worth including in the theory. But if it is not included in the theory, to report explained variance which includes it inflates the statement of the predictive utility of the theory.

Avoidance of "strong" models often stems from the fear that they are spuriously precise. But spurious precision in theory is not generally produced by unwarranted strong assumptions (which simply cause explained variance to be low), but by acceptance of random or idiosyncratic events as representatives of general laws. One must guard against abstracting some particular effect from a specific body of data and elevating it to general theory, unless there is some reason to believe that the characteristic really does have some generality. Suppose it is found, for example, that the effect of rank on satisfaction is slightly curvilinear in Columbus, Indiana, but not in the other cities. Should the fact that clerical workers are slightly less satisfied than either craftsmen or technicians be carried as an essential part of the general theory, or should only the general proportionality between rank and satisfaction be selected as the aspect of the particular empirical results to be asserted generally? The latter is the more conservative procedure, and we shall follow it except in instances where the results suggest a different empirical regularity.

As befits a tentative first approximation, linear additive multidimensional models are easily modified to take other kinds of effects into account. If some nonadditive or curvilinear effect should appear regularly in some context, it can be introduced into the equations of the original model. For example, the absolute value of the difference between father's occupation and son's occupation may be entered as an additional predictor in such an equation. For another example, if some dependent variable proves to be a step-function of a given rank variable, that rank variable can be entered into the equation as a dichotomy, or can be broken up into a series of "dummy" variables.

We express ignorance in our models as a portion of the error term. To assert that, for example, the association between intolerance and education is linear means that as far as our model is concerned, departures from the linear trend are unpredictable and as such are consigned to the error term. When increased knowledge makes it possible to predict such departures, they can be included in the model as a nonlinear component, in which case the variance due to the predictable aspect of the nonlinearity will be *explained* rather than *unexplained*.

Our models should be regarded as tentative in another sense. As we mentioned above, we have no direct measures of such potential underlying dimensions as power or prestige. The results in this and succeeding chapters are thus open to a number of possible interpretations, in terms of direct effects of the observable rank dimensions alone or in terms of the effects of two or more unmeasured dimensions which perhaps mediate the effects of the observable dimensions in a number of ways. (However, the data do rule out models in which all effects pass through a *single* underlying dimension.)

Our models can be easily extended by writing equations specifying the existence and role of certain underlying dimensions. The results of our analyses may even supply some leads in writing such extensions. And any model extended in this way can be initially tested by our results. For example, if an extended theory specifies that education acts on a dependent variable only through prestige, then the product of the supposed effects of education on prestige and of prestige on the dependent variable must equal the direct effect of education on the dependent variable observed in our data.

Even without specifying the nature of any possible underlying dimensions, however, our results as they stand have several considerable implications for the individual effects of inequality in the U.S.

One main conclusion from the analyses above is that social mobility and status inconsistency have few if any unique effects upon individual attitudes and behavior. In contrast to the effects of the rank variables themselves, mobility and inconsistency effects appear rarely, tend to be weak, and do not replicate well across communities. This conclusion is based on our results ruling out nonadditive effects and upon our findings that rank effects of opposite sign were present in only about one-third of our regressions, were not strong, and could not be accounted for by one (or a few) types of mobility or inconsistency.

This result suggests that some of the reasoning behind these hypothesized mobility and inconsistency effects must be wrong. For example, one reason for hypothesizing these effects is the assumption that different rank positions carry clear expectations which conflict when a person holds noncomparable ranks (Meyer and Hammond 1971). Perhaps, in our communities, such expectations never become strongly attached to ranks on the various dimensions. If the expectations for a doctor are not very different from those for other job-holders and the expectations for the poor do not differ sharply from those for the rich, being a low-income doctor should cause few conflicts of expectations.

Another interpretation is that mobility and inconsistency do produce conflicting expectations and these are stressful for the individual, but the social arrangements and cultural prescriptions in the U.S. allow the person to quickly resolve or adjust to those difficulties. The relative ease of making new friends in a suburban setting, the success ethic which supports a decision to move to a better job in another state, and the relatively open access to many formal organizations are examples of such adjustive mechanisms. A related view is Wilensky's (1966a:132–133) "consolation prize 'theory' " of mobility: that down-mobiles may be compensated for their occupational failure by marrying a high-status spouse or by a relatively good income (meaning that inconsistency assuages the stress of mobility). Studying mobility and inconsistency effects, then, would be akin to studying atomic particles with short half-lives—any population at a given time would contain mainly people who either never had such problems or who had experienced them and quickly adjusted. Only men still in the brief adjustment phase would exhibit any effects.

For both of these reasons, the relatively high rates of mobility and inconsistency in our communities should weaken the effects of these experiences. Such flexible systems make it difficult for people with different ranks on a given dimension to behave, or be expected to behave, in clearly different ways. Similarly, the frequency of mobility and inconsistency probably promotes mechanisms to ease the problems of these experiences. Some kinds of discrepancies between ranks, such as upward mobility, are probably even supported by the value structure in our cities.

By this reasoning, mobility and inconsistency may have powerful effects upon individuals in more rigid stratification systems, or possibly among extraordinarily mobile or inconsistent persons in the U.S. but would not appear in a study of the general U.S. population. Reasons exist, then, for not discarding these hypotheses altogether, but our data, supported by the above lines of argument, lead us to conclude that such effects are rare in contemporary U.S. communities.

The results in this chapter also have substantial implications for two other problems: (a) the extent to which communities develop unique contexts for rank effects, which is relevant to the larger issue of national versus community-level stratification; and (b) how various attitudes and behaviors are distributed throughout the stratification structure as a result of multidimensional rank effects. However, we shall wait until the last chapter for a full discussion of these topics. The next six chapters will furnish a good deal of concrete detail on how various rank dimensions affect specific dependent variables and these results will allow us to discuss the above implications more fully.

In Chapter 1, we discussed feelings of deprivation and social participation as two possible major variables mediating effects of specific rank positions upon a variety of dependent attitudes and behavior. The next chapter treats deprivation and dissatisfaction and the two chapters following that analyze informal and formal social participation.

6

SATISFACTION: BALANCING
ASPIRATIONS AND SUCCESS

It would be difficult to reason in the field of social stratification without assuming that low rank is experienced as depriving and high rank is experienced as rewarding. In fact, this assumption is definitional since high rank is possession of or access to some socially defined value. Therefore the assumption is not open to question. And yet Richard Cory put a bullet through his head.

The unhappiness of the favored—the wealthy, the successful and the respected—is a recurrent theme in literature and the mass media. The basic reason for general interest in this theme is, of course, the lower social rank of the audience. Envy accompanied by spite is a pervasive element of social stratification. Yet an equally general phenomenon in communities and societies is the need of people below the top to justify and accept their relative rank. In consequence, social ideologies often provide beliefs which make it easier to accept lower status. For example, high rank may be regarded as intrinsically undesirable or coming at too high a price ("Who would want all that worry and responsibility?"; "Doctors can never get away from their work"; "Alpha children . . . work much harder than we do"). The scientific question is whether such views are only fabrications designed to soothe the feelings of the less fortunate or whether they have some truth to them, requiring us to qualify the assumption that high rank is rewarding.

Theory in social science has provided a number of reasons why persons of high rank might be seriously uncomfortable, even accepting the assumption that high rank is intrinsically rewarding. An example is Durkheim's analysis (1897:252–253) of social contexts in which the social limits on desires are swept away by abrupt experiences of success. Under the extreme hypothesis that success only increases the desire for more success, the more of a good thing people have, the worse they feel the lack of more of it.

Another, probably more generally applicable, version of this theoretic orientation simply defines satisfaction as the amount of gratification of some kind (wealth, deference, etc.) in relation to the amount of gratification aspired to (see Morse 1953; Kleiner and Parker 1963). This approach retains the idea that social motives arise through socialization without implying that rank is inversely related to (or unrelated to) satisfaction. It also leads to the proposition that people may increase satisfaction either by striving for greater gratification or by lowering aspirations. In this process, people adjust to their social ranks.

Satisfaction, rather than absolute or immediate gratification, should be especially relevant in mediating the effects of social stratification on the individual, since it is the extent to which humans are content with their lot. But satisfaction has many components and it is reasonable to think of most individuals as satisfied in some respects but not in others. Very specific dissatisfactions, however, can be met with very specific responses, such as moving out of a neighborhood, getting divorced, or writing a letter to the editor. Moreover, they can be balanced by other satisfactions (see Institute for Social Research 1974:4–5). One may decide to ignore unpleasant neighbors if the school district is excellent. But chronic dissatisfaction *in general* with many aspects of one's station in life and with the style of living that it allows should affect the motivation for other social behaviors such as political activity, participation in mass movements, conservatism, and scape-goating. Therefore it is *general satisfaction* that is of prime concern for the theory of social stratification.

How should social rank be related to general satisfaction? Rank should affect both the gratifications accruing to an individual *and* the past and current socialization experiences which form aspirations for gratification. Adjustment to a given level of rank is partly an idiosyncratic experience, but is also built into the system of stratification. One's level of origin and early attainments not only provide rewards but also manipulate the individual's horizons and focus attention upon the rewards that are plausibly available (see, for example, Sewell et al. 1970; and Woelfel and Haller 1971). The idea of relative deprivation itself suggests that though deprivation is partly caused by inequality, stratification automatically provides some adjustment for felt deprivation, insofar as same-rank reference groups are perceived.

To the extent that a status system is institutionalized, an ideology supporting this kind of adjustment is often provided culturally. Thus middle-class children may be taught to regard the debutante's coming-out party as ridiculous and to think of high political positions as exacting exorbitant costs in terms of moral compromise, loss of privacy, and so on.

The effects of various social ranks upon satisfaction, then, depend upon several processes. First, how much gratification (deprivation) is caused by high (low) rank per se on various dimensions? If a given value is distributed very unequally (if the dispersion of a rank variable is high) its effect on gratification should be increased. Further (as the ideology about politicians suggests) some high ranks may come equipped with offsetting costs. Or, when high rank eliminates one source of discomfort, it may only provide the opportunity to contemplate others. A second process is the effect of rank on aspirations. If a system of class subcultures has formed about bounded classes the effect on aspirations will be greater than if everyone is taught to aspire to the same goals, whether realistically attainable or not. A third factor is the extent to which various other sources of gratification (or deprivation) are organized by rank. There are sources of pleasure in life that are not necessarily bound up with social rank. If the society or community is one in which these pleasures or pains are distributed randomly with respect to rank (compatible spouses, for example) or distributed uniformly across the board (certain public services and taxes), then the relationship of rank to satisfaction will be reduced. Compensatory allocation, in which gratifications are deliberately funnelled to those low in rank, will of course reduce the relationship even further.

Our initial assumption, that high rank is intrinsically rewarding, is now seen in a more complex light. In attempting to see how this general principle works out in specific social circumstances, we are led to a series of questions for analysis: Does being better off in a material sense have a simple correspondence to satisfaction, or does having some only whet the appetite for more? Do high ranks of all kinds have the same sorts of effects on satisfaction? How can the pattern of effects be interpreted in terms of the balance between aspirations and gratifications? To what degree does rank determine satisfaction? Does the social context of the community affect satisfaction? (see Bradburn and Caplovitz 1965:129). Do social ranks influence satisfaction in different ways depending upon the community context?

THE MEASUREMENT OF GENERAL SATISFACTION

General satisfaction represents the acceptability of the match between goals and achievements. In consequence, satisfaction may be achieved either by lowering aspirations or by being more successful, although most people would prefer the latter method and would find it difficult to practice the former beyond some minimal "floor" point. In asking respondents how satisfied they are, we are inquiring about the comfort with which they have adjusted their aspirations to their actual accomplishments, or vice versa. The condition under study is neither the height of the goal nor the absolute amount of achievement, but the gap between the two.[1]

[1]Two of our measures of satisfaction are framed in just this manner. We assume, however, that the other two (stated in "how satisfied are you with . . ." form) normally get this kind of

Global questions on satisfaction are hard to answer, however, because they separate the respondent from concrete experiences. At the same time a list of specific satisfactions could be endless. We compromised by asking somewhat general questions within four different areas of experience: work, "success," income and enjoyment of life:

Thinking of all the things about your job, how satisfied or dissatisfied are you with it?

Would you say that you have been as successful in life as you wanted to be?

Are you reasonably satisfied with your family income, or do you feel you need a higher income?

In general, have you been able to get as much enjoyment out of life as you wanted to?

The questions were asked in different parts of the interview schedule, as the general topics of work, income, etc., were covered.

These four areas of satisfaction are distinct, yet not entirely independent. When each item was scored[2] and each pair of items related, the resulting zero-order correlations were all positive, but not strong: almost all of them fell between .10 and .30. One implication of this is that few people are satisfied or unsatisfied across the board: Most satisfaction in one area is balanced by dissatisfaction in another.

To measure *general* satisfaction we constructed an index for each respondent by summing his scores on the four types of satisfaction.[3] As a check, we answer anyway because respondents have to answer in relation to some standard, which is probably their level of aspiration.

[2]The four items were scored as follows:

Job: Dissatisfied or very dissatisfied (0)
      Satisfied (1)
      Very satisfied (2)
      Completely satisfied (3)
Income: Need more (0)
         Satisfied, but could use more (2)
         Satisfied (3)
Success: No (0)
          Successful, but wanted more (2)
          Yes (3)
Enjoyment in life: No (0)
                    Yes (3)

[3]The index therefore ranges from 0 (dissatisfied) to 12 (satisfied). The zero-order correlations between each component and the index are:

Job: .5
Income: .7
Success: .7
Enjoyment: .6

Thus the items received about the same weight, with slightly higher weights for success and income satisfaction.

performed most of the analyses discussed below for each of the components as well as for the index. The results were the same—no area of satisfaction behaved in a significantly different fashion from the others, except that the relationships involving the index were somewhat stronger, presumably because random measurement error was reduced and idiosyncratic causes of this or that type of satisfaction were averaged out.

SOCIAL RANK AND GENERAL SATISFACTION

In the broadest terms, people of higher rank are more satisfied. Our general rank index is positively related to general staisfaction (see the bottom panel of Table 6.1), although the relationship is very weak. This happens, as we shall see, because some rank variables affect satisfaction positively and others negatively, and the general index cannot reflect these oppositions. This is one instance in which a very weak unidimensional rank effect conceals stronger effects of specific ranks. Even the pattern of specific rank effects varies between communities.

We began analyzing the separate effects of rank variables by looking at the regression (described in the last chapter) of satisfaction on the set of 17 rank variables, separately within the six cities. We found, first, that majority racial–ethnic rank produces notable satisfaction only in Indianapolis, that is, being black (the minority in that city) reduces satisfaction. The other cities, with mainly Mexican–American minorities, yielded no effect of majority rank. We have, then, an interaction effect by city: Majority affects satisfaction only in Indianapolis. Our next step was to simultaneously examine other rank effects and compare the patterns of effects across cities, using an analysis of covariance. Since majority racial–ethnic rank is defined differently in the cities and since we had already obtained an interaction with respect to that variable, the analysis of covariance was done only for men of majority status. To avoid cluttering up the analysis with trivial effects we also (as explained above in Chapter 5) dropped all rank variables that did not produce a significant beta of at least .10 in at least one city. The interviewer ratings were also dropped. The results are shown in Table 6.1.

The strongest and most regular effect is that income increases satisfaction. It appears that the pleasures of being well off materially are not offset by ever-increasing desires for wealth or by worries and concerns caused by higher income. The rating the respondent gives his neighborhood and the class rating he gives himself also seem to contribute to satisfaction independently of other rank variables, although not in every city. The picture we have is one of present material affluence and its expression in consumption and self-conception contributing positively to satisfaction.

The positive effects, in two cities, of father-in-law's job on satisfaction can be taken as a trace finding, suggesting that marrying a woman of high family

Table 6.1 General Satisfaction Regressed on Rank Variables (Racial-Ethnic Majority Only)

Rank variables	Regression coefficients: Unstandardized and standardized (in parentheses)[a]						
	Average within-city	Indianapolis	Columbus	Linton	Phoenix	Yuma	Safford
Self-placement	.257 (.11)*	.464 (.20)*	.279 (.12)*	b	.352 (.14)*		.219 (.10)
Family income	.009 (.16)*	.012 (.22)*	.007 (.12)*	.008 (.15)*	.009 (.16)*	.011 (.20)*	.008 (.16)*
R's neighborhood rating	.286 (.11)*	.237 (.09)	.514 (.22)*	.286 (.13)*	.344 (.12)*		
First friend's job		.012 (.08)	.010 (.07)	-.007 (.06)		-.008 (.06)	.021 (.17)*
Education		.044 (.05)	-.112 (.13)*	-.110 (.12)			-.205 (.25)*
Wife's education		-.266 (.19)*		.065 (.05)			.099 (.09)
Father's education		-.100 (.12)*	.063 (.06)				
Father's occupation	-.007 (.05)*	-.009 (.06)			-.019 (.12)*		-.010 (.06)
Father-in-law's job			.007 (.06)				.034 (.22)*
R^2	.07	.14*	.15*	.04	.09*	.05	.12*
Mean		6.9	7.0	7.3	6.5	6.9	7.0
Adjusted mean[c]		7.2	7.0	7.4	6.6	6.9	6.7
N	2032	272	354	282	596	287	241
Proportion of the variance explained by[d]							
General rank index[e]	(+).06*	(+).06*	(+).10*	(+).01	(+).04*	-.02*	(+).01*
17 variable regression	.17*	.17*	.17*	.07	.11*	.15	.10*

[a] Asterisked coefficients are those with associated t-values of 1.65 or higher; hence, significant at about the .10 level (two-tailed test). Asterisked correlation coefficients are those significant at the .05 level.

[b] When the standardized coefficient is both nonsignificant and less than .05 it is not shown.

[c] Means on general satisfaction calculated after statistically equalizing the cities on the rank variables. These adjusted means are significantly different (p<.05). Interaction by city was significant (p<.05).

[d] These analyses were run for the total sample, not just men of majority status.

[e] Signs in parentheses show direction of relationship with general rank.

status provides gratification to some men. This in turn recalls Wilensky's "consolation prize" notion (Wilensky 1966b:41–42) discussed in the last chapter.

The negative effects of specific ranks are interesting, but less consistent from one community to the next. Satisfaction seems to be *reduced* by education and by father's occupation. Although the details vary from city to city, social background and early attainment variables seem to contribute negatively to satisfaction. Our earlier discussion suggests an explanation: high rank on these variables set high levels of aspirations, which in turn (when achievement is controlled) reduce satisfaction.

Oddly enough, neither current nor first occupation appear in this analysis because neither had a sufficiently large effect in any city in the initial regression, even though job satisfaction was one of the components of our General Satisfaction index. Occupation evidently affects satisfaction mainly by contributing to a man's income and style of life. In Chapter 4, we also showed occupation to be a major influence on self-placement, so this is another major mediating variable. Plausibly, then, occupation had little direct effect in this analysis because we have included the major variables through which it affects satisfaction.

Our hypotheses about the process of rank effects on satisfaction are summarized in the diagram in Figure 6.1. Income and occupation increase gratification indirectly, through the man's assessment of his own standing and that of his neighborhood. Income also has a notable direct effect on gratification. High family rank and educational achievement indirectly raise gratification, but directly they act to raise aspirations. The balance of gratifications vis-à-vis aspirations is then reduced by higher aspirations and raised by higher gratification. Finally, this balance positively affects the man's general satisfaction. The effect of minority racial–ethnic rank, noted in Indianapolis, is presumably to directly reduce gratification, net of the effects of income, self-placement and other variables.

This model corresponds to what we called a difference model in the last chapter, because satisfaction is supposedly finally affected by the balance between gratification and aspiration. Another way to state the conclusion we are drawing from these findings is that persons whose affluence exceeds their expectations are particularly satisfied, while those whose expectations exceed their affluence are relatively dissatisfied, controlling for level of status. Theoretically, this is a little different from saying that affluence tends to increase satisfaction and high aspirations to decrease satisfaction, but without some measured intervening variable to demonstrate different results, the statements are empirically equivalent.

We must remind the reader, however, that rank is at best able to explain only 15% of the variance (and the explanation only rises a little in the full 17-variable regression which includes the full sample and the majority and

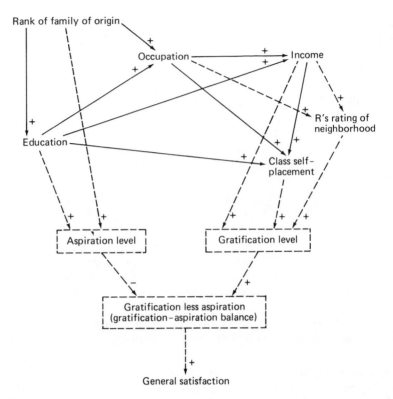

Figure 6.1. *Hypothetical process of rank effects on general satisfaction (unmeasured variables and effects are given in dotted lines).*

interviewer rating variables). The model depicted in Figure 6.1 may reflect real effects upon satisfaction but these effects fall far short of determining satisfaction. Measurement error, of course, accounts for part of the failure, but much of the unexplained variance is no doubt due to a host of other pains and pleasures which are not related to the system of stratification.

EFFECTS DUE TO CITY AND TO CONTROL VARIABLES

The above discussion focussed on the general picture of rank differences, as reflected in consistent effects across cities and in the average within-city regression. We want now to briefly discuss the differences between the cities and then to examine the results of introducing a number of control variables into the analysis.

The ways in which rank affects satisfaction do differ from city to city. We have already noted that the racial–ethnic effect occurs only within Indianapolis. Even within the majority sample, however, the hypothesis of no interaction can be rejected at the .05 level. The six separate regressions (for the majority men) shown in Table 6.1 are different enough to add 3% to the explained variance (beyond the 7% explained by the average regression).

The separate regressions show some similarity, despite the significant interaction. The most consistent effect is, of course, that of family income, usually accompanied by positive effects of self-placement and/or neighborhood rating. We would have expected from our findings in previous chapters that the respondent's raing of his neighborhood would have little to no effect in the small towns, but a substantial effect of this variable appeared in Linton.

The negative effects of origin and early attainment variables appeared less regularly, and the particular variables having this effect varied considerably from city to city. However, the general pattern of positive effects for affluence and consumption variables and negative effects for background and/or education variables appeared in every city except one: In Yuma the only substantial effect was that of income. The cities also varied in the degree to which the rank variables explained satisfaction: multiple R^2's were especially low in Yuma and in Linton. The variations in effects from city to city do not suggest to us any clear explanation in terms of city size or region or other attributes of the community context. Yuma illustrates a town where a small correlation with general rank is not greatly increased by multidimensional analysis, but Safford illustrates a town where an even smaller bivariate correlation conceals a substantial multidimensional effect.

In spite of the varying rank effects, the average level of satisfaction did not differ greatly from one community to the next. The general satisfaction scale varied from 0 to 12, with an overall standard deviation of about 3.2. The highest and lowest city means differed by less than one point. Like Bradburn and Caplovitz (1965), we find no dramatic differences in average levels of satisfaction in our cities. This result does not change when the city means on satisfaction are adjusted for city differences in composition on the rank variables (although this adjustment must be read tentatively, since it is not strictly legitimate when there is a significant difference between the city slopes). Communities appear to differ not so much in the average satisfaction of inhabitants, as in the extent to which rank affects satisfaction and in the specific manner in which rank affects satisfaction (save for the consistent effect of family income).

The next step in the analysis was to introduce several control variables in order to see if any of the rank effects found above might be spurious (data not shown). For example, older people have lower rank on education and the social background variables. If older people also tend to be more satisfied, then the negative effects of education and social background we observed above could be spurious, due only to age variations.

The variables we entered as controls into our regressions were: age, number of children, stage of the family life cycle (a set of dummy variables), home ownership, mother's religion, whether the respondent was reared in the South, and whether he was native to the community or a recent or a long-ago migrant (another set of dummy variables).

Adding these control variables to our regressions did not change our general conclusions about the effects of rank variables. Linear adjustments for these variables only slightly altered the partial standardized regression coefficients for the rank variables. The only exception involved the regression for Safford, in which the beta for family income fell from .16 to .08 and the beta for education from −.25 to −.04 when the controls were added. Only in this city, then, did some of the rank effects turn out to be partly or wholly spurious.

The effect of age itself deserves notice, since it was as strong and as consistent as that of family income: In every city, older men were more satisfied than younger men (with the other variables controlled).[4] This suggests that as a man grows older he is able to bring his aspirations into line with his success more effectively, so a higher level of satisfaction results.

A final analysis suggests a further complication: The effects of education upon satisfaction may vary with age. Table 6.2 reports a regression for the total sample in which we sought the effects of four rank variables upon satisfaction within five age categories. As before, income has a strong effect and occupation and majority little or no effect.

Education affects satisfaction positively for the youngest men, but more and more negatively as age increases, except after age 65 when the effect switches to positive again. The interaction is significant at the .01 level. Evidently, the situation is not as simple as we suggested above—education does not only affect satisfaction by setting aspirations. We can offer an explanation of this result, but it should be taken as both post hoc and tentative.

Any rank variable—perhaps especially education—may have many different meanings. Education probably acts as a direct source of gratification, yielding prestige, for example. We have suggested above that it also sets levels of aspiration. At the younger ages, it probably also affects a man's predictions about his future level of gratification. Before age 35 higher

[4]One might think that the relationship between general satisfaction and age or variables related to age (e.g., education) would best be explained by family life cycle. Adding age and three life cycle dummy variables to the rank predictors, however, yields an increase in explained variance of four percent at most, and one percent at least. Much of the rank- and age-related variance explained in satisfaction is probably redundant, then, and only a small portion of explained variance can uniquely be ascribed to age or life cycle. Moreover, the regression coefficients for age are all positive and strong in all six cities, while those for life cycle categories, net of age, are moderate at best, and their pattern varies from one community to the next. The interaction with age presented below in Table 6.2 shows that the impact of education shows a regular curvilinear variation according to age, but even in that analysis the independent effect of age itself is remarkably stable. We conclude that stage of family life cycle may be an interesting condition for some rank effects—notably education—on satisfaction, but that the most regular and strongest effects are those of income and age itself.

Table 6.2 *General Satisfaction Regressed on Rank Variables within Age Categories (Total Sample)*

Rank variables	Regression coefficients: Unstandardized and standardized (in parentheses)[a]				
	Age 20 - 34	Age 35 - 44	Age 45 - 54	Age 55 - 64	Age 65 and over
Family income	.015 (.16)*	.011 (.19)*	.015 (.34)*	.012 (.28)*	.011 (.20)*
Occupation	b	-.006 (.05)	.008 (.06)		
Education	.165 (.14)*	-.024 (.03)	-.053 (.06)	-.085 (.10)	.119 (.16)*
Majority					.552 (.05)
R^2	.08*	.03*	.11*	.06*	.12*
Mean	6.2	6.7	6.6	7.4	7.7
N	509	475	442	328	261

[a] Asterisked coefficients are those with associated t-values of 1.65 or higher; hence, significant at approximately the .10 level (two-tailed test). Asterisked correlation coefficients are significant at .05 level.

[b] When the standardized coefficient is both nonsignificant and less than .05 it is not shown.

education may produce satisfaction because it yields prestige and leads a man to expect future gratification; these have positive effects on gratification level which are stronger than the (negative) effect on aspirations. Specifically, young well-educated men may have aspirations higher than their current levels of success, but they can easily reconcile this discrepancy because they expect success in the future. As a man grows older and moves further into his career, education may be less directly salient as a source of prestige since occupation and income come into play as more immediate indexes of success. Likewise, education must affect estimates of future gratification less and less as a man uses up more and more of his future. As age increases, then, the meaning of education shifts from direct gratification and promise for the future to unreachable aspirations from the past, so the negative effect of education on satisfaction through aspirations becomes more and more powerful.

Some discontinuity evidently occurs at retirement. When employment ends education evidently becomes less important in fixing aspirations to be fulfilled in the working, income-getting world. Its importance as a source of prestige probably does not increase, but it may assume importance as a resource to draw upon in filling the new idleness—a source of prestige as well as interests and activities beyond those once provided by occupation. Education at this stage should thus increase satisfaction. In other words, we see the discontinuity at age 65 as deriving from retirement rather than simply advancing age. Some confirmation of this was obtained by doing the regression in Table 6.2 separately for employed and nonemployed men over 65.

The effect of education remained negative (−.08) for the employed men over 65 but shifted to positive (+.20) for the unemployed men.

SUMMARY AND CONCLUSIONS

Our major empirical results can be summarized as follows:

1. The general rank index has a small positive relationship to general satisfaction.

2. Income, class self-placement and one's rating of his neighborhood all increase general satisfaction.

3. Satisfaction seems to be reduced by more education and by higher social origin, especially father's occupation. Education may have this negative effect only for men in their middle and later working years.

4. The total effect of rank on general satisfaction is moderate at best; rank never explains as much as 20% of the variance and sometimes much less.

5. The average levels of satisfaction in our cities were similar, but the cities displayed somewhat different patterns of rank effects, and in varying degrees. The effect of income appeared in all communities and the effects of self-placement and neighborhood rating in most communities, but the particular education and origin variables having negative effects on satisfaction varied considerably from city to city. Majority racial–ethnic rank increased satisfaction only in Indianapolis (where the minority is black). The cities also varied in the extent to which rank explained satisfaction. These variations are not simply ordered by size or region.

6. Introducing a set of nonrank control variables did not alter our findings about rank effects (except in one city, Safford).

7. As men grow older they become more satisfied, net of any rank effects.

These results lead us to the basic interpretation that satisfaction depends upon the balance of aspirations and gratification: Men whose affluence exceeds their aspirations are satisfied, while those whose aspirations exceed their affluence are relatively dissatisfied. Rank variables mainly affect this balance by affecting gratification: Our strongest and most consistent effects on satisfaction are those of income and other variables that plausibly increase gratification and hence improve the balance between gratifications and aspirations. But the data also contained persistent suggestions that educational rank (at least under some conditions) and origin rank variables increase aspirations and hence have the net effect of reducing satisfaction.

The effects of age and of city are also consonant with this interpretation. The age effect can be interpreted as meaning that as men age they tend (if they fail to achieve to the level of their aspirations) to reduce their aspirations to match their achievements, and hence become more satisfied. The absence of a clear relationship, when rank composition is controlled, between average community prosperity and average community satisfaction suggests that community prosperity neither acts as a direct reward nor as a salient reference group for the evaluation of individual rewards. If men derive gratification from their success mainly by comparing that success to others, then, the "others" are not the entire community but some subset of the community (siblings, peers, etc.), or some extracommunity reference group (professional colleagues, for example), or some national standard (perhaps sponsored by the mass media).

Our formulation is that being well-off is not sufficient for satisfaction— what is important is the discrepancy between gratification desired and gratification achieved. On theoretical grounds, then, we arrived at a type of difference model in which rank variables do not have separate additive effects on a dependent variable but rather each affects the balance between aspirations and gratifications, which in turn influences satisfaction. Such an interpretation could be stated in terms of the effects of mobility and inconsistency as well as in terms of the effects of the rank variables per se. Upward mobility presumably involves gratification greater than the level of aspiration set earlier in life and hence should increase satisfaction; downward mobility implies the opposite. High educational rank combined with low income rank implies greater aspirations than achievement, thus this type of inconsistency produces dissatisfaction. Our earlier rejection of hypotheses of mobility and inconsistency effects must therefore be qualified, with respect to the dependent variable of satisfaction, since an additive difference model of mobility and inconsistency effects seem to fit these data reasonably well.

What are the implications for the distribution of satisfaction throughout the stratification structure of a community? Let us suppose that in a given community the various rank dimensions were very highly related, so almost everyone held consistently high ranks, or medium or low ranks, on the various dimensions. Further, suppose that all rank dimensions affected satisfaction positively. Finally, suppose that these effects were very strong and controlled most of the variance in satisfaction. If all these conditions held, "upper-class" people would be much more satisfied than "middle-class" people who in turn would be much more content than members of the "lower class."

None of these conditions are met in our data. The relationships between rank dimensions are not high; many people who have to contend with low rank on one dimension can perhaps draw upon resources due to high rank upon some other dimension. High rank on some dimensions promotes satisfaction; high rank on others reduces satisfaction. People with uniformly high or low ranks would therefore tend to have medium levels of satisfaction. Only poorly educated, well-paid men from humble origins who live in neighborhoods they rate highly are receiving consistent positive inputs to their satisfaction. Finally, even such men are not guaranteed a high level of satisfaction—the low R^2's mean that many are dissatisfied, while many men whose patterns of rank mitigate against satisfaction are nevertheless generally satisfied, due to the effects of factors not related to rank.

We conclude, then, that chances for satisfaction are not sharply different at different places in the stratification system. The causal processes of multidimensional stratification yield a tendency for few people to be found at the extremes of satisfaction and dissatisfaction and for these extremes not to be closely associated with the extremes of any given rank (see Hodge 1970, for a similar conclusion). A man with high income only *tends* to be more satisfied than a poor man. If he has high ranks on education and origin, his satisfaction will be reduced; he may rank lower on self-placement or neighborhood rating, which will also reduce his satisfaction; and even well paid men without these handicaps will range widely in satisfaction, because so many other factors randomly related to rank affect satisfaction powerfully. It is no surprise, then, that the zero-order r^2 between income and satisfaction is no greater than .05 in any city.

This means we must alter our notions, set out in Chapter 1, about satisfaction as a major mediating variable between rank and other sorts of behavior and attitudes. We can no longer believe that rank closely controls satisfaction, which in turn closely controls other forms of behavior. The effects of rank on satisfaction are not strong at all. If satisfaction does closely control other sorts of behavior and if indeed most rank effects act primarily through satisfaction, then rank effects on other forms of behavior will be even weaker than those on satisfaction. On the other hand, if rank does strongly affect various dependent variables, then satisfaction is not the major intervening variable. One possibility is that some component of the above system is a major intervening variable—for example, gratification per se, rather than an aspirations–gratification balance, may control other sorts of behavior. Another possible intervening variable, which we discussed as theoretically important in Chapter 1, is social participation. Rank effects on both informal and formal participation are examined in the next two chapters.

7

INFORMAL SOCIAL
PARTICIPATION:
VISITING AND FRIENDSHIP

This chapter begins with a general discussion of the role of individual participation in the social networks of interaction (and therefore communication) through which humans organize themselves. It considers the implications of types of social participation for community organization and for the extent to which social classes exist as organized entities. We then present findings on visiting as an instance of informal social participation, on values regarding visiting, and on differential association—the degree to which men choose as friends men of the same social rank.

SOCIAL PARTICIPATION AND COMMUNITY
SOCIAL STRUCTURE

The structure of any social organization consists of the regular relationships among its component social roles. Any such organization must be maintained through a system of communication. The network of communication parallels the social structure, partly because that is how regular relationships between roles are established and maintained in the first place, and partly because the organization of activities, prescribed by the roles, determines who will be able to communicate with whom.

Communities (and social classes, for that matter) exhibit social structure and networks of communication (both formal and informal), but they differ in important ways from aggregates such as large-scale complex organizations. The basic reason for the differences, of course, is that the charter of a corporation, for example, specifies a few activities or products as goals and organizes behavior in relation to them, while the "charter" of a community is much more general, since communities are fundamentally ecological entities embracing a wide sphere of activities. They consist of families and individuals who live and work in the same territory, and who share the same resources in the daily or weekly round of life.

Although some proscriptive laws exist, relationships among community members are ordinarily not closely prescribed by norms. The detailed coordination of the millions of activities, from peeling carrots to tending lathes, that go on in a community each day is more a matter of economic or functional integration rather than normative integration. Members of most contemporary urban communities are bound together by mutual dependence (and the differences between members, as between manager and worker or husband and wife) more than they are by consensus on goals or values (and the similarity between persons which gives rise to consensus).

In such a setting, communication networks have an infinite number of purposes, since in the absence of consensus any issue can become something that it is important for people to communicate about. When an issue presents itself, the organization to deal with it does not suddenly appear, but must be constructed out of previously existing communication networks. For the most part, those previous networks are *generalized* in nature, because there are so many different specific purposes that they are (or might be) used for.

The community social structure can be described, therefore, by the recurrent interactions within a population defined by a common territory and economic interdependence.

To the extent that organized social classes with distinctive subcultures exist within communities, their perpetuation depends on associated social networks. One should never expect a class to be as tightly organized as a bureaucracy unless it is unusually small. Like communities, levels of social rank tend to include large numbers of people and their organization is largely informal. In consequence, communication is apt to be indirect: A speaks to B who speaks to C who speaks to D, connecting A and D though the two may never communicate directly. The the social structure of a class is diffuse unless the class is so small that it is possible for each member to know each other member personally.

Small groups are considered cohesive if the ties among members are all strong and reciprocated, but the cohesion of such large entities as classes or communities paradoxically depends on the frequency of *weak* interpersonal ties (Granovetter 1973). The formation of solidary cliques may give individuals an enhanced sense of belongingness and social participation, but the very solidarity and exclusiveness of such cliques may militate against the development of an extensive network of communications within some larger collectivity, and clique interests may oppose those of the collectivity as a whole.

The social structure of a community (or of one of its component social classes), is as important for what it *might* be used for at some time in the future as it is for what it *is* being used for at the moment. *Potential* organization or *potential* channels of communication are important because when some new issue confronts a population and a new organization has to be built to contend with the issue, it is much easier to build the new organization on the basis of present used or unused relationships than it is to start from scratch. Generalized structures, within the community or a class, are always available as means to mobilize public action. Each new issue creates its own public, and in that sense people are organized by events, but each new public grows up out of previous segments of community structure, and in that sense social structure organizes human perception of, and response to, events.

Community social structures are not noted for fast and efficient action (except for bureaucratic components such as the fire department) Such action is possible for armies, hospitals, football teams precisely because the social structure is so observable, clear-cut and reliable; coordination is based on planned mutual understandings about how team members will act. But collective action at the community level may be extremely slow and/or highly disorganized. Often the problem is not one of implementing goals that are agreed upon by all, but one of finding out what the different goals within a population are, so that they can slowly be compromised.

The strong point of community social structure is ability to contain conflict, and this strength depends on the looseness of the network. Since communities are defined by territory, they are apt to include very real conflicts stemming from differences of interest or from major cultural differences. Conflicts are plausibly minimized when a communication network is connected enough to allow opponents to indirectly exchange views, but loose enough to make their direct personal contact unlikely. Thus as structures go, communities tend to be loosely integrated, yet capable of mobilizing vast numbers of involved individuals when the occasion demands.

Social structures and their associated communicative networks, then, are aggregate phenomena which consist of large numbers of actions by individuals. The social process which can be described as a social network from the community perspective consists of social participation from the perspective of the individual. Paradoxically, it is difficult to observe social structure and social participation at the same time, though the terms refer to the same reality. A sample survey of the individuals who make up the population misses the connectedness of the structure and omits detailed description of groups that are statistically minute, yet of enormous importance in community affairs. A study of elites, on the other hand, cannot describe participation within the population at large. Like most past studies, our procedure here will be to infer features of the structure of the community (regarding which we will have no direct data) from patterns of individual social participation (which we study directly).

The data we have gathered from individual family heads on their social participation represents potential exposure to communicative acts, under specified conditions. They indicate, that is, the extent to which a particular individual can be reached in his normal round of life through the different more or less organized channels of communication available in the community. These data interest us both as an instance of the effect of rank on individual behavior and as a basis for inferring characteristics of the communication networks that exist in the different communities. Some channels of communication are entirely missing in these data, simply because the interview could not be endless. Most notable among these were communications that come to a family head at work or through the mass media.

Informal social participation will be the subject of this chapter; the next chapter will deal with formal participation. Theoretic interest in both chapters is in the extensiveness of an individual's social network (how many people does a relationship put one in contact with?) along with the individual's ability to use the network to get information and communicate to others. Formal participation, as in churches, associations, political parties and government, allows one to influence (and to be influenced by) large numbers of persons beyond the reach of personal contacts. Such organizations maintain some small means of mass communication, even if it consists of no more than a list of addresses and a mimeograph machine. On the other hand, informal participation affords the possibility of strong personal impact and may also be important simply because the operation of the network may not be as observable to community members as, for example, the mass media.

Formal and informal participation do not, of course, operate in isolation from one another. Formal organizations sometimes cannot accomplish their goals without the informal organizations that grow up within and around them. Conversely, part of the importance of formal structures in a community lies precisely in the fact that they can generate and maintain informal ties. Thus becoming an officer in the Neighborhood Improvement Association not only gives one access to the membership list, the machinery of meetings, the power to decide what goes into the monthly bulletin and the authority to speak for the association, but also provides the basis for personal friendships and acquaintanceships that might otherwise be hard to arrange.

SOCIAL PARTICIPATION AND HIERARCHY

Theoretically, if social networks of individuals are generally restricted to people of similar social rank, community rank differentiation becomes the differentiation of that population into a set of social strata. This occurs because similarity is the general condition for social interaction (and therefore communication) and communication is the condition for the development and perpetuation of culture or subculture.

Any form of social differentiation—by race, occupation, sex, ideological position, etc.—is potentially a barrier to communication, because it entails some difference in perspective, language, interests and previous experience. To the extent that rates of interaction across the lines of differentiation are high, social differences are not likely to be concretized in cultural differences, but to the extent that communication ceases across those lines, cultural differences are apt to emerge, yielding groups which do not interact with one another, and which differ culturally as well as socially.

Another crucial question is who holds central positions in the community network of communication. This depends both on the extent of differential association and on the extent to which persons of high rank participate at higher *rates* than those of low rank. Centrality in communication is an important resource in exerting power in community affairs (Secord and Backman 1974:148–154). If high rank on income, occupational prestige, etc., affords such a central position, it thus confers an additional degree of power. The question is not simply one of the connectedness of networks at specific levels of rank, but of potential influence within the community network.

For the stratification system to be also a controlling, organizing and governing system, individuals of high rank must hold central communicative positions. This will happen if persons of high rank can both draw information from the entire community and can communicate with each other more freely and frequently than is possible for those at other levels.

The optimum conditions for this, in turn, are that rank be positively related to rates of participation and that the degree of differential association be moderate. If individuals of high rank participate more in social interaction, their positions will, in general, be more central since they will be in contact with more people. But if differential association is very high, their contacts will be restricted to others of high rank. If differential association is moderate, however, they can draw from information from other levels, but there will also be easy communicative contact among persons of high rank by virtue of their small numbers. In fact, given moderate differential association, those high in the social rank hierarchy would have communicative centrality even if rank were unrelated to rates of participation, because the number of persons to be communicated with is vastly lower at the very high levels of social rank.

With increasing social rank, we expect that the individual has access to an increasingly wide segment of the community, (a) by increasing the total amount of social participation and (b) by selecting and emphasizing those types of participation that yield the widest communicative access. Of the two, we should expect the total amount of participation to vary least by social rank, since (if for no other reason) individual participation is limited to less than 24 hours a day, regardless of rank. The type of participation should vary more strongly with rank.

Type of participation has many dimensions, but one of the most important is the formal–informal distinction. The attainment of achieved social rank in American society is above all a matter of demonstrated ability in the use of formally structured organizations. Indeed, two important measures of achieved rank, namely education and occupation, represent for the most part success in formal organizations and under contemporary conditions the same is often true of income. These skills and interests useful in preparing for and producing income may be expected to operate outside of working hours as well and increase rates of voluntary formal participation.

We now turn to our analyses of informal participation. Formal participation will be dealt with in Chapter 8.

RATES OF VISITING AND VALUES ABOUT VISITING

Visiting, spending an evening together on a family basis within the "territory" of one party, is only one of many possible loci for sociable interaction, but it allows us to conveniently compare rates of different types of informal participation.

Several features make visiting particularly· interesting to the student of stratification:

1. Visiting specifically implies equal status interaction. Even when the boss invites a worker to dinner because of the boss–worker relationship, the norms governing the interaction are that the two and their wives are to treat each other more or less as equals for that evening. It would be intolerable for the boss to order his worker around and embarrassing for the worker to show too much deference.

2. The families are involved or represented as status units.

3. Visiting is one link between the public and private spheres of behavior. Normatively, visiting itself is socially private, yet the community status context cannot be totally ignored by the participants. Some commitment in the eyes of the community is implied in visiting—consider the difference between being polite to a couple in passing on the street, and having them over for dinner. In answering the question on visiting neighbors (quoted in the following section, many respondents themselves distinguished between visiting and "over the fence" contacts, implying an important distinction between the two.

4. The nature of interaction during visiting may or may not be superficial, but it is generalized: people are to be treated as people, not just as role segments.

Rates of Informal Participation

To distinguish different bases for visiting, we asked the following questions: "Do you have relatives in the (community) area—aside from those living with you?"; (If yes) "How often do you get together with them?"; "How often do you get together with people you work with—away from the job?"; "About how often do you get together with your neighbors—either in your home or theirs?"; "Outside of relatives and neighbors, about how often do you visit with friends?"[1]

Our results agree with several past studies that the traditional bases for informal contacts, namely visiting with relatives and neighbors, have not withered away into nothingness with urbanization. Over half the men with relatives in the area visit them once a week or more often (see Table 7.1). The corresponding figure for neighbors is about 30%. However, rates of visiting with (nonrelative, nonneighbor) friends is a little higher—about 35–40% visit friends once a week or more.

The same ordering of rates of visiting—relatives, then friends, followed by neighbors, then work associates—is found in all cities. There are some variations from city to city (e.g., there is less visiting of neighbors in Colum-

Table 7.1 *Extent of Four Kinds of Informal Participation*

	Percentage who visit once per week or more often					
People visited	Indianapolis	Columbus	Linton	Phoenix	Yuma	Safford
Relatives[a]	56	51	60	55	67	62
Friends	35	28	37	40	46	38
Neighbors	b	19	30	27	35	28
Work associates	b	15	22	18	28	18

[a] These are percentages of those men with relatives in the community area.

[b] The questions on visiting neighbors and work associates were not included in the Indianapolis survey.

[1] The responses offered the respondents to the questions on frequency of visiting, and the scores assigned to each, were:

Several times a week (0)
About once a week (1)
A few times a month (2)
Once every month or two (3)
A few times a year (4)
Once a year or less (5)
Never (a volunteered response) (6)

Because high scores indicate low rates of visiting these variables were called "*infrequency* of visiting . . ." in Chapter 5. In this chapter, however, the scores are reversed so high scores will indicate high rates of visiting and a positive regression coefficient will indicate that men of high rank visit more than men of lower rank.

bus), but they do not seem to be clearly due to city size or region. Small town visiting patterns are not clearly different from large city patterns. There does seem to be slightly less visiting with relatives living in the area in the three mostly highly industrialized and prosperous communities (Indianapolis, Columbus, and Phoenix).

Rank Effects on Visiting Relatives and Friends

Visiting relatives, as opposed to visiting friends, is a major contrast in our analysis. We initially expected visiting relatives to illustrate a kind of informal participation that is largely irrelevant to rank, while visiting other friends would be especially common among high ranking family heads.

The possibilities of visiting relatives are incommensurable with those of visiting friends in one respect. Most men can expect to find friends of one kind or another in any community to which they move. The same is not necessarily true of relatives. Therefore, data on visiting relatives and friends will be presented as follows: First the question of whether the family in question *has* relatives in the area will be examined, and then rank effects on the frequency of visiting relatives *if there are any in the area* will be contrasted to rank effects on the frequency of visiting friends.

The overall effect of general rank on the presence of relatives in the local area is clear: The higher his general rank index score, the less likely a family head is to live in an area where he has relatives. The correlation coefficients (squares of which are reported in Table 7.2), though weak and somewhat variable, are all negative (within rounding error of 0 in Phoenix).

Allowing the rank effect to be multivariate generally produces much better prediction than the unidimensional analysis (compare row 1 to rows 2 and 3 in Table 7.2). Much of this improvement is because the pattern of rank effects is rather different from city to city and the multivariate predictions can capture these variations while the general rank index does not.

The cities are different both in the strength of the prediction and in the patterns of effects. The 17-variable R^2's vary from .05 to .20, the weaker relationships appearing in Linton, Phoenix, and Yuma. The pattern of effects (see Table 7.3) also varies considerably across cities (as the last chapter showed, the analysis of covariance for *relatives in the community area* yielded an interaction term significant at the .05 level). Hence, what we present as conclusions below are relatively small, although apparently real, signals embedded in a great deal of random noise. Table 7.3 reports a regression employing those rank variables having noticeable effects on the dependent variable.

The major consistent effect is that men of prestigious occupations are less likely to have relatives living nearby. A substantial negative effect of occupation appears in each city. The other evident effect, although less consistent, is that indicators of the rank of the couple's families of origin (father's

Table 7.2 *Visiting Relatives and Friends: Variance Explained by Rank Variables*

Dependent and independent variables	Percentage of variance explained (r^2 or R^2)					
	Indianapolis	Columbus	Linton	Phoenix	Yuma	Safford
Relatives in the area						
General rank index[a]	(-).02*[b]	(-).11*	(-).01	.00	(-).02*	(-).01
17 rank variables[c]	.13*	.20*	.07	.05*	.08*	.14*
9 rank variables[d]	.10*	.18*	.06	.02	.05	.07*
Frequency of visiting relatives						
General rank index	.00	.00	.00	(-).01*	.00	.00
17 rank variables	.08	.09	.11	.10*	.06	.11
5 rank variables	.08	.06	.07*	.09*	.06	.10
Frequency of visiting friends						
General rank index	(+).03*	(+).05*	.00	(+).01*	.00	(+).01
17 rank variables	.12*	.10*	.05	.04	.07	.07
9 rank variables	.11*	.06*	.01	.02*	.02	.03
Rather visit relatives than friends						
General rank index	(-).06*	(-).08*	(-).09*	(-).08*	(-).05*	(-).07*
17 rank variables	.12*	.18*	.24*	.11*	.10	.14*
7 rank variables	.10*	.12*	.18*	.05*	.05	.16*

[a] The signs in parentheses in this row indicate whether the general rank index is positively or negatively related to the dependent variable.

[b] Asterisks indicate that the regression is significant at the .05 level.

[c] These are the 17 rank variables employed in analyses in Chapters 2 and 5.

[d] These are the rank variables selected for the analyses of covariance in Chapter 5. These analyses were performed for men of majority racial-ethnic rank only, and included only rank variables which had a standardized regression coefficient of at least .10 and an associated t-value of at least 1.65 in any one city in the corresponding 17-variable regression.

occupation, father's education and wife's education) also generally have negative coefficients. This may mean that high status parents are less likely to exert pressure to keep their children in their home town or that socioeconomically high occupations more often require migration, but it may also indicate that even if such a couple remains close to home, their parents and/or siblings often move away. Negative effects of occupation and origin, then, are mainly responsible for the negative general rank effect in Table 7.2.

These relationships were also considered in a further analysis with controls introduced for nonrank variables which may also affect the presence of relatives in the community. These were number of siblings, migration, age,

Table 7.3 Rank Effects on the Presence of Relatives in the Community Area

Rank variables	Regression coefficients: Unstandardized and standardized (in parentheses)[a]					
	Indianapolis	Columbus	Linton	Phoenix	Yuma	Safford
Self-placement	b	.026 (.08)				.043 (.13)*
Family income		.005 (.05)			.012 (.13)*	
Occupation	-.004 (.24)*	-.003 (.18)*	-.003 (.18)*	-.002 (.10)*	-.002 (.10)	-.002 (.09)
Education	-.020 (.18)*	-.035 (.27)*	.021 (.16)*			
Wife's education			-.013 (.07)	-.018 (.10)*	-.017 (.09)	
Father's occupation	.002 (.12)*	-.002 (.11)*	-.001 (.05)	.001 (.06)	-.002 (.08)	-.005 (.19)*
Father's education	.007 (.07)		-.008 (.06)		-.013 (.10)*	
Majority	.064 (.05)	.212 (.06)		-.115 (.08)*	-.058 (.05)	-.088 (.07)
R^2	.09*[c]	.15*	.05	.03*	.05*	.07*
N	322	376	298	686	375	306

[a]In this and following tables in this chapter, asterisked regression coefficients are those with associated t-values of 1.65 or higher; hence, significant at about the .10 level (two-tailed test).

[b]In this and following tables in this chapter, coefficients are not shown when the standardized regression coefficient is both non-significant and less than .05, i.e., for relatively weak effects.

[c]In this and following tables in this chapter, asterisked R^2's are significant at the .05 level.

and stage of family life cycle. Such variables as number of siblings could produce a spurious correlation between rank and having relatives in the area; other variables, such as migration, may be affected by rank and in turn affect the dependent variable in question. It is therefore mildly surprising (especially for the control on migration) that including these controls did not change the above results in any substantial fashion. Evidently, high-ranked occupations separate men from their relatives, not because they involve movement per se, but because the movements are independent of family ties. Lower status men may move, but are apparently more likely to move to a community where some of their kin already live.

These findings do not necessarily imply that men with higher-ranked jobs are *socially* separated from their relatives. The geographical separation may simply force an organizational adaptation. For example, the nuclear family whose head works in middle or high levels of a national concern or who has specialized in a nationally organized profession must expect to move around the country for occupational reasons. Extended families, in a somewhat modified form, continue to exist in these circumstances to the extent that their members are trained and willing to use of means of communication other than face-to-face talking. Their communal life occurs by post and telephone rather than frequent visiting.

How does rank affect visiting relatives, given that relatives are available to be visited in the area? The major answer to this question is that there are vast fluctuations from city to city in the pattern of rank effects. In Chapter 5 (Table 5.2), we found that the interaction term (reflecting city differences in slopes) for the rate of visiting relatives was significant at the .05 level and explained three times as much variance (6%) as the average within-city regression.

Examining the pattern of effects (in a table not given here) tells us that the coefficients for most rank variables fluctuate in both size and sign from city to city, and that within any given city about half the rank variables have positive effects and about half negative. The variations do not seem to follow any simple pattern of city size or region effects, as far as we can tell. Indeed, many of them are probably random. We see in Table 7.2 that the multivariate R^2's, although ranging from .06 to .11, usually are not statistically significant since the sample is reduced to include only those men with relatives in the area (about 70% of the respondents, in general). Given these fluctuations, it is not surprising to see that the general rank index, which assumes that all rank effects act in the same direction and have the same pattern in all cities, has essentially no relationship to the frequency of visiting relatives.

The sole effect consistent from city to city is that, with other rank variables controlled, families with higher incomes seem to visit less with relatives. This effect appears in every city (and five of the betas are larger than $-.05$). When the controls mentioned above were included the effect remained, although it was weakened somewhat (three of six betas larger than $-.05$).

This effect may mean that high income families have less leisure for visiting relatives, or that they put their leisure to other uses. It may represent a reluctance to visit relatives (a topic analyzed below), since relatives are likely to have a smaller family income and the difference in levels of consumption is sufficiently embarrassing to slightly inhibit visiting. However, the finding is not substantial or consistent enough under controls to be considered as anything more than a trace finding to be followed up in later research.

The analysis so far, then, shows that men of higher occupations are substantially less likely to have relatives in their community area but that if men have relatives nearby rank has essentially no effect on how often they are visited (though high income perhaps inhibits visiting slightly). These findings are consistent with those of Klatzky (1972) who reported that the only occupational effect was greater visiting among farmers. Farmers would enter the present analysis as a low status occupation, but their number was too small to influence the regression equations.

Rank effects on visiting friends are more consistent from city to city than effects on visiting relatives, but the relationships are still fairly weak and show some variability across cities. The general rank index is positively (but weakly) related to visiting friends in four cities and unrelated in the other two (see Table 7.2). We shall see, however, that this overall positive relationship is an average of opposed positive and negative effects.

Several effects appeared with some consistency across the cities (Table 7.4). Higher rates of visiting friends are generally found among men who are either well educated themselves or, especially, married to well educated wives. However, men whose fathers held prestigious jobs are *less* likely to visit friends. In fact, with few exceptions, all forms of education (respondent's, wife's, father's) promoted visiting while all forms of occupation (respondent's, father's) generally produced lower rates of visiting friends. These conclusions were not altered by including controls for number of siblings, migration, age, and stage in the family life cycle.

Some mild city differences appear in these effects—our analysis of covariance in Chapter 5 yielded an interaction term significant at the .25 level. First, the cities vary in the strength of the association: Social rank seems to explain more about visiting friends in the two most industrialized cities, Indianapolis and Columbus (but, even in these two cities, explanation does not much exceed 10%). The effects described above also are present in only some cities. Respondent's education increases visiting in the large cities, but wife's education has the main effect in the medium and smaller communities. The effect of father's occupation is more evident in Arizona than in Indiana.

The opposed effects of education and occupation were not expected.[2] We

---

[2]This instance of opposed effects was, incidentally, not picked up by our analysis in Chapter 5 because it is so inconsistent. A clear opposition of respondents' education and occupation, for example, appears only in Indianapolis.

Table 7.4 Rank Effects on the Frequency of Visiting Friends

Rank variables	Regression coefficients: Unstandardized and standardized (in parentheses)					
	Indianapolis	Columbus	Linton	Phoenix	Yuma	Safford
Rating	-.064 (.05)	.090 (.06)		.208 (.12)*		
Family income		.017 (.05)				
Occupation	-.004 (.06)	.006 (.10)	-.006 (.09)		-.005 (.07)	
Education	.141 (.30)*			.037 (.08)		
Wife's education		.106 (.17)*			.082 (.13)*	.084 (.17)*
Father's occupation		-.004 (.06)		-.006 (.08)*	-.005 (.07)	-.009 (.10)
Father's education			.055 (.09)		.053 (.12)*	
Majority	-.343 (.07)				.487 (.12)*	
R^2	.10*	.07*	.01	.03*	.05*	.03
N	320	367	295	656	371	301

can speculate that education provides a person with confidence and trust, skill in making friends, and the motivation to do so. If the wife is typically given the role of initiating and maintaining friendships (especially in the smaller cities?), then *her* education would be more important than her husband's in affecting rates of visiting.

The negative effect of father's occupation initially suggests a mobility effect—with respondent's occupation held constant, the higher the father's occupation the more downwardly mobile (or less upwardly mobile) the respondent. The negative effect of father's job thus might mean that downwardly mobile men are less likely to visit friends and upwardly mobile friends more likely. This would be a more convincing explanation if the coefficients for respondent's occupation were generally positive, or at least zero. Instead, they are generally negative also. This suggests that net of education, income, etc., high status occupations per se reduce the tendency to visit friends. In the conclusion to this chapter, we will offer a possible interpretation for this effect in terms of strain between informal participation and the demands of high rank. The direct negative effect of father's occupation suggests either the mobility effect outlined above or that fathers holding prestigious jobs themselves visited less and thus presented less gregarious role models for their sons to follow when they established their own families (Hodge and Treiman 1968b).

Thus rank would seem to be of greater relevance in visiting friends than in visiting relatives, but the effect on visiting friends is still (a) small, (b) comprised partly of opposing rank effects, and (c) variable from city to city.

Preferences for Visiting Relatives Rather than Friends

Although actual visiting patterns were only weakly related to social rank and the relationships varied markedly with the community context, we find that rank has moderately clear and consistent effects on *values* about visiting: As rank increases, men are less and less likely to prefer visiting relatives as opposed to friends. Higher ranking family heads would *prefer* to spend an evening with friends rather than relatives, but they are constrained by their life circumstances. The relationship between *preferring* to visit relatives rather than friends and *actually* visiting relatives is weak (the r^2's vary from .05 to .00 in the six cities). Hence, rank can affect preferences for visiting and yet be only weakly related to actual visiting.

If a cultural or normative mechanism is proposed for rank differences in visiting patterns, then values regarding visiting patterns ought to vary with rank at least as strongly as the actual rates of visiting do. But rank effect on preferences could also arise simply from attempts to avoid deprivation. Low rank may be punishing in the kind of quasipublic informal interaction represented by visiting with friends. Visiting friends means entering an arena in which low status is open for inspection and comment. Visiting within a family, on the other hand, may not present these threats. Family ties may provide protections and sources of support that are absent in visiting friends. Within the family community rank is less relevant than the status ascribed by family membership.

To study these values, we asked, "On the whole, would you rather spend an evening with friends or with relatives?" The question was asked of all respondents, whether or not they had relatives in the community area, and all respondents are included in the following analysis. The responses were given numerical scores.[3]

General rank affected preference for visiting relatives the same way in all six cities: The higher the rank, the less likely the preference for visiting relatives (see Table 7.2). The relationships were moderately strong, but were increased substantially by allowing a multidimensional definition of rank. In general, the variance explained is higher than for the actual rates of visiting relatives or friends.

The major rank variables affecting preference were education and occupation with the education effect especially showing consistency. Family income and mother's education revealed smaller and/or less consistent effects (Table 7.5). Evidently, then, preference for visiting relatives is especially decreased by high achieved rank. The pattern of these effects is reasonably similar in the six cities (in Table 5.2 we saw that the interaction term for this variable was only significant at the .25 level and added about 3% to the explained variance).

As in previous analyses, controls for age, number of siblings, stage in the family life cycle, and migration were added to help us to see if any of the effects were partially or wholly spurious. For example, men with many brothers and sisters are disposed to visit relatives rather than friends. Since number of siblings is also related to origin rank (mother's education, in this case) and other rank variables, it, like the other control variables, might be producing spurious effects in Table 7.5. Controlling the multivariate relationship between rank and preference for visiting relatives modifies the general relationships described above in only one respect. Controlling for "life situation" characteristics of the family head seems to reduce the education effect only minutely and to increase the occupation effect minutely, while income effects are not changed at all. However, the effect of mother's education is considerably reduced in all cities but Yuma.

---

[3]Men answering "friends" were scored "0" and those answering "relatives" were scored "2." If a man indicated that he preferred the two equally he was scored "1." In the three regressions reported in Table 7.2, men in this third group were omitted, but they were included in the regressions reported in Table 7.5. Omitting this third group decreases the size of the sample by as much as one-third, but sharpens the contrast within the cases included. The result is to increase the proportion of the variance explained, but to reduce the likelihood of attaining statistical significance.

Table 7.5 *Rank Effects on the Preference for Visiting Relatives Rather than Friends*

	Regression coefficients: Unstandardized and standardized (in parentheses)					
Rank variables	Indianapolis	Columbus	Linton	Phoenix	Yuma	Safford
Self-placement	.037 (.06)		.042 (.07)			-.044 (.07)
Family income	-.017 (.10)		-.019 (.14)*		-.008 (.05)	
Occupation	-.006 (.17)*	-.004 (.14)*	-.001 (.05)	-.003 (.09)*		
Education	-.018 (.08)	-.033 (.15)*	-.048 (.19)*	-.030 (.13)*	-.027 (.12)*	-.033 (.16)*
Wife's education		-.019 (.06)				-.022 (.08)
Mother's education	-.018 (.06)			-.016 (.06)	-.030 (.12)*	-.017 (.07)
Majority	.203 (.07)			-.171 (.07)		-.146 (.07)
R^2	.07*	.08*	.10*	.07*	.06*	.09*
N	310	372	292	654	373	296

Some variations across cities should be noted. Local community details include an unusually low education effect in Indianapolis, where occupation plays an unusually important part, an unusually high income effect in Linton, and the unusually strong effect of mother's education in Yuma. Apart from these qualifications, the general model is relatively invariant in different communities, even after adjustment for the set of control variables.

Values regarding whom to visit, then, were more strongly and consistently affected by social rank than were actual frequencies of visiting. The communities were quite similar in rank effects on individual preferences regarding informal participation. Actual visiting behavior, on the other hand, appears to have been influenced by concrete life circumstances (including recency of migration, age, size of family of orientation, phase of family life cycle, etc.) than attitudes about visiting. Many of these circumstances clearly depend on the local community context, including such things as climate, homogeneity of neighborhoods, time and distance to be travelled, and social composition of the community. In consequence, the way in which values, which are in part effects of social rank, get translated into actual behavior varies from one community to another. In this analysis, then, the theoretical significance of the community context appears to be not so much a matter of contrasting status systems, but rather a matter of how the implications of social rank come to be applied under local conditions.

Visiting Neighbors and Work Associates

Rank variables had negligible effects on rates of visiting neighbors and work associates in most of the five cities in which these rates were measured (these questions were not asked in Indianapolis). Rank affected visiting neighbors in only one city and visiting work associates in two.

In general, frequency of visiting with neighbors did *not* vary with rank. The proportion of variance explained by several rank variables was only 3–4% in four of the five cities. In Safford, seven rank variables explained about 8% of the variance, the major effects being that current achieved ranks decreased visiting, while self-placement and wife's education increased it. Since these effects only appeared in one city, we think the best general conclusion is that visiting with neighbors is not structured by rank.

In three of the five cities for which data were available, rank also has little effect upon visiting work associates. The regressions in Linton, Phoenix and Yuma were not significant and explained 2–4% of the variance, and even this explanation was partly due to the effects of control variables. In Columbus and Safford, however, substantial rank effects emerged. Regressions of visiting work associates on eight rank variables explained 14% of the variance in Columbus and 7% in Safford and most of this explanation is over and above that provided by possible control variables. In both cities, men of highly ranked occupations visit work associates markedly more than other men. The other consistent effect is a moderate positive effect of class self-placement. Introducing controls does not change this conclusion. Therefore, men high on these two rank dimensions do tend to visit work associates more often, but these effects only appear in two of five cities.

DIFFERENTIAL ASSOCIATION: A BASIS FOR CLASS CULTURES?

Class subcultures based on informal relationships (rather than on socialization by the mass media or such institutions as school or church) imply differential association (homophily), that is, imply that men of similar rank are more likely to associate with one another than are men of dissimilar rank. If families befriend, visit, and marry into families of similar rank and remain socially distant from families higher or lower in the social scale, they may potentially develop a distinctive style of life.

In Detroit, Laumann (1973) did not find the tightly knit informal social networks that could convert numbers of people at the same level of rank into status groups with private subcultures. Though his respondents showed some tendency to choose friends from the socioeconomic level of their own occupations, that tendency was slight enough that the resulting social networks were "relatively heterogenously composed" by occupational rank. Laumann concluded that "Considerations such as these . . . go far toward explaining the absence of rigidly differentiated social structures in the United States with correspondingly highly differentiated class and/or status subcultures (Laumann 1973:82)."

Still, this heterogeneity of social networks might be precisely the difference between Detroit and Boston, say, or Newburyport. The problem of this chapter segment is to describe the extent to which communities differ in terms of differential association by occupational rank. Are Americans generally subject to local structures of informal relationships as loose as that described for Detroit? Is the reverse true, with Detroit notable as an exception? Is every community a law unto itself?

This problem is immediately complicated by the possibility that homophily may be greater at some levels of rank than at others. For example, Curtis (1963) and Laumann (1966:85) reported data from Detroit and Cambridge–Belmont respectively, indicating less homophily in the middle of the occupational structure than either in the top or the bottom, with the very highest rates near the very top. Curtis speculated that a *middle mass* existed in Detroit, within which families associated according to their incomes and consumption styles, but not according to the occupational ranks of their friends. Laumann suggested that instead of locating friends out in the community, persons in the center of the occupational hierarchy associated with their relatives, who were occupationally heterogenous.

Thus the informal structures may differ among communities not only in the extent to which rank is relevant to the choice of friends, but also in the relationship between rates of homophily and occupational rank itself.

The data reported below are entirely descriptive. If the question under study had dealt with the causal process relating rank to a propensity to choose friends from the same rank, then some of the social conditions we report would have been statistical artifacts. For example, a wider choice of friends in the middle than in either the top or the bottom of the occupational structure might simply be a "ceiling or floor" effect: Top men and bottom men can only choose in one direction, while middle men can choose in both directions. Similarly, skilled workers might be expected to choose themselves more frequently than professionals choose themselves simply because there are so many more skilled workers to be chosen. For present purposes, however, it does not matter whether a friend was chosen because he was available, because he held the right status, or by coincidence: We are concerned with the resulting social networks.

Our measure of homophily is the extent to which men choose friends who resemble them in the rank of their occupations. Our survey questions on this topic were: "Now I'd like you to think about a man who is one of your best friends. . . . What kind of work does he do for a living?" "Now I'd like you to think about another man who is a good friend of yours. . . . What kind of work does he do for a living?"[4]

After scoring the respondent's occupation and those of his two friends on the Duncan socioeconomic index of occupations, we formed several indicators of heterophily, the reverse of homophily (see Table 7.6). The first was calculated by finding the absolute differences between the respondent's occupation (scored on the Duncan index) and those of his two friends and taking the mean of the two differences. This gives his average distance from his friends in "prestige units." This measure, of course, might vary from city to city simply because of variations in the shapes of the community occupational distributions. It is conceivable, moreover, that friendship is based on relative standing rather than on the distance metric implied in the Duncan index. To obtain a standardized or relative measure, we converted each man's and each friend's Duncan index score to a percentile score, indicating their standing in the cumulative distribution of resondent's Duncan index scores in their own community.[5] We then constructed a second measure, a

---

[4]These were the questions used in the five city survey. In Indianapolis the questions were somewhat different: "Outside of relatives, think of the one person you talk with and visit with the most. . . . if R's friend is male: What does he do for a living? If R's friend is female: What does the head of her family do for a living? . . . "Besides relatives, is there any specific person or family you feel you could turn to in time of need?" . . . "Now we'd like for you to think about another person who is a good friend of yours, outside of the person (two people) you just mentioned. What does he (the head of the family) do for a living?" The occupations of *visit with most* and *another good friend* were scored and used to measure differential association.

Table 7.6 *Occupational Heterophily in Six Communities*

Measure of heterophily	Indianapolis	Columbus	Linton	Phoenix	Yuma	Safford
Mean absolute difference between R's job and the jobs of his two friends, measured by						
Duncan index scores	16.6	17.8	20.6	18.2	18.0	18.1
Percentile scores[a]	18.8	20.3	23.4	21.7	22.2	21.1
Proportion of variance *not* explained by R's occupation[b] in						
First friend's job	.74	.69	.81	.80	.81	.74
Second friend's job	.56	.80	.93	.85	.84	.83

[a]To obtain these scores, we converted the distribution of respondent's occupation in Duncan index scores to a percentile distribution separately within each city. Each respondent's and friend's Duncan score was then converted into a percentile score, using the percentile distribution for the appropriate community. Mean absolute differences were then calculated from these percentile scores.

[b]This is simply 1 minus the square of the correlation coefficient between the respondent's job and the friend's job.

mean of the absolute *percentile* differences of a man from his two friends. This measure indicates average distance between a man and his friends in percentile terms based on the occupational distribution of his particular community. A third type of measure was calculated from the correlation coefficients between a man's occupational Duncan index and that of each of his two friends. From these we get the proportion of variance in a friend's occupation *not* explained by respondent's occupation ($1 - r^2$), showing the extent to which a friend's job is independent of respondent's occupation. For all three measures, a high value indicates low homophily.

Moderately low levels of homophily are indicated by the data in Table 7.6. The average occupational distance between a man and his friends is about 18 points on the Duncan scale, or 20 percentile points. Men do not appear to restrict their friendships to men close to them in occupation. The correlational measures reinforce this picture—usually upwards of 75% of the variance in friend's occupation is unexplained by the respondent's occupation. Men appear to show some propensity to choice of friends by rank, that is, but that propensity does not result in homogeneous social networks.

[5]We prefer to standardize by the distribution of respondents' occupations rather than the reported occupations of their friends because the former distribution is our best estimate of the occupational distribution of all males in the community. Distortion can be introduced by standardizing by the distribution of *choices*.

The differences between cities are not great, although roughly the same pattern appears for all the measures—homophily is about the same in the three Arizona cities, but increases with city size in Indiana. Results are similar for measures based on the percentile scores, suggesting that the city-size effect in Indiana is not due to differences in the shapes of the occupational distributions in Indianapolis, Columbus and Linton. Even with such differences controlled, homophily plausibly should be higher in large cities because the sheer number of men of similar occupational standing available for friendship should be greater there. But no such effect appears in Arizona, so our data in general offer little support for this as a general proposition.

Still, similarities or differences among community structures of informal relations might lie within specific occupational strata, as suggested earlier. To search for such a pattern, we divided the respondents from each community into five occupational categories ranging from low to high. For the men in each category we calculated an aggregate measure of homophily. We did this by calculating the distance (absolute values of differences in percentile scores) between a man and each of his two friends and taking the mean of these two distances. This yielded, for each man, his distance from his "average friend." Our measure of aggregate homophily for each occupational category is the percentage of men in that category within 20 percentile units of their average friend. The percentages within each city (Table 7.7), show fluctuations, but no consistent pattern.

Where earlier we found that friend's occupation was not strongly related to respondent's occupation, we now find that homophily is only weakly related to occupation in those cities where the relationship exists at all. In Table 7.7, the six communities show six different patterns, including no relationship (Phoenix), greater homophily towards the top (Indianapolis),[6] at the bottom (Safford), and in two different middle groups (Columbus and Linton).

In summary, we find that communities do vary a little in the extent to

---

[6]One might interpret the positive relationship in Indianapolis (Table 7.7), as well as the higher total percentage of homophily in that city, in the light of the different question asked about *first friend* (see Footnote 4, above). It would seem reasonable that greater homophily, and a more consistent relationship of homophily to occupational rank, would appear with the more realistic *person you talk to and visit with most* than with the vaguer *one of your best friends*. The former might be a better indicator of the actual structure of interpersonal contacts, that is, while the latter allowed more room for fantasy. However, the question about *second friend* in Indianapolis was quite similar to the question about both friends in the other five cities (though the interview context was different), and it is specifically the *second* friend that is responsible for the relatively high rates of homophily in Indianapolis (compare unexplained variance for first and second friend in Table 7.6). The more realistic question is in fact responsible for greater heterophily, rather than the reverse. If anything follows from this difference between questions, it is that answers closer to the actual structure of informal contacts show even less differential association, and that predispositions to choose same-status friends are indulged by the vaguer questions.

Table 7.7 Homophily by Occupation and City

	Indianapolis		Columbus		Linton		Phoenix		Yuma		Safford	
	\%	N	\%	N	\%	N	\%	N	\%	N	\%	N
Occupation[a]												
0 – 15	39.3	(28)	44.0	(25)	43.5	(46)	48.2	(56)	43.4	(53)	61.2	(67)
16 – 32	55.6	(63)	57.6	(59)	65.1	(43)	53.7	(95)	53.5	(71)	61.9	(42)
33 – 48	54.5	(33)	65.0	(40)	45.9	(37)	48.8	(127)	53.7	(80)	50.0	(42)
49 – 65	68.4	(57)	75.6	(41)	40.4	(47)	54.8	(115)	57.4	(54)	43.1	(51)
66 – 98	74.3	(70)	44.9	(78)	38.9	(36)	54.0	(161)	58.3	(60)	50.0	(36)
Total	61.8	(251)	56.4	(243)	46.9	(209)	52.3	(554)	53.5	(318)	53.8	(238)

Percentage within 20 percentiles of average friend

[a]Duncan SES scores classified so as to prevent small cells.

which rank is translated into an informal structure, and substantially in the pattern the structure takes, but that the heterogeneity of social networks is so great as to render the variability irrelevant. Fundamentally, this set of communities does not include any in which friendships are significantly restricted to a band of occupational rank.

SUMMARY AND CONCLUSIONS

The analyses in this chapter yield the following major empirical conclusions:

1. Rates of informal participation—visiting—are moderately high in all of our communities. A little over half our respondents visit with relatives once a week or more (if they have relatives in the area); about 35% visit with friends this often. Relatives were visited most often, followed by friends, then neighbors, then work associates. This order held in all six cities.

2. Men of highly ranked occupations are less likely to have relatives in the same community area; high origin also has this effect, but less consistently across cities. These rank effects on the presence of relatives in the community area are not strong.

3. Rank variables have little or no general effect on the frequency of visiting relatives though there is variability from city to city. The data contain a suggestion that in most cities increased family income may reduce visiting with relatives.

4. Rates of visiting with friends are increased somewhat by higher class self-placement and higher education (of self or wife), but decreased by respondent's occupation or father's occupation. These effects are not strong and vary somewhat across cities.

5. Rank effects on visiting preferences (for relatives versus friends) were stronger and more consistent from city to city than effects on actual visiting rates. Men of high achieved rank, especially education and occupation, prefer to visit friends rather than relatives.

6. Rank variables did not affect rates of visiting neighbors, but occupational rank increased visiting with work associates in two of five cities.

7. Differential association or homophily—the tendency to choose friends similar in occupational rank—is moderately low in our cities. The cities do not differ very much in overall rates of differential association, and exhibited no consistent stratum-specific pattern of homophily.

One general conclusion from these findings is that the effects of social rank on informal participation, especially actual rates of participation, are weak and somewhat unstable across samples. By contrast, sociological theory has generally held social status to be of central importance in affecting social participation and thereby community social structures, and a number of past empirical studies have reported rates of informal participation that differ by social class. We believe these past findings exaggerate the size of the relationships, for several reasons.

First, the effect on social structure (the sociological concern) does not require a close association between rank and participation at the individual level. One easily draws conclusions regarding the former without qualifying them with conclusions regarding the latter. Second, most previous studies have sought only to demonstrate the *existence* of some connection between rank and participation, not the strength of the relationship, and certainly not the extent to which status was more closely related to participation than some alternate set of predictors. Where attempts to do so have been made, the results have been bland. Hodge and Treiman (1968b) report, for example, that three rank variables explain about 6% of the variance in visiting friends (however, their dependent variable—the number of *different* friends recently visited—was somewhat different from ours). A third reason for the common belief in a strong relationship between individual rank and social participation was the widespread practice of reporting data in the form of percentage tables. Such tables allow the reader unwittingly to take advantage of nonlinearity and even departures from monotonicity, even when his theory affords him no basis at all for doing so. More importantly, the strengths of percentage associations were generally not calculated and reported using a proportional reduction of error measure even roughly comparable to explained variance.

Rank effects on informal participation were not only weak, but often varied among our communities, or only appeared in some community contexts (e.g., the occupation effect on visiting work associates). Partly this means that local conditions affect visiting patterns more than they do the process of rank attainment. Partly, it may be interpreted to mean that the social significance of rank for sociable behavior may depend on local definitions and practices. Clearly there is no powerful general social consequence of rank (e.g., that lower class men are isolated), but to some minor extent, sociability may be patterned by rank in some particular community. From this point we can only go on to speculate that the weak and variable relationships are consistent with the notion of opposing forces associated with rank: Some predisposing towards more visiting with higher rank, and others predisposing towards less.

The aspects of high rank increasing participation can be gathered under the heading of resources. Developing and keeping informal, voluntary ties with other people requires energy, time, some money perhaps, and a level of security and a history of past security that allows one to trust others. We can argue that high standing on various rank dimensions yields more of these resources than low rank. In Chapter 10, we will partly support this proposition by showing lower rates of anomia (higher rates of trust) among men of higher achieved rank, especially of higher education. For these reasons, with all else held constant, participation should vary positively with rank.

On the other hand, high achieved rank may also complicate intense personal contacts. In certain ways, the nature of a primary relationship is contradicted by the kind of stance a family head must take in public in order to attain or preserve high achieved rank and the public image that accompanies such rank. Ideally, primary relationships are permanent rather than temporary, are local (socially, if not geographically) rather than cosmopolitan in orientation, require investment of the total person rather than a segment of his social personality, are maintained on the basis of *who* the person is rather than on the basis of what he has accomplished, devalue personal achievement in relation to collective good, require treatment of others as valuable entities rather than as means to ends, and insist that the other be treated as a special individual rather than as a member of a category. Under industrial–urban conditions, however, success often requires temporary relationships, cosmopolitan orientations in space and time, segmental interaction, achievement criteria, individualism, manipulation of others, and the universalistic application of norms.

The problem of resolving these contradictory implications for behavior is none the less real for being soluble. One solution is rigid segregation of the private sphere from the public sphere, so that one may be thought of as a different kind of person within each sphere. A more feasible, adequate and common solution is to modify the extent and the quality of one's informal participation so that it does not hinder, or perhaps even enhances, the chances for high rank.

The solution in interpersonal relations that the family head who has (or aspires to) high rank is constrained to seek is one that yields the power of communicative centrality, yet does not compromise his autonomy. He must be able to move, to relate to culturally different individuals, to devote his interest to problems area-wide, regional, national or even international in scope, to manipulate others without being manipulated and to retain a respectable public face, and to "get along well with others" at the same time. The solution, of course depends on very personal skills and capacities, but tends to involve relatively heavy participation in formal associations (to be treated in the next chapter), a cosmopolitan style of participation and a *personal network that lacks the power to control his behavior.*

What determines the extent to which an individual's informal social network can control his behavior is the strength of the emotional ties, the frequency of contact, and the tightness of the network. A tight network is defined as one in which each member tends to interact with each other member as opposed to a loose network, in which members are related to one another through intermediate participants. Loose networks expose the individual to less unanimity in the pressures brought to bear on him (Blum 1964) and thus leave him more autonomy. Autonomy also increases when contact is infrequent and/or emotionally attenuated.

This concern for autonomy can be seen in status differences in the conception of social debt. Muir and Weinstein (1962) found that lower class respondents were more apt to express a kind of familial mutual-aid orientation to a variety of social debts, while the orientation of higher status respondents was more apt to resemble a financial transaction. In consequence, the lower status person is always under obligation, while the person of higher status may feel it legitimate to refuse to accept an obligation by having "paid off his debts" in advance.

In *Street Corner Society* (1955), William F. Whyte described the interpersonal problems required by upward mobility out of an ethnic neighborhood. Bettering oneself in education, occupation and income entails a kind of egocentrism that runs counter to the norms of extremely close networks. What this means to the individual is not that he no longer sees his former friends, or that they no longer care for him, but that he cannot accept the *control* exercised in such intimate groups. Members of Doc's gang were controlled by the norm of reciprocity, while members of Chick's gang avoided such control either by staying out of "debt" or by denying the legitimacy of its control over their behavior. It could be countered that Chick's gang were controlled by the occupation-income reward system, but that is simply to locate their allegiance in the larger system of social status.

Persons of high rank, then, are pressed to form a pattern of informal contact involving a wider number of more disparate individuals (many of whom are not connected to each other), attenuated emotional ties, and less interdependence. Since less frequent contact both promotes these characteristics and in and of itself reduces the strain between high rank and primary ties, we can expect, all other things held equal, *lower* rates of visiting with higher rank.

Essentially the above argument is that informal participation costs those of high rank less in terms of the resources required, but more in terms of threats to and contradictions with the requirements of their high rank. Our findings are at least roughly consistent with such a view. Preferences for visiting should not be affected by resources, since the resources required to visit friends and relatives in the area should be about the same. But contacts with relatives pose more threats to autonomy and so are less preferred by high-status men. Actually visiting relatives requires relatively fewer resources for high status men but imposes more costs, producing a weak and unstable effect of rank on this form of participation. For the same reason, visiting friends is also weakly related to rank. The above line of argument also throws some light on the opposing effects of education and occupation on visiting friends. Education, representing resources more than the demands of an organizational or a community position, promotes such visiting, while occupation, representing more clearly the pressures of current position, hinders it.

Our results suggest that informal participation cannot be a major variable mediating the effects of rank upon other forms of behavior. As was true of satisfaction in the analysis in Chapter 6, rates of visiting are not strongly enough related to the rank variables to explain the effects of rank on other attitudes and actions. If men of high rank vote differently or are more or less prejudiced than men of low rank, it is not because they are more or less interpersonally isolated or because they visit or befriend markedly different kinds of persons.

Finally, we should briefly set out the implications of our findings for class or stratum formation. The amount of homophily indicated by our data would seem to be less than is required to support a cultural embodiment of rank differentiation in terms of clearly different and bounded strata. In this way, the results in this chapter support those of our analysis of class consciousness.

We do not even find any particular evidence that denser networks of friendship are causing culturally distinctive groups to emerge at the top or the bottom of the stratification system. Yet, as we remarked earlier, (and as developed by Granovetter 1973) this loose network allows more widespread influence to be exerted by opinion leaders. Centrality in such a network could result in greater community power than in a set of status-defined cliques, with cultural recognition of the statuses. We shall see in the next chapter that participation in formal associations does vary with rank, and therefore might promote centrality for men of higher rank.

8

FORMAL SOCIAL PARTICIPATION

In the last chapter, one primary concern was how informal social participation forms a network of communication in a community assuming that a central position within that network confers influence. This chapter continues that concern, but focuses instead on the role of *formal* social participation.

We are interested in how social rank affects formal participation because we assume that formal participation is another means by which men can exercise influence in the community. Perhaps the context for this chapter can be given most clearly by a graph of the particular causal relationships which interest us:

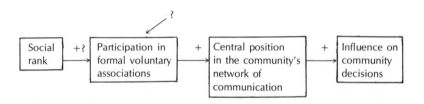

Our analysis will deal only with the effects marked with questions, namely, the nature of rank effects and the extent to which participation is independent of rank. The last two effects, about which we can only speculate, provide a motive for the analysis: If participation does indeed increase centrality and centrality increases influence, then how social rank affects participation becomes an important question from the perspective of community organization. Thus our study of the effect of the individual's social rank on his formal participation is intended to shed light on the extent to which, and the processes by which, positions of communicative centrality and influence tend to be taken by persons of high rank.

ASSOCIATIONS, THE COMMUNICATION
NETWORK, AND COMMUNITY INFLUENCE

The broadest set of communicative acts which can be observed in the modern community are those of the mass media. Mass communication provides a unique basis for community organization because individuals of different rank use the mass media differently (Hollingshead and Redlich 1958:398 ff.). Although not included in this study, this is another significant way in which rank affects an individual's participation in community social life.

Formal associations have several features which make their role in the community communication network different from that of the mass media. First, formal participation affords the opportunity not only of sending messages, but of receiving them as well. It provides a communication structure which links the grass roots to positions of real power in the community and therefore not only gets information and "orders" from the top of the structure to the bottom, but also sends reactions back to the top. Second, the mass media usually subject a large number of persons to the same stimulus without taking into account differences between the various community segments in the audience. A candidate for office, on the other hand, can insert three different messages into the communication network that will eventually reach large numbers of voters by speaking to three different clubs or church groups the same evening. He would be unwise to contradict himself clearly, but he can vary his emphasis greatly according to his audience. Third, formal participation, in contrast with the mass media, allows private dialogues: Until the newspapers catch wind of it, for example, public school officials may exchange views with representatives of a minority community without having right-wing neighborhood members reacting to each move and counter-move.

Overlapping memberships in formal organizations form a vital part of the community's communication network over and above the ties formed by informal contacts. These memberships *allow* people to communicate either through a formal apparatus such as a club newsletter or in face-to-face interaction at a meeting or some other function of an association. Like informal ties, associations are important to community organization as a *potential* means for mobilizing individuals who are otherwise unconnected in their usual day-to-day activities. The P.T.A., for example, is unlikely to do anything of great significance on any given occasion, but if an issue for which there is no standard or official route of communication suddenly receives widespread and deep concern, then the P.T.A. *can* become the organizational vehicle for its public airing. Thus some local P.T.A. meetings could have been no more than dull lectures to a handful of dedicated parents, with cookies afterward, for 30 years, but when the city announces busing for racial balance, the organizational apparatus of that same P.T.A.

can be used as a forum for public discussion or as a tool to convert an otherwise disorganized neighborhood into a disciplined and solidary association for political combat.

In this view, the significance of associations often stems not from the efficiency of their own organizations, but specifically from the lack of any alternative. It is the absence of community organization with respect to some purpose that makes any association *potentially* useful to a population attempting to organize for collective action. Publics arise whenever some new issue of collective concern divides a population into those in favor and those opposed. Decision-making requires those in favor to be able to communicate among one another and to debate publicly with those opposed, but since the issue is new there may well be no structure of communications which parallels the new division. Whatever structure of communications grows up for the purpose of communicating selectively about the issue will probably be based on what *does* exist, which, in great part, is the network of overlapping memberships in associations.

In summary, it is the communicative network among the members of many associations of different types, no matter what the purpose of the associations, that is of greatest use in mobilizing a public in the absence of institutionalized channels of communication (Greer and Orleans 1962). Organizations with overlapping memberships constitute a structure through which information flows in informal as well as formal interaction (Young and Larson 1965). The information may or may not be relevant to the charter or formal purpose of the organizations. Participation in formal associations serves to attach the individual to a network of communication with many indirect links. Such a network is very loosely knit, but extremely extensive (Babchuck and Booth 1969). Thus, members of the Woodsmen of the World are part of a chain of communication linking their nonmember friends, neighbors and work associates to the nonmember friends of Cub Scout den fathers. Apart from the mass media and the direct actions of city government, the communicative structure of a community may consist of little more than this network.

We assume that a central position in this network is ipso facto a position of potential power in community affairs. The communication network based on formal participation (with effects spread more widely through subsequent informal contacts) is what operates in community decision-making, so people at central locations in the network can both gather more information useful in guiding their actions and also to some extent modify and shape information sent to others. Communication about political and parapolitical issues is especially vital because these issues are explicitly questions of collective action.

We assume, then, that membership and participation in formal associations tend to involve one in the flow of information and persuasion in a community and hence confer a certain measure of community influence.

Participation, particularly office-holding, in formal associations may also allow more direct control of certain decisions. First, a formal association, representing some mobilized segment of the community, may put pressure upon governmental and private officials to make decisions favorable to its membership. In addition, certain community decisions may actually be given over to such an association. We have in mind such matters as the allocation of charity proceeds or the provision of fire protection, which in some communities are not left to the vagaries of individual decisions or to the market's "invisible hand," but have not been vested in an official governmental body either. Hence, in swaying the decisions of others and in allocating certain community resources, associations directly own a portion of community power, which is exercised by the membership generally, but especially by the officers.

TYPES OF FORMAL PARTICIPATION

The types of membership and activity analyzed below are in churches, in formal voluntary associations other than churches, and in political campaigns. All such activity has content, and is organized in relation to relatively specific purposes, but the topic of this investigation is simply the extent to which individual community residents are "reachable" through the network of communication based on formal participation. We are concerned with the relationship between rank and church attendance, for example, and not with that between rank and religious belief. By the same token, rates of participation in the political arena—such as voting, regardless of whom the vote was cast for—are presented in this chapter, and political ideology is taken up in Chapter 9.

Membership in an association must be distinguished from activity or involvement in that association, because the two may be quite different forms of participation in the communication network, just as they may have different importance to the association itself. Mere membership may imply very little about involvement and may be of little importance to the association, but it is potentially of great importance from the perspective of reachability through the communication network. Having broad contacts through a variety of associations (e.g., a tennis club, P.T.A., Neighborhood Improvement Association, V.F.W. and church) may be of greater significance to communication than the amount of effort expended in any one area (e.g., how often a person plays tennis). Amounts of activity are also limited by the fact that no one has more than 24 hours per day, while the upper limit of the number of mailing lists one may be on is hard to specify. Finally, simply belonging to a tennis club indicates formal organizational skills and interests as much as it does interest in tennis, but frequency of playing tennis much more strongly indicates specific interest in tennis. That interest, too, may be related to social rank, but if it is, the reason is different from the reason for the relationship between rank and having many social contacts.

Formal Voluntary Associations

The prime indicator of the extensiveness with which an individual is exposed to the communication network based on overlapping memberships is the number of memberships he reports. We asked, "Now I'd like to ask you about organizations and clubs. What associations or organizations do you belong to?" If the respondent said, "None," the interviewer continued, "Well, how about fraternal organizations, or business or civic groups, or a union, or charitable organizations: Do you belong to any groups like that?" Church membership was considered later in the interview, and was not supposed to be included here, although about 1% of the respondents did mention a church in response to this question. Because this question measures total associational activity, we thought it appropriate to include unions in the count, even though plausibly union membership is negatively related to rank variables while other memberships may be positively related. Because of the limited interview time devoted to the question, we suspect that participation is underestimated for those reporting more than three, four, or five memberships, but that the relative ordering of respondents is basically correct.

About two-thirds of the respondents reported membership in at least one organization and hence are connected to the structure of associations in their community.[1] Well over a third of the men in each city have two or more memberships and thus represent overlapping links between associations. The frequency distribution of number of memberships, presented in Table 8.1, drops off rapidly from the mode (no or one memberships), reaffirming the position that many persons belong to very few assocations while a very few persons belong to many associations.

Some small differences appear between the cities (a mode of no memberships versus a mode of one; a higher mean number of memberships in Indianapolis), but the general picture is one of rough similarity. Certainly the data offer little support for the thesis that voluntary associations are a special feature of life in large cities (Wirth 1938; Wright and Hyman 1958; Schnore 1967:173ff.). The differences which do appear between the cities are not arranged by either city size or region.

Beyond this simple amount of belonging, we also investigated frequency of participation, friendships within the context of associations, and office-

---

[1]For comparison with results of other studies, it should be remembered that the respondents were male household heads; that churches are not included, but unions are; and that the variable is the sum of all memberships, not the number of different types of memberships. For a summary of other studies and a discussion of comparisons, see Smith (1975).

holding. Because of limitations on interview time, however, we asked these questions about only one association. If a man named only one membership, we used that as the context for succeeding questions. For men with two or more memberships we asked "Which of the organizations you belong to would you say is the *most* important to you?" and used that organization as the context for these further questions (if the respondent didn't answer this, the organization he named first was used). The base N for these questions, of course, is the number of men who reported at least one membership.

Attendance at meetings, it must be admitted, is a rather minimal sort of activity, but it renders activities of very different kinds, from stamp collecting to partisan politics, comparable. Each type of activity is expressed as the number of times the individual encounters it in the formal setting of meetings.[2]

Membership in formal voluntary associations very generally results in personal friendships with other members. Concerning the respondent's *most important organization,* we asked, "Have you become friends with other members, as a result of joining?" Approximately 85% of the men who reported at least one membership said they had such a friend. These can be enduring contacts. Of those reporting such a friend, less than 5% said that they never got together with this friend, outside of meetings. The modal frequency of seeing association friends, however, was "a few times a year," indicating that belonging to an association implies infrequent participation in a loose but possibly lasting network of friends encountered in formal settings.

Holding office in a voluntary association is a rather specialized form of participation, but one that is of particular importance in forming loose social networks, by making the office-holder visible to other members of the association and by requiring him to participate in the formal communication apparatus of the association and to coordinate with members and other officers. Also, office-holding implies greater influence, perhaps in determining the role of the association in the community, but at least in giving one a place in the chain of communication from which true community leaders

---

[2]Frequency of attendance was measured by asking: "How often do you attend meetings of (most important organization)?" The responses and the scores given them were:

Several times a week (0)
About once a month (1)
A few times a month (2)
Once every month or two (3)
A few times a year (4)
Once a year or less (5)
Never (volunteered) (6)

Since high scores mean low attendance, this variable was referred to as "infrequency of attending most important association" in Chapter 5. In this chapter, however, we will reflect the scores, so a positive regression coefficient will mean that high rank produces higher attendance.

derive their power. However, many of these positions are not highly sought after and have the reputation of making busy people even busier. This is less a measure of community leadership on a grand scale than an indication of numerous social contacts. Our question was: "Have you ever held any office or position in (most important organization)?"

Office-holding of this kind is relatively common (see Table 8.1). From three-fifths to a half of the association members had held office, meaning that about a quarter of all the male household heads in each community had been an officer. In this case, the results are neatly ordered by region and city size: For each pair of cities of similar size, office-holding (among members) is more likely in Arizona. Within each region, office-holding is negatively related to city size. The simplest explanation is that associations tend to be smaller in total size in smaller communities, but probably have about the same number of official positions to fill. Hence no tendency toward greater democracy within small-town associations is necessary to explain the city-size finding, although such a tendency could be a contributing factor.

Church Membership and Attendance

Apart from economic production, church is the single most prevalent context for formally structured social participation. Two-thirds of our entire sample reported church membership, and less than 10% reported no attendance whatever.[3] Now this may represent fairly minimal involvement, but it does provide the basis for an extremely broad and highly differentiated network of contacts. The existence and social importance of this network is real, whether the person belongs and attends for religious or for social reasons, and whether the denominational doctrine is one of specific disregard for worldly affairs or one of militant social action.

Church attendance is more widespread than church membership (in contrast to most associational attendance), and the link between them depends somewhat on denominational identification. Yet both are forms of participation which in some way render the family head accessible to communication in a formal context, though the type of communication implied by the two is probably different. Nonattending members receive mailings and may participate (to varying degrees) in church government or at least feel some concern for the affairs of the church. Frequent attenders who do not claim membership are subject to the communications directed at them in, or along with, the service, and of course they have the opportunity for regular interaction with others in the congregation.

[3]After a series of questions on religious preference, we asked: "About how often do you attend religious services?" and "Do you belong to a church (synagogue)?" Frequency of church attendance was scored in the same way as frequency of attending the man's most important association (see footnote 2).

Table 8.1 *Memberships and Offices Held in Formal Associations*

	Indianapolis	Columbus	Linton	Phoenix	Yuma	Safford
Memberships						
Distribution (%)						
None	30	40	27	33	26	39
1	25	26	30	30	29	27
2	18	14	19	19	21	13
3	10	8	10	9	11	7
4	6	5	6	4	7	7
5	4	3	6	3	4	6
6 or more	8	4	1	2	1	1
Mean	1.9	1.4	1.6	1.4	1.6	1.4
Percentage of members who have held an office in their most important association	29	37	38	38	45	49

Political Activity

The place of individual participation in community action is shown more clearly in political activity than in any other type of formal participation. What the individual contributes is an extremely small portion of his time and resources, and his individual contribution is a negligible portion of what goes into a community decision. Yet the aggregate consequences of such individually negligible contributions can weigh heavily in collective decisions. The behaviors we have studied—registration, voting in local and national elections, and contributing time and/or money in a campaign—are of just this sort; they do not represent political power until they have been concentrated by aggregation. Yet these are the activities which, when organized behind an issue, candidate or broker of political influence, *constitute* power.

In our sample, political activity formed a natural empirical cumulative scale. We converted political actions[4] into an *index of political activity* by assigning 0 to those who were not locally registered to vote, 1 to those

[4]The questions used in the five-city survey were: "Do you happen to be a registered voter in (community)?" . . . "There are many reasons why people aren't able to vote in every election. Did you get to vote in the last presidential election in 1964 when Johnson ran against Goldwater?" . . . "Did you vote this past November 8th?" . . . "Have you contributed time or money during a political campaign any time from 1960 on?" The questions in the Indianapolis survey were similar, except that the final question about contributions referred only to the last political campaign.

registered, 2 to those who reported voting in the last national election (1964), 3 to those who reported voting in the last local election, and 4 to those who reported contributing time or money "during a political campaign any time from 1960 on." Each man was given the highest score he earned, for example, a man who gave money, but who didn't vote, still received a score of 4. Ninety-five percent of the sample were *scale types* in that they reported *all* levels of activity up to their highest—in general, men who contributed time and/or money to a campaign were registered and had voted in both types of election, those who had voted in local elections had also voted in national elections, and those who had only voted in a national election were registered.

EFFECTS OF RANK ON FORMAL SOCIAL PARTICIPATION

Formal Voluntary Associations

Several forms of achieved rank positively affect the number of memberships a man has accumulated, with the result that a substantial proportion of the variance in memberships is explained by rank. The data are presented in Table 8.2. The dimension having the strongest effect, and the effect most regular across cities, is family income. Self-placement and the respondent's first job also have rather strong, regular effects. Respondent's current occupation and education also generally increase belonging.

Evidently, then, high current achieved ranks (especially family income) and early achieved ranks (especially first job) both increase memberships. These results are consistent with those of past studies (Hodge and Treiman 1968b; Hyman and Wright 1971). The explanation offered in the last chapter for rank effects on informal participation can also be applied to these findings. Men of high rank have more resources to apply to organizational membership. However, unlike informal participation, there is no systematic strain between holding a position of high rank and holding a formal associational membership. Hence, the only effect which emerges is that of higher resources, producing the pattern we see of a number of rank variables all positively related to belonging. In addition, high occupational rank may carry with it expectations for joining associations. The strong effect of first job suggests that some memberships are contracted for this reason early in the career and endure even if the man changes his occupational rank.

However, part of the relationship (net of other variables) between belonging and income may be due to a *reverse* causal order, that is, belonging may increase income. It seems reasonable to assume that union memberships tend to increase income, while memberships in a variety of associations may

Table 8.2 Rank Effects on Number of Associational Memberships

Rank variables	Regression coefficients: Unstandardized and standardized (in parentheses)[a]					
	Indianapolis	Columbus	Linton	Phoenix	Yuma	Safford
Self-placement	.075 (.05)	.282 (.20)*	.204 (.18)*	b	.157 (.14)*	.163 (.13)*
R's neighborhood rating	.333 (.18)*	.084 (.06)	.179 (.15)*			-.130 (.09)*
Family income	.008 (.20)*	.009 (.22)*	.007 (.25)*	.007 (.28)*	.006 (.20)*	.007 (.23)*
Occupation	.010 (.11)	.004 (.06)	.005 (.08)			.008 (.11)*
First occupation	.013 (.13)*		.007 (.10)	.010 (.15)*	.013 (.18)*	.014 (.19)*
Wife's education	-.057 (.06)		.068 (.10)		.060 (.10)*	.052 (.10)
Education	.067 (.11)	.093 (.17)*	.036 (.07)	.049 (.12)*	.036 (.08)	-.020 (.05)
Mother's education	.066 (.08)					-.023 (.05)
Father's occupation						.021 (.22)*
Majority[d]	-.817 (.12)*		7.056 (.10)*			
N	320	372	297	686	372	305
R^2	.27*	.25*	.34*	.23*	.27*	.34*
Proportion of the variance explained by						
General rank index	(+).21*[c]	(+).21*	(+).28*	(+).16*	(+).23*	(+).29*
17 variable regression	.29*	.30*	.36*	.25*	.30*	.39*

[a] In this and following tables in this chapter, asterisked coefficients are those with associated t-values of 1.65 or higher; hence, significant at approximately the .10 level (two-tailed test). Asterisked R^2's and r^2's are significant at the .05 level.

[b] In this and following tables in this chapter, coefficients are not shown when the standardized regression (path) coefficient is both nonsignificant and less than .05, i.e., for relatively weak effects.

[c] In this and following tables in this chapter, the sign in parentheses indicates the direction of the relationship between the general rank index and the dependent variable.

[d] Reflected Bogardus scores in Columbus and Linton.

benefit businessmen, especially those, like insurance agents, whose prosperity depends upon a wide range of contacts.

Origin ranks (mother's education, father's occupation) seem to have few direct effects. A theory advanced by Hodge and Treiman (1968b) holds that a pattern of memberships is to some extent passed on from generation to generation, partly through "inheritance" of membership in specific ethnic, fraternal, or religious organizations. Our data provide little support for this proposition, except in the city of Safford, where father's occupation has a large direct relationship to belonging. Hyman and Wright (1971) also found little relationship between origin and memberships in their national sample, once current rank was controlled.

The effect of majority rank on belonging depends considerably on the type of minority. In Indianapolis, where the minority is black, racial–ethnic rank has an effect, but no effect appears in the Arizona cities, in which the minority group is substantially or entirely Mexican–American.

In Indianapolis, once other rank variables are controlled, blacks belong to *more* associations than whites. Here is another instance of rank effects of opposing signs—although most rank variables are positively related to memberships, the effect of racial–ethnic rank is negative.

The finding that blacks belong to more organizations than whites, with rank adjusted, has been noted in other research.[5] The finding can be explained in different ways. The important point here is that their higher participation does not necessarily mean that blacks are disproportionately represented in the network of overlapping memberships which constitutes the "core" of the associational structure of a community. Rather, they may have constructed a parallel structure of formal organizations, being denied access to the existing majority associations in the community. The result of such a parallel structure has traditionally been that the black community was reachable indirectly through its formal associations. Although the rate of informal interaction between whites and blacks in a community could be very low, the community could remain organized in that community leaders could come into communication with the black population through black brokers who held large numbers of memberships and officerships in key black organizations. It may well be that this pattern is currently changing radically with (a) somewhat increased access of blacks to the associational network of the community as a whole, and (b) the growth of many new black associations which are not dominated by the "old" organizational style, but are more separatist.

Several control variables were introduced into the above analysis to see whether any of the rank effects were spurious. These variables were: age,

---

[5]Babchuck and Thompson (1962), Orum (1966), Olsen (1970), Ross and Wheeler (1971), Antunes and Gaitz (1975), Williams et al. (1973). Hyman and Wright (1971) found little difference between races with rank *not* adjusted. Since rank measures are lower among blacks, adjustment would probably have produced estimates much like ours.

stage of family life cycle, migration, rural versus urban background, and an *index of incapacitation* (reflecting hindrances due to old age, retirement, unemployment, and/or physical problems). Adding these control variables produced only minor changes in the rank effects. In most cities, the standardized coefficient reflecting the effect of income decreased slightly and the coefficient for education increased, but the pattern of effects described above was unchanged.

The relationships between rank and number of memberships seem to take about the same form in the six cities. Hodge and Treiman (1968b: 739), in comparing their results from a Washington, D.C. suburb to those for Detroit innercity and suburban samples, conclude that, " . . . the comparative evidence suggests the need for taking ecological and structural variables into account when building a theory of the linkages between social inequality and voluntary association." However, the similarities between our cities suggest that different patterns may occur more often between ecological subunits of a single community than between whole communities.

Some of the city differences deserve brief mention. The differences in racial–ethnic effects from city to city have already been discussed. Among majority men only, an analysis of covariance (discussed in Chapter 5) yielded a significant interaction effect due to different community slopes, but these city differences added only an additional 4% to the 24% of the variance explained by the common within-city regression equation. The interaction seems to be due to fluctuations across cities in the effects of such variables as the respondent's rating of his neighborhood, wife's education, and the origin variables. Also, the effects of self-placement were negligible in the two large cities.

The general level of belonging was not substantially different in the six cities. Although the analysis of covariance revealed a significant difference (with the rank variables controlled) between cities in the number of memberships, it accounted for only 1% of the variance and was unpatterned by city size or region. However, the *strength* of the relationship between rank and belonging does vary clearly—rank is a more important determinant of joining in small towns than in the other cities. Since heavy union membership should reduce the relationship between rank and belonging, it might be thought that the strong relationships in the small towns are due to low levels of union membership there. But this is not true. Membership in unions is highest in Linton (26%) and although the level is low in Safford (12%), it was lower still in Columbus (9%) at the time of the survey.

The variance in number of memberships explained by a unidimensional rank model (our general rank index) is substantial. Indeed, this dependent variable is the strongest correlate of the general rank index which we encountered. Although the multidimensional models explain more than the general rank index (compare the R^2's and the R^2's in Table 8.2), the differences are proportionately smaller than for most other dependent variables.

The reasons for this are that there are several strong rank effects on membership, most rank effects are in the same direction, and community differences, such as they are, tend to be which of a set of similar and related measures carries the effect most strongly in a given community. In consequence, the general rank index tends to average out detailed community differences, but not to lose much in cancelling out opposing effects.

In vivid contrast to the effects of belonging, we find only weak and unstable rank effects on frequency of attending meetings of the respondent's most important association (data not shown). We regressed attendance upon the 10 rank variables shown to be most important in the 17-variable analysis. Because of the nature of the results, we will briefly describe them rather than presenting a table. The proportion of the variance explained in these runs was below .10 for all cities except Linton (where the R^2 was .17). The rank effects were both weak and varied markedly from city to city. Often the effects of a given variable changed in sign from city to city; even if this did not happen, most rank variables had noticeable effects in only one or two cities (and different cities for different variables). No city-size or regional pattern appeared in these variations. Only two rank effects appeared with some consistency. A high class self-rating accompanied higher attendance in four of the six cities. In the three Indiana cities, men of higher occupational rank reported more attendance. The effects of majority racial–ethnic rank were variable. In Indianapolis, the minority men (blacks) attended more frequently than whites, with other rank variables controlled. The results for the Arizona cities were mixed. In Phoenix, minority men (blacks and Mexican–Americans) attended more than whites, but the reverse was true in Safford, where the minority is mainly Mexican–American. All these results held unchanged when controls were introduced.

We should note that these weak results on attendance may be a function of the question we asked. Since our question referred only to attendance at the man's most important association, it would not yield a high score for a man who belongs to many associations and attends meetings nearly every night of the week, but spreads his attendance thinly over his memberships. This may be a characteristic pattern of attendance for men of higher rank, but our measure was not capable of picking it up.

As we pointed out above, however, membership is probably more important in establishing a potential communication network than sheer rate of activity. High activity in a formal voluntary association not only requires greater commitment, it probably indicates a devotion to the special purposes of the association more than a tendency to communicate with a large number of other members. Holding (or having held) an office in one's most important association probably also reflects some concern with the specific purpose of the association, but in addition directly indicates a portion of power in the organization and a central place in the network of communication.

Office-holding is more strongly related to rank than is attendance, although it is less strongly related than the number of memberships. We report
in Table 8.3 the results of an analysis of covariance between rank variables
and office-holding. Those rank variables were included which showed up as
potentially important (having a significant beta of .10 or more in at least one
city) in the 17-variable regressions. Since majority was not such a variable,
we omit it and do the analysis only for men of majority rank.

High occupation seems to be the strongest and most consistent source of
office-holding. Other variables which also yield a consistent increase in
office-holding are a favorable rating of one's own neighborhood and high
occupation of the father. A prestigious first job also increases office-holding.
Evidently occupation is especially important in choosing officers in associations. This may partly be due to the social skills which accompany high-
ranked occupations as well as special occupational skills (accountants undoubtedly are more likely to be chosen as treasurers).

Other possibilities are that high occupations yield power which enables
men to gain organizational office and/or that office-holding tends to be
restricted to men presumed to act responsibly and high occupation may be
taken as a sign of responsibility. The net effect of father's occupation may
mean that fathers with high occupations were more likely to hold office and
hence socialized their sons to think such behavior is feasible, rewarding, etc.

Despite these more or less consistent effects, considerable differences
appeared between the cities. The interaction term, although only significant
at the .25 level, explained 3% of the variance, compared to the 6%
explained by the average within-city equation. The interaction stems in large
part from the regression in Safford, which departs markedly from the pattern
generally established in the other cities. Within each region the explained
variance is higher in the small towns.

Our final analysis of associational participation investigated our notion
that the use of formal voluntary associations as a basis for primary relationships would be a skill especially developed among higher status men. This
did *not* prove to be the case. Having a friend within the organization (if a
member) was generally unrelated to social rank, and the frequency of
visiting that friend, if there was one, was also unrelated to rank. Thus high
ranking men have more association-based friends because they belong to
more associations, not because they are especially sociable as members.

Church Membership and Attendance

Although the cities differ substantially in rank effects on church membership
and attendance, some rank variables have reasonably consistent effects.
Men of high education, married to well-educated women and living in
neighborhoods they rate as prestigious, tend to participate more in church

Table 8.3 Rank Effects on Office-Holding (Association Members of Majority Racial-Ethnic Rank Only)

Rank variables	Average within-city	Indianapolis	Columbus	Linton	Phoenix	Yuma	Safford
	Regression coefficients: Unstandardized and standardized (in parentheses)						
R's neighborhood rating	.042 (.10)*	.048 (.12)	.053 (.13)*	.069 (.18)*	.030 (.07)	.062 (.14)*	-.037 (.08)
Occupation	.003 (.13)*	.005 (.28)*	.004 (.20)*	.004 (.23)*	.002 (.07)	.003 (.12)	.002 (.09)
Second friend's occupation			-.003 (.16)*	.002 (.09)	.001 (.05)	-.001 (.06)	
First occupation	.001 (.07)*	-.003 (.16)*	.001 (.06)	-.002 (.10)	.003 (.14)*		.004 (.18)*
Wife's father's occupation				-.002 (.07)			
Mother's education		.026 (.15)*				-.010 (.06)	.006 (.24)*
Father's occupation	.002 (.07)*		.002 (.08)	.005 (.21)*	.002 (.07)	.002 (.12)	-.002 (.09)
R^2	.06*	.12*	.08*	.15*	.07*	.05	.12*
Mean	.41	.31	.37	.40	.39	.47	.53
N	1367	180	207	200	407	225	148
Proportion of variance (total sample, members only) explained by							
General rank index	(+).08*	(+).08*	(+).04*	(+).06*	(+).08*	(+).04*	(+).08*
17 variable regression	.14*	.14*	.10	.17*	.11*	.10	.16*

organizations, while men of majority racial–ethnic rank tend to participate *less*.

Rank effects on belonging to a church are reported in Table 8.4. The major factors which increase belonging are education, wife's education, and the man's rating of his own neighborhood. In contrast, *minority* racial–ethnic rank appears to increase belonging, net of other rank effects, in the four cities with substantial minority populations. To examine these findings further we introduced controls for stage of the family life cycle, migration, rural versus urban background, age, the incapacitation index discussed above, and religious preference (a dummy variable representing Catholic preference). Introducing these controls did not change the above conclusions. Indeed, the education rank effect became somewhat stronger and more consistent when the controls were added. A small negative effect of first occupation was slightly strengthened in five of the six cities. The only other change of note was that the majority beta dropped to −.07 in Yuma but jumped to −.21 in Safford, probably as a result of adjusting for Catholic preference.

The above description sets forth the effects that were consistent in some degree from city to city, but the city differences were substantial. In the analysis of covariance for majority men (discussed in Chapter 5), the interaction term was significant in the .01 level and added an additional 3% of explained variance to the 5% explained by the regression equation common to all cities. Notable among the differences in effects across cities is that occupation affects membership positively in the Indiana cities, but negatively or not at all in Arizona. In contrast, the effects of education are stronger in Arizona. Finally, the degree to which rank determines church membership, although nowhere more than moderate, is especially low in Phoenix.

Rank variables have some moderately strong and stable effects on church attendance, unlike their effects on attending the man's most important voluntary assocation. Most of these effects are similar to those reported above for membership. Major factors which consistently increase attendance are again education, wife's education and the neighborhood rating (see Table 8.5). The man's self-placement is also positively related to attendance, but part of this could be an effect in the reverse direction: Frequent attendance could add to a man's feelings of respectability and place in the community and thus perhaps make him more likely to think of himself as middle or upper-middle class. As was true for belonging, majority racial–ethnic rank has a negative effect on attendance—minority men attend church more, net of other rank effects. This effect is reduced somewhat in the Arizona cities when the controls listed above are introduced, but the effects persist (betas, after controls, are −.05, −.09, and −.10). Introducing the controls erases the small negative effects of father's occupation which appear in Table 8.5. Finally, under controls a small negative effect of income

Table 8.4 Rank Effects on Church Membership

Rank variables	Regression coefficients: Unstandardized and standardized (in parentheses)					
	Indianapolis	Columbus	Linton	Phoenix	Yuma	Safford
Self-placement	.043 (.13)*	.042 (.13)*	.022 (.06)			
R's neighborhood rating		.053 (.15)*		.039 (.10)*	.050 (.12)*	
Family income	.001 (.08)		.001 (.10)			-.001 (.05)
Occupation	.003 (.18)*	.001 (.06)	.003 (.18)*			-.002 (.10)
First occupation		-.001 (.07)				-.002 (.12)
Wife's education		.016 (.09)		.011 (.07)	.027 (.14)*	.022 (.15)*
Education				.013 (.10)*	.020 (.15)*	.026 (.24)*
Mother's education	-.013 (.07)	.024 (.13)*	.018 (.08)	-.013 (.09)*		.008 (.06)
Father's occupation	-.001 (.07)		.002 (.09)			-.004 (.18)*
Majority[a]	-.289 (.21)*			-.214 (.14)*	-.264 (.22)*	-.135 (.12)*
Mean	.64	.73	.61	.65	.59	.73
N	322	373	297	686	372	305
R^2	.11*	.13*	.08*	.04*	.07*	.09*
Proportion of variance explained by						
General rank index	(+).04*	(+).14*	(+).09*	(+).01*	(+).01*	.00
17 variable regression	.13*	.16*	.14*	.06*	.08*	.12*

[a] Reflected Bogardus scores in Columbus and Linton.

Table 8.5 Rank Effects on Church Attendance

Rank variables	Regression coefficients: Unstandardized and standardized (in parentheses)					
	Indianapolis	Columbus	Linton	Phoenix	Yuma	Safford
Self-placement		.170 (.13)*	.134 (.09)		.090 (.06)	.121 (.08)
R's neighborhood rating	.172 (.12)*	.339 (.24)*		.192 (.12)*	.153 (.10)*	.238 (.14)*
Family income			-.003 (.09)		-.003 (.09)	
Occupation	.006 (.09)	.004 (.05)	.007 (.09)		.006 (.07)	-.015 (.18)*
First occupation		.004 (.05)	-.008 (.08)		.071 (.10)	.006 (.07)
Wife's education	.071 (.09)					.042 (.07)
Education	.069 (.14)		.088 (.14)	.025 (.05)	.056 (.10)	.109 (.23)*
Mother's education		.040 (.05)	-.039 (.05)	-.084 (.14)*	-.050 (.09)	.041 (.07)
Father's occupation	-.008 (.09)	-.007 (.09)	.006 (.06)		-.005 (.06)	-.008 (.07)
Majority[a]	-1.27 (.23)*		-4.690 (.05)	-.615 (.10)*	-.881 (.19)*	-.714 (.14)*
R^2	.11*	.14*	.04	.05*	.08*	.10*
Proportion of variance explained by						
General rank index	(+).02*	(+).12*	(+).02*	.00	(+).01	(+).02*
17 variable regression	.15*	.18*	.07	.06*	.11*	.12*

[a]Reflected Bogardus scores were used in Columbus and Linton; a positive coefficient means that high racial—ethnic rank accompanies high attendance.

205

appears in every city.[6] The positive effects we found for education and wife's educatior are consistent with earlier findings reported by Hodge and Treiman (1968b). They report that income has only a negligible effect, however, whereas after controlling we find a small negative effect. Their findings of a substantial effect of occupation seem to be city-specific—we find that occupation (slightly) increases attendance only in the Indiana cities.

As was true for church membership, rank effects on attendance vary considerably from city to city. In the analysis of covariance for majority men, the interaction term (reflecting differences in slopes across the cities) was significant at the .01 level and allowing each city to have a distinct pattern of effects added 3% to the 5% of the variance explained by the common equation. Most of the city differences are scattered fluctuations. Two regularities are that occupation (as for membership) has a positive effect on attendance in Indiana and no or negative effects in Arizona, and that the effect of self-placement is absent in both of the large cities. The cities also vary in the strength of the rank effects. Four cities have moderate R^2's (between .14 and .08), but explanation seems especially weak in Linton and Phoenix.[7]

One of our main findings, then, is that a man's education and the education of his wife both independently promote participation in church. This is consistent with our findings above on the effects of education on visiting friends and on holding memberships in voluntary associations, and can be understood in the same way—that education furnishes resources in terms of trust and social skills which promote participation. The finding, however, argues against any view that education promotes a secular and/or scientific view of the world which makes educated men take religion and religious activity less seriously. Either this effect simply doesn't occur, or is confined to men with very high education or certain types of schooling, or is overpowered by the opposing effect of the resources for participation provided by education.

[6]In Table 5.2, we reported an example of opposed rank effects in the average within-city equation in an analysis of covariance for majority men only. This took the form of education and neighborhood rating increasing church attendance and mother's education decreasing it. As Table 8.5 makes clear, this is not a consistent result across cities. Mother's education does have a negative effect in three cities, but a positive effect in two others. The data do contain two consistent opposed effects however. In a context of generally positive effects, the net effects of majority rank and (perhaps) family income are negative.

[7]The standardized coefficients reported here are roughly comparable to those reported in Mueller and Johnson (1975). Their conclusions appear to differ somewhat from ours, largely because their question is "What are the causes of church attendance?" while ours is "Does rank affect church attendance?" They note a substantial interaction, however, that would not be corrected by our "Catholic" dummy variable, namely that rank affected attendance of Catholics only among the unmarried. Had we performed separate analyses, we might have found sharper rank effects on attendance among "everyone else," and no effects (or negligible effects) among married Catholics, who comprised a significant portion of our sample.

Political Activity

Rank effects on political activity are similar to those on the number of associational memberships—a number of reasonably strong, reasonably stable positive effects, plus a negative effect of majority racial–ethnic rank in Indianapolis. In contrast to our previous analyses, we present in Table 8.6 the regression coefficients for rank variables *after* controls were applied for migration, age, family life cycle, incapacitation, and rural versus urban background. We follow this procedure because rank effects on political activity were altered somewhat by introducing the control variables and the effects net of the effects of the control variables give a clearer picture, we believe, of the actual rank effects. For example, age should be controlled because older men both have less education and are more politically active and this combination of effects therefore masks or diminishes any direct positive effect of education.

High rank on a number of dimensions increases political activity. The strongest and most consistent effect is that of education—in every city better educated men reported higher levels of activity. Wife's education also had substantial and reasonably consistent effects. The positive effect of occupation was also reasonably strong in most cities. Other variables increasing political activity were income, father's occupation and class self-placement (although this latter effect, once again, may partly reflect some reversed causation—political activity may enhance a man's notion of his place in the community).

In striking contrast, racial–ethnic rank has a *negative* effect on political activity in Indianapolis. Blacks, the minority group in this city, are more politically active than whites, controlling for other rank variables and the several control variables. This is consistent with prior findings by Orum (1966) and Olsen (1970).[8]

Some city differences appear in the regressions, although they are not as substantial as in some earlier analyses. The degree to which rank determines activity is relatively high in most cities, but it drops to .07 in Linton (and rises to .27 in Safford). The most marked city difference, of course, is the effect of majority racial–ethnic rank, which is confined to Indianapolis. Other differences worth noting are that the respondent's education seems to have stronger effects in Arizona than Indiana, and that the effects of occupation disappear in the two large cities.

___

[8]As indicated in the text, the result of introducing the five control variables was to strengthen the effects of education (and father's occupation), probably due to the effects of age. Introducing the controls also *weakened* the effects of occupation, class self-placement and, especially, income. It is possible that high income partly fosters political activity by reducing the chance of being incapacitated, thus the effect of income was reduced by controlling for a variable that mediates its effect on activity.

Table 8.6 Rank Effects on Political Activity (Net of Control Variable Effects)

Rank variables	Regression coefficients: Unstandardized and standardized (in parentheses)[a]					
	Indianapolis	Columbus	Linton	Phoenix	Yuma	Safford
Self-placement		.108 (.13)*		.073 (.08)*	.067 (.07)	.111 (.13)*
R's neighborhood rating	-.066 (.07)	.079 (.09)*	.076 (.10)*	.054 (.05)		.001 (.06)
Family income	.002 (.09)			.001 (.07)		
Occupation		.004 (.10)	.008 (.20)*		.006 (.10)*	.005 (.11)*
First occupation	.003 (.06)	.002 (.05)		.023 (.05)		
Wife's education	.076 (.14)*	.049 (.12)*			.096 (.25)*	.054 (.14)*
Education	.060 (.18)*	.026 (.08)	.026 (.09)	.081 (.23)*	.067 (.17)*	.068 (.24)*
Mother's education		.035 (.08)				
Father's occupation	.004 (.08)				.005 (.08)	.004 (.07)
Majority[b]	-.748 (.20)*	2.640 (.07)				
R^2 ("net" R^2)[c]	.33* (.16)	.30* (.16)	.26* (.07)	.19* (.11)	.33* (.20)	.40* (.27)

[a] These are the regression coefficients in an analysis in which the listed variables are entered *plus* six control variables: migration, rural versus urban background, an incapacitation index, age, stage in the family life cycle, and Catholicism. The coefficients thus reflect rank effects net of the effects of these control variables.

[b] Reflected Bogardus scores were used in Columbus and Linton; a positive coefficient means high racial-ethnic rank accompanies high activity.

[c] This is the *additional* proportion of the variance explained by the rank variables, beyond joint variance or that explained by the control variables.

RANK, FORMAL PARTICIPATION, AND POLITICAL ACTIVITY

Formal participation may generate further formal participation, quite apart from the effects of social rank. Once a man has been induced to join two or three associations (say, because of his job) he may find that he enjoys and/or profits from the memberships so much that he joins several more associations, not because of his high rank, but because he joined the first three. We have suggested that participation connects the individual with a network of communication and potential communication. This could be a vehicle for political influence in community affairs. Perhaps political activity is enhanced only among men of high rank who take formal participation seriously (but see Erbe 1964; Olsen 1972; Greer and Orleans 1962; Burstein 1972 for elaboration of this issue).

The above argument motivates us, in this section, to investigate whether a given type of participation increases other types. (We cannot analyze whether participation of a given kind produced more of the same kind, since we do not have over-time data.) We begin by assuming that participation in voluntary associations (number of memberships) may act independently and directly to increase participation in religious activities, and that belonging to many associations and participating in church may increase political activity. In addition, we assume that social rank may have direct effects, unmediated by other forms of participation. The general scheme of these effects, which will guide our analysis below, can be sketched as follows:

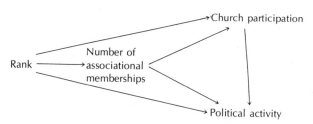

Although several of these effects might conceivably be reciprocal (political activity might increase simple joining, for example, as well as vice versa), we assume here that the "return" arrows we have omitted represent only minor effects. This assumption stems from a notion that the number of memberships, reflecting the general amount of formal participation, probably affects the other two specific forms of participation rather than the other way around, and that if church participation and political activity are causally linked, political activity is much more likely to be affected by, than to affect, church participation.

Two important, interrelated substantive issues are raised by this causal scheme. The first is whether the rank effects we reported above on church participation and political activity might turn out to be partly or entirely mediated by another form of participation. In particular, do men of high rank go to church more often because their community rank leads them to do so, or mainly because men of high rank belong to more (nonchurch) associations and this activity motivates them to be more active in the religious area? Or, are men of high rank (excepting racial–ethnic rank) more active politically mainly because they participate more in voluntary association and/or churches and these memberships bring them into contact with political issues and other stimulants to political participation? These questions amount to asking whether the arrows flowing directly from rank to church and to political participation should be erased.

The second issue is whether there are sources of participation independent of rank. For example, we will ask whether voluntary association participation has an important direct effect on political activity. Since rank falls far short of determining joining, men of low rank may have high membership rates. If memberships then have a strong direct effect on political activity, they represent a source of political activity which is to some extent independent of rank.

Our first empirical conclusion, from an analysis of the direct and mediated effects on church membership and attendance, is that the rank effects on these variables are *not at all* mediated by number of associational memberships. Number of memberships, introduced into the regression equations explaining these two forms of church participation, adds less than one percent of explained variance in any city. Among the 12 tests (six cities, two dependent variables), the regression coefficient for memberships was nonsignificant 9 times.

We conclude, therefore, that the amount of general joining does not directly increase either kind of church participation. The effects of rank on church participation are direct and not mediated. Evidently, whatever resources or encouragements which high rank provides for participation lead men both to join associations and to join and attend church. Further, these two direct effects of rank seem to almost completely account for any correlation between associational and church participation. This result suggests, in turn, that no other unmeasured factor, such as gregariousness or sociability, is acting (independently of rank, at least) to promote both types of participation.

In analyzing effects on political activity, we expected, in contrast, to find substantial effects of other forms of formal participation. This expectation was based on previous research results and the theoretical explanations advanced for those results. For example, in a summary and replication of much previous research Erbe (1964) showed that socioeconomic status and organizational involvement had independent as well as joint effects on political activity and that, if anything, the effect of other forms of formal participation was greater than the status effect. In explanation, Erbe suggested two possible mechanisms: (a) Formal associations select members who are politically active and (b) members of formal voluntary associations are subject to adult socialization encouraging political activity (partisan or not), no matter what the manifest goals of the particular association (our causal scheme assumes the first mechanism is the weaker of the two). He argued that the effect of organizational membership on political activity was cumulative, in that meeting the same active people in organization after organization would reinforce their influence. In our view, this is precisely what establishes a communication network which carries the detailed information used in political (and other kinds of community) activity.

In a more recent study of Indianapolis, Olsen found that social rank, participation in formal voluntary associations, and church activity all independently affected political activity. Political attitudes failed to explain these effects. He concluded that social participation influences voter turnout:

> This theoretical explanation, derived from the mobilization version of social pluralism theory, argues that active involvement in voluntary, special-interest, nonpolitical organizations—including voluntary associations, community activities, and churches—tends to bring individuals into contact with political issues, actors and affairs, and provides them with information and skills necessary for voting and other kinds of political participation [1972:331].

In a cross-national study, Burstein (1972) found that the effects of socioeconomic status on political participation occurred only indirectly, through the operation of "organizational involvement" and use of the mass media, in four of the five countries studied. This failed to contradict either Erbe (1964) or Olsen (1972) in that the exception was the United States, where an independent direct effect of rank on participation was found (as also in the present study). While the data are not strictly comparable, all these investigations show that social status influences the level of political activity both directly and indirectly through other forms of social participation such as religious activity, formal voluntary association memberships and use of the mass media.

These past results and explanations, then, lead us to believe that other forms of participation should directly increase political activity, both because a man active in associations may be motivated to seek further fields, including politics, for participation, but also because other forms of participation should guide a man's future activity specifically into political channels. To check on the accuracy of this idea, we regressed political activity on a set of rank variables and control variables, just as we did above in Table 8.6, but added two participation variables, memberships and church attendance (and a measure of political potency, to be discussed).

Number of memberships in formal voluntary associations and church attendance each increase political activity independently of rank and also explain part of the effect of rank on political activity. But substantial direct effects of rank remain.

The findings are given in Table 8.7. The effects of memberships and church attendance are among the strongest and most consistent in the table. In every city, *each* of these forms of participation acts to increase political activity, net of the effects of the other rank and control variables. These net effects mean that formal participation encourages political activity even among men who do not hold high social rank. The hypothesis that participation of other sorts leads to political participation is strongly supported.

We saw above that social rank affects both number of memberships and church attendance. Since they each in turn affect political activity, our results indicate that some of the effects of rank on political activity are mediated by these other forms of participation. We can see which rank effects are mediated, and how much, by looking for the rank regression coefficients which drop in size from Table 8.6 to Table 8.7. The rank variables whose betas seem to decrease notably when participation variables are added are education and (in Indianapolis) majority. Evidently, educated men and minority men participate in voluntary associations and attend church more often and this partly explains why such men are more active politically. The extent to which formal participation explains the effect of rank on political activity is measured by the size of the drop in rank betas from Table 8.6 to Table 8.7. For example, the education effect dropped from .23 to .14 in Phoenix, but only from .24 to .22 in Yuma. The degree of mediation seems moderate at best.

Both education and majority retain substantial direct effects on political activity. Direct effects of self-placement, occupation and wife's education also appear with some consistency across cities. Clearly, then, rank has substantial effects on political activity which are not mediated by other types of participation. The direct effects of participation are comparable in magnitude to those of rank. Even in Safford, the exception, the participation effects yield two betas of .09, and the rank effects five betas of .12, .18, .13, .11 and .06, so that while political activity is dominated by rank in Safford, formal participation still affords an avenue to political activity that is independent of rank.

Indianapolis, as a community in which organizational participation affects political activity more strongly than any rank variable, is the strongest contrast to Safford. The only significant positive rank effect on political activity in Indianapolis is the beta of .13 for education. Church attendance and number of memberships add effects estimated at .16 and .19 respectively, and being white *reduces* political activity (with a −.16 beta). In Indianapolis, in other words, formal participation, which explains part but not all of the effect of rank on political activity, also yields a significant means by which men not distinguished by their rank are encouraged to political activity.

The above analysis was also designed to give evidence on the influence of feelings of political potency, an attitude which plausibly should enable

Table 8.7 Effects of Rank, Participation, and Feelings of Potency on Political Activity (Net of Control Variable Effects)

Independent variables	Regression coefficients: Unstandardized and standardized (in parentheses)[a]					
	Indianapolis	Columbus	Linton	Phoenix	Yuma	Safford
Self-placement		.063 (.08)		.067 (.07)		.099 (.12)*
R's neighborhood rating	-.083 (.08)	.066 (.08)	.044 (.06)			.011 (.06)
Family income	.002 (.09)					
Occupation		.004 (.10)	.006 (.17)*		.004 (.07)	.005 (.11)*
Wife's education	.052 (.10)	.062 (.14)*				.050 (.13)*
Education	.045 (.13)*		.016 (.06)	.052 (.14)*	.083 (.22)*	.050 (.18)*
Mother's education	-.033 (.07)	.026 (.06)			.072 (.18)*	
Father's occupation	.005 (.08)				.003 (.06)	
Majority[b]	-.609 (.16)*	3.676 (.10)*				
Number of associational memberships	.105 (.19)*	.073 (.13)*	.088 (.15)*	.117 (.14)*	.142 (.17)*	.063 (.09)
Church attendance	.108 (.16)*	.067 (.11)*	.043 (.09)*	.074 (.11)*	.077 (.11)*	.054 (.09)*
Political potency		.106 (.10)*	-.095 (.10)*	.124 (.09)*		
R^2	.38*	.31*	.29*	.22*	.34*	.42*

[a]These are the regression coefficients in an analysis employing the listed variables *plus* five control variables: migration, rural versus urban background, an incapacitation index, age, and stage in the family life cycle. The coefficients thus reflect effects net of the effects of these controls.

[b]Reflected Bogardus scores were used in Columbus and Linton; a positive coefficient means high racial-ethnic rank accompanies high activity.

213

political participation. Our notion was that high social rank might encourage potency which in turn might increase actual rates of political activity. Our question on this matter, "Do you think public officials care what men like *you* think?" is adapted from a political potency battery and is intended to indicate whether the respondent feels that he has any potential impact in democratic political organization. Responses were scored from 0 to 4, depending upon the vigor and direction of the response; a score of 4 was given for an emphatic "Yes" (e.g., "You bet they care . . . if they don't they better start caring") for a "Yes" with one or more illustrations of how they care.[9]

Rank variables were positively related to potency in similar ways in all six communities. The analysis of covariance for majority men showed that the interaction term was insignificant, and rank accounted for 6% of the variance at the least (Yuma) and 19% at most (Columbus). The significant betas for the average within regression were education (.21), income (.09) and neighborhood rating (.07): That equation accounted for 9% of the variance for the whole sample. High social rank, then, does seem to promote feelings of political potency.

However, the second link is missing in our chain of effects: Political potency has no clear net influence on actual political activity. In Table 8.7, we see that in only three cities does potency have coefficients worth noting and they change in sign from city to city. Men of high rank report both feelings of potency and high rates of political activity, but, so far as we can tell, potency does not contribute to the activity. This failure of an attitudinal variable to explain the effects of rank on political participation is consistent with the results on attitudinal effects in the studies by Erbe (1964) and Olsen (1972). Such results suggest that participation is not explained by the apparently relevant attitudes of the participants. Rather, the relationships among rank and various forms of formal participation are sustained more directly by the resources made available by high rank and by the reinforcing experiences of the participation itself.

SUMMARY AND CONCLUSIONS

The major results of our analyses in this chapter are:

1. In all cities, most of the men belong to few associations, while a minority belong to many. The modal number of memberships is zero or one

[9]The detailed coding was as follows:

(0) No, and gives an example of their not caring.
(1) No
(2) Qualified caring: They care at some times and not at others, etc.
(3) Yes
(4) Yes, and gives an example of their caring.

in all cities. However, over a third of the men in each city belong to two or more associations.

2. Between 30% and 50% of men who belong to at least one association have held office in the association most important to them. Officeholding is more common in the Arizona cities, and within region, is more common the smaller the city.

3. Participation in church is very widespread. About two-thirds of the men are church members and over 90% attend church at least occasionally.

4. The main effects of rank on the forms of participation we studied are shown in Figure 8.1. In general, high rank on subjective status dimensions, on current achieved dimensions and on early achieved dimensions promote participation, but origin ranks have little effect. In contrast, *low* racial–ethnic rank promotes participation (although often only in Indianapolis). Participation in voluntary associations seems most affected by income and occupation (both current and first job), while participation in religious and political associations is affected more by education (of the man and of his wife). The effects described are those remaining after imposing controls appropriate to the analysis, including age, migration, incapacitation, religious preferences, etc.

5. The participation variables most strongly affected by rank are the number of memberships and the degree of political activity. Even for these, over 70% of the variance usually remains unexplained by rank effects. For the other participation variables, the unexplained variance is generally above 85% or 90%.

6. Although the rank effects described above appear with some consistency, the pattern of all rank effects varies considerably from city to city. This variability is especially marked for the four participation variables least well explained by rank, while the rank effects on number of memberships are most consistent across cities. Most of the city differences seemed to follow no clear pattern. A major exception is the effect of racial–ethnic rank. For several forms of participation, minority men were found to participate more *only in Indianapolis,* suggesting that this effect holds for blacks, but does not extend to Mexican–Americans. Another trace pattern that appeared in the city differences was that the positive effects of occupation often were stronger in Indiana cities than in Arizona, but that the opposite was true for education effects.

7. Participation of one kind sometimes promotes participation of other kinds. One pattern of such effects which fit our data is presented in Figure 8.2. We find that the effects of rank on church participation are not mediated by a man's degree of participation in voluntary associations. However, part of the effect of rank on political activity *is* indirect: Rank affects the number of memberships and church attendance and these in turn promote political activity. The net effects of these other forms of participation on political activity are as strong as the remaining direct rank effects.

	Number of associational memberships	Associational attendance	Associational office-holding	Church membership	Church attendance	Political activity
Self-placement	++	+			+	+
R's neighborhood rating	+++		++	+	++	
Family income	+	+	++	+	−	+
Occupation	++		+	−		
First occupation				++		
Wife's education				+	+	+
Education	+				++	++
Father's occupation			+			− (Ind'pls only)
Majority	− − (Ind'pls only)	− (Ind'pls only)		− (Ind'pls only)	−	− (Ind'pls only)

Figure 8.1. Summary of rank effects on forms of formal participation ("+" indicates a positive effect and "−" a negative effect; the number of signs indicates the strength of the effect and how consistently it appeared across the cities).

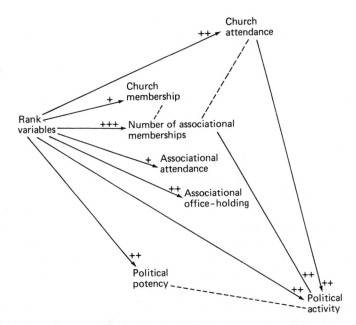

Figure 8.2. *Effects of rank on various forms of participation and effects of forms of participation on each other (dashed lines indicate hypothesized effects which are* disconfirmed *by the data).*

8. High rank appears to promote feelings of political potency, but such feelings do not have any marked effect on rates of political activity.

The scheme of rank effects on participation summarized in Figure 8.1 could be taken as an initial statement of a theoretical framework relating these variables. But it is probably better regarded as a set of findings the theory should account for, as calling for an explanation—why does rank affect participation in these ways?

Some reasons why high status may increase formal participation have been mentioned in the presentation of findings above. They are of two sorts: High rank may *motivate* or encourage participation and may independently provide *resources* necessary for participation. That is, if men were equally endowed with the resources for participation, men of high status might nevertheless participate more because their standing encourages them to use their resources in this rather than other ways. Likewise, if all men were equally motivated to participate, high status men might actually participate more because they have more of the resources that make participation feasible.

Such a theoretical approach may allow us to explain several features of our findings. First, we found that rank effects on formal participation are stronger and more consistent across communities than are the rank effects on informal participation we described in the last chapter. We argued there that the ways in which high rank promotes informal relationships are outweighed to some extent by the contradictions and costs of such ties for men of high rank. Formal participation, by contrast, should not present any serious contradictions to the requirements of holding high rank, so in studying formal participation we do not as often see weak rank effects suggesting simultaneous encouragements and hindrances to participation.

A second feature of our findings is that each form of participation is usually affected by a constellation of rank variables rather than by only one or two. This is just what should happen if participation is simultaneously affected by several kinds of resources and motives which in turn are provided by several different rank variables.

Third, we can tentatively offer an explanation for our finding that income and occupation exercise the major effects on voluntary association participation while education mainly affects church and political participation. Our line of argument suggests that membership and office-holding in one or more of a variety of voluntary associations require a variety of resources and motives, but do *not* require the resource of high levels of trust (which, presumably, is provided by education) and may be more a matter of responding to community and/or corporate pressures than to any sense of values taught in the educational system. Church participation and political activity seem to be stimulated by somewhat different processes. Resources of money and social skills are not required as much for such acts as attending church or registering and voting, accounting for smaller income and occupation effects. The strong educational effects suggest, on the other hand, that values learned in the educational system, while not motivating membership in general, do promote a feeling of specific obligation to participate in religious and political affairs.

Although the effects discussed above appeared with some consistency across cities, we also found that rank effects on formal participation do vary to some degree with the community. Neither formal nor informal social participation is distributed by social rank the same way in all cities. The reason would appear to be that while attitudes and values about social participation are consistently patterned by rank, the ability to express those attitudes and values in behavior depends upon the local conditions. In the last chapter, this conclusion was suggested by our analysis of preference for visiting friends versus relatives. In this chapter, the analysis of political potency comes to a similar conclusion. Feelings of political potency were related to rank in very much the same way in all cities whereas rank effects on actual political participation varied somewhat.

We would speculate however, that these varying patterns of rank effects tend to produce, in all the cities, an associational network in which high ranking men are proportionately overrepresented in the central positions of communication and in which communication links are denser among higher than among lower ranking men. Many of the community differences in rank effects are matters of which particular rank variables are positively related to participation. In all communities, men of high rank participate more (excepting racial–ethnic rank). Higher ranking men, being more frequent joiners, are more likely to hold overlapping memberships. These, together with the associational offices they are more likely to hold, probably give them positions of centrality in the network of actual and potential communication in the community. In addition, the number of high ranking men is smaller, so that fewer links are required to construct a communication net among them.

Still, these findings do not indicate whether or not there is, in fact, a unified power elite based on social rank (see, for example, Mills 1956) in any given community. To begin with, high ranking men are few in number, meaning that many positions of control and communicative centrality in associations must be held by lower ranking men. Second, many other factors besides rank have an important effect on formal participation (or, to put it the other way around, the effects of rank fall far short of determining participation) and there are effects of one form of participation on another, independent of rank. Therefore, associational membership, though a primary mechanism for the development of a rank elite, is at the same time the mechanism through which other community residents (no matter what their ranks) have a voice in community affairs. Finally, the fact that several different rank dimensions have additive effects on each form of participation means that any associational elite is not dominated by high rank along any one dimension. A social elite *could* develop, not because it controlled the formal associational structure, which it does not, but because the formal associational structure affords it a tighter grip on the network of communication than is available to any other status group. But the fact that several kinds of rank are typically involved probably means that a clear basis in personal interest is lacking; rich men and college graduates are high in their respective rank systems, but rich men (insofar as they are *not* also college graduates) have different interests from college graduates (insofar as they are not rich). The communicative advantage would only be used for action on issues where the interests of different types of high ranking men tend to coincide.

Thus it would appear that an elite *could* mobilize rapidly, given the right kind of issues, and that it would be more difficult for any lower ranking group to do so. What we think happens more frequently (since the relevance of social rank for political and community issues is usually not clear, varies from issue to issue, and depends on the rank system involved) is that men of high rank serve disproportionately to organize publics within the community—publics largely composed of somewhat less active men not distinguished by rank. It is mainly in this sense that we think individual social rank is related to individual social power.

The next three chapters deal with political attitudes, anomia, and intolerance as further consequences of social rank. These variables were chosen for analysis both because theoretical discussions and past research suggest that they are primary correlates of rank and because they are the only other major dependent variables in our study which actually turned out to be strongly related to rank. In the analyses below we shall include formal participation as an intervening variable. Our results in this chapter raise the possibility that, unlike feelings of dissatisfaction and rates of informal participation, some types of formal participation are strongly enough affected by social rank to serve as important mechanisms by which rank might affect other attitudes and types of behavior.

9

POLITICAL IDEOLOGY AND
PARTY IDENTIFICATION

Most generally, ruling classes can be expected to have a stake in the status quo and in the political party or parties which support it. But the application of this extremely broad generalization to any particular historic situation is neither simple nor straightforward. Both the unique political context and the unique configuration of social rank must be specified. This chapter applies this generalization to a specific dimension of political attitudes and to party identification under the specific conditions of the six communities investigated. Therefore, the problem of this chapter is not so much *whether* the generalization is true, but *how* it applies.

The above generalization expresses a theory of class interests. Any stratified society involves class interests, but they may vary greatly from society to society in the form of their expression. Class interest itself is the common fate of people who share a broad level on some rank dimension. What they have in common, initially, is a particular stake in the social process according to which rewards and positions are allocated. They *may* organize themselves for collective action to defend or improve their position. Yet class interest is always potentially relevant to political activity, whether classes have given rise to self-conscious organizational expressions of the interest or not.[1]

---

[1] Notice that persons at the same level of social rank *have* a common interest by definition. How that interest ought to be implemented, however, is a matter of legitimate debate, even among those who share the interest. Which side of the debate is "demonstrably correct" is not for social scientists to say, though the popular notion of "false class consciousness" implies just such a judgment. For example, some elite members saw the propagation of individualistic norms and policies as the salvation of their class, during the 1930s, while others favored New Deal programs which might head off revolution. Neither posture was an instance of "false class consciousness" unless clairvoyance is the test of true loyalty.

The mechanisms through which classes express their interests and mobilize their memberships are found at the level of individual attitudes and orientations. Specifically, political ideology and party identification are, *among other things*, vehicles for the expression of class interest and for organizations to implement it. They relate to social rank, ultimately, at the level of individual political attitudes and individual preferences for a party label. Like many social phenomena requiring organized and coordinated action, the order at the group level (coherent ideology and party organization) is produced by mechanisms which appear nearly chaotic at the individual level (political attitudes and party stance of the average person). Nevertheless, the individual level is the place to show *how* order at the group level comes about.

The relationship between social class and political ideology or party affiliation is an extremely regular aspect of social life, but not necessarily a strong one, even at the group level. The reason is that class interests are only one among a set of causes underlying political orientations, and the causal chain may be quite long and indirect. Thus the special importance of social class in political life stems from ubiquity and causal priority, not from its power in *determining* political behavior.

CONSERVATISM AND CLASS INTERESTS

Conservatism can relate to social rank in several different ways, not only because different causal mechanisms are available (e.g., class interest, class culture, differential exposure to media), but also because conservatism refers to several different things politically. It covers stances in foreign policy, civil rights, domestic welfare policies, traditional symbolism, and even generalized resistance to social change, and there is no reason to expect social rank to be associated with conservatism the same way in all these areas. Lipset (1959a) has shown, for example, that, while men of high rank oppose liberal welfare policies, they nevertheless support liberal civil rights positions.[2]

Thus people may have interests in common whether they know or care about them or not. Those interests are defined by shared position, and not by anyone's conception of the implications of that position. To call these "class interests" in no way implies that persons sharing the interest are organized or culturally defined.

[2]For an extensive discussion of the subsequent debate over Lipset's position, see Hamilton (1972), especially Chapter 11. In summary, the debaters do not in general challenge the assertion that workers may take "liberal" positions on one set of issues and "conservative" positions on another. Whether the evidence for "working class intolerance" of one kind or another is strong, moderate, or equivocal seems to depend on the sample, the methodology, and the interests of the writer. Lipset's expectation that current "working class authoritarianism" could be explained by childhood socialization is questioned by findings (supported by the present investigation) that such intolerance is not much affected by parental status, net of current status characteristics.

In sociological theories of stratification, class interest has traditionally been the basic causal mechanism relating high rank and conservatism. Marx was not alone in viewing political struggles as a direct expression of class interest. In the class conflict view, higher classes are naturally *conservative* in the sense that they normally attempt to prevent privilege and legitimate power from falling into the hands of men of lower rank. In this specific meaning, "conservative" could refer to an independent ideology which provides the organizing principle for a variety of issues, that is, a coherent stance in relation to foreign policy, civil rights, property laws, etc. But class interests are what ultimately determine the definition of a "conservative" position.

The terms *left*, *right*, and *center* are less confusing ideological tags in that they are historically more obviously derived from class interest definitions of ideology:

> The political and sociological analysis of modern society in terms of left, center and right goes back to the days of the First French Republic when the delegates were seated, according to their political coloration, in a continuous semi-circle from the most radical and egalitarian on the left to the most moderate and aristocratic on the right. The identification of the left with advocacy of social reform and egalitarianism, the right with aristocracy and conservatism, deepened as politics became defined as the clash between classes. Nineteenth-century conservatives and Marxists alike joined in the assumption that the socio-economic cleavage is the most basic in modern society. Since democracy has become institutionalized and the conservatives' fears that universal suffrage would mean the end of private property have declined, many have begun to argue that the analysis of politics in terms of left and right and class conflct over-simplifies and distorts reality . . . [Lipset, 1959b:348].

Therefore "conservatism" or "rightism," as concepts that organize issues into an ideological position, should be expected to bear a systematic relationship to social class only in societies in which class interests do, in fact, strongly organize political issues. To the extent that issues are organized according to interests of region, age, religion, type of philosophy, or something else, one should not expect "conservatism" of all types to bear the same relationship to social rank. The salience of class interests among the social characteristics which define and relate political issues varies from one society to another and also varies through time in a given society. Thus the problem of "conservatism and social class" becomes a question of the extent to which class interests are the basis for the current political divisions, compared to other sources of political contention (see Campbell et al. 1960).

The salience of class interests in politics is probably a function of two general considerations: (a) the extent and organization of class conflict, and (b) the urgency of other concerns (war, crime, environmental problems, etc.). Of course the specific class conflict may vary: It may be management versus labor at one time, inner-city blacks versus suburban whites at another, and the "respectable" versus the poor and unemployed at still another. Conflict should be reduced by high rates of inconsistency and mobility in the societal stratification system, but in addition any one rank dimension may be more or less polarized. Events may deepen the gulf between rich and poor at one time, for example, forcing middle income people increasingly to identify in one direction or the other, but allow the gulf to close on other occasions.

For much of American history, neither the "conservative–liberal" dimension of ideology nor the organization of the major political parties has been very tightly or exclusively based on class interest. The Democratic party has often offered itself as the "party of the working man," but in most election years this is not nearly as direct an identification with class interests as that made by European Socialist parties. Since (a) the policies of the "left"-seated delegates of the First Republic are mostly embodied in the U.S. Constitution, and (b) Democrats, as well as Republicans, have held national power for extended periods, it would be a serious mistake to equate either political "conservatism" or Republican identification with a philosophical opposition to social change in general.

Certain economic conditions, such as the Great Depression, can increase the salience of class interests in the organization of ideology and in the significance of party membership. For example Richard Centers (1949), writing in the context of the management–labor conflicts immediately following World War II, found it appropriate to summarize many political issues in a single "conservatism–radicalism" dimension which combined leanings toward government expansion, welfare programs and increased power for working people in government. He theoretically connected this dimension to the issue of social change in two ways: (a) It represented an ideological epiphenomenon of the great social revolution, and (b) it represented acceptance of the changes wrought by the New Deal in response to problems of the Depression and of the enormous expansion of federal government during the war, as opposed to the "anti-change" ideology of return to the "normal" conditions of the 1920s. Centers interpreted the campaign of Roosevelt versus Dewey as a more or less "class" election: Would the U.S. swing back toward pure capitalism after the wartime necessity for collective action? Thus the way different ideological elements combine in a single dimension is explained by historical political and economic circumstances and the dimension is not necessarily appropriate to altered circumstances, even in the same country.

However, class interests are always of *potential* significance, whether they happen to be dominating the operation of the body politic at a given moment or not. When religious conflicts dominate, for example, correlations between rank and items of political ideology probably decline somewhat, but can be expected to rise again when religious harmony returns.

Even where class interests are salient, individual social rank and individual political attitudes will not necessarily be strongly related. Since humans are much more than members of classes, their individual attitudes are affected by all sorts of things, from family history to gout, in addition to social rank. Individuals may correctly perceive, on occasion, that what is good for them is not good for their class.

Therefore, we expected to find that men of high rank are motivated to protect the status quo politically, but that the relationship, although broadly applicable, is not compelling in strength. The details of how this generalization applies may be more interesting than the fact of its nonrejection.

DOMESTIC LIBERALISM AND PARTY IDENTIFICATION

Unlike the circumstances under which Centers considered a single dimension of conservatism–radicalism appropriate, the political atmosphere in the middle 1960s, when our interviews were conducted, was one of ideological reorganization. Many of our respondents thought of the political world in "Roosevelt versus Dewey" terms, but others, particularly the younger men, were reacting to vastly different alignments of issues. Dominant concerns were shifting from worker–management disputes to such areas as the Vietnamese War, drugs, crime in the streets, civil rights, government responsiveness, urban blight, and the "environment." To grossly summarize the mood, this was the period when the post-Kennedy "consensus of affluence" began to crumble.

Converse (1964) argues that the connections among the issues which make up an ideological position are often historical or social rather than logical or philosophical in nature. For example, attitudes concerning long hair were probably correlated with attitudes toward drug use during this period, not by virtue of any intrinsic aesthetic logic connecting hair and drugs, but because a symbolically important category of youths, about whom citizens had strong feelings one way or the other, both wore long hair and used drugs. According to Converse, crystallized political ideologies operate according to their own inner logic only among a very small minority of the politically most active voters. For others, issues are related to one another by their implications for group interests, by group membership, by political party, or by the social base of their support. For many voters, opinions on various issues are more or less independent, rather than different expressions of a coherent underlying social philosophy.

The connection between issues with which we are concerned here, of course, is that provided by class interest. To reflect class interest in a relatively stable way, we selected for analysis two rather specific political orientations, attitudes toward *domestic liberalism* (Federal welfare policies) and *party identification*. This avoids confusing ideology with group membership and identification.

Voting, to be sure, is a more direct and decisive sort of political behavior, but it tends to confound more or less stable predispositions, such as might be generated by class interest, with the particular idiosyncratic issues and personalities that are involved in any given campaign. Thus Campbell et al. (1960) analyze elections as a combination of the "normal vote" and the specific features of the campaign. Though predispositions ultimately have political effects only through political actions such as voting, the attempt to read those predispositions from a particular vote may be as hazardous as interpreting tea leaves. The last national election before this study, for example, was the Goldwater–Johnson presidential election, in which some Indiana respondents who normally vote Republican probably crossed over the line while some Democratic Arizonans probably crossed the other way from regional loyalty. Thus the more stable aspects of the relationship between social rank and politics could have been obscured by studying the vote.

Party identification, a number of studies have shown, is influential in determining one's vote, tends to be passed on from parents to children, and is apt to change only in certain watershed times of national stress, such as the 1930s depression. It represents an attachment to a party symbol with affective and cognitive connotations and organizes voting decisions and other political activities. Thus, it represents an orientation to the party label rather than to any particular ideological stand or to the content of any issues that may be currently espoused by the party.

We measured this variable by asking, "Do you generally consider yourself a Republican, a Democrat, some other party, or what?" If a man did not place himself in one of the two major parties in answering this question, he was asked, "Do you consider yourself closer to the Republican or to the Democratic Party?" The responses were scored to produce a 5-point scale from clearly Democratic (high score) to clearly Republican (low score).[3]

The domestic liberalism scale, on the other hand, is issue oriented, but rather than focusing on a single narrow issue or averaging responses on a wide variety of issues, it reflects the respondents' trend of thinking through a series of related policy questions: whether the government should undertake a wider scope of tasks, especially to reduce inequality and provide security against economic threat. In the context of this scale, "conservative" does not

[3]A score of 4 was given to respondents who answered "Democrat" on the first question, 3 to men who would not identify with one of the parties on the first question but chose "Democratic Party" on the second question, 2 to men who would not identify with a party in answering either question (about 6% of the samples), 1 to men answering "Republican" to the second but not the first question, and 0 to men identifying with the Republican party in answer to the initial question.

connote general opposition to change, constitutionalism, or traditionalism, but only resistance to Federal expansion and government welfare programs.
    This scale was constructed from the following items:

1. The government ought to make sure that everyone has a good standard of living.
2. Federal government aid in the medical area is certain to result in inferior service.
3. The government should give a person work if he loses his job because a machine is brought in to do his job.
4. Poverty programs, aimed at giving aid to the poor, only encourage people to expect something for nothing.
5. If it looks like a depression is about to start, the government should do something at once, such as a program to build highways and schools to give people jobs.
6. (Community) should not accept federal aid to schools because then the government will try to control the school system.

The responses were scored and summed to form a 25-point scale, with high scores reflecting an attitude that the government should take a more active role in the society in behalf of the disadvantaged.[4]
    Though it is often reasonable to ask whether the unity of an ideological dimension has been imposed by the conceptual scheme of the investigators, rather than by the respondents' attitude patterns, there are some empirical reasons to regard the domestic liberalism scale as a functional unity. First, though the correlations among the six items are low (mostly .2 or lower, but occasionally reaching .4), they are all in the appropriate direction. Second, the correlations of the items with the total index score are in the .5 to .6 range, always correct in sign (the "reversed" items correlated negatively with the total index), and very regular from city to city, indicating that the scale has a similar internal structure in each of the communities. Third, a factor analysis for Indianapolis (Stirling 1973) of 38 attitude items reflecting a variety of domains, such as anomia, authoritarianism, political liberalism, political dogmatism, and intolerance of deviance, provides further support for the functional unity of the index. Domestic liberalism emerged as one of the (orthogonal) factors. All six of the above items loaded on the factor, four of them (numbers 1, 2, 4, 6) with loadings above .5. These four items did not load as highly on any other factor, nor did any of the other 32 items load above .3 on this factor.

---

[4]Responses were scored 0 for strongly disagree to 4 for strongly agree, except that scores on the second, fourth, and sixth items were reversed so a high score would reflect favorableness toward welfare state policies. Scores on the six items were then summed for each respondent to obtain his overall scale score. Since three of these questions have been reversed (that is, a person favoring governmental action would have to "disagree" rather than "agree") this index should not have been influenced by an acquiescence response set.

A final analysis dealt with the question of whether domestic liberalism and party identification are in turn parts of a broader central dimension of favorability to social change in general. To get at this issue, we employed three items from our interview schedule which were meant to reflect attitudes toward more or less apolitical sorts of change. They were:

1. Many people find the *Star-Spangled Banner* difficult to sing. If a new and appropriate national anthem were written, would you object to substituting it for the *Star-Spangled Banner?*
2. Some words in the English language are hard to use because they aren't spelled the way they sound. I mean words like "enough" and "height". Would you be in favor of changing the spelling rules and the dictionaries so that words like these are spelled the way they sound?
3. Some people think that the United States is just wasting money trying to land men on the moon. Do you feel that the United States should spend billions of dollars on this program?

To search for a generalized attitude toward social change which underlies political ideology, we combined the first two items into an index entitled *opposes change*, leaving the third item as a separate variable. We then computed zero-order correlations among domestic liberalism, party identification, *opposes change*, and the *moon* item. The correlation between Democratic party identification and domestic liberalism was positive in all cities, varying from +.28 in Yuma to +.41 in Indianapolis. But all other pairs of variables were essentially unrelated, with most correlations below .10 and sometimes varying in sign from city to city. Thus domestic liberalism and Democratic identification are distinct but positively related, and what they have in common does *not* appear to be a generalized favorability to social change.

These results are precisely what we would expect from a perspective, like that of Converse, in which the links between attitudes are produced and maintained socially rather than by some underlying logic. The time and effort devoted to political and philosophical thinking is low in our population, and efforts to teach people some coherent, closely constructed view of social change are minimally supported and generally ineffective. While we would expect that such correlations as those above might be higher for certain segments of the population, say those highly educated *or* intensely interested in politics, we certainly cannot attribute an ideological logic to the bulk of our sample.

RANK EFFECTS ON POLITICAL ORIENTATIONS

The basic multidimensional model of rank effects on domestic liberalism is that majority racial–ethnic rank, followed by high occupation and income, all tend to produce conservatism (see Table 9.1). The effects hold in every city. In other words, government intervention in favor of the disadvantaged is favored, logically enough, by men presently disadvantaged—it is *current* life chances which affect these attitudes. Further, "current" ascribed rank has an even stronger effect than achieved rank. Minority men might logically be expected to be liberal on issues of prejudice and civil rights, but their handicaps also affect attitudes in the economic realm, making them more liberal than majority men of the same income, occupation, etc.

The aspects of social rank that are more closely associated with socialization or culture have notably weak and/or variable effects. Education, for example, has negative effects in three cities, but a positive effect in Indianapolis. Support for a negative education effect is therefore ambiguous. On the other hand, the data do more or less rule out a positive education effect, suggesting that education (controlling current achievement) does *not* exercise any liberalizing influence. The effects of the parental ranks are weaker and more variable than those of education. The aspect of ideology we have called domestic liberalism seems to respond more to immediate prospects of gratification or deprivation than it does to attitudes learned in a previous time or condition.

These effects, although among the strongest in our study, are still only moderate in absolute terms. Rank variables explain about 10% to 20% of the variance in domestic liberalism. The unexplained variation may be due to random responses on the part of politically uninterested respondents or due to other variables not included in this model, but it is clear that social rank falls far short of determining this aspect of liberalism.

Most socially-based political theory deals with a single vertical dimension of stratification. Therefore, our findings most applicable to past thought are the correlates of general rank (see the lower panel of Table 9.1). The results are predictable: *lower* general rank is associated with welfare liberalism in all cities. This single dimension of vertical rank represents rank effects on domestic liberalism moderately well, explaining substantially less than our seven-variable regression only in Indianapolis (where a substantial positive effect of education appears).

The most consistent and important effect on Democratic party identification, as on domestic liberalism, is minority racial–ethnic rank (see Table 9.2). Low occupational rank and low educational rank also predispose men to identify with the Democrats, but income has only weak and variable effects. Unlike domestic liberalism, party identification is affected by parental rank, in particular father's education and occupation. In general, the effects of these origin variables are not as strong as those of majority, occupation or education.

Rank is not as strongly related to party identification as it is to domestic liberalism; the variance explained is about 10% in all cities except Linton, where it drops to 3%. As in the previous analysis, general rank index effects

Table 9.1 Domestic Liberalism Regressed on Rank Variables

Rank variables	Regression coefficients: Unstandardized and standardized (in parentheses)					
	Indianapolis	Columbus	Linton	Phoenix	Yuma	Safford
Family income	-.010 (.15)*[a]	-.004 (.06)	-.004 (.08)	-.005 (.09)*	-.010 (.16)*	-.009 (.15)*
Occupation	-.027 (.19)*	-.014 (.12)*	-.014 (.11)	-.018 (.13)*	-.020 (.14)*	-.025 (.16)*
Education	.133 (.14)*	-.163 (.19)*	-.115 (.11)	b	-.092 (.10)	-.152 (.15)*
Father's education	-.056 (.06)		.072 (.06)		.095 (.10)*	
Father's occupation			-.024 (.14)*	.013 (.08)*		
Mother's education	-.117 (.09)	-.086 (.07)			-.089 (.09)	.098 (.09)
Majority	-2.575 (.24)*	--c	--c	-1.963 (.18)*	-1.192 (.15)*	-2.081 (.23)*
R^2	.19*	.12*	.09*	.08*	.16*	.19*
Mean	12.7	11.5	12.1	11.6	12.1	11.4
N	309	345	281	656	349	265
Proportion of the variance explained by						
General rank index	(-).11*[d]	(-).11*	(-).09*	(-).07*	(-).12*	(-).18*
17 variable regression	.21*	.14*	.12*	.12*	.20*	.22*

[a] In this and remaining tables in this chapter, asterisked regression coefficients are those with associated t-values of 1.65 or higher; hence, significant at approximately the .10 level (two-tailed test). Asterisked correlation coefficients are those significant at the .05 level.

b In this and remaining tables in this chapter, coefficients are not shown when the standardized path coefficient is both non-significant and less than .05, i.e., for zero or relatively weak effects.

c In this and remaining tables in this chapter, the majority racial-ethnic variable is omitted in the regressions in Columbus and Linton, since these samples contained almost no men of minority rank.

d The direction of the relationship with the general rank index is given in parentheses.

Table 9.2 (Democratic) Party Identification Regressed on Rank Variables

Regression coefficients: Unstandardized and standardized (in parentheses)

Rank variables	Indianapolis	Columbus	Linton	Phoenix	Yuma	Safford
Family income			-.003 (.09)	-.001 (.05)	-.002 (.05)	.001 (.05)
Occupation	-.013 (.19)*	-.007 (.09)	-.004 (.06)	-.010 (.13)*		
Education		-.099 (.20)*		-.047 (.09)*	-.048 (.10)	-.075 (.18)*
Father's education		-.045 (.08)	-.071 (.11)	-.045 (.09)*		-.039 (.08)
Father's occupation	-.005 (.07)	-.004 (.05)			-.009 (.11)*	-.005 (.05)
Mother's education				-.037 (.06)	-.046 (.08)	.043 (.09)
Majority	-.811 (.16)*	--	--	-.552 (.09)*	-.548 (.12)*	-1.137 (.26)*
R²	.10*	.11*	.03	.11*	.09*	.13*
Mean	2.28	1.89	2.65	2.15	2.64	2.82
N	318	349	287	670	367	296
Proportion of the variance explained by						
General rank index	(-).11*	(-).12*	(-).03*	(-).08*	(-).06*	(-).06*
17 variable regression	.16*	.14*	.06	.11*	.12*	.10*

are in the same direction in all cities. Except in Safford, general rank explains about as much as our seven-variable regression.

The diagram below allows a rough comparison of rank effects on liberal ideology and party identification.

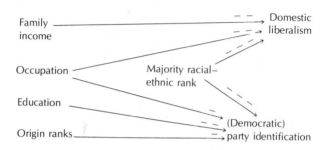

Both dependent variables are affected by racial–ethnic rank and by occupation, but liberal attitudes are also reduced by income, while Democratic party identification is reduced by high education and/or origin rank.

The differences in the two patterns of effects suggest that the immediacy of expected reward or deprivation is more relevant in forming political attitudes, while socialization and other longer-term implications of rank are more relevant to party identification. The effects we found of parental statuses on identification partly arise spuriously because the respondent's party depends partly upon his parents' party which in turn was related to the education and occupation of the father. Whether this is the entire source of these effects, or whether origin ranks have small continuing direct effects, the relevance of rank for political party identification has a much longer time dimension than its relevance for political ideology.

For both dependent variables, however, the processes are similar in that all effects have the same direction. High rank on one relevant dimension produces the same (negative) result as high rank on another. For this reason, our multidimensional models often did not improve explanation substantially over the unidimensional general rank index.

More than many other attitudes, political phenomena may be expected to reflect the up–down dimension of each rank system in the same way. Being systematically or chronically rewarded or deprived along any dimension is what defines class interest in relation to government policy, and what defines the embodiment of class interest in political parties. Which rank systems are salient in this kind of reward or deprivation at a given point in history, however, can only be seen by observing multidimensional effects.

The results described above represent the average picture of effects across the communities. In the main, this averaging seems justified, for the pattern of effects is fairly consistent from city to city. In Chapter 5 (Table 5.1), we found that the rank effects on domestic liberalism and party identification only differed enough across cities to add about two percent to the variance explained (and attain significance at the .25 level). The major exception to this picture of similarity is the effect of majority racial–ethnic rank, but only in the sense that it simply does not operate in Columbus and Linton because those cities have so few minority men. Only a few other city variations seem worth mentioning. Education has a *positive* effect on domestic liberalism in Indianapolis, in contrast to its generally negative effect. With respect to party identification, we find that the negative effects of occupation are mainly confined to Indiana cities, while the effects of education mainly occur in Arizona communities.

The strength of the effects also vary somewhat from city to city. This is most marked with respect to domestic liberalism—the R^2's vary from .08 to .19. Their pattern is puzzling: The variance explained by the rank variables rises with city size in Indiana and falls with city size in Arizona. However, city variations in the determination of party identification are much smaller. R^2's are .10 or a little more in all cities except Linton. Except for the varying effect of racial–ethnic majority, we can offer no explanation for the city differences either in the pattern or in the strength of the effects.

Thus the cities are more or less similar in the existence of a general process by which multidimensional rank affects domestic liberalism and another by which it affects party identification, and they are quite similar in the size of the effect on party identification. The strength of the rank effect on ideology is the same as that on party identification in some cities and substantially stronger in others.

What is the outcome of these processes in terms of electoral contests? Can these similarities and differences be explained by the patterns of partisan politics in these cities? Are some of the cities one-party towns in which real conflicts are prevented from adjudication at the polls?

Both presidential and off-year elections between 1956 and 1972 show evidence of vigorous and real party conflict in the counties containing these cities. (Since the counties include large populations not in the cities, these figures tell us more about the general local context of politics than about the particular political line-ups in the cities.) Only rarely did the percentage cast by the losing major party go below 30% and in a majority of the elections the loser's percentage was greater than 40%. Also in only one of the six cities (Phoenix) did the same party win all five of the presidential elections between 1956 and 1972.

The six cities include a fair spectrum of types of political context, though no Democratic bastion is represented. The Phoenix area is generally the most Republican. Indianapolis, Columbus and Safford are Republican, but less so. The counties containing Linton and Yuma have the most even contests. Thus the similarities among the processes relating rank to politics in the different cities cannot be explained by there being no real political contest in the cities selected or by the cities all representing a single type of political context.

A final step in this portion of the analysis is to introduce controls to find out if any of the rank effects we have observed are spurious. The control variables are age, religion, being born in the South (as an indicator of early training in Southern political thinking), urban versus rural origins, and the experience of being fully employed versus being retired or unemployed.[5] In order to simplify the analysis somewhat, father's education, the origin variable most reliably related to political orientations in the previous analyses, was retained as the only indicator of rank origin. Table 9.3 gives the net effects of rank variables on domestic liberalism, *after* controls have been imposed; Table 9.4 gives the same results for party identification.

The pattern of rank effects described above is only altered in detail by introducing these controls. No effect is completely spurious and most effects are substantially unchanged. Majority racial–ethnic rank continues to have the strongest effect on domestic liberal attitudes, although the effects are slightly reduced in the Arizona cities (see Table 9.3). The effect of high occupation in reducing liberalism is not changed by the controls. In five of the six cities, after controlling, occupation has more influence than family income, whose effects were reduced somewhat by introducing the controls. This reduction is probably due to the effect of full employment, since this is the only control variable correlated with family income to any extent. However, income still has a substantial negative effect on liberalism in four cities, net of the controls.

Introducing these same controls changes our notions of the rank effects on party identification (Table 9.4) in only one respect—the net effect of majority racial–ethnic rank is substantially reduced in the Arizona cities. Evidently part of the effect observed before was due to religion—Catholics tend to be both Mexican–American and Democratic in Arizona, and this spuriously inflated the effects of majority in the previous analysis. However, majority racial–ethnic rank still has a considerable effect even after controlling,

---

[5] In this analysis, age is scored in years. Religion is scored as Catholic versus Protestant versus persons of other religions or no preference, except that in Linton (where there are very few Catholics) the variable is defined as fundamentalist Protestant and Baptists versus other Protestants versus persons of other religions or no preference. In Safford, the division is between Catholics versus Mormons versus other Protestants. We measured experience in the South by the region of the respondent's birth, on the grounds that a man born in the South was likely to be raised by parents with a Southern point of view, whether he was actually raised in the South or not. Our size-of-place-of-origin variable was scored 2 for men growing up on a farm or in the country, 1 for those raised in a small town or small city, and 0 for those raised in or about a medium or large city. Full employment was scored 1 for those in this condition, and 0 for those (mostly retired, plus some unemployed) who were not.

Table 9.3 Rank Effects on Domestic Liberalism (Net of Control Variable Effects)

Rank variables	Regression coefficients: Unstandardized and standardized (in parentheses)[a]					
	Indianapolis	Columbus	Linton	Phoenix	Yuma	Safford
Family income	-.008 (.12)* reduced[b]	reduced	reduced	-.003 (.05) weaker	-.006 (.10)* weaker	-.009 (.15)* same
Occupation	-.037 (.26)* stronger	-.012 (.10) reduced	-.018 (.14)* increase	-.015 (.10)* reduced	-.021 (.15)* same	-.019 (.12) reduced
Education	.178 (.18)* increase	-.225 (.26)* stronger	-.171 (.16)* stronger	.049 (.05) increase	weaker	same
Father's education	-.102 (.11)* stronger	-.083 (.08) increase	same	same	weaker	-.105 (.10) weaker
Majority	-2.574 (.24)* same	--	--	-1.606 (.14)* reduced	-.963 (.12)* reduced	-1.800 (.19) reduced
R²	.22	.17	.11	.08	.18	.19

[a]These are the regression coefficients in an analysis employing the listed variables *plus* five control variables: age, religion, born in the South, size of place in which raised, and being fully employed. The coefficients thus reflect rank effects after these other variables have been controlled.

[b]Terms below the regression coefficients represent the way in which the effects changed as a result of introducing the controls (i.e., how these coefficients compare to those in Table 9.1). "Weaker" indicates a drop in beta of .05 or more. "Reduced" indicates a smaller drop. Similarly, "stronger" indicates a rise in beta of .05 or more, and "increase" means a smaller rise. "Same" indicates no change.

Table 9.4 Rank Effects on (Democratic) Party Identification (Net of Control Variable Effects)

Rank variables	Regression coefficients: Unstandardized and standardized (in parentheses)[a]					
	Indianapolis	Columbus	Linton	Phoenix	Yuma	Safford
Family income	same[b] same	same	-.003 (.09) same	-.002 (.07) increase	-.002 (.07) same	.002 (.08) increase
Occupation	-.012 (.08)* same	-.009 (.12)* increase	-.004 (.06) same	-.010 (.12)* same	same	.003 (.05) increase
Education	-.041 (.09) increase	-.127 (.25)* stronger	same	-.036 (.07) reduced	-.096 (.18)* stronger	-.069 (.16)* reduced
Father's education	same	-.042 (.07) same	-.070 (.10)* same	-.060 (.12)* increase	same	reduced
Majority	-.793 (.16)* same	--	--	-.296 (.05) reduced	-.320 (.07) weaker	-.907 (.20)* weaker
R^2	.16	.15	.05	.14	.14	.14

[a] These are the regression coefficients in an analysis employing the listed variables *plus* five control variables: age, religion, born in the South, size of place in which raised, and being fully employed. The coefficients thus reflect rank effects after these other variables have been controlled.

[b] Quantities below the regression coefficients represent the way in which the effects changed as a result of introducing the controls (i.e., how these coefficients compare to those in Table 9.2).

especially in Indianapolis and Safford. The introduction of controls altered the effects of occupation and education little, if at all.

On the whole, then, the rank effects on political ideology and identification we originally described do not appear to have been inflated or deflated much by the effects of these various control variables. The diagram of effects presented previously needs to be modified in only two ways: (a) The effect of income on liberalism is not as strong as indicated, and (b) the effect of majority on party identification is weaker than shown. But in both cases much of the original effect remains after controlling.

The variable of parents' party identification was, unfortunately, not included in our interview schedule. However, introducing it would probably not affect our account of rank effects very strongly. Parents' party identification has strong effects on the party identification of the son, but it is poorly related to the parents' social status. National sample data show that status of the family of origin explains only 2–3% of the variance in mother's and father's party identification (Knoke 1972). The correlations between race or current ranks and parents' identifications are even lower. This is consistent with the data for our respondents, for the party identifications which they will pass on to their children will also be only mildly related to the social rank of their children's parents. Hence, adding this control to the analysis would undoubtedly improve our predication of party identification, but it would change our estimates of rank effects little, if at all. At most, such a control would reduce the already unstable effects of origin rank still farther.

MEDIATING FACTORS: WHY DOES RANK AFFECT POLITICAL ORIENTATIONS?

Since the controls we introduced above failed to explain most of the effects of rank on political orientations, we provisionally conclude that these effects are genuine, if moderate. But the question still remains of how, or through which intermediary channels, rank affects political ideology and identification. Our intent in this section, then, is not to see if rank effects are spurious, but to identify important intervening variables.

The variables we introduce should therefore potentially be both caused by at least one form of social rank and should in turn potentially influence one of the forms of political orientation. We chose seven variables as possibly intervening in this way. They fall into three sets, the first of which consists of a single variable, our measure of general satisfaction (discussed above in Chapter 6). The rationale is that low rank may mean a variety of dissatisfactions based on deprivation (although this hypothesis was severely qualified by our findings in Chapter 6) and dissatisfaction in turn may lead men to favor governmental intervention in favor of poorer people and the political party more likely (on the national scene) to implement and encourage such intervention.

The second set of possible intervening variables is composed of subjective views of rank and the rank system, mainly from our analysis in Chapter 4. The first variable in this set is our index of legitimacy, indicating whether the respondent sees success in America as coming from legitimate sources (e.g., hard work) rather than nonlegitimate sources (e.g., "knowing the right people and pull"). Our hypothesis (once again severely qualified by the results in Chapter 4) is that low rank leads to views that success is nonlegitimate which in turn lead a man to favor "liberal" policies and parties.

The second subjective rank variable is Centers's question on class self-placement. The analysis in Chapter 4 showed that objective rank affects a man's perception of his place in the class system; we ask here if self-placement in turn affects political orientation. If so, two men with different objective ranks may have different subjective ranks and *for that reason* hold different political attitudes. Such effects would also imply that if two people of different objective rank for some reason had the same subjective rank, then their political orientations would not differ.

The third subjective variable is labeled *businessmen agree* in Tables 9.5 and 9.6. This scale measures whether the respondent sees different groups as lining up on different sides of questions like Medicare and Federal aid to education, and if so, which group he most resembles. The questions employed are those used in Chapter 4 to measure class dissensus, but a changed scoring method is used. A high score is given to a man who feels that businessmen would agree with his opinions on certain matters of public policy and workingmen would not; a low score is given to a man with the opposite set of perceptions, and a medium score to all others.[6]

Finally, we introduce a set of variables dealing with formal and informal social participation. The first of these quite simply measures the *amount* of formal participation by the number of associations the respondent belongs to. Perhaps centrality in communications reflected by this kind of participation affects political orientations. Second, we introduce union membership as a possible catalyst which provides the political education or propaganda necessary to forge a link between low rank and political orientation.[7] As

[6]For this analysis, the scoring was as follows:

Businessmen agree, but workingmen do not   2
Businessmen disagree, but workingmen agree   0
All other responses, including saying both agree or both disagree or answering "don't know" to one or both questions   1

For the total sample (all cities combined), the mean on this variable was .96 and the standard deviation .51.

[7]For an extended discussion of the rationale for this possible intervening mechanism, see Wilensky (1966b), especially pp. 23–26.

measured here, the variable refers not to simple membership, but to naming the union as one's most important association (or one's only association). Finally, we introduce the Duncan prestige score for the occupation of the respondent's first-named friend as an indicator of the rank position of the persons he associates with, since *level* of social participation may exercise some direct effect on political orientation.

To estimate the effects of these variables on political orientations and to see whether they mediate the effects of rank on political orientations, we ran the two regressions reported in Tables 9.5 and 9.6. In each, one of the political dependent variables was regressed on the five rank variables used above and the seven possible mediating variables. The three control variables found in the prior analyses to have the strongest effects on political orientations were also included, although coefficients for them are not reported in the table. These three variables are religion, being fully employed, and being born in the South. Therefore, all results discussed below are net of the effects of these factors.

In general, the effect of adding the seven possible mediators to the analysis was substantially to increase the explained variance in domestic liberalism, and somewhat to increase the variance explained in party identification, but (with one major exception) not to *explain* the effects of rank on political attitudes. Some of the introduced variables simply had no direct effect on political attitudes and hence were shown to be irrelevant.

Domestic Liberalism

The substantial improvement in the explanation of domestic liberalism can be seen in the proportions of explained variance (R^2) in Table 9.5 as compared to those in Table 9.3. These increase by one-third to two-thirds in five cities; R^2 doubles in one city. The proportion explained now ranges from 16% to 31%, still being lowest in Linton and Phoenix. This indicates that the role of the seven variables introduced is not entirely intervening. That is, substantial amounts of the variation they explain is *not* controlled by rank variables (something we knew from earlier chapters). If they were nothing but passages for the effects of rank, the R^2's would not have altered, but the regressions coefficients would have. This increase in the R^2 means that they also act on their own and/or as passages for the effects of other exogenous variables not explicitly included in this regression. Hence these variables may mediate the effects of rank, but they may also mute or obscure rank effects by their independent influence on political orientations.

The regression coefficients for the mediating variables (see the second panel of Table 9.5) indicate the *direct* effects of these variables on domestic liberalism. In general, satisfaction decreases liberalism, but the effects are both weak and irregular.

Table 9.5 Domestic Liberalism Regressed on Rank Variables and Intervening Variables (Net of Control Variable Effects)

Rank and intervening variables	Regression coefficients: Unstandardized and standardized (in parentheses)[a]					
	Indianapolis	Columbus	Linton	Phoenix	Yuma	Safford
Family income	weaker[b]	same	same	weaker	-.011 (.17)* stronger	-.012 (.20)* stronger
Occupation	weaker	-.008 (.07) reduced	-.019 (.15)* same	-.013 (.09)* same	-.018 (.13)* reduced	-.030 (.20)* stronger
Education	.149 (.15)* reduced	-.188 (.21)* weaker	-.119 (.12) reduced	.068 (.07) increase	same	.123 (.14) stronger
Father's education	-.127 (.13)* increase	weaker	.114 (.10) stronger	same	same	-.145 (.14)* increase
Majority	-2.935 (.26)* increase	---	---	-1.179 (.10)* reduced	-1.120 (.13)* same	-1.089 (.11) weaker
General satisfaction	-.081 (.07)	-.107 (.10)*	.054 (.05)			-.059 (.05)
Legitimacy	-.530 (.09)	.224 (.05)		-.338 (.06)		-.723 (.13)*
Self-placement	-.221 (.08)	.169 (.07)	-.305 (.14)*			-.130 (.05)
Businessmen agree	-1.382 (.22)*	-1.245 (.21)*	-1.120 (.14)*	-1.772 (.28)*	-1.695 (.24)*	-1.860 (.26)*
Number of association memberships	-.120 (.08)	-.156 (.10)		.185 (.08)*	.117 (.06)	.138 (.06)
Union membership	1.013 (.10)	-1.286 (.10)*	-.584 (.08)		1.188 (.14)*	.913 (.07)
First friend's job		-.016 (.12)*			.010 (.08)	
R^2	.30	.23	.16	.16	.24	.31
N^c	237	254	207	527	288	215

[a] These are the regression coefficients in an analysis employing the listed variables plus three control variables: religion, being fully employed, and born in the South. The coefficients thus reflect effects after these three variables have been controlled.

[b] Quantities below the coefficients represent the way in which effects changed as a result of introducing the intervening variables (i.e., compared to effects in Table 9.3).

[c] The number of cases is lower than in Table 9.1 mainly because of missing data on first friend's job.

The first two variables in the subjective set, legitimacy and class self-placement, have similarily weak and irregular negative effects. In contrast, the effects of businessmen agree are consistent across cities and relatively strong. Men who say that businessmen agree and workingmen disagree with their policy views are much less likely to have liberal attitudes in all six cities.

Although this is one of our strongest "effects, "the causal interpretation is not clear. The variable may reflect an awareness of conflicting groups in society which leads men to subscribe to the ideology associated with the group they align themselves with. But another obvious interpretation posits the opposite causal order: Men with liberal opinions, for example, are simply likely to be aware that most businessmen disagree with them. They may just be reporting accurate perceptions of agreement, based on the mass media, experience in political discussions with men of similar or different rank, etc.

For data that are highly comparable to these in many respects, see Guest (1974), who found a very similar "status awareness" effect. Interpreting his data and ours at the same time, objective rank has an effect on political attitudes, some small part of which is mediated by self-placement. Self-placement additionally has a smaller, independent effect, generally in the same direction. Status awareness, and especially "businessman, anti-worker" class awareness, though not strongly related to objective rank, has a substantial and independent effect in reducing domestic liberalism. Guest's measure of status awareness, however, is not subject to the simple reversed explanation that weakens our interpretation of the businessmen agree effect. It is possible, of course, that people feel membership in a class *because* they hold attitudes attributed to it, but this is not the simple matter of perceiving who does or does not agree on political matters.

These data appear to support partially Centers' (1949) original contention that identification with a social class, more than objective class membership, is a cause of certain political attitudes, but the data call for two qualifications. First, Centers' own measure of identification can more profitably be interpreted as self-placement: an opinion as to where one stands, *not* a feeling of shared destiny with a social category. Second, objective rank and subjective class identification *both* affect political attitudes, and the effects are independent.

The three social participation variables showed effects that were so weak and that fluctuated so much in direction from city to city that no clear case for their influence on domestic liberalism can be made. With rank variables (and controls) held constant, the number of associational memberships affects political ideology, but the effects are negative in the Indiana cities and positive in the Arizona cities. Thus formal participation cannot explain rank effects which are generally in the same direction in all cities. While the effect of formal association on political *participation* was positive in all six cities (see Chapter 8), its significance for ideology differs by local context (for reasons we cannot guess). The effect of union membership also fluctuates (although not regularly by region or city size) and the prestige of friend's job has no perceptible effect in most cities.

But do these satisfaction and subjective rank variables act as mediating variables and so explain why rank affects ideology? Mostly not. In the first place, of the four added variables with at least moderately stable effects on ideology, only class self-placement is solidly related to objective rank. As Chapters 4 and 6 showed, legitimacy and general satisfaction are only weakly related to the rank dimensions. Nor, surprisingly, is the businessmen agree variable related to objective rank—its zero-order correlations with various rank variables were almost always less than .20 in the various cities. Hence, the only variable that could mediate is class self-placement, and its direct effect on domestic liberalism is not very strong or regular.

We can also attack this question by comparing the standardized regression coefficients for the rank variables in Tables 9.3 and 9.5. These rank coefficients represent direct effects, so if one of them is less in Table 9.5 than in Table 9.3, it suggests that part or all of the effect of that rank variable is indirect via one or more of the mediating variables introduced in Table 9.5. As Table 9.5 shows, however, there were no patterns of regular increase or decrease in these beta's across cities. For example, introducing the mediating variables wiped out the effect of income in Indianapolis but strengthened the same effect in Safford.

The effects of occupation in Table 9.5 are only a little weakened, on the average, by the newly introduced variables. Majority racial–ethnic rank has reduced effects in two of the Arizona cities, but continues even in those cities to substantially reduce liberalism. The effects of income, quite regular in Table 9.1, have by now disappeared in four of the six cities, but it is not clear why. Different processes may be operating in different cities. For example, the drop in the coefficient for income in Indianapolis could be due to the role of class self-placement, since this variable has a direct negative effect on domestic liberalism in that city, but this cannot be the explanation for the reduction of the income coefficient in Phoenix, since class self-placement does not affect domestic liberalism there.

Our conclusion, then, is that some of the seven additional variables do add significantly to the explanation of domestic liberalism, but that none of the new variables (with the possible exception of class self-placement) seems to be an important mediator between rank and political ideology. We can put our final, if tentative, conclusions about these rank effects on domestic liberalism in the form of a graph, including "?'s" by those effects which are somewhat irregular across cities:

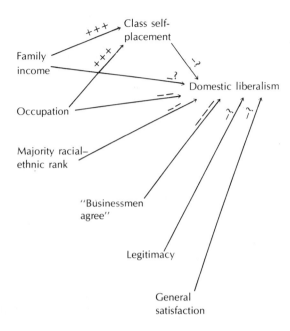

(Democratic) Party Identification

Introducing the seven additional possible mediating variables improves the prediction of party identification substantially, although less than for domestic liberalism. Proportions explained now range from 8% to 27% (see Table 9.6). Increases over the previous amount explained (in Table 9.4) are generally about 5 percentage points, although in Safford the additional explanation is 13 points. Here again, these increases mean that the additional variables serve not simply as intervening variables for the effects of social rank, but also as independent influences in and of themselves.

Four of the seven added variables seem to have direct effects on party identification and thus qualify as potential intervening variables, but they are not the same four as affected domestic liberalism. General satisfaction appears to be negatively associated with Democratic identification, although the effect disappears in the small towns. Of the variables reflecting subjective perceptions of status, only the businessman agree variable affects party identification, and as before these effects are quite strong and consistent, but raise questions about causal direction. Thinking that businessmen agree with one on policy issues (and that working men do not) either makes one more likely to identify with the Republicans, or Republicans are more likely to perceive this particular pattern of agreement and disagreement, or both.

Guest's (1974) findings, not subject to this problem, are again parallel,

Table 9.6 (Democratic) Party Identification Regressed on Rank Variables and Intervening Variables (Net of Control Variable Effects)

Rank and intervening variables	Regression coefficients: Unstandardized and standardized (in parentheses)[a]					
	Indianapolis	Columbus	Linton	Phoenix	Yuma	Safford
Family income	.002 (.06) increase[b]	.002 (.07) increase	-.002 (.08) same	reduced	-.003 (.09) increase	.003 (.08) same
Occupation	weaker	weaker	reduced	-.005 (.06) weaker	same	reduced
Education	-.037 (.08) same	-.103 (.19)* weaker	same	-.038 (.07) same	-.120 (.21)* increase	-.067 (.15)* same
Father's education	same	-.039 (.06) same	weaker	-.057 (.11)* same	-.028 (.06) increase	-.044 (.09) stronger
Majority	-1.030 (.19)* increase	--	--	reduced	-.404 (.08) increase	-.492 (.10) weaker
General Satisfaction	-.039 (.07)	-.072 (.12)*		-.038 (.07)	-.032 (.06)	
Legitimacy	.164 (.06)	-.110 (.08)				-.350 (.13)*
Self-placement						-.178 (.14)*
Businessmen agree	-.476 (.16)*	-.417 (.12)*	-.363 (.08)	-.717 (.21)*	-.482 (.13)*	-1.105 (.31)*
Number of association memberships	-.063 (.08)	-.066 (.07)				.111 (.10)
Union membership	.539 (.11)*		.654 (.16)*	.316 (.06)	.366 (.08)	-.374 (.06)
First friend's job	-.009 (.12)*	-.009 (.12)	-.004 (.06)	-.007 (.08)*	.007 (.10)	
R^2	.23	.19	.08	.20	.18	.27
N^c	240	258	206	526	295	237

[a] These are the regression coefficients in an analysis employing the listed variables plus three control variables: religion, being fully employed, and born in the South. The coefficients thus reflect effects after these three variables have been controlled.

Quantities below the coefficients represent the way in which effects changed as a result of introducing the intervening variables (i.e., compared to effects in Table 9.4).

[b]

[c] The number of cases is lower than in Table 9.2 mainly because of missing data on first friend's job.

except that he investigated Democratic voting rather than party identification. As in the case of domestic liberalism, Democratic identification (or voting) was relatively strongly affected by class awareness, which did not simply carry the effect of rank.

In contrast to the effects on domestic liberalism, party identification is affected by the social participation variables: Union membership is associated with Democratic identification, while claiming a friend of high occupation produces Republican identification, net of one's own occupational standing. These influences testify that party identification is partly structured by the nature of the groups and friends with which a man is involved.

Do these four variables act to transfer the effects of rank onto party identification? We can rule out two of them for this role immediately. General satisfaction is only weakly related to rank, as Chapter 6 showed, and, as we said above, the zero order correlations between businessman agree and the rank dimensions are so low as to argue that this attitude, too, is relatively unaffected by rank and hence cannot mediate the effects of rank. On the other hand, the occupation of the first-named friend and union membership are both, predictably enough, consistently related to the respondent's occupation, although these correlations are moderate at best.

We must conclude, therefore, that part of the effects of occupation on party identification occur because men of high occupation are less likely to be union members and more likely to have friends with "good" jobs, and both of these attributes in turn reduce the likelihood of Democratic identification. As Table 9.6 shows, introducing these variables practically erases the direct effects of occupation, suggesting that *all* or nearly all of its effects on party identification are mediated by these two variables.

The standardized regression coefficients for the other rank variables do not seem to have been consistently affected by introducing the mediating variables. Education continues to have a substantial net direct effect in depressing Democratic identification, and father's education continues to have a moderate negative effect. Minority men are still generally more likely to identify themselves as Democrats. This effect remains strong in Indianapolis, where minority men are nearly all black, but has been reduced somewhat in two of the Arizona cities. Our conclusions from this analysis can be summarized graphically as follows:

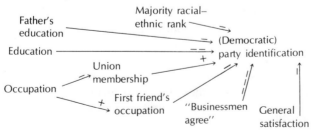

SUMMARY AND CONCLUSIONS

The analyses in this chapter aimed at estimating the effects of various dimensions of social rank on two types of political orientation, domestic liberalism (favoring Federal intervention in favor of the disadvantaged) and identification with the Democratic party. The major findings are:

1. Neither domestic liberalism nor identification as a Democrat is part of any broad attitude of favoring or opposing social change in general. These two political orientations are essentially unrelated to attitudes toward several types of apolitical change and, indeed, are only moderately related to each other.

2. Low occupational rank and minority racial–ethnic rank have the main direct effects in promoting domestic liberalism. These two effects are net of each other, of other rank variables and of controls for various nonrank variables (such as age, religion, and being born in the South). Family income may also have a direct negative effect on domestic liberalism. These effects are summarized in graphic form earlier in this chapter. Education and origin ranks have only weak and/or unstable effects on domestic liberalism, suggesting that current rank status is more important for this dimension of ideology than previously learned attitudes.

3. Rank variables explain only 10% to 20% of the variance in domestic liberalism.

4. A small part of the effects of occupation and income on liberalism may be mediated by the respondent's self-placement in a class. With this one partial exception, the variables we introduced as possible mediators failed to pan out, being either unrelated to rank or to liberalism, or both. The effects of occupation and racial–ethnic rank therefore remain substantially uninterpreted. These effects are not explained by the intervening effects of satisfaction, subjective views of stratification (except for a weak mediating effect of class self-placement), or levels or types of social participation.

5. Democratic party identification is directly increased by minority racial–ethnic rank, by a low status origin (indexed by father's education), and, most strongly, by lower education. These are all direct effects. Occupation has a substantial mediated effect on party identification. These effects (which are net of each other and of control variables) are presented in graphic form earlier in this chapter.

6. Rank variables explain only about 10% of the variance in party identification.

7. In analyzing mediating variables, we had some limited success. Men of high occupation tend not to belong to unions and tend to have friends of high occupation; both of these factors tend to make such a man more Republican, and all of the effect of occupation on party identification

seems to work through these two factors. All other effects, of education, father's education and racial–ethnic rank, appear to be direct and cannot be interpreted by the three types of intervening variables we introduced.

Can this pattern of findings be taken as evidence that political orientations are organized by considerations of class interest? To begin with, the directions of the effects bear out this interpretation. *All* of the effects which are of some size and stable from city to city are negative in direction—men of high rank on various dimensions are less likely to approve federal intervention in favor of the disadvantaged and are less likely to identify with the party commonly thought of as the "party of the common man."

But when we attempt to apply this general interpretation to the specific patterns of rank effects, some qualifications and complexities intrude themselves. As a main example, a class interest argument might plausibly imply that income would be a major predictor of political orientations, but its effects turned out to be unstable and not as strong of those of other rank variables. Hence, our results provide little support for any "embourgeoisement thesis"; by our analysis, higher income for working men has only moderate effects at best upon their political attitudes and less, if any, on their choice of political party.

The effects of racial–ethnic rank, on the other hand, can clearly be interpreted in terms of interests. In the middle part of this century, and especially in the few years preceding our survey, blacks and other minorities could see that relief from their handicaps was best available from the federal government directly, fueled by policies of the Democratic party at the national level. Hence, attitudes favoring domestic liberalism and the Democratic party made the most practical kind of sense for men in this position. This would be especially true for blacks, which matches our finding that the effect of the majority variable was strongest in Indianapolis, where the minority men were predominately black.

The negative effects of occupation on domestic liberalism and (indirectly) on identification with the Democrats can also be interpreted from a class-interest point of view: men with lower-ranked jobs feel they would be best served by an active federal government run by the Democrats. This effect is net of other ranks, however, so it is not traceable to the lower incomes of these jobs. One plausible guess is that the interest involved concerns security more than income. The possibilities of layoffs and shutdowns are more salient for men in lower ranked jobs. This provides a direct reason for such men to rate high on our domestic liberalism scale, which included two questions explicitly on job security and other questions involving guarantees of a certain level of services to all citizens. Evidently being in such an occupational position is enough to directly produce agreement with such attitudes—the effects are not mediated by other variables we introduced. However, social influence is evidently necessary to bring men in lower jobs to identify with the Democrats; these jobs only produced such an inclination when the man was a union member and/or had friend(s) of similarly low occupational rank.

The association between social rank and political behavior is not simple and straightforward, however, and cannot wholly be covered by a class interest explanation. Consider the negative effects of education on Democratic identification. In many ways, men of high education (net of their other standings) cannot be said to possess an interest either way in government intervention or a rational connection to either political party. It is hard to see what they as a group would stand to gain or lose if the Republicans came to power with a definite program of self-help and government limitation. And indeed, we find that education has no stable effect on domestic liberalism. But added years of education do make a man more likely to think of himself as a Republican. This effect is net of other current and origin ranks, and does not appear to be mediated by any of the intervening variables we introduced.

It does appear that political attitudes of the domestic liberalism sort are more directly affected by one's current status struggles, so that attitudes grow directly and unmediated out of experience. On the other hand, party identification is not affected by income, is affected by occcupation only via social relationships, is affected by education perhaps via socialization into subcultural political stances, and is affected by origin possibly as a proxy for the inheritance of party identification from parents. These facts suggest that identification with a concrete political organization is more a matter of social influence and cultural transmission and less a direct response to current experience. Party identification appears to be taught and supported by social contacts much more than domestic liberalism.

The translation of objective rank into political orientations does not appear to depend very much upon men forming accurate perceptions of their rank position. A man's inclination to place himself in a particular class certainly depends somewhat upon his rank, as Chapter 4 showed, but this perception in turn has only weak and irregular effects on political ideology and no stable effects at all on party identification. Viewing the system of success attainment as nonlegitimate also leads to small increases in domestic liberalism, but this perception does not act to mediate rank effects either.

One form of perception, that which sees the community as divided into opposing camps of businessmen and workers who disagree on public policy, and place themselves in one of these camps, *is* closely associated with ideology and party identification. Men who feel that businessmen would agree with their policy attitudes while workingmen would not are much more likely to be nonliberal and Republican. However, this perception is so poorly related to objective rank that it does not mediate any of the rank effects, and its effects on political attitudes and party identification are in addition to (and independent of) the rank effects.

Finally, a class interpretation of political orientations must be qualified by considering the extent of status polarization, or the extent to which people of different status levels line up in opposing political stances. In any sense of the term, polarization seems limited in our samples, for two reasons. First of all, most of the variance in ideology and identification is not controlled by social rank; many other kinds of personal attributes evidently also affect these orientations. While the forms of social rank are more strongly related to domestic liberalism than to party identification, even for liberalism the variance explained by rank is usually one-fifth or less. This means that the attitudes of "middle-class" people must overlap substantially with those of "working-class" people.

Secondly, both ideology and identification are affected by several rank dimensions independently rather than by just one type of rank such as income or occupation. Further, these rank dimensions are themselves only moderately associated, as we saw in Chapters 2 and 3. These high levels of mobility and inconsistency also militate against status polarization, because they mean that a great many people have different levels on different rank dimensions, giving each of them some reasons for "liberalism" and some for "conservatism." Furthermore, and more importantly, this situation means that the groups in the population who differ on income are not the same as those defined by occupation and both differ from the groups defined by educational levels. Thus superiority (or inferiority) of a given kind is not socially reinforced by other kinds. These cross-cutting differences make it harder for political groups to polarize about social class differences.

The hypothesis implicitly stated above is that when several forms of rank independently affect political orientations, political groups based on class interests are more likely when two conditions are *both* met: Rank must affect political orientations strongly, and the different forms of rank must be so highly correlated that most people will have stable and consistent profiles of rank. Neither condition appears to be met in the communities we studied.

10

ANOMIA

Norms play an important part in integrating community life. At some level, the members of the community must agree on a common set of norms, use them to control their own behavior, and rely on them to regulate the behavior of others. Such an integration through the norms distinguishes people bound up in a communal life from a simple ecology in which segments of a population compete for the resources of a common environment.

Anomia, as we will use it here, is a situation in which an individual does not perceive a system of norms that he can use to guide his own behavior or rely on to guide the behavior of others. Anomia is therefore a form of alienation that questions the very basis of social organization.

Anomia has many possible sources, including rapid social change that outmodes a former system of norms, great heterogeneity in the society, and inadequate methods for effectively socializing new members of the society. Our major concern in this chapter, however, is whether levels of anomia are systematically affected by levels of social rank, and, if so, how these effects occur and with what consequences for community organization.

ANOMIA, SOCIAL RANK, AND COMMUNITY INTEGRATION

By *anomia*, we do not mean simply a personal alienation in response to punishing life circumstances, as most often measured by sociologists (e.g., by the attitude scale introduced by Srole 1956). Rather, the empirical measure used here is intended to tap one component of a multidimensional attitude domain (Seeman 1959; Dean 1961), namely one that is sometimes called *normlessness* to distinguish it from other components (for a summary of the complex and voluminous literature on alienation studies and the nature of different components, including normlessness, see Seeman 1975). The specific definition of what we call anomia is given below in the section on measuring anomia.

In order to compare the results of various studies of anomia or alienation, it is wise to rely on the operational definitions, because the terminology in this domain is quite confusing. For example, *anomie* is often used to refer to alienation in general, to Durkheim's (1897) usage (whatever that means empirically), to some operational definition of Merton's (1957) means–ends schema, to the Srole (1956) scale, or to a normlessness component of the domain, as in the present instance. Terminological inconsistencies are not limited to the use of the generic term, but extend to the components of alienation, and even to presumed causes, effects or correlates of variables within the domain. In the most recent study to which our results can be compared, for example (Otto and Featherman 1975), the components measured are *powerlessness* and *self-estrangement,* but an examination of the questions asked suggests that self-estrangement in the Otto and Featherman study is almost the same thing as general satisfaction in our study. Moreover, all investigators in this area (no matter what their operational definitions) are theoretically interested in alienation in general, as well as in its special forms.

Among the special forms, normlessness is of particular interest in the attempt to trace the causal patterns by which individuals react to their own social ranks. It is easy to see how underreward might lead individuals directly to pessimism, self-estrangement, feelings of powerlessness, or general alienation from society, but disbelief in the normative system is an additional link in the causal chain from social rank to behaviors associated with rank through individual attitudes.

This variety of anomia is also a potential theoretic link between individual characteristics and the operation of social stratification at the societal level. There is no universal law relating individual rank to alienation; the relationship itself varies from one society to another (Form 1975). The extent to which attachment to the normative system depends on rank is a societal characteristic affecting the way in which activities can be organized in the society. For example, a society in which high ranking members trust the norms but low ranking members do not is one in which both social integration and social control must operate very differently at the bottom of the structure than they do at the top.

Why should anomia be related to rank at the individual level? In general form, the simplest argument is that low rank alienates people and that one form this alienation takes is anomia, the failure to perceive and rely on a system of norms.[1] But we must specify more exactly what is involved in this

[1]Following Durkheim (1951:246–254), some writers use anomia in the sense of limitless

general argument. We will briefly summarize here several ways in which social inferiority might produce anomia. Each of these points will then be spelled out in more detail as evidence for (or against) it is presented in the analysis section below.

An initial, and straightforward, possibility is that low rank punishes and deprives the person in various concrete and objective respects, and this deprivation in turn leads to anomia and other forms of alienation. Conversely, the rewards that accompany high social rank give the person a stake in the social system of the community, one form of which is a greater commitment to the system of norms. This point of view supposes that the effect of social rank on anomia is mediated by experiences of objective reward or deprivation.

But low rank might also produce anomia by affecting the person's social relationships. In the first place, low rank might isolate people and reduce their levels of informal or formal social participation. This means the person would have fewer chances to trade information with other people or be involved in relationships of mutual interdependence and trust, thereby producing higher levels of anomia. An alternative role of social relations turns on the degree of homogany (see Simpson and Miller 1963). If anomia, for one of the reasons mentioned above or to be mentioned below, is more endemic among lower class people, then persons in frequent contact with people of low rank would be more likely to observe anomic behavior around them or to directly "catch" this attitude about social life. If friendship and other forms of contact are mainly status-bound, so that men of low rank are mainly in contact with people of equally low rank, this would strengthen the tendency for anomia to be negatively associated with rank.

In addition, low rank may lead to anomia because low rank is defined as failure to meet the person's own goals of success. For instance, a person's feeling of being unsuccessful and/or his feeling that he did not get a fair chance to succeed may lead him to place less reliance in an evenhanded normative system. But feelings of legitimacy may also be involved—failure might lead one to conclude that rewards are not distributed fairly in the community at large, and that much success is gained by nonlegitimate means. This lack of faith in the norms of attainment, this feeling that success is often obtained by cheats and scoundrels, could be naturally extended to norms in general and thus produce high levels of anomia. On the other hand, if one thinks that rewards are, in general, handed out by fair proce-

---

desires (the person's belief system places no limit on what it is reasonable to want). This situation presumably arises at times of rapid improvements in prosperity or at least with respect to individuals who experience a rapid rise in success. This would imply a positive relationship between rank and this form of anomia. Prosperity in the 1960s did not have this "boom" character, nor do we have many cases of rapid and radical upward mobility, hence anomia is unlikely to be positively related to rank in our data. Also, our scale measures anomia more in the sense of normlessness than goallessness.

dures to deserving people, he may retain his faith in the normative system even if he himself experiences failure.

Of course, this process at the individual level is strongly affected by the belief systems in the society at large. For example, Merton (1957) has argued that men are socialized more or less universally in success goals, while legitimate means for attaining success are less avilable to men from low rank origins. This implies that the relationship between rank and anomia would be reduced if either legitimate opportunities were equally available or if beliefs about what it is reasonable to want were adjusted to circumstances, so those less likely to succeed could adopt more realistic goals.

Of course, anomia can also be reduced by other belief systems that offer an explanation for reality and a firm guide to behavior. Religious beliefs would be one example, especially if most people in the community were also believers, so a person could count on such beliefs to regulate the behavior of others. Such alternate systems can include beliefs about stratification, either norms of legitimacy (success is a sign of divine grace) or alternative goals (salvation has far more significance than mere worldly goods).[2] If these alternate belief systems are found more often in the lower classes, the relationship between rank and anomia should be reduced.

The extent of the relationship between personal rank and personal anomia has crucial implications for the integration of the community. Inequality is clearly present in the social structure of the six communities studied here, meaning that losing is logically part of the structure of the game. Therefore, personal alienation because of low rank is potentially a serious problem to be met by the social organization of these communities.

If men of low rank are anomic, and if sociological theory on anomia is correct, then important consequences for the community follow. Men in the lower classes would then have less trust in their fellow men and the social institutions of the community, they would participate less and be less committed to civic and associational life, and they would be more likely to engage in various sorts of deviant behavior. Hence the relationship between anomia and rank has implications for the integration of the community, whatever the specific reasons underlying that relationship. The extent to

[2]The relevant set of norms need not be those related to the legitimacy of the stratification system per se. It could be religion (in even a nontheocratic society), as described by Weber: The concept of the calling motivated men to carry out their daily work in spite of the possible illegitimacy of the system around them. It could be collective purpose: In World War II, for example, millions of men took orders from officers they regarded as inferior, in order to win the war. It could be philosophical humanism, in which the exigencies of social life demand some subordination to social principle. It could be ethnic solidarity, in which identification with a group is a justifying principle. It could be the extension of personal charisma, in which a deed is good if it is done in the name of the prophet. All of these, and numberless others, imply some normative system which can be used for justification, for evaluation and for the assignment of meaning to human rank relations. While they differ widely, they will provide a conceptual and moral order.

which men of low rank are more anomic than men of high rank is an important facet of the community's social life.

If we take a multidimensional perspective on stratification, thinking in terms of social rank on several different dimensions instead of (as in the above discussion) low or high rank in general, several implications follow for our study of anomia. For example, we are led by a multidimensional view to ask which forms of rank are most highly related to anomia. If only one or two of the rank dimensions are related to anomia and others are not, the nature of the related rank dimensions may offer some clues about why low rank causes anomia. For example, if occupation and income were the most important determinants of anomia, it would suggest that the man's definition of his success is a crucial factor in the process. However, if other dimensions have a stronger net effect, the above arguments in terms of success would be weakened.

We also know, from Chapters 2 and 3, that the rank dimensions are not highly related to one another. Hence, a man's rank on one dimension does not totally determine his opportunity for high or low rank on another. This implies that many or most people will have medium scores on anomia, because few people will have the uniformly high or low ranks that would produce a low or high anomia score. Most people will be inclined toward anomia because of low rank on one dimension but this will be offset by higher rank on a second dimension. However, if only one of the rank dimensions actually produces anomia, the high levels of status inconsistency will not affect the distribution of anomia in the community. In this case, we would expect a greater dispersion in anomia scores and a greater concentration of high anomia scores among men low on the particular salient rank dimension.

Let us now give a quick preview of the questions to be addressed in this chapter. A major, consistent finding from past research is that anomia scores are higher for people of successively lower social status. Our first object is to see whether this same result appears in our data. Then we wish to extend this rather simple result by asking in addition which particular forms of social rank are most related to anomia and whether these effects continue to hold when certain control variables are introduced. We also wish to get a more precise notion of the strength of the relationship between social rank and anomia than has been afforded by most previous studies. Assuming that some forms of rank do indeed produce anomia, we will then ask why rank should have this effect. By trying a succession of intervening variables suggested by some of the above discussions, we can hopefully discover which ones do indeed mediate the rank–anomia relationship. Finally, we will have questions about the effects of the community context on this process. We will ask whether the level of anomia is different in different communities and whether social rank affects anomia in different fashions within different cities.

The discussion below, therefore, begins by describing how we measured anomia, then relates rank dimensions to anomia within the six cities, and then adds a number of possible intervening variables to try to explain the effects of rank.

MEASURING ANOMIA

We tried to design our index to measure anomia as closely as possible, independently of other forms of alienation. We built the index from the following items, most of which have appeared in previous research studies.

1. There are so many ideas about what is right and wrong these days that it is hard to figure out how to live your own life.
2. The trouble with the world today is that most people don't really believe in anything.
3. Everything is relative and there are no definite rules to live by.
4. These days a person doesn't really know who he can count on.
5. The world is a jungle and if you want something you have to fight for it.
6. In spite of all the terrible things that happen these days, most Americans have very clear ideas of right and wrong and live by them.
7. The world is so complicated these days and things are changing so fast that it's hard to understand what's really going on.
8. Most people today live lives that do not have any real meaning.

The respondents answered by choosing from a set of fixed responses ranging from "Strongly agree" to "Neither" to "Strongly disagree." These responses were scored and combined into a numerical index ranging from 0 (low anomia) to 32 (high anomia).[3]

The items refer to normative characteristics of "the world," "most Americans," or "most people" in general, and to the respondent's feeling that he can place himself in that world. The items deal with the potential for order in the respondent's social world: order as established by clear beliefs, by trust in others, and by well-understood and widely shared normative standards for behavior. Whether the respondent feels he can use the normative order as a basis for cognitively organizing the world around him, or for establishing standards for evaluation, is picked up by phrases such as "hard to figure out," "hard to understand," and "(no) real meaning." More importantly, most of the items ask the respondent whether norms are available that either guide his own behavior or which he can rely on to guide the behavior of

[3]The possible responses to each item (strongly agree, agree, neither, disagree and strongly disagree) were assigned scores of 4, 3, 2, 1, and 0, respectively (except that for item 6, in which agree means low anomia, the scores were reversed). The anomia index score for each person was then simply calculated by adding up his eight scores on the individual questions. Hence a high score reflects high anomia.

others. In short, this set of items indicates *whether the person sees around him a reliable normative and belief system which makes social life both possible and understandable.*[4] Among the various types of personal alienation, such as those analyzed by Seeman (1959), what we have tried to measure here is closest to normlessness, but also includes some *meaninglessness,* in the sense of being unclear about beliefs involving moral standards (see Seeman 1959:786).

Certain items that might be considered to be part of the anomia domain were deliberately left out, both to obtain a more conceptually pure measure and to make our results easier to interpret and less open to the charge of tautology. For these reasons, we rejected possible items that might simply reflect the deprivation inherent in low rank. We also omitted items dealing with legitimacy, or the norms of success attainment, so that any relationship between this scale and our scale of legitimacy would not be confounded or tautological. What this index as a representation of anomia *underemphasizes,* then, is specifically the feeling of deprivation allied to low reward allocated unfairly by an alien "system." If such items *were* included in the index, any anomia–rank relationship could be suspected of tautology, but since they are not, this aspect of the theory of anomia can receive a strong test.

Another aspect of the feeling of anomia that was not directly included in our measurement is pessimistic future-orientation. Adequate moral order provides confidence in one's ability to deal with tomorrow at least as well as today has been dealt with. The anomic person cannot be surprised by what terrible thing could happen tomorrow, because he sees no moral stability. This is indirectly implied in the items of our index, in that each item refers to something which *might* ensure stability, if it existed. Taking the index literally, then, we have not identified anomic people by their lack of faith in what lies in store, but by their failure to see a moral order that might provide that faith.

Our claim that this index does indeed measure anomia is based substantially on the manifest content of the items. That is, we rely heavily upon face validity, since we think the items add up to the theoretically interpretable dimension outlined above. Without such theoretical coherence, the most statistically reliable scale is relatively useless, in our view.

However, we can also present some statistical evidence for the unity of these items. Although the 28 intercorrelations of the items are rather low, mainly .20 and below, all but two are in the proper direction. Further

---

[4]This conclusion may appear to be overintellectualizing our respondents. We do not mean to say that our respondents consciously employ such a global concept as the one we ascribe to this index. The attitude being tapped here is probably not a conscious part of the respondent's thinking apparatus, but it should strongly affect his reaction to others and the way he chooses to play his roles in society.

evidence comes from a factor analysis of 38 items using the data (including female respondents) from Indianapolis (Sterling 1973). On both orthogonal and oblique rotations, our eight anomia items loaded on the same factor, with only small loadings on other factors. Also, only one or two other items loaded on this factor. All loadings were positive, except for the one reversed item. Since the original 38 items in this analysis included a great variety of attitudinal questions, the emergence of these 8 items as a coherent cluster helps to support our use of them in a single index.

The most commonly used measure of anomia is Srole's scale (1956), which has produced remarkably regular results in different research settings. It is a scale of 5 items:

1. There's little use writing to public officials because often they aren't interested in the problems of the average man.
2. Nowadays a person has to live pretty much for today and let tomorrow take care of itself.
3. In spite of what some people say, the lot of the average man is getting worse, not better.
4. It's hardly fair to bring children into the world with the way things look for the future.
5. These days a person doesn't really know whom he can count on.

Since most of what is empirically known about anomia is based on application of this scale, it behooves us to come to terms with it.

Srole sees the scale as tapping the "individual's generalized, pervasive sense of 'self-to-others belongingness' at one extreme compared with . . . 'self-to-others alienation' at the other pole . . ." (1956:711). However, this meaning is not clearly reflected in all of the questions. The first and fifth items refer more or less directly to the person's attitudes toward other people, but the middle three can be connected to this domain only indirectly. Meier and Bell (1959:191) characterize the scale as referring to *despair;* others see it as tapping pessimism and cynicism. It is clear why these disparate interpretations have arisen: The scale has little conceptual integration.

Conclusions based on the use of our index should be expected to parallel those based on the Srole scale, then, only in that we focus on one aspect of the several tapped by the Srole scale. Indeed, we adopted Srole's question number 5 (substituting "who" for the aristocratic "whom"), intending to emphasize that aspect of the alienation concept dealing with confidence in, and reliance on, social relationships and the normative system. Hopefully, the more precise scope of our index should make for clearer interpretations.

Another potential problem in measuring anomia, and one that also seriously affects the Srole scale, is the bias introduced by an acquiescence response set. That is, some respondents may be inclined to agree with any statement presented to them. Such people will show up as highly anomic on any scale in which most of the statements are phrased so that "agree" denotes anomic. In Srole's scale all five of the items are phrased this way.

Worse, this mismeasurement may systematically affect the relationship between anomia and other variables. First of all, if another scale is also phrased so that a string of "agree's" will lead to a high score, it will be spuriously related to anomia due to acquiescence response set. Second, the rank–anomia relationship may be affected. Men of low rank are known to adopt acquiescence as a means of contending with persons of higher rank, using agreement as a protective device in a potentially threatening situation. Since most interviewers are middle class and white, low-ranked respondents may be inclined to agree with statements because of the status differences built into the interview situation. Lenski and Leggett (1960) and Carr (1971) have shown that this form of status-induced acquiescence can produce a negative relationship between rank and anomia (as measured with Srole's scale) that is partly spurious.[5]

However, some of the agreement induced by an interviewer of superior status may not be spurious, but actually represent anomia. Respondents may agree with statements made in the interview because they feel powerless and unable to rely on a strong normative system to protect them from persons of higher rank (see Carr 1971:291–292). For low-rank men who define the situation this way, one response is to agree pleasantly with everything the interviewer says and wait patiently for her to leave. (Most of the interviewers were women—how this affects acquiescence we cannot tell).

Therefore, when questions are set up so that agreement is scored as anomic, acquiescence is both a hazard in properly estimating the rank–anomia relationship and a theoretical correlate and indicator of anomia. In terms of a casual scheme:

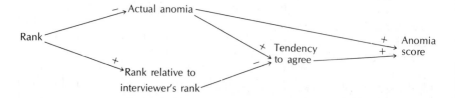

We want to estimate the path from rank to actual anomia, but since this is not directly measured, we must use the relations between rank and the

---

[5] Another possible response bias is that a principal consequence of modern mass education is learning to answer false (or disagree), on multiple choice examinations, to all statements that are vague or overgeneral. Better-educated people would then score low on anomia scales such as Srole's, spuriously producing a negative relationship between anomia and rank. The procedure we used to control acquiescence would not correct for this type of bias.

anomia score to do so. However, this relation might be affected by acquiescence, and so yea-saying must be controlled (although to the extent that true anomia causes yea-saying, controlling will underestimate the effects of rank on anomia).

In designing the questions for the survey, we intended to meet the acquiescence problem by including three anomia questions which were phrased so that "disagree" meant anomic. By using such items, a person would have to answer several "disagree's" as well as "agree's" in order to be scored as highly anomic. One of the questions is listed as the sixth item in the scale above. The other two were: "In our society, very few people are lonely and isolated from their fellow human beings," and "A man who lives by his moral principles won't have any trouble being successful and getting ahead in the world today." These two items were omitted from the index because they either were uncorrelated with the other eight anomia items or related in the wrong direction (i.e., were positively correlated, even though they were reversed in format).

Why this failure? Anomia items may be peculiar in that reversing their direction seems to change the meaning of the questions over and above the simple reversal in direction. Agreeing that most people are lonely, for example, should be the same as disagreeing that few people are lonely, but apparently it is not the same to respondents. It may be that reversing such items loses the negative tone of the question, and the respondent's feelings of anomia and alienation that may be called forth by the original phrasing do not emerge and cause a disagree response to a positively phrased question.

It is also possible that these two items did not correlate with the other anomia items because they are less accurate indicators of anomia per se. The first question deals with interpersonal isolation, but not necessarily with the lack of normative guidance, and the second deals with norms only in the sphere of success attainment. Our decision to drop these items, then, might have been taken on theoretical grounds even if they had related properly to the other items. If an item reflecting interpersonal relations and another reflecting feelings of legitimacy had been included in the scale, we would have introduced some artifactual effects into the analyses below dealing with the mediating effects of isolation and legitimacy.

Use of only one reversed item called for an additional attack on the problem of response set. We tried to identify the *acquiescers* and discard them before analysis. To do this, we pulled out people with anomia scores of 20 or higher, indicating a general tendency to agree to most questions, either because of anomia or because of response set. Of that set of people, who are scored as high in anomia, we identified those who agreed or strongly agreed that ". . . most Americans have very clear ideas of right and wrong and live by them." We felt that a person who agreed to a number of the other items indicating anomia and also agreed to this one (indicating low anomia) was likely to be one of the people affected by a tendency to agree with the interviewer. All such people (203 of them in the six cities taken together) were omitted from the following analysis.

As the above discussion about status-induced acquiescence would imply, the people dropped were lower on most rank dimensions than the respondents retained. Also, as we shall see below, dropping these yea-sayers did indeed weaken the relationship between rank and anomia to some degree, suggesting that some of the original relationship was spurious. We do not believe that this control for acquiescence is fully adequate,[6] but we do think that the bias is substantially reduced.

WHICH SOCIAL RANKS AFFECT ANOMIA?

The basic model of multidimensional rank effects is one in which current high achieved ranks—education, occupation, income—result in lower anomia. Of these, education has the strongest effect. Majority status (where minority populations exist) also reduces anomia considerably. The evidence for these conclusions is shown in Table 10.1.

The cities all show medium overall levels of anomia. The anomia means (shown in the second panel of Table 10.1) range only a little above and below a central value of about 14. Since our scale of anomia varied from 0 to 32, our samples on the whole exhibited medium levels of anomia as we measured it.

The rank dimension that most strongly influences anomia is education: In each community the net effect of low education was to produce a considerable increase in anomia. Family income and the respondent's occupation have similarly negative effects on anomia, although neither is as strong nor as consistent as the effect of education. In three of the four cities in which our sample included men of minority racial–ethnic status, this variable also affects anomia. In particular, blacks in Indianapolis seem to be considerably more anomic than would be predicted from their status on occupation, education, and the other rank dimensions.

The effects of background status seem to be both weak and scattered. The occupation of the father and the education of the father and the mother have effects on anomia that are sometimes positive, sometimes negative, and frequently too trivial to be counted in Table 10.1. There is a suggestion that high family background has a continuing net effect in reducing anomia in

---

[6]Indeed, no solution to this problem is fully adequate, since acquiescence is related to the independent and dependent variables theoretically as well as practically. It seems to be unusually difficult to get low-rank anomics to answer "no" to anything, so that even if an index could balance positive and negative answers, men with high scores would constitute a special category within "lower class anomics," namely men willing to disagree with several statements. If such a category were used for the purposes of inductive theory construction, it could yield peculiar generalizations, since it would be composed of lower-class men who eschewed a typical lower-class pattern of adaptation (see Carr 1971:291).

the two small towns, where background may indeed be an aspect of present status. Still, the data seem to rule out any general hypothesis that a person's view of the reliability of the social system is mainly formed in childhood as a result of parental influence, or at least that such views persist into later life unaltered by the current experiences of the man involved.

Finally, two other variables that appear to have little or no effect should be mentioned. First occupation has effects in Table 10.1 that are both relatively weak and fluctuating in direction. In a separate analysis (not shown here), we also found that the social class in which the person places himself has little net effect on his level of anomia.

Anomia is about as strongly related to social rank as any other social attitude we have encountered in this study. The eight rank variables considered in Table 10.1 explain between 12% and 21% of the variance in anomia. This also indicates, of course, that the effects of rank fall far short of determinacy: Evidently, many things about individuals besides their social ranks affect feelings of anomia. Yet relative to most other variables treated in this study, anomia is one of the primary correlates of social rank.

How would these results have changed if we had not removed acquiescent individuals? The bottom panel of Table 10.1, which reports results of analyses including the acquiescent respondents, suggests that correcting for acquiescence reduces the proportion explained by eight rank variables by 5 or 6 percentage points. Hence, there does appear to be a real relationship between social rank and anomia, but in studies in which acquiescence is not somehow controlled or adjusted the effects of rank are probably overstated in some moderate degree.

In terms of the effects of particular rank variables, restoring acquiescent respondents to the analysis in Table 10.1 would mainly increase the effects of education and family income, which are already two of the more important rank variables. Therefore, the pattern of rank effects is not basically affected by dropping acquiescent respondents.

The effect of a general continuum of social status, reflected by our general rank index, is also shown in the bottom panel of Table 10.1. The general rank index is negatively related to anomia in all six of the cities. General rank explains about as much of the variance in anomia as the eight specific rank variables included in Table 10.1, mainly because the effects of the individual rank variables are all or almost all in the same, negative direction.

The six communities are very similar with respect to almost all of the above results. The only important differences from city to city in the effects of the individual rank variables are, first, the trace suggestion that family background may have an effect upon anomia in the small towns and, second, the shifting effects of majority racial–ethnic rank across cities. This is partly because the cities differ in minority composition. In the analysis of covariance involving only majority men (reported in Chapter 5), the city interaction term was clearly nonsignificant (probability greater than .25), indicating that the rank variables affect anomia in more or less the same way in all six communities. The proportion of the variance explained by the rank variables also is similar from city to city, although somewhat higher in Safford than in the other cities. Even the mean anomia levels differ but little from city to city. These differences are unpatterned by size and region, except for a slight suggestion that mean anomia goes down as city size rises; even this trace pattern disappears in the analysis of covariance when the mean anomia scores for the communities are adjusted for differences between them in average income, education, etc. It would appear, therefore, that American social institutions set the conditions for anomia, and that the only effect of the local community is to provide minor idiosyncratic variations.

The final analysis in this section gives us some assurance that the rank effects discussed above are not spuriously produced. In Table 10.2, we show the results of an analysis in which the four rank variables having the most substantial effects are entered, plus controls for age, the size of the community of origin, and religious preference. The first two controls are entered on the hypotheses that anomia might increase with age and, further, be greater for men who were raised in large cities. Since both of these variables are to some extent related to rank variables, their effects might thereby potentially produce spurious rank effects. Religious belief systems, of course, have long been thought to influence anomia. First, having a strong coherent set of religious beliefs constitutes low anomia to some degree in and of itself. Second, some religious systems provide a more systematic and ordered view of the world than do others. Third, the social organizations, formal and informal, that are associated with different religions may have varying potentials for reducing anomia.

The results suggest that neither age nor the size of community of origin have strong or consistent direct effects on anomia and therefore could not act to spuriously produce rank effects. Religion, on the other hand, does seem to have a considerable independent effect on anomia. Since the religious composition of the cities varies somewhat, the religious effect is different in the different communities. The general conclusions supported by the religion rows of Table 10.2 seem to be: (a) Catholics are usually less anomic than Protestants; (b) Mormons are less anomic than Catholics (this result is supported only by data from Safford); (c) fundamentalist Protestants are more anomic than other Protestants (this supported only by data from Linton). From least to most anomic, then, the rough ordering then seems to be (with some exceptions): Mormons, Catholics, church Protestants, sect Protestants.[7]

---

[7]This pattern of religious effects holds throughout the rest of the analysis, despite the variety of controls that are added. The third, reference category in these analyses includes persons of no religious preferences and persons with preferences for a religion other than the two explicitly listed in Table 10.2. This category included from 3% to 8% of the samples in five cities and 31% of the Safford sample.

The main rank effects are little altered, however, by the controls for religion and the two other variables. The top rows of Table 10.2 show much the same pattern of rank effects as in an analysis (not shown) in which only these four rank variables were introduced. The only effect of adding the three control variables was to reduce the effect of education slightly in some cities. Even with this reduction, however, the effect of education on anomia is still the strongest and most consistent of the four effects.

WHY ARE MEN OF LOW RANK MORE ANOMIC?

We have now confirmed in our data the typical, negative relationship between social rank and anomia, and, further, have specified that relationship in more detail by showing that current rank, and especially education, is much more strongly related to anomia than is the class standing of the respondent's family while he was growing up. The next step in the analysis is to see if we can discover the principal intervening mechanisms between social rank and anomia, that is, to see if we can find out *why* "lower class" people are more anomic than "middle class" or "upper class" people. To do this, we introduce a number of variables that our earlier discussions suggest might plausibly mediate between rank and anomia. Only two of these variables, it turns out, actually appear to play an intervening role; and they fall far short of explaining why low rank produces anomia.

We begin by adding, one at a time, three sets of possible intervening variables to the analysis of the relationship between anomia and the rank variables. These sets are: *(a)* indexes of deprivations that accompany low rank; *(b)* indexes of social isolation; and *(c)* measures of the extent to which the respondent is in contact with lower class people. These are, in general, indicators of objective life circumstances that potentially vary with social rank. Later in this section, we will consider various possible subjective, attitudinal mediating variables. To conserve space, we do not show the tables in which each of the three sets of possible objective intervening variables were added to the rank–anomia analysis. However, those variables from the three sets which showed some consistent relationship to anomia were then included simultaneously in a single analysis, which is displayed in Table 10.3.

Conditions of Deprivation

One meaning of low rank is that life is hard and troubled, and insecurities abound. For example, satisfaction with work and the possibility of investing oneself in one's work is lower for people of lower occupational rank. We include three variables in this set of possible intervening measures: An index of work satisfaction, whether the respondent reports a physical or health

Table 10.1 *Anomia Regressed on Rank Variables*

	Regression coefficients: Unstandardized and standardized (in parentheses)					
Rank variables	Indianapolis	Columbus	Linton	Phoenix	Yuma	Safford
Family income	-.009 (.12)*[a]	-.005 (.07)	-.005 (.07)	-.010 (.17)*	-.009 (.12)*	-.007 (.11)
Occupation	b	-.015 (.10)	-.026 (.17)*	-.009 (.05)	-.010 (.07)	-.010 (.07)
First occupation	.009 (.05)			-.013 (.08)	.011 (.06)	-.018 (.11)
Education	-.396 (.34)*	-.263 (.24)*	-.127 (.10)	-.109 (.10)*	-.306 (.26)*	-.130 (.14)
Father's education	-.059 (.05)	-.058 (.05)				-.278 (.27)*
Father's occupation	.010 (.05)			-.010 (.06)	-.008 (.05)	.032 (.16)*
Mother's education	.144 (.09)			.092 (.07)		
Majority[c]	-2.281 (.17)*	-.006 (.05)	-.356 (.21)*	-1.509 (.11)*	-.772 (.07)	
R²	.17*	.12*	.14*	.13*	.14*	.21*
Mean	13.5	14.3	14.4	14.1	14.2	14.7
Standard deviation	4.4	3.6	3.9	3.8	3.9	3.7
N[d]	280	307	236	545	310	224
Proportion of the variance explained in anomia without removing acquiescent respondents						
Above 8 variables	.22*	.17*	.15*	.19*	.21*	.25*
General rank index	(-).19*[e]	(-).15*	(-).10*	(-).16*	(-).18*	(-).20*
17 variable regression	.25*	.20*	.20*	.20*	.24*	.27*

[a] In this and remaining tables in this chapter, asterisked regression coefficients are those with associated t-values of 1.65 or higher; hence, significant at approximately the .10 level (two-tailed test). Asterisked correlation coefficients are those significant at the .05 level.

[b] In this and remaining tables in this chapter, coefficients are not shown when the standardized path coefficient is both non-significant and less than .05, i.e., for zero or relatively weak effects.

[c] In this and remaining tables in this chapter, the (reversed) Bogardus racial-ethnic social distance scores (described in Chapter 2) are used in the regressions in Columbus and Linton. The majority racial-ethnic variable could not be used in these cities, since these samples contained almost no men of minority racial-ethnic rank.

[d] The N's are lower than in some previous analyses partly because respondents affected by acquiescence response set were dropped (as explained in the text).

Table 10.2 Anomia Regressed on Rank Variables and Control Variables

Rank variables	Regression coefficients: Unstandardized and standardized (in parentheses)					
	Indianapolis	Columbus	Linton	Phoenix	Yuma	Safford
Family income	-.007 (.10)	-.005 (.07)	-.004 (.06)	-.010 (.18)*	-.011 (.14)*	-.006 (.10)
Occupation	-.017 (.10)	-.017 (.12)*	-.028 (.18)*	-.011 (.07)		-.016 (.10)
Education	-.218 (.19)*	-.267 (.25)*	-.120 (.09)	-.147 (.13)*	-.276 (.23)*	-.205 (.22)*
Majority	-1.938 (.15)*	-.006 (.05)	-.010 (.06)	-1.610 (.12)*	-1.573 (.15)*	-.514 (.05)
Age	.031 (.10)		.032 (.13)*			
Size of community of origin	-.142 (.08)		-.179 (.06)	-.126 (.07)		
Religion						
Catholic[a]	-1.667 (.13)	-.901 (.08)	.894 (.11)	-1.020 (.11)	-.753 (.09)	
Protestant[a]	-1.725 (.15)	-.510 (.05)	.543 (.07)	-.811 (.10)	.456 (.06)	-.827 (.11)
R^2	.18*	.14*	.12*	.13*	.15*	.15*
N	259	294	236	535	306	205

[a]In Linton the two religious groups are defined as Fundamentalists and Baptists, and Other Protestants. In Safford, the religious groups are Catholics and Mormons.

265

Table 10.3 Anomia Regressed on Rank Variables and Intervening Variables (Net of Control Variable Effects)

Rank and intervening variables	Regression coefficients: Unstandardized and standardized (in parentheses)[a]					
	Indianapolis	Columbus	Linton	Phoenix	Yuma	Safford
Family income	weaker[b]	weaker	reduced	-.005 (.09)* weaker	-.005 (.07) weaker	weaker
Occupation	-.011 (.06) reduced	-.011 (.08) reduced	-.029 (.18)* same	reduced	same	-.019 (.12) increase
Education	-.193 (.16)* reduced	-.163 (.15)* weaker	-.104 (.08) same	-.106 (.09)* reduced	-.208 (.18)* weaker	-.176 (.18)* reduced
Majority	-1.656 (.12)* reduced	same	-.009 (.05) same	-1.723 (.13)* same	-1.466 (.14)* same	-.822 (.08) increase
Work satisfaction	-.328 (.07)		-.200 (.05)		-.450 (.10)*	
Physical problems	.194 (.06)	.829 (.09)		.523 (.06)	.578 (.06)	1.163 (.15)*
Fully employed	-1.461 (.11)	.765 (.06)	-1.067 (.10)	-1.436 (.13)*		-1.659 (.09)
Living with spouse	-1.522 (.08)	-.896 (.05)		.792 (.06)		-1.193 (.15)*
Children at home					-.441 (.05)	
Informal participation	-.506 (.08)		-.406 (.07)		-.521 (.09)	
Number of association memberships				-.292 (.12)*		
R's neighborhood rating	-.247 (.07)	-.346 (.12)	-.268 (.10)	-.237 (.07)		
Interviewer's area rating	-.281 (.09)	-.358 (.10)	.381 (.10)		-.510 (.13)*	-.376 (.11)
R²	.22*	.16*	.14*	.16*	.19*	.22*
N	251	296	223	531	295	201

[a] These are the regression coefficients in an analysis employing the listed variables plus two control-variables: age and religion (categorized as described in Table 10.2). The coefficients thus reflect effects after these two variables have been controlled.

[b] Quantities below the coefficients for the rank variables represent the way in which their effects changed as a result of introducing the intervening nine variables listed above (i.e., compared to the effects in Table 10.2). "Weaker" indicates a drop in the beta of .05 or more.

266

problem, and whether or not he is fully employed. The hypothesis is that men of lower rank will be more exposed to these various kinds of hardships and insecurities and these may in turn lead to anomia in various ways. First, we have suggested above that the deprivations of low rank are inherently alienating. Further, unemployment and physical illness may *incapacitate* a man in the sense of barring him from participating fully in social life, which may in turn make him less likely to see a reliable normative order. Also, these various forms of deprivation may prevent men of lower rank from enjoying the luxury of trusting in their fellow men, since they have a smaller margin of safety to protect themselves from the disappointments and reversals that trust sometimes brings.

Experiencing some form of physical illness does seem to increase anomia among men in most of the cities, although this effect is not overly strong relative to other effects in Table 10.3. There is some indication that being fully employed and satisfied with one's work reduce anomia, but these effects do not appear consistently in a majority of the six communities. It appears, then, that only one variable in this set of deprivation conditions, experiencing physical problems, has enough of an effect upon anomia to be a candidate for a possible mediating variable between social rank and anomia.

Social Isolation

A second possible reason for the negative relationship between social rank and anomia is that trust in one's associates and in a reliable social system tends to be built up in the process of formal and informal social participation. If so, isolation would mean the person is deprived of supporting social relationships, which in turn would lead to a decay in his perceptions of a reliable social system. If isolation is more likely among members of lower ranks, then this might in whole or in part account for the negative rank–anomia relationship. Our previous finding (in Chapter 7) that people of low rank have about the same levels of informal participation as people of higher rank implies that informal participation (which, a priori, seemed the most logical connecting link) is not acting in this way. However, rates of formal social participation might well be. Indeed, formal participation, which offers an instructive experience in the voluntary, organized interaction of a wide variety of otherwise unrelated people, might well be important in convincing a person that the social structure has some reliable order.

To test these notions, we introduced five indicators of social isolation into the analysis of the relationship between social rank and anomia. These indicators were: (a) whether the respondent lives with his spouse; (b) if he does, whether children are also present in the home; (c) the length of time he has lived in the community (on the theory that newcomers are less likely to have developed social ties); (d) the amount of informal social participation (measured by an index of frequency of visiting with relatives, neighbors, work associates, and other friends); and *(e)* the number of formal voluntary associations to which the respondent belongs.

In general, the results indicate that being socially isolated does not affect anomia enough to explain the rank–anomia relationship. Length of residence did not have even the minimally consistent effects on anomia required to be included in Table 10.3. The effects of the other isolation variables tend to be in the predicted direction (participation reduces anomia), but most of the effects are weak and do not appear consistently from city to city. None of the isolation variables have a consistent effect on anomia in a majority of the six cities.

We conclude, therefore, that although the data presents some trace support for the proposition that social contacts make a man a little more likely to perceive a reliable normative system, none of the social isolation variables has a sufficiently strong or consistent effect to qualify as an intervening variable between rank and anomia.

Contact with Lower Class Environment

The simplest argument to account for high anomia scores for lower class people is that when answering such questions, they are merely reporting accurately what they see about them. If it were true that lower class people are less reliable (in a normative sense), have less clear ideas of right and wrong, and are more confused in their beliefs, then any man of low rank would be likely to agree to most of our questions just as a result of generalizing to the community or the society as a whole from his daily observations of the people around him. In other words, *anomie* varies by rank, and anomia is the perception of it. This notion leads to the prediction that a man's anomia score should vary with the rank of the people he contacts, as well as with (or possibly more than with) his own rank standings.

(Note, in passing, that a Pandora's box of interpretations has been opened by entertaining the very real possibility that perceptions of anomia might depend both on the perceptual apparatus of the individual and the actual amount of anomie in the social surroundings. In addition to the above interpretation, the actual amount of societal anomie might be high at all levels of rank (the world might actually *be* a jungle), but it is to the advantage of highly rewarded persons to rationalize rewards as normatively just, rather than as spoils accruing to tooth and claw. Again, societal anomie might be low and constant, with poorly rewarded persons simply uninformed of their surroundings. Yet again, the "rules of the game" might actually be what is sustaining some in higher ranks, and might be reliable to others only in keeping them down.)

The same prediction, that anomia depends on the rank of one's contacts, can be advanced on somewhat different grounds (see Simpson and Miller

1963). Here the argument is that people learn views of the world directly from the people they contact in neighborhoods, in friendship groups, etc. If so, then people, whatever their own class, who associate with lower class people, will develop an added increment of anomia. Hence, low rank leads to anomia perhaps directly, but perhaps also indirectly by lowering the rank of the man's associates.

To test this prediction we included in the rank–anomia analysis three measures of the extent to which the respondent comes into contact with lower class people. These were: (a) the occupational prestige score of the respondent's best friend; (b) the respondent's rating of his neighborhood; and (c) the interviewer's rating of the respondent's neighborhood (these last two ratings are described in Chapter 4).

The data offer some support for the notion that the social rank of one's surroundings affects anomia, net of one's own ranks. Although the prestige of the occupation of the respondent's best friend did not have sufficiently consistent effects to warrant its inclusion in Table 10.3, the social class ratings of the respondent's neighborhood do seem to be, in general, negatively related to anomia, over and above the effects of the rank variables and other variables included in Table 10.3. The interviewer's rating of the neighborhood appears to have the stronger effect (although it is reversed in Linton), possibly because it is the more objective measure and hence more likely to accurately reflect the "lower-class-ness" of the neighborhood.

Although this finding supports the above line of argument, it does not by any means prove it. Something else associated with the estimated rank of neighborhoods could be responsible for the finding. A reverse causal effect is also possible: Neighborhoods rated as lower class may be more likely to select or attract anomic individuals, some of whom may appear among our respondents. With these qualifications, however, the straightforward interpretation is that living in a lower-ranked neighborhood produces anomia, over and above the effects of the ranks of the resident. The social rank of the neighborhood is therefore the second variable we have located which has a sufficiently consistent effect upon anomia to qualify as a possible intervening variable that mediates the effect of rank upon personal anomia.

To this point, then, we have presented data to suggest that two other life circumstances beyond objective rank positions have a direct and consistent effect upon anomia. Before we can conclude that these two factors actually are mechanisms by which rank positions are translated into anomia-producing experiences, we must show that these variables are related to rank position and that the relationship between rank and anomia is reduced when these variables are added to the analysis.

With respect to the second point, introducing these 9 potential intervening variables reduced the direct effect of income and education on anomia, but did not change the direct influences on anomia of occupation or of the majority racial–ethnic variable. The terms in parentheses under the first four lines of Table 10.3 show reduced effects in all six cities for the rank variable of family income and reduced effects in five of six cities for education. However, the effects of occupation and majority were not consistently altered in the six cities. The added potential intervening variables evidently did not explain the effects of occupation and majority on anomia, but did partly explain the effects of education and income.

However, only one of the two possible intervening variables, the interviewer's rating of the area, is strongly enough related to both income (r = .41) and education (r = .39) to explain part of the rank–anomia relationship. The experience of physical problems is related to rank much more weakly and hence cannot mediate the effects of rank. We conclude, then, that education and income partly affect anomia because high rank on these variables tends to allow and/or motivate a man to live in a better neighborhood, and this in turn tends to lower his level of anomia. To this limited extent, then, the hypothesis is supported that the individual's contact with lower class persons helps to explain the rank–anomia relationship. Our hypotheses about the intervening roles of social isolation and deprived life conditions are *not* supported.

Most of the effects of the four main rank variables, therefore, turn out to be direct and not mediated by any of the intervening variables introduced so far. Table 10.3 shows that even with control variables and intervening variables introduced, education continues to have a major and consistent negative effect on anomia, as does majority racial–ethnic status in the cities with substantial numbers of minority men. High rank on occupation also reduces anomia, although the effect is not as strong or consistent.

The direct effect of income has disappeared in Table 10.3 except in two cities. This is somewhat misleading. The data suggest that the income effect was controlled out by different variables in different cities, so that its effect on anomia is not consistently mediated by the same intervening variables. In an anlysis including only the four main rank variables and the three additional variables so far found to have consistent effects on anomia (physical problems, the interviewer's rating of the area, and religion) income is seen to have a consistent, although modest, negative net effect on anomia.

FRUSTRATION AND PERCEPTIONS OF OPPORTUNITY AND LEGITIMACY AS INTERVENING VARIABLES

Our search for mechanisms which translate rank deprivation into the normless form of alienation brings us now to a major line of sociological thought relating anomia to social rank, namely the argument that derives anomia from the societal condition of anomie (Merton 1957; Cohen 1955). In this argument, anomie, a condition of the society, results from socializing a population widely to accept success goals and values, while failing to make the legitimate opportunity structure open to all who have internalized these goals. Such a situation is said to weaken the controls that norms exercise on behavior in the society. Weaker normative controls are especially likely among people of low social rank, since the legitimate opportunity system is most closed to those people and hence they are most likely to resort to unapproved means to gain the success they have been taught to value.

The negative rank–anomia relationship per se cannot be said to provide a very strong test of this line of thought, however, since (as we have seen above) any number of other lines of theory predict the same relationship. We can make a somewhat stronger test in this study by introducing measures of some of the intervening variables mentioned above, in particular, measures of frustration, feelings of being blocked, and feelings of legitimacy. We tapped feelings of frustration by introducing four items:

> *Success satisfaction:* "Would you say that you have been as successful in life as you wanted to be?"
>
> *Income satisfaction:* "Are you reasonably satisfied with your family income, or do you feel you need a higher income?"
>
> *Income expectations:* "In five years, do you expect that your family income will be much larger than it is now, somewhat larger, about the same or less than it is now?"
>
> *Job expectations:* "In five years, do you expect that you will have a much better job than you have now, a somewhat better job, or about the same kind of job you have now?"

The respondents' feelings of being blocked were measured by a single item:

> "Have you sometimes felt that you have not been given the chance to show what you can do?"[8]

To gauge the extent to which low rank produces a general perception of normative unreliability by leading men to see unreliability in the system of success attainment, we introduced the measure of legitimacy used in Chapter 4:

> "Which of these do you think are the main reasons behind a man's success in America today?"

The reader will recall that this item was scored according to the extent to which the man replied "hard work," "ability," and "drive and initiative" rather than "opportunities his family gave him," "knowing the right people and pull," and "good luck."

---

[8]In the Indianapolis survey, this question took the form: "Do you feel sometimes that you are not given the chance to show what you can do?"

The attitudinal intervening variables were added to a regression anaysis involving anomia on the one hand and the four main rank variables on the other. This regression also included controls for the three variables which were found in previous analyses to have a consistent direct effect on anomia (defined as betas greater than .05 in the same direction in at least four of the six cities). The results are shown in Table 10.4. The data suggest that current satisfaction (or frustration) has little consistent effect upon anomia. Income satisfaction affected anomia, weakly, in only two cities, while the effects of satisfaction with success were not even consistent from city to city.

The two items on expectations were introduced on the grounds that not expecting success in the future might increase current frustration and so increase anomia. No such result appears for occupational expectations, but expecting no improvement in income did tend to increase anomia in three of the five cities for which this measure was present. These effects are relatively small, however.

Even though men frustrated by lack of success are not in general more anomic, the data clearly show that if a man sees that his "failure" is due to *denial of opportunities* he will be more likely to develop anomic attitudes. The feeling of being blocked from opportunity, "not . . . given the chance to show what you can do," produces moderate increases in anomia in five of the six cities. This effect occurs with perceptions of legitimacy held constant, indicating that the experience of being blocked from success intrinsically produces anomia, *apart from* the individual's perception of whether the general success attainment system is or is not legitimate.

Finally, legitimacy also shows a substantial and highly consistent net effect on anomia. Apart from social rank and other factors affecting anomia and even apart from whether the man feels that he personally has or has not enjoyed a chance for success, the feeling that rewards in the U.S. are not actually distributed according to legitimate principles also produces increments in anomia.[9]

To what extent do the variables of income expectations, feeling that one has not been given a chance, and legitimacy, explain the effect of rank on anomia? The first requirement to be met for those variables to mediate this rank effect is that they themselves be affected by rank. We know from the analyses in Chapter 4 that perceptions of legitimacy are consistently increased by high income, occupation and education and also by majority

[9]The reader might question the above results on the grounds that these six added items are bound to be very highly intercorrelated, and hence the regression coefficients indicating their effects will be unstable and not open to clear interpretation. This suspicion has only limited grounds. The highest intercorrelation among these variables is between the two forms of expectations: about .50 in each of the five cities in which they were measured. The relationship between the two forms of satisfaction ran between .25 and .30 in the six cities. All of the other correlations between these items were below .20. The degree of multicollinearity does not seem large enough to affect the interpretation of the effects which we have made above.

Table 10.4 Anomia Regressed on Rank and "Attitudinal" Variables (Net of Control and Intervening Variable Effects)

Rank and attitudinal variables	Regression coefficients: Unstandardized and standardized (in parentheses)[a]					
	Indianapolis	Columbus	Linton	Phoenix	Yuma	Safford
Family income	reduced	.004 (.05) increase	-.004 (.06) same	-.008 (.13)* reduced	-.006 (.08) reduced	-.003 (.05) same
Occupation	same	reduced	-.026 (.17)* reduced	-.010 (.06) same	same	-.021 (.13) same
Education	-.256 (.23)* same	-.180 (.17)* same	-.195 (.14)* same	-.095 (.08) reduced	-.279 (.22)* increase	-.140 (.14) reduced
Majority	-.881 (.07) weaker	reduced	reduced	-1.954 (.15)* increase	-1.493 (.14)* increase	reduced
Success satisfaction			.208 (.07)	-.212 (.08)*		
Income satisfaction		-.302 (.10)*	-.188 (.06)			
(Low) income expectations	c	.414 (.09)	.365 (.07)	.274 (.05)	.274 (.05)	.328 (.07)
(Same) job expectations	c		.631 (.14)*	-.334 (.07)	-.334 (.07)	-.312 (.06)
Not given a chance	.370 (.08)	.332 (.09)		.294 (.07)*	.532 (.12)*	
Legitimacy	-1.262 (.19)*	-.846 (.16)*	-.633 (.10)	-.641 (.11)*	-1.017 (.16)*	-.644 (.10)
R^2	.21*	.18*	.15*	.16*	.25*	.20*
N	248	281	222	505	281	188

[a] These are the regression coefficients in an analysis employing the listed variables *plus* three control and intervening variables: interviewer's area rating, physical problems, and religion (categorized as described in Table 10.2). The coefficients thus reflect effects after these three variables have been controlled.

[b] Quantities below the coefficients represent the way in which effects changed as a result of introducing the "attitudinal" variables listed above (i.e., compared to an analysis (not shown) including only the four rank variables and the three control and intervening variables).

[c] These variables were not measured in the Indianapolis survey.

racial–ethnic rank (especially in Indianapolis where the minority group is largely black). However, these effects were not large and explained only a very small proportion of the variation in legitimacy. The zero-order correlations between occupation and education on the one hand and income expectations on the other indicate that men high on these rank dimensions are somewhat less likely to expect lower future incomes. These two variables, then, appear to be affected by rank to some extent. The perception of being blocked from opportunity, of not being given a chance, seems to be much less strongly related to rank. Its zero-order correlations with the major rank variables are always below .15 and fall below .10 in most cities, which seems to rule out this variable as a mediating factor. We conclude that unfavorable expectations of future income and feelings that the system of success attainment is not legitimate may act to mediate the effects of rank on anomia, but that these mediating effects are not very strong, both because the links between rank and these variables are not strong and because the effects of these variables in turn on anomia are not overly substantial.

When we look at how the effects of the rank variables change as a result of introducing these potential intervening variables, we become even more uncertain about their mediating role. These changes are shown in the terms below the first four lines of Table 10.4. The effect of income is reduced in some cities, but the effects of occupation and education are, in general, not changed by adding these mediating variables. The changes in the racial–ethnic effects are not consistent, but the major change is a strong drop in Indianapolis. In general, education continues to reduce anomia strongly and income, occupation and racial–ethnic rank continue to have noticeable effects.

What can we conclude? Expecting a lower income probably does not mediate the effects of rank to any significant extent. It is related only to occupation and education, yet the effects of these variables did not change in any consistent way in those cities in which income expectations affected anomia. Presumably, a man's feelings that the success system is not legitimate does mediate some of the effect of income, since this variable did decrease its direct effects in three cities. The feeling of legitimacy also presumably mediates much of the effect of majority rank in Indianapolis. In this city (as shown in Chapter 4), the black minority tend to deny that the system is legitimate and this in turn (as shown in Table 10.4) has a substantial effect in increasing levels of anomia. This accounts for the substantial drop in the direct effect of majority racial–ethnic rank on anomia in this particular city.

We must therefore conclude that the interpretation advanced above, resting on the relationship between societal anomie and individual anomia, is far from adequate. Of the variables presumed in this line of argument to mediate the rank–anomia relationship, only feelings of legitimacy in fact does so, and it is by no means the major way in which rank affects anomia. Most of the rank effects are direct and remain unexplained.

SUMMARY AND CONCLUSIONS

This chapter has attempted to determine which rank variables affect anomia and, further, the degree to which these rank effects are mediated by a variety of possible intervening variables. Our major conclusions are:

1. High ranks of various kinds act to reduce anomia. The strongest and most consistent of these net effects is that of education. Majority racial–ethnic rank has a similar effect in those cities in which minority communities exist, especially in Indianapolis, where the minority is black. High income and prestigeous occupation also reduce anomia to some degree. In general, however, the effects of background origin are weak and unstable. This pattern of effects is not altered by introducing controls for age, size of community of origin, and religious preference, although religion does have an additional direct effect on anomia.

2. Our index of general rank is related negatively to anomia in all cities.

3. To try to find the reasons why high rank reduces anomia, we introduced three sets of potential mediating factors: three variables reflecting conditions of deprivation, five indicators of social isolation, and three measures of the extent to which the respondent comes into contact with people of low rank. Most of these variables had little effect on anomia and so failed to qualify as intervening variables. The only two exceptions were that reporting a physical or health problem and a low social class rating of the neighborhood were both associated with higher anomia. The former variable was not strongly enough related to rank to serve as a mediator. Neighborhood rating, however, does serve to mediate some of the effects of income and education on anomia. To a limited extent, then, the individual's contact with a lower class environment seems to partly explain why low rank leads to anomia. Deprivation and social isolation do not seem to be mediating variables.

4. A next attempt to find mediating variables led us to introduce four measures of success frustration, a measure of feelings of being denied opportunity, and a measure of the legitimacy of the system of success attainment. Three of these six variables had consistent direct effects on anomia: low income expectations, feelings that opportunities were denied, and feelings of legitimacy. Of these, however, only feelings of legitimacy appeared to partly mediate the effect of income and, at least in Indianapolis, the effect of majority racial–ethnic rank on anomia.

5. The controls and intervening variables fall far short of completely

accounting for the effects of rank on anomia. Even when they are introduced, education continues to have a substantial and consistent direct effect
in reducing anomia; and income, occupation, and majority racial–ethnic
rank continue to have noticeable effects.

Our conclusions on the effects of rank variables, control variables and
potential intervening variables are represented graphically in Figure 10.1.

6. Rank variables by themselves explain from 12% to 21% of the variance;
including rank, control, and potential intervening variables all together
raises the percent explained to the 15–25% range.

7. The patterns of anomia and its relation to rank are very similar from
city to city. Average anomia is at about the same medium level in all communities. The pattern of rank effects is similar, with two exceptions: The
effect of racial–ethnic rank varies because of the racial–ethnic composition
in the cities, and there is a suggestion that family background might have
some effect on anomia in the small towns. The variance explained does
range some from city to city, but the differences are not patterned by region
or community size.

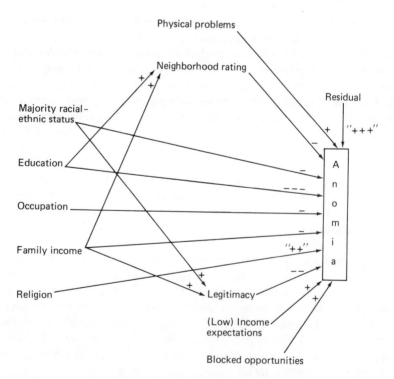

Figure 10.1. *Summary of direct and mediated effects of rank on anomia.*

INTERPRETATIONS

What general implications can we draw from these specific findings? As will become obvious below, our results can be interpreted in many ways, and in that sense many questions remain about the effects of rank upon anomia. On the other hand, we have made some progress in the sense that the results disconfirm, or at least severely sprain, a number of possible hypotheses about the rank–anomia relationship. Let us turn to these first.

Anomia does not persist as a reflection of rank of origin or some previous rank, nor as a result of socialization at some earlier rank level. It is apparently a reaction to present life conditions (except possibly in small towns, where background rank may be involved in present reputation). Past social rank is related to anomia mainly through its effect on present rank. One might have supposed that a secure and rewarded childhood would teach reliance in a normative system, but such learning is apparently not resistant to the actual conditions of later life. At the same time, men who presumably did not learn trust in the moral order in their families of orientation, but who have since acquired high rank, apparently tend to be convinced by the events of their careers.

Hypotheses that upward or downward mobility or status inconsistency increases anomia are also rejected by our data (see Chapter 5). Incongruity between past and/or present social ranks or an imbalance between investments (or expectations) and rewards, as opposed to the simple extent of current reward, seem to have little or no effect on anomia. This follows, first because rank effects on anomia involve little interaction: Anomia was one of the most additive dependent variables in our analysis. Second, there are practically no rank effects of opposing sign: All forms of social rank that affect anomia appear to affect it negatively.

Thirdly, it is apparently *not* isolation from interpersonal contact that accounts for feelings of anomia. The only form of social contact which mediates the rank–anomia relationship seems to be the experience of living in a high or low status neighborhood. Lower education or income have the effect, for obvious reasons, of prodding men to live in neighborhoods of lower standing; this in turn seems to increase feelings of anomia, in and of itself. One interpretation of this result, suggested above, is that *contagion* occurs: Daily contact with lower class people leads a man to take on more strongly their (presumably anomic) attitudes. The independent effect of neighborhood may also arise because the normative system is actually less reliable in lower class neighborhoods, and the respondent is simply reporting what he sees about him. There may be more crime or other sorts of deviance among the neighborhood residents, and in addition a range of institutional protections, such as police service, may function more erratically in such neighborhoods. The larger community may systematically provide less support for moral stability in lower-class neighborhoods.

Finally, the data throw considerable doubt on the hypothesis that low rank causes anomia because anomia is mainly a result of accepting high goals and then failing to achieve them (though some operation of Merton's mechanism is supported by the "illegitimacy effect"). This notion that failure is a central mediating variable has several implications which are not borne out by the data. It implies, first, that occupational and income rank, as the most direct measures of success, should have more effect on anomia than such dimensions as education, but this does not turn out to be true. The "failure" hypothesis also implies that such variables as satisfaction with success or feelings of not being given a chance should intervene in the anomia–rank relationship, but they do not.

If the man's own lack of success, however, leads him to conclude that the means for attaining success in the U.S. today are largely illegitimate, then this feeling *does* tend to be translated into attitudes of anomia. But failures to achieve are not the only sources of feelings of illegitimacy; men of minority racial–ethnic rank, whether successful or not, also tend to feel that much success is due to unapproved means. We must also raise here the question of reciprocal effects. Our basic interpretation is that low rank causes men to lose faith in the norms of success attainment, which then spreads to a more general doubt in the reliability of the normative system as a whole. It may be, however, that the opposite effect also occurs: A feeling that the norms in general are unreliable, arising from whatever source, leads to the specific feeling that the norms of success attainment are not effective.

Our data indicate that rank variables, and especially education, have substantial direct effects on anomia, not mediated by a number of plausible intervening variables which we introduced into the analysis. This throws doubt on a number of hypotheses about the sources of anomia, as we have just pointed out. But how can these direct effects of rank be interpreted?

We begin by suggesting several plausible ways in which the effect of education on anomia might arise, since this effect is the strongest in our data. The education effect is net of occupation and income, and hence it is not simply a matter of providing skills which are in turn converted into other forms of high rank. Low educational attainment increases anomia directly, either because education is an especially salient type of rank or because of other characteristics of education which are especially important for normative alienation, even though they are not *evaluated* aspects, that is, they do not contribute to the superiority–inferiority aspect of educational attainment.

As an initial explanation of the effect of education, it could be postulated that education is *the* institutionalized means to rank attainment in the U.S. This institutionalization is in the hands of employers who use degrees as universalistic hiring criteria, or as criteria for even entering the race for promotion. Therefore, low educational rank means that a man is blocked from the legitimate opportunity structures. Further, this restriction is more or less permanent, since few people are able to improve their educational rank after becoming adults. In this view, then, educational level opens or closes the door to future success. For men of high education, such factors as drive, initiative, ability, and hard work lead to rewards, and the individual therefore sees a reliable normative system around him. For men of low education, on the other hand, effort and sterling personal qualities do not lead to reward, but rather to fatigue, and the man therefore feels in a personal and immediate sense that the system of norms is not operating reliably.

However, several aspects of our results seem to disconfirm this point of view. If this explanation of the educational effect were true, it would imply that feelings of legitimacy and feelings of being "given the chance to show what you can do" should have certain mediating roles. However, they did not. Also, this view implies that men of low education who are able to attain some measure of success with respect to income or occupation might well recover their faith in a reliable normative system (unless, of course, they achieved this success in some illegitimate manner). Yet, the relationship is additive, showing that low education increases anomia even for men with good jobs and high income. Hence, we must seek another interpretation for the direct effect of education.

A second possible hypothesis is that formal education systematically protects men from many of life's difficulties and from the alienating behavior of others. "Years of education" can be understood as the age at which a man leaves this protective environment and exposes himself to a competitive world that is not formally dedicated to his personal enhancement. In this view, the world outside the school tends to produce disillusionment and cynicism and low education produces anomia simply because poorly educated men have been exposed to this world for a longer period. If this were true, however, age, which is much more strongly related than education to the time a man has spent outside the sheltering confines of the school, should have a strong positive effect on anomia, with education controlled. This it does not have, so this second hypothesis must also be regarded with some doubt.

A third hypothesis is that the educational institution teaches people various forms of conceptual order, including normative order. Schools teach that norms do exist and do organize life, but education also teaches a eunomic approach to life and to problem-solving in general. The educated man's approach to anything is to arm himself with a conceptual apparatus that orients him and gives meaning to a problem and through the use of which he can deduce a solution. For the uneducated man, a stable conceptual order in the social universe may be essentially irrelevant to life. Therefore, the farther a man goes in formal education, the more he has been taught, and encouraged to think, that the world is ordered in a reliable fashion.

A fourth possibility is that the school teaches trust in the norms not only by open instruction but also by reinforcement. Presumably, one's belief in the reliability of a normative social system is, like most other behaviors, strengthened by periodic reward. Those people who have placed some reliance on the social system in the past and have been rewarded tend to continue to subscribe to the view that the system is reliable. That is, when one invests energy or time or money expecting that a reliable social system will yield a return on the investment, a payoff tends to reduce anomia. By the same token, the opposite experiences tend to promote anomia. This kind of reinforcement through involvement in a reliable and rewarding social system could be expected to promote faith in a wide range of social arrangements, and not only those involving attainment of success in the outside world. Therefore, this effect of rank would not totally be mediated by such variables as feelings of legitimacy.

Men who have spent more years in school have had precisely this kind of reinforcement. They have placed their trust in an interdependent social net, assuming that the norms are reliable enough to insure that their effort will be rewarded. By definition, the reward has been granted, as prepromised. Further, in the educational system, especially in the later years, the time span between investment and reward is often relatively great and this should tend to make a man's belief in the reliability of the system even more tenacious. On the other hand, men who have spent fewer years in school have not received this kind of reinforcement and indeed may have defined their experience with the educational system as essentially punishing.

A fifth possible hypothesis to account for the effect of education in reducing anomia is one of a reverse causal direction. Stated generally, it may be that men who have little faith in a reliable social system, and who therefore have low levels of trust, are seriously handicapped in attaining high rank in our society. For example, the decision to delay gratification is based on the belief that rewards will indeed be forthcoming as a result; if one has little faith that the social system will deliver, he is unlikely to make the commitments that are often required for success. This argument implies that the school system essentially selects and retains nonanomic individuals, since people who are anomic (for whatever reason) will not have the level of trust required to motivate the effort involved in higher levels of education. Quite possibly, a reciprocal relationship exists in which continuing education promotes trust, but trust also allows education to continue.

High education may also reduce anomia because it provides security. High rank per se should not be expected to produce trust in the social system and its future behavior if the high rank is unstable or insecure. Education is unlikely to change much during the work life of an adult and so high education is essentially irrevocable. Further, it involves the skills and resources that themselves tend to guarantee the future. The education that enables one job will enable another. As long as ability is difficult to evaluate directly, and as long as universalistic criteria are demanded on a mass basis, a man may expect to be evaluated (initially) on the basis of education. In this sense, our results indicate the effects of immediate social rank less than they do *entrenchment* in a social rank. To attain a high rank is to entrench, and higher levels of education are the most entrenched kinds of rank.

No matter what features of education are responsible, we are led to the general conclusion that if rank is generally associated with alienation of various kinds, it is especially education that is associated with anomia in particular (compare the model shown in Ottó and Featherman 1975). Since religion, too, affects anomia, the late adolescence–adult socialization explanation for perceptions of reliable norms is supported. We found in Chapter 6 that education had an opposite effect on satisfaction in setting aspirations higher than possible achievements, which can be viewed as a kind of alienation. Here we find that, at the same time, persons who have been taught to rely on a normative system, either by exhortation or by experience, in fact place greater reliance on that system. (Independently, for all we know, people could be right or wrong about whether the normative system is in fact reliable).

Some of the above hypotheses also provide possible explanations for the direct effects of the other rank dimensions—income, occupation, and racial–ethnic status. For example, high prestige jobs are more likely to involve a man in rewarding interaction with a reliable social system (either in the professions or in large corporate organizations) and hence reinforce trust in the normative system. The same argument may be applied to the effects of racial–ethnic status. Being defined as a black or a Mexican–American increases the chances that "promises" made by the social system will not be kept, that is, that the norms will not consistently regulate the behavior of other people. Indeed, a major argument of Myrdal's *An American Dilemma* (1944) is that powerful American norms are routinely contradicted in the treatment of blacks. Hence, feelings of trust are less likely to be reinforced by rewards for minority men.

Similarly, the argument that anomia affects rank as much as rank affects anomia may apply to occupational and income rank as well as to education. Good jobs and high pay probably tend to require some willingness to rely on social regularities and to trust other people to some extent. Anomic individuals, unwilling or unable to make such commitments, would therefore tend to collect in the lower reaches of these rank dimensions.

Finally, the hypothesis that high rank affords security and thereby reduces anomia certainly applies to occupational and income rank as well as to education. Lower-ranked occupations have not only less prestige, but less stability as well, even of employment itself. Moreover, the incomes that are high in these samples are probably more secure than the lower incomes because of obvious features of income maintenance, even though they are not explicitly measured in this study.

In addition, sheer reward may explain some of the effect of high rank in reducing anomia, especially the privilege allowed by high incomes and the prestige afforded by high occupations and majority racial-ethnic rank. In the first place, people receiving high levels of rewards, whether in response to their own efforts or not, probably tend for that reason alone to be more attached to and less alienated from the social system in general, including its norms. Secondly, as we suggested above in our discussion of the mediating effect of neighborhood rank, social life probably *is* more reliable for men that are highly rewarded. A good job, a good salary and an Anglo-Saxon face all confer to their fortunate possessor a certain degree of power and control over the environment. If only for this reason, others are likely to act according to his expectations, and he is thus more likely to perceive a reliable social world.

What implications do our findings have for relationships at the level of the community? Especially, what are the consequences of stratification for normative integration? A first result is that the cities are similar in general levels of anomia and in the way in which social rank is related to anomia. Possibly because they are not exceptionally different with respect to stratification systems, these cities do not seem to form unique contexts for the growth of normative alienation. There is little evidence in our data that attributes of the community have a significant effect on the levels of anomia experienced by residents.

Within each community, different levels of anomia are found at different levels of rank. This relationship is far from determinate, because many individual-level idiosyncratic factors affect anomia. Also, in some cases other social structures such as religion will supply a normative system to those of low rank. Even so, anomia is more heavily affected by rank than almost any other dependent variable considered in this study.

Since the effects of education, occupation, income, and racial–ethnic status are independent and additive, status inconsistency between these dimensions has the effect of spreading anomia out through the class structure in the community. Thus, status inconsistency in the system of stratification reduces the association between a unidimensional definition of status and anomia. However, this spreading out effect is much less than for some other variables we have considered in this study because the effect of education is so much stronger than the effect of the other three rank dimensions. To some degree, educational differences do tend to override differences in other forms of status and to establish a clear range from eunomic, secure, and rewarded persons at the top of the structure to less secure, anomic persons at the bottom.

There is a tendency, therefore, toward a situation in which the moral order is more effectively able to organize behavior of higher ranked (educated) people, while this form of integration is less effective at the bottom because low-ranked people are less likely to believe in the organized efficacy of the moral order. To the extent that this is true, then, American institutions have not dealt effectively with the integrative problems posed by the intrinsically punishing character of rank deprivation.

11

INTOLERANCE

We deal here with a range of negative feelings that individuals have about other groups or about people who behave in ways they regard as wrong or improper. We shall describe and analyze four forms of these negative attitudes below. The word *intolerance* will be used here as an umbrella term for this range of attitudes.

One major reason that intolerance is socially significant is its reflection in the treatment accorded an ethnic group or a status group by other members of the population. At the community level this is a problem in intergroup relations, that is, the treatment of blacks by Mexican–Americans, of Catholics by Protestants, of Orientals by Anglo–Saxons, and so on. Simple cultural differences between groups are one thing, but such differences can be transformed into social strata affecting life chances, insofar as the differences come to be associated with wealth or influence. Intergroup relations are bound up with stratification in two ways: In the fact that a group, such as WASPs, is given high or low evaluation by other groups in the community, but also in the fact that persons of high rank may treat members of a given group differently than do those of low rank.

Hence the possibility of discrimination is what makes the distribution of intolerance in a population socially important. The transformation of individual intolerance into socially significant acts of discrimination between groups depends very strongly on the historic social and economic context. But to understand the conditions for the eruption of intergroup hostility at different levels within the status structure of a community, we must learn how social rank is related to intolerant attitudes.

The various forms of intolerance are cognitive styles which are employed socially in thinking about intergroup relations. They vary from highly abstract qualities such as tolerance for ambiguity (which could be socially transformed into reluctance to adopt an available racial stereotype) to particular attitudes such as distrust of Jews (which could be transformed into membership in a restrictive club). Whether they are lifelong personality traits or recently assumed cultural traits, they have the same importance at a point in time, namely, the fact that they can be transformed into a personal basis for intergroup discrimination. The distribution of intolerance according to rank at a point in time indicates the way in which social stratification will be relevant if some specific problem in intergroup relations emerges in the community.

A second major reason why intolerance is socially significant concerns its potential effects on the political process. Lipset (1960:108) has suggested that

> Acceptance of the norms of democracy requires a high level of sophistication and ego security. The less sophisticated and stable an individual, the more likely he is to favor a simplified view of politics, to fail to understand the rationale underlying tolerance of those with whom he disagrees, and to find difficulty in grasping or tolerating a gradualist image of political change.

He suggests that people of low status, lacking this "rich, complex frame of reference" (1960:116), are prone toward extremism. Working class authoritarianism or intolerance, then, represents a danger to democratic institutions:

> The social situation of the lower strata . . . predisposes them to view politics as black or white, good or evil. Consequently, other things being equal, they should be more likely than other strata to prefer extremist movements which suggest easy and quick solutions to social problems and have a rigid outlook [1960:90].

This point of view has been disputed by several researchers, most vigorously by Hamilton (1972:399–506). He maintains that some evidence shows that working class people are in some respects more tolerant or just as tolerant as people in other strata. He also suggests that some of the evidence of greater working class intolerance is spurious, caused by such factors as a higher proportion of working class men being raised in the South. Finally, he contends that these intolerant attitudes result not from early socialization in the working class but rather from outside causes, such as the content of the mass media. Our results, relating the multiple dimensions of rank to various forms of intolerance, will provide some evidence on this controversy.

EXPECTATIONS FROM THEORY

Social rank should be related to or affect various forms of intolerance for a number of reasons. It is convenient to group them roughly under four headings, because the four explanations have somewhat different implications for the way in which rank should be related to intolerance and for the specific forms of intolerance which should be most affected by rank.

Economic deprivation or insecurity is a major suggested source of intolerance. Being at a disadvantage in one or more economic markets, this argument runs, promotes frustration and hostility that may be displaced onto an outgroup in the form of prejudice and/or discrimination (Bettelheim and Janowitz 1964). Alternately, economic deprivation may produce feelings of insecurity and anxiety (Hamilton 1972:452) and this may produce or facilitate intolerance or extremist responses. Finally, a person or group may be at an economic disadvantage because of competition with some identifiable minority group (Blalock 1967a:73–108). Such competition would lead naturally to feelings of hostility toward this outgroup.

What sorts of rank effects on intolerance should economic deprivation produce? We would expect primarily negative relationships (the higher the rank the less the intolerance), and the rank variables most directly involved should be income and occupation.

A second major mechanism possibly relating rank to intolerance is the attempt to strengthen one's claim to prestige or to avoid its loss. Honor and deference are the prime motivators here, rather than economic status (Blalock 1967a:51–70), so individuals systematically avoid and reject contact with those of lower rank in order to preserve their own prestige. One hypothesis implied by this position is that prejudice should be more common among individuals of *higher* rank: "One would generally anticipate that the greater the status gap between two individuals involved in an equal-status contact, the greater the loss in status for the higher-status individual" (Blalock 1967a:61–62). Persons of higher rank, having more prestige to lose, would therefore tend to be less tolerant of contact with any given other group. The forms of tolerance most affected by rank should be those involving low status groups and especially attitudes about intimate equal-status contact with such groups. The forms of rank most closely tied to intolerance by this argument should be those which most closely reflect general prestige. It can be argued that these dimensions are occupation, income and racial–ethnic rank and, subjectively, class self-placement.

A third possible major source of intolerance concerns the emotional and cognitive style of the individual. Emotional rigidity and hostility, on the one hand, and an unsophisticated and over-simplified grasp of social affairs on the other, both predispose the person toward intolerant attitudes (Lipset 1960:87–121). Lipset argues further that lower class people are raised in a situation of tension, aggression, and physical punishment which leads to hostility and a lack of emotional flexibility. Lower class people also tend to have limited perspectives and are isolated from heterogeneous environments (see Schooler 1972), preventing them from acquiring a sophisticated understanding of, for example, the political system. This reasoning suggests that the social rank of origin and education should be the most salient dimensions in affecting intolerance. Furthermore, it suggests that intolerance is a general interpersonal orientation, which could be displayed in a variety of specific forms. Therefore, the prediction would be that rank of origin and education should have substantial effects on all forms of intolerance.

Finally, it may be that attitudes of intolerance and prejudice (or of tolerance) mainly reflect norms embedded in certain cultures or subcultures. By this view, a person is tolerant or intolerant because he has internalized norms of prejudice or tolerance early in life, or has been taught them as part of his formal schooling (Davis 1975; Whitt and Nelson 1975). Further, these processes of learning will usually nominate particular targets for prejudice.[1] Therefore, a level of social rank may be the social occasion of some subculture, but the height or depth of the level may not be a factor in the extent to which the subculture carries norms of prejudice or tolerance.

It must be remembered that both types of norms may affect one's level of tolerance; norms of forebearance and goodwill may be as powerful at some rank levels as norms of prejudice are at others. It is plausible, for example, that additional years of education would include more or less explicit support for norms of tolerance, perhaps accompanied by systematic disparagement of norms of prejudice. Whatever these norms, however, if it is true that they are mainly internalized in the family of origin and during education and are little changed thereafter, the major effects on forms of intolerance should be carried by the dimensions of origin rank (including ethnicity) and education.

The discussion above suggests some general connections between rank and intolerance, but it must be emphasized that the effect of some form of rank on some kind of tolerance may well depend on or vary with particular sets of historical conditions. While most authors concede the relevance of rank for racial discrimination, for example, the mechanism for the relationship is held to be complex, depending on sociohistorical conditions, political climate, etc. Among the many reasons why an individual's rank might influence his intolerance, that is, some will be made salient by historic circumstance while the effect of others will be suppressed.

The evidence provided by past studies[2] on the relations between rank and

---

[1]Different groups espouse approval or disapproval of different things. In a comment on this manuscript, Richard L. Simpson pointed out that tolerance, as measured in most studies (including this one), confounds two questions: (a) "What do you disapprove of?" and (b) "How tolerant are you regarding things of which you disapprove?" The cogency of this comment will be apparent in the questions we asked. Its implication is that the results we (and others) report probably include both a weak relationship between social rank and a general willingness to "live and let live in spite of wrongheadedness," and a specification of persons, attitudes, behaviors, and characteristics more approved of (or less disapproved of) by higher ranking persons than by lower ranking persons.

[2]Past studies on racial and ethnic prejudice include Greenblum and Pearlin (1953), Bettelheim and Janowitz (1964), Silberstein and Seeman (1959), Williams (1964), Hodge and Treiman (1966), and Treiman (1966). Several of these studies are mainly concerned with the

intolerance is not completely adequate. Most studies have concentrated on a specific dependent variable such as attitudes toward blacks or attitudes about the civil liberties of various kinds of deviant persons (Stouffer 1955:26–57). In general, education has usually been found to be related to higher levels of tolerance, but the findings on income, occupation and social rank of origin have not been completely consistent. This may be because most studies have included only one or two forms of social rank simultaneously, leaving other forms of rank uncontrolled. Other potentially important variables, such as age and being raised in the South, which may spuriously produce or mask relationships between rank and intolerance, are also often left uncontrolled. Our analysis below will attempt to provide improved evidence, relating a number of forms of rank simultaneously to several forms of intolerance, controlling for at least some of the important potentially confounding variables.

FOUR VARIETIES OF INTOLERANCE

We are primarily interested in the effects of rank on a generalized attitude of intolerance (*if* such an attitude exists) rather than intolerance limited to any one behavior or attitude. We should like to investigate a quality more general than anti-Semitism, racial discrimination, or anti-Catholicism, yet one which may be manifested in any of these ways. Therefore, we shall attempt to replicate across dependent variables as well as across communities.

Our focus, then, is on generalized tolerance for behaviors, points of view, alien individuals or groups, unpopular ideas and so on, although we are in no position to measure it directly and have no reason to regard it as necessarily unidimensional in any case. Therefore, we shall examine four different instances of tolerance, giving special attention to commonalities in the relationship between each of them and social rank. The four varieties of tolerance were selected to represent a wide range of variation. Generalized tolerance, however, should not be taken as an independent concept, but rather as an indefinite set of which the four types of responses studied are members.

Racial prejudice is our first form of intolerance. It is our guess that Americans accept racial–ethnic stereotypes (based on socio-political thought and ideology but unmotivated by direct personal experience) much less than before in our history (see Bettelheim and Janowitz 1964; Campbell 1971). However, they are strongly motivated by certain specific issues in

---

effects of social mobility or status inconsistency, but their data can be examined for the main effects of various rank dimensions. Dogmatism and related cognitive styles were investigated by Rokeach (1960). Stouffer's (1955) study is the original analysis of punitiveness toward deviant groups (see also Davis 1975). Lipset (1960:Chapter 4) and Hamilton (1972:Chapter 11) both present data on several forms of intolerance.

racial relations, as exemplified now by busing and proportional representation in hiring and in political organization.

To represent the area of prejudice and discrimination as realistically as possible within the interview context, we focused on residence, and where possible, on actual experiences. Following open questions on what makes a good area, and whether there are groups or types of people the respondent would not like moving in, we asked, "Are there any Negroes living in this neighborhood? (If yes,) How do you feel about this? (If no,) How would you feel if a Negro tried to move into this neighborhood?" Blacks were not asked these questions.

The respondents' replies were rated and scored on a scale from 0 (reflecting approval involving action) to 4 (reflecting the willingness to act in a disapproving way), with intermediate scores given to remarks indicating attitudes of approval or disapproval not accompanied by statements about action.[3] We labeled this variable *disapproval of Negroes as neighbors*. This scale appeared to be the most effective of the items we used in the domain of racial attitudes; other questions proved to be more responsive to such different issues as states' rights, constitutionalism, and property rights.

Since this item was pointed so specifically at the issue of blacks living or moving into the respondent's neighborhood, we wanted other items that might also show the effects of generalized tolerance, but under different conditions. Behaviors, as well as persons, can be the objects of intolerance. The rigidity of norms and the sanctions attached to them are also relevant. The other three aspects of intolerance we chose were conventionalism, dogmatism, and attitudes toward deviant behavior.

By *conventionalism* we mean the extent to which respondents see people as limited by normative conventions attached to their social positions, especially where the deviance was mild or the definition of the position highly conventional. We asked:

Here are some situations that some people in other communities think are wrong. Please tell me how you feel:

How do you feel about a college professor who uses swear words in public places?
How do you feel about an elementary school teacher who visits a bar in the evening with an escort?[4]
What would you think of a minister who divorced his wife?

---

[3]The categories used to classify respondents were: approving response involving action ("Would try to help them"); approving response restricted to an attitude ("Would like it, fine with me"); contingent or neutral response ("OK if they are friendly"; "Wouldn't make any difference to me"); disapproving response not involving action ("I'd hate it"; "I'd just have to adjust"); disapproving response involving action ("I'd sell"; "Run them out"). These were scored respectively from 0 to 4, so a high score indicates strong disapproval of Negro neighbors. If a respondent made several remarks, he was given the score appropriate to most disapproving response of the first three remarks he made.

[4]In Indianapolis this question was worded differently: "Do you think it is right for an elementary school teacher to visit a bar in the evening with an escort?"

For each of these questions, the respondent was given a score of 0 if he said "right," of 1 if he said "neither right nor wrong" or "it depends," and of 2 if he said "wrong." The index is simply the sum of these scores, so it varies from 0 to 6 with a high score indicating disapproval of these unconventional acts. In Chapter 5, we called this variable the index of adherence to conventional norms, but for simplicity we shall here label it *conventionalism*.

A third aspect of intolerance is preference for a rigid authoritarian hierarchy in which rules from above are not questioned. We call this variable *dogmatism*. Our measurement is relatively weak, since we used only two questions (both taken from Rokeach 1960:78–79). Both asked the respondent to agree or disagree: "Any group that tolerates too many differences of opinion among its members cannot exist for long," and, "Governing a country this large is so difficult that the only thing we can do is to trust our leaders and their experts to do what is right." Each of these questions was scored 0 for "strongly disagree" to 4 for "strongly agree." The dogmatism index is simply the sum of these two scores, so a high score indicates high dogmatism, or intolerance toward generalized sociopolitical dissent.[5]

Our fourth measure deals with intolerance toward four attitudes and/or behaviors often considered deviant. Our questions (based on, and extending, those asked by Stouffer in *Communism, Conformity, and Civil Liberties* 1955:26–57) were:

> There are always people in any community whose behavior is considered strange or undesirable by others. We would like to ask you several questions about some people like this.
>
> First of all an atheist. Should an atheist—a person who doesn't believe in God—be allowed to make a speech in (community)? Suppose an atheist is a high school teacher. Should he be allowed to keep his job? Should the city government try to get an atheist to leave the community? Should an atheist be punished?

Other "deviants" concerning whom the same questions were asked included drug addict, nudist, and Communist.[6] The responses were scored to form a scale from 0 to 56, the high score indicating most intolerance.[7] This measure differs from those above in avoiding the issue of social rank (atheists

---

[5]Because of a technical error in the Indianapolis results for dogmatism, only the findings for the other five communities are reported here.

[6]In the Indianapolis survey, the wording was slightly different. The main differences were that the word "atheist" was used without supplying the definition, " . . . a person who doesn't believe in God." Similarly, in the five-city survey, the respondent was given a definition of a nudist as "a person who goes to nudist camps where they don't wear any clothes," but in the Indianapolis survey the word "nudist" was used without any additional explanation or definition.

Note that, as suggested by Simpson (Footnote 1), we failed to ask about tolerance of radical rightists, whether it is alright to drink beer in an undershirt, or whether a public school teacher could espouse the doctrine of racial inferiority.

[7]To establish weights for the degrees of punitiveness, a factor analysis of the items was carried out (Fairbank 1973:92). This preliminary analysis indicated that not allowing a deviant to speak and not allowing him to teach were roughly equivalent, while making him leave the community

or nudists could be rich or poor, white or black, well or poorly educated), in dealing with forms of deviance usually thought more serious, and dealing specifically with the severity of sanctions to be imposed, rather than simply asking about general reactions toward the behavior. We label this variable *punitiveness toward deviants.*[8]

The intercorrelations between the four varieties of intolerance suggest that it is a domain of weakly connected attitudes. Punitiveness toward deviants is a central measure, moderately related both to dogmatism and conventionalism, and, less strongly, to disapproval of Negroes. Dogmatism and conventionalism are mildly related to one another, but neither is related to disapproval of Negroes. This pattern of relationships is reproduced with remarkable similarity in each of the cities. We can graphically represent the arithmetic average of the intercorrelations (exluding Indianapolis) as follows:[9]

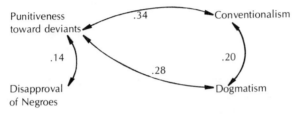

was more severe and punishing him still more severe. Points were assigned to responses as follows:

	"No"	"It depends"	"Yes"
Allowed to speak?	2	1	0
Allowed to teach?	2	1	0
Made to leave?	0	2	4
Punished?	0	3	6

The points were then summed to yield the respondent's index score. The index thus varied from 0 to 56, with a high score indicating greatest intolerance and greatest tendency to punish these forms of deviance.

[8]The dogmatism index is directly subject to the problem of acquiescence response set because respondents who said "agree" to both questions would receive high dogmatism scores. However, since the question on Negro neighbors was "How would you feel . . . ?" simple acquiescence was obviated. To receive high conventionalism scores, respondents would have to say that specific behaviors were wrong, which is a far cry from universally answering "true" on a true–false test. The punitiveness toward deviants index was balanced: to attain the highest intolerance score, the respondent had to answer, "no, no, yes, yes", for each type of deviance. Thus, three of the four intolerance measures were guarded against the acquiescence response set problem in three different ways. Dogmatism was not, but whatever dogmatism has in common with the other three aspects of intolerance cannot be explained by acquiescence response set.

[9]The omitted correlations (disapproval of Negroes by conventionalism and dogmatism respectively) are .03 and .06.

These results suggest that intolerance toward deviant, unconventional, or dissident behaviors does tend to form a complex of attitudes which tend to be found together. However, a person's position on this rough dimension is not, in general, well related to his prejudice toward a raci?, group of low rank.[10] These data cast doubt on our initial notions of tolerance as a single generalized stance toward social objects, and on the causal relevance of intolerance for racial hostility.

EFFECTS OF RANK ON FOUR FORMS OF INTOLERANCE

We begin by presenting the results from four analyses, each one using seven rank variables to predict one of the forms of intolerance. These analyses also include controls for several variables that we thought might confound or muddle the effects of rank on intolerance. For example, older people tend to be less well educated; if growing old also makes one less tolerant, then age would produce a spurious relationship between education and tolerance (better educated people would appear to be more tolerant, simply because they were younger). To get more accurate estimates of how rank affects intolerance, then, we controlled in the following analyses for five variables which were strongly related to one or more of the forms of intolerance: age, whether the respondent was raised in the South, the size of the place in which he was raised, the length of time he had lived in his community (for a rationale for this list, see Whitt and Nelson 1975), and general satisfaction. What we will see in the tables below, then, are the net effects of rank after these five variables have been statistically held constant.

Disapproval of Negroes as Neighbors

Two forms of current rank are consistent in their effect on the respondent's tendency to disapprove of Negro neighbors, but these effects are in opposite directions: Higher education consistently and strongly reduced disapproval, while higher family income tends to encourage this form of intolerance (see Table 11.1). The effects of rank of origin (father's occupation and mother's education) are scattered and vary in direction from city to city.

In the three Arizona cities, majority men are much more likely to disapprove of Negroes as neighbors. The minority men in this comparison are primarily Mexican–American since this question was not asked of blacks and therefore they do not appear in Table 11.1. With other rank variables

[10]For a more detailed discussion of these (and other) components of intolerance, see Fairbank (1973), who comes to the same conclusions on prejudice against blacks. She warns, however, of a possible artifactual explanation of the correlation among components: quality of measurement. Punitiveness probably contains the least random error, with conventionalism second.

held constant, then, we find that Mexican–American men are much more willing to have Negroes as neighbors than are men of majority racial–ethnic rank.

We see, their that one rank variable, education, affects this form of intolerance negatively, while two other ranks, income, and racial–ethnic status, are positively related. We will consider possible explanations for these opposed effects in the concluding section below.

Disapproval of Negroes as neighbors differed from the other three forms of intolerance in being substantially less predictable from rank. In five of the six cities, the seven rank variables added only a modest contribution to explained variance, over and above the variance due to the control variables. One reason for this may be that disapproval of Negroes was measured by answers to a single item, and hence is probably affected more by random measurement error than some of our other scales derived from several averaged items. Furthermore, this form of intolerance refers to a specific attitude directed at one group rather than representing a general orientation. Therefore, one might expect many variables (e.g., dyspepsia, experiences with blacks, friends' attitudes, etc.) to affect this form of intolerance in ways not explainable by social rank. Since in each city some rank effects were positive and others were negative, the general rank index, representing an overall averaging of the person's social positions, was related very poorly to disapproval of Negroes. Indeed, general rank was related to this form of intolerance positively in some cities and negatively in others.

The respondents' scores on this dependent variable averaged out between 2 and 3 in each of the six cities, indicating moderate disapproval. The greatest disapproval was found in Indianapolis and Linton, and the least in Columbus, Yuma, and Safford. These differences were changed very little when the cities were equalized statistically with respect to the seven rank variables and the control variables. The variation in the adjusted means, although statistically significant, does not appear to be patterned clearly by region or by size of city, nor by the presence of blacks in the community. For example, Indianapolis, with a substantial black subcommunity, and Linton, with almost no black residents, exhibited equally high adjusted means.

Within a framework of rough similarity, there was some variation from city to city in the pattern of the rank effects. The analysis of covariance in Chapter 5 (restricted to majority men only) showed that rank effects on disapproval of Negroes were different enough from city to city to produce interaction significant between the .05 and .25 level. Although many of the variations across cities appear to be random and unintelligible, several can be singled out for mention. First, the effects of current achieved rank were entirely missing in Linton, meaning in that city rank explains almost none of the variance in the extent to which men disapprove of Negro neighbors. Second, the difference in this form of tolerance between majority and minority men appears to be especially large in the city of Safford. A special

Table 11.1 Disapproval of Negroes as Neighbors Regressed on Rank Variables (Net of Control Variable Effects)

	Regression coefficients: Unstandardized and standardized (in parentheses)[a]					
Rank variables	Indianapolis	Columbus	Linton	Phoenix	Yuma	Safford
	b					
Self-placement				.042 (.07)	.056 (.10)	
Family income (00s)	.001 (.06)	.001 (.08)			.002 (.13)*[c]	.002 (.15)*
Occupation	-.002 (.07)	.005 (.16)*		-.002 (.05)	-.003 (.07)	
Education	-.045 (.20)*	-.033 (.14)*		-.014 (.06)	-.049 (.21)*	-.023 (.12)
Father's occupation	.003 (.09)	-.003 (.08)	.002 (.05)			-.005 (.11)*
Mother's education	.030 (.09)		-.027 (.08)		.035 (.14)*	
Majority[d]			.003 (.09)	.518 (.19)*	.232 (.11)*	.783 (.38)*
Proportion of the variance explained by						
Above rank variables	.05	.04	.04	.04*	.08*	.18*
Rank variables, net[e]	.04	.04	.01	.03*	.07*	.14*
17 variable regression	.09	.10*	.09	.06*	.11*	.20*
General rank index[f]	(-).03*	(+).00	(-).01	(+).00	(+).00	(+).02*

294

Means

Unadjusted	2.68	2.33	2.65	2.40	2.33	2.33
Adjusted[g]	2.65	2.32	2.61	2.42	2.33	2.34
N	240	327	266	638	324	285

[a] These are the regression coefficients in an analysis employing the listed rank variables *plus* five control variables: age, raised in the South, size of place in which raised, time lived in the community, and general satisfaction. The coefficients thus reflect rank effects after these five variables have been controlled.

[b] In this and remaining tables in this chapter, coefficients are not shown when the standardized coefficient is both nonsignificant and less than .05, i.e., for zero or relatively weak effects.

[c] In this and remaining tables in this chapter, asterisked regression coefficients are those with associated *t*-values of 1.65 or higher; hence, significant at approximately the .10 level (two-tailed test). Asterisked correlation coefficients are those significant at the .05 level.

[d] In this and remaining tables in this chapter, the majority racial-ethnic variable is replaced by the (reversed) Bogardus social distance score in Columbus and Linton since these samples contained almost no men of minority rank.

[e] In this and remaining tables in this chapter, this is the proportion of the variance explained by the seven rank variables beyond that explained by the five control variables (that is, the R^2 for all 12 variables less the R^2 for the five control variables alone).

[f] In this and remaining tables in this chapter, the direction of the relationship with the general rank index is given in parentheses.

[g] Means on disapproval of Negroes as neighbors after statistically equalizing the cities on the seven rank variables (substituting Bogardus social distance scores for majority racial-ethnic rank in all six cities to allow cities to be compared) and four control variables of age, raised in the South, size of place in which raised, and time lived in the community. These adjusted means are significantly different (*p*<.01).

analysis (not shown) indicated that this marked effect occurs not because the Mormons in Safford, who make up a substantial proportion of the majority men, have especially disapproving attitudes toward Blacks, but because minority men in Safford were unusually approving. Third, the only statistically significant effect of social rank of family origin occurs in Safford. This effect also occurs for each of the other three forms of intolerance. Clearly, a social background of higher status in this particular town appears to increase all forms of tolerance. Although the effect is remarkably regular, we cannot explain why it works the way it does or why the effect should only appear in this community and not in the other five.

Conventionalism

The tendency to insist that members of certain occupations should live up to conventional norms seems to be reduced consistently by several forms of social rank (see Table 11.2). In general, education reduces conventionalism most, but majority racial–ethnic rank and higher income also have moderate negative effects. In most cities, coming from a home of higher status (as indexed either by father's occupation or mother's education) seems to have a small net effect in reducing conventionalism. One result of these consistently negative rank effects is that the general rank index is negatively related to conventionalism in each of the six communities.[11]

The means in all six cities ran between 3.5 and a little over 4.0, indicating, overall, mildly conventional attitudes. The data suggest that, even after adjusting for a number of rank and control variables, attitudes of conventionalism may be most pronounced in small towns. However, the highest single mean on conventionalism appeared in Columbus, providing an exception to this pattern.

The patterns of rank effects are somewhat different from city to city. The analysis of covariance dealing with majority men, in Chapter 5, yielded an

[11]We pointed out in Chapter 5 that in almost all of our analyses the effects of rank variables on a given dependent variable assumed an additive form. That is, the data did not require an explanation in terms of special effects of social mobility or status inconsistency. However, the data do include a trace suggestion that one form of status inconsistency may possibly affect conventionalism. When we related this dependent variable to racial–ethnic rank and occupation, interaction was significant in three of the six cities (see Jackson and Curtis 1972:709–710). The deviations of observed means from those predicted by the additive model assumed the same plausible form in Yuma and in Safford: People who have an occupational rank which is either much higher or much lower than their racial–ethnic rank are less likely to condemn unconventional behavior than are people with more consistent positions on these two rank variables. The same pattern of deviations also tends to appear in the other four cities, even though interaction was usually not statistically significant.

Considering that we did not hypothesize this particular effect of status inconsistency, that other forms of mobility or inconsistency did not affect conventionalism, and that some such results might well turn up solely by chance in a large number of analyses, we should probably regard this finding as no more than suggestive.

Table 11.2 Conventionalism Regressed on Rank Variables (Net of Control Variable Effects)

Rank variables	Regression coefficients: Unstandardized and standardized (in parentheses)[a]					
	Indianapolis	Columbus	Linton	Phoenix	Yuma	Safford
Self-placement		.060 (.05)			.065 (.06)	
Family income (00s)	-.004 (.13)*			-.003 (.14)*	-.002 (.07)	-.003 (.12)*
Occupation	.004 (.05)		.005 (.07)			-.008 (.12)
Education		-.076 (.17)*	-.077 (.15)*	-.039 (.09)*	-.091 (.20)*	-.016 (.16)*
Father's occupation		-.003 (.05)		-.005 (.08)*		
Mother's education	-.037 (.06)		.046 (.07)	-.030 (.06)	-.033 (.07)	
Majority	-.396 (.08)		-.005 (.07)	-.688 (.14)*	-.455 (.12)*	
Proportion of the variance explained by						
Above rank variables	.10*	.13*	.05*	.17*	.13*	.16*
Rank variables, net	.03	.03	.02	.13*	.08*	.09*
17 variable regression	.15*	.18*	.07	.18*	.16*	.20*
General rank index	(-).04*	(-).07*	(-).02*	(-).12*	(-).08*	(-).12*
Mean						
Unadjusted	3.44	4.03	4.16	3.47	3.53	4.12
Adjusted[b]	3.59	4.09	3.94	3.58	3.49	3.83
N	271	338	266	641	330	237

[a] These are the regression coefficients in an analysis employing the listed rank variables plus five control variables: age; raised in the South, size of place in which raised, time lived in the community, and general satisfaction. The coefficients thus reflect rank effects after these five variables have been controlled.

[b] Means on conventionalism after statistically equalizing the cities on the seven rank variables (substituting Bogardus social distance scores for majority racial-ethnic rank in all six cities to allow cities to be compared) and four control variables of age, raised in the South, size of place in which raised, and time lived in the community. These adjusted means are significantly different (p<.01).

297

interaction term significant at the .05 level. The effects of education, income, and majority racial–ethnic rank, although somewhat consistent, do not appear in some cities, although these fluctuations are difficult to explain. The effect of income appears mainly in the Arizona communities, and is missing from Columbus and Linton. Majority racial–ethnic rank tends to reduce conventional attitudes, but this effect is missing in two communities. The absence is understandable in Columbus, since the comparison there involves only majority men of various national origins, but it is hard to understand why there is no effect of majority versus minority rank in Safford. Finally, we note again that the largest effect of father's occupation in reducing conventionalism appears in Safford.

These patterns of effects produced some differences between cities in the ability of the rank variables as a set to explain variance in conventionalism. The added amounts of explanation ranged around 10% in the three Arizona cities, but were only 2% or 3% in the three Indiana cities. Presumably, this is because the effects of income, father's occupation, and majority rank all tended to be smaller in the Indiana cities than in the Arizona cities.

Dogmatism

The effects of social rank on dogmatism, like conventionalism, are mostly negative. Additional years of education lead to the most substantial reductions in dogmatism, but higher occupational rank also has consistent negative effects.[12] In two of the cities in which a comparison is possible, men of majority racial–ethnic rank are less dogmatic than minority men. The data (in Table 11.3) also contain a suggestion that men from higher status homes, as indexed by father's occupation and mother's education, may be somewhat less dogmatic. Since most rank effects are negative, the respondent's average rank represented by our general rank index is negatively related to dogmatism in all five cities reported.

The patterns of rank effects on dogmatism show considerable similarity from city to city. The effects of both education and occupation, although they fluctuate somewhat in size, appear in each of the five communities. Many of the differences in rank effects from city to city appear to be scattered and random in nature. We can note, however, that once again a substantial negative effect of father's occupation appears in Safford, while majority

---

[12]The figures shown here may slightly underestimate the effect of education. The reader may remember that in Chapter 5 we found the relationship between education and dogmatism to be somewhat curvilinear, in that increasing education lead to smaller and smaller decreases in dogmatism (i.e., dogmatism decreased at a decreasing rate with increases in education). However, the curve relating education and dogmatism was significantly nonlinear in only three cities and even there the gain in explanation allowed by permitting a curvilinear relationship was relatively small (1% to 3%). Therefore, we feel that the coefficients for education in Table 11.3 do not seriously misrepresent the effects of that rank variable.

Table 11.3 Dogmatism Regressed on Rank Variables (Net of Control Variable Effects)

Rank variables	Regression coefficients: Unstandardized and standardized (in parentheses)[a]				
	Columbus	Linton	Phoenix	Yuma	Safford
Self-placement	.135 (.12)*		-.063 (.05)		-.132 (.11)*
Family income (00s)			-.003 (.12)*		-.002 (.06)
Occupation	-.010 (.15)*	-.004 (.07)	-.011 (.15)*	-.008 (.13)*	-.007 (.10)
Education	-.141 (.31)*	-.104 (.24)*	-.084 (.17)*	-.082 (.20)*	-.076 (.19)*
Father's occupation				-.003 (.05)	-.013 (.14)*
Mother's education	-.068 (.11)*	.027 (.05)			-.026 (.06)
Majority		-.005 (.09)	-.391 (.07)*	-.691 (.19)*	
Proportion of the variance explained by					
Above rank variables	.21*	.11*	.21*	.20*	.25*
Rank variables, net	.14*	.05*	.16*	.16*	.19*
17 variable regression	.24*	.13*	.24*	.22*	.30*
General rank index	(-).14*	(-).07*	(-).17*	(-).13*	(-).20*
Mean					
Unadjusted	4.55	5.14	4.52	4.81	4.67
Adjusted[b]	4.66	4.99	4.60	4.73	4.48
N	333	270	644	347	273

[a]These are the regression coefficients in an analysis employing the listed rank variables *plus* five control variables: age, raised in the South, size of place in which raised, time lived in the community, and general satisfaction. The coefficients thus reflect rank effects *after* these five variables have been controlled.

[b]Means on dogmatism after statistically equalizing the cities on the seven rank variables (substituting Bogardus social distance scores for majority racial-ethnic rank in all six cities to allow cities to be compared) and four control variables of age, raised in the South, size of place in which raised, and time lived in the community. These adjusted means are significantly different ($p < .01$).

racial–ethnic rank has no effect in that city. The reader will recall that this same configuration of effects appeared in Safford in the analysis of conventionalism.

The relationship between rank and this form of intolerance (net of control variables) seems to be stronger than the relationship between rank and either disapproval of Negroes as neighbors or conventionalism. The rank variables explain about an additional 15% of variance in four of the cities, although the net explanation drops to a lower level in Linton.

Punitiveness Toward Deviants

Several forms of social rank also appear to reduce the tendency to deny privileges to or punish deviants. In each city, better educated men are much less likely to be punitive than poorly educated men. Higher income and occupation have similarly negative effects on punitiveness, although these effects are smaller. Finally, the data (in Table 11.4) suggest that men of majority racial–ethnic rank tend to be less punitive than minority men. In five of the six cities, however, a contrasting positive effect appears: Net of objective status position, men who rank themselves higher in the class system tend to be more rather than less punitive. We will examine possible explanations for these opposing effects below. Because most rank effects are negative, our index of general rank is negatively correlated with punitiveness in each of the communities.

These patterns of rank effects are very consistent from city to city, even though we found in Chapter 5 that the between-city interaction term was minimally significant. In that analysis, allowing for different patterns of effects in the different cities added two percent of explained variance to the 17% explained by the common within-city model. The reason for this low amount of additional explanation is clear; most of the important effects appeared consistently in most of the cities. The negative effects of education and occupation were found in all six cities and the negative effect of income and the positive effect of self-placement were found in five of the six cities. City differences worth mentioning include the significant negative impact of father's occupation which appears, once again, in the city of Safford, and the absence of an effect of majority racial–ethnic rank in Indianapolis. The data suggest that blacks and whites do not differ in punitiveness, but that in the three Arizona cities the Mexican–Americans are somewhat more punitive in their attitudes towards deviants than are Anglo men.

The means on punitiveness ranged between 17 and 22 in the six cities. This indicates an average answer slightly more punitive than prohibiting each of the deviant persons (atheists, nudists, etc.) from speaking publicly or teaching, but allowing them to remain in the community, unpunished. The differences between city means persist when the cities are statistically

Table 11.4 Punitiveness Toward Deviants Regressed on Rank Variables (Net of Control Variable Effects)

Rank variables	Regression coefficients: Unstandardized and standardized (in parentheses)[a]					
	Indianapolis	Columbus	Linton	Phoenix	Yuma	Safford
Self-placement	.807 (.09)	.938 (.10)*	.635 (.07)		.390 (.05)	.711 (.08)
Family income (00s)	-.026 (.12)*		-.012 (.05)	-.010 (.06)	-.011 (.05)	-.013 (.06)
Occupation	-.036 (.07)	-.045 (.09)	-.026 (.05)	-.037 (.08)*	-.064 (.13)*	-.059 (.11)
Education	-.899 (.27)*	-1.626 (.46)*	-.953 (.23)*	-.968 (.31)*	-1.343 (.41)*	-.968 (.31)*
Father's occupation	.036 (.06)					-.074 (.10)*
Mother's education	-.375 (.08)	.361 (.07)			.167 (.05)	.250 (.07)
Majority				-4.774 (.14)*	-2.546 (.09)*	-5.851 (.17)*
Proportion of the variance explained by						
Above rank variables	.18*	.24*	.12*	.21*	.29*	.25*
Rank variables, net	.11*	.15*	.06*	.18*	.23*	.22*
17 variable regression	.22*	.27*	.16*	.22*	.32*	.27*
General rank index	(-).09*	(-).10*	(-).08*	(-).15*	(-).19*	(-).16*
Mean						
Unadjusted	20.1	19.2	22.1	16.8	17.5	21.6
Adjusted[b]	20.9	19.8	20.9	17.8	16.6	19.7
N	281	343	272	655	353	289

[a] These are the regression coefficients in an analysis employing the listed rank variables plus five control variables: age; raised in the South, size of place in which raised, time lived in the community, and general satisfaction. The coefficients thus reflect rank effects after these five variables have been controlled.

[b] Means on punitiveness toward deviants after statistically equalizing the cities on the seven rank variables (substituting Bogardus social distance scores for majority racial-ethnic rank in all six cities to be compared) and four control variables: age, raised in the South, size of place in which raised, and time lived in the community. These adjusted means are significantly different (p<.01).

301

"made equal" on the rank and control variables. The city differences suggest that punitiveness is generally higher in the Indiana communities than in Arizona, and that punitiveness is curvilinearly related to community size, being lowest in the medium size cities.

Social rank is more strongly related to this form of intolerance than to the other three already considered. The seven rank variables contribute between 10% and 20% of additional explained variance in most cities, net of the effects of the control variables. However, the effect of rank on punitiveness appears to be stronger in Arizona than in Indiana cities, and is especially weak in the city of Linton. Presumably, one main reason for this is that relatively strong effects of majority rank appear in the three Arizona cities but are absent in the Indiana cities.

Intervening Variables

We initially thought that at least some of these effects of rank on certain forms of intolerance might be explained by either satisfaction or by rate of social participation. That is, we suspected that men of high rank would be more satisfied or would participate relatively more either in formal or informal social networks and either of these experiences might lead them to be more tolerant. However, the data give us no encouragement for any of these hypotheses. When measures of satisfaction or of various forms of social contact were introduced into analyses involving rank and the intolerance measures, the rank effects were not reduced. Usually the supposed intervening variables were not in fact related to dependent variable. Only slight effects appeared. For example, the average standardized regression coefficient of general satisfaction was +.04 in affecting conventionality, +.05 in affecting punitiveness, and −.03 in affecting disapproval of Negroes. In addition, the paths from rank to the intervening variables were small, so the intervening variables essentially explained little or none of the original effects of rank. These data argue that something else about education and other forms of social rank other than general contentment or social participation is the reason that intolerance varies with social rank.[13]

A promising line of thought not addressed in these data suggests that cosmopolitanism, or "breadth of world view" is specifically the intervening variable that relates formal education to less dogmatism, conventionalism, punitiveness or related aspects of intolerance (Gabennesch 1972; Schooler 1972). The same might also be true for disapproval of Negroes as neighbors.

[13]In an earlier exploratory analysis (Curtis, Timbers and Jackson 1967), we had suggested that possibly intolerance might be decreased by participation in formal associations and increased by certain kinds of contacts with primary groups. These hypotheses were not borne out in analyses of the present data (see Fairbank 1973).

SUMMARY AND CONCLUSIONS

The major results from our analysis of the effects of social rank on four forms
of intolerance are as follows:

1. Most forms of high rank tend to reduce most types of intolerance. A
detailed display of rank effects is given in Figure 11.1. Additional years of
education strongly reduces all four forms of intolerance. Higher-ranked
occupations tend to reduce dogmatism and punitiveness toward deviants.
The effects of income and majority racial–ethnic rank are generally negative, but high rank on these two variables *increases* disapproval of Negroes
as neighbors. Self-placement does not affect most forms of intolerance, but
has a positive effect on punitiveness. The effects on intolerance of social
rank of origin are generally weak, but higher father's occupation did appear
to reduce both dogmatism and conventionalism in at least some of the cities.

All rank effects on conventionalism and dogmatism, then, were negative;
the same is true of punitiveness except for the positive effect of self-
placement. Disapproval of Negroes as neighbors was, however, reduced by
more education and increased by higher income and majority racial–ethnic
rank.

2. The general rank index, our approximation to an average SES or class
position scale, was negatively related to conventionalism, dogmatism, and
punitiveness toward deviants, because rank effects on these forms of intolerance were generally negative. For disapproval of Negroes, where this was
not true, the relationship between the general rank index and intolerance
was both weak and varied in direction.

3. The set of rank variables explained only modest amounts of variance in
conventionalism and disapproval of Negroes, but relatively substantial
amounts of variance in dogmatism and punitiveness.

4. Our communities differed significantly in the mean levels of each of
the four forms of intolerance, even after they were statistically equalized
with respect to the various rank variables and control variables. In general,
Indiana communities had higher averages on all forms of intolerance than
Arizona communities of the same size.

5. The pattern of certain rank effects was the same in all communities
(e.g., education) especially for effects on dogmatism and punitiveness, although there were often additional effects that varied from city to city (e.g.,
father's occupation). Statistical interaction was at least minimally significant
for all the forms of intolerance. Some of the differences between cities
depended upon the different racial–ethnic compositions of the cities. For
example, majority rank had no effect on punitiveness in Indianapolis where
the minority men are all almost entirely black. The effect of majority rank
was usually different in Safford from that effect in other cities; the effect of

	Forms of Intolerance			
	Disapproval of black as neighbors	Conventionalism	Dogmatism	Punitiveness toward deviants
Self-placement	(+)			+
Family income	+ (+)	– (–)	(–)	– (–)
Occupation	(+)	(–)	– – (– –)	– (–)
Education	– – (– –)	– – (– – –)	– – (– – –)	– – (– –)
Father's occupation	(– –)	–? (–)	–? (–)	(–)
Mother's education	(– –)	(–)	(–)	(–)
Majority	+ + + (+ + +)	– (–)	– (–)	– (–)
Average net R^2 due to rank	.06	.06	.13	.16

Figure 11.1 *Summary of observed and expected rank effects on forms of intolerance ("+" indicates a positive effect and "–" a negative effect; the number of signs indicates the strength of the effect and how consistently it appeared in the six cities. Signs in parentheses are effects predicted by the model in Figure 11.2)*

majority was stronger in Safford for disapproval of Negroes as neighbors and for punitiveness and disappeared with respect to conventionalism and dogmatism. Finally, a negative effect of father's occupation on each of the forms of intolerance regularly appeared in Safford. Social background appears to be especially salient for intolerance in this community.

6. For all of the forms of intolerance, the set of social rank variables explained more of the variance in intolerance in the Arizona communities than in the Indiana cities. Intolerance appeared to vary more strongly with social rank in Arizona.

7. Satisfaction and various forms of informal and formal social participation *do not* appear to act as intervening variables mediating the effects of rank on the various forms of intolerance.

The basic fact that most intolerant attitudes are inversely associated with most forms of social rank is clearly reflected in all cities and may be regarded as an established empirical generalization for social conditions such as those investigated in this study. However, the effects of some forms of social rank, notably education, are stronger than the effects of others. Also, the way in which rank affects attitudes toward Negro neighbors is much different from the pattern of effects on other forms of intolerance. We will therefore try to go beyond the broad generalization just stated and present a more detailed, though speculative, explanation of why rank affects intolerance. This explanation will help account for some of the substantial departures from the general pattern of overall negative effects.

As a first step, let us note that our four forms of intolerance fall conceptually into two fairly distinct groups. The question about attitudes toward Negro neighbors taps the respondent's feelings, not only toward a social category explicitly defined as low in (racial–ethnic) rank, but also his feelings about associating intimately with members of such a group. A question of this kind, dealing with close social contact with persons of low rank, raises the threat of loss of prestige. However, this is not true of the items on conventionalism, dogmatism, or punitiveness toward deviants.

A second major difference among the four types of intolerance concerns the nature of the behavior to which the respondent is asked to react. For the questions on conventionalism, dogmatism, and punitiveness toward deviants, some form of deviant or improper behavior is always involved, either behavior counter to a norm or behavior counter to the edicts of authority (as in the dogmatism question). This is not true of the question concerning disapproval of Negroes, since the behavior there consists of the commonplace activity of moving into or living in a neighborhood.

The two basic categories into which our dependent variables can be divided, therefore, are attitudes toward a status-threatening contact with a low ranked but nondeviant group (the disapproval of Negroes as neighbors question) and attitudes toward deviant behaviors which raise no particular threat to prestige. The reader may remember that the zero order correlations among these four forms of intolerance cluster them into precisely these two groupings.

Since the two categories of intolerant attitudes are substantially different in nature, the way in which rank affects them, and the reasons for these effects, might also be quite different. Figure 11.2 presents some possible patterns of effects.

At the beginning of this chapter, we suggested four kinds of variables which might exercise more or less direct effects on various forms of intolerance, and therefore might serve to mediate the effects of rank on intolerance. These potential mediating variables are listed in the center column of Figure 11.2. We suggest here that a deprived or insecure economic position will tend to increase both of the types of intolerance outlined above. The same is true of the global category of rigid and/or unsophisticated emotional or cognitive stances. However, we suggest that the person's concern about losing prestige should only affect the variable of disapproving of Negro neighbors, since the other forms of intolerance treated here do not imply intimate social contact with a low-ranked group. In the abstract, atheists and professors who swear in public do not present any threat to status.

We have divided the factor of normative effects, arguing that learning norms of racial intolerance would specifically produce disapproval of Negro neighbors, while having little or no effect on conventionalism, dogmatism and punitiveness toward deviants. (Of course, this also implies that learning

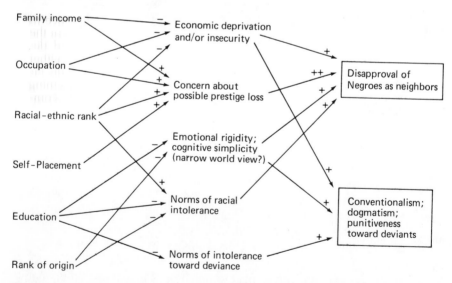

Figure 11.2 *Hypothetical pattern of effects of rank on forms of intolerance through intervening mechanisms.*

norms of racial *tolerance* would tend to decrease one's disapproval of Negroes as neighbors.) However, the opposite pattern of effects should result from the extent to which the person has internalized norms which identify nonusual behaviors as bad and which urge the person not to condone such behavior in others. Our suggestion, then, is that variations in the way different ranks affect different forms of intolerance may partly be due to the fact that the several mediating variables do not affect all types of intolerance in the same way.

Our suggesions about the ways in which various forms of social rank affect the supposed intervening variables are graphed on the left-hand side of Figure 11.2. High income and occupation both obviously reduce a man's sense of economic deprivation, but, since both are attributes which are evaluated in determining a man's current status or reputation in the community, they both increase his prestige and hence his concern about possible prestige loss. We suggest that majority racial–ethnic rank, net of the effects of other rank variables, should decrease economic deprivation, but should increase concern with prestige loss and also lead one to learn racially intolerant norms. Since we are dealing here with net effects, a man's self-placement in a social class represents the extent to which he places himself higher or lower than most other men with the same income, occupation, education, etc. Therefore, a high self-placement represents a rating of oneself which is, in this sense, objectively unwarranted, and therefore should plausibly increase a man's concern about prestige loss.

The pattern of effects above contains one interesting paradox. The disapproval of Negroes as neighbors is represented as being increased, at the same time, by low economic standing and by high prestige. That is, with respect to economic standing, it is low rank which produces intolerance. However, with respect to prestige, the effective variable is one's concern about losing high rank. We further suggest that honor may be more precarious than economic rank, so the defense of high prestige standing may even have a stronger effect on at least this particular form of intolerance than does the experience of low economic standing.

One effect of formal education, we suggest, is to reduce rigid and over-simple modes of thought and feeling (or to produce cosmopolitanism: a broad world view). Also, greater education can be expected to decrease learning of norms of both types of intolerance, or put conversely, to teach the person universalistic norms. This may partly be only historical accident: Today's high-brow norms dictate at least verbal tolerance, but tomorrow's may dictate verbal bigotry. Beyond this, structural factors may also be involved. If formal education in the United States is formally structured as an achievement-oriented, universalistic system, both with respect to the stated values of the system and with respect to much of its actual operation, then those persons who have been most successful within the system (men with high education) would probably have had universalistic attitudes and behavior reinforced to some extent during their educational careers. Finally, the graph represents Lipset's (1960:106–116) idea that child-rearing patterns in the lower class produce children more likely to have rigid and oversimplified stances toward the world.

If the processes graphically illustrated in Figure 11.2 are at least roughly accurate, what kinds of effects would we expect to find when directly relating various forms of social rank to various forms of intolerance? These hypothesized or derived effects are given in parentheses in Figure 11.1.

Clearly, the effects of some forms of social rank depend upon the way in which they operate *simultaneously* through several intervening variables. For example, income and occupation can each be expected to reduce the disapproval of Negro neighbors through the link with economic deprivation, but to increase this disapproval due to the mediating effect of concern with the loss of prestige. Since we posit that possible prestige loss affects this dependent variable more strongly than economic deprivation, we emerge with the conclusion that income and occupation should both have an average positive effect on this variable; that is, high income and high occupation should both increase disapproval of Negro neighbors. These forms of social rank should, however, each decrease the other forms of intolerance since they are linked to conventionalism, dogmatism, etc., only through their negative effect on economic deprivation.

The hypothesized pattern of effects yields a prediction that high self-placement will lead to more disapproval of Negroes as neighbors, but will have no effect on the other forms of intolerance, since it operates only through the intervening variable of prestige concern. Majority racial–ethnic rank illustrates the averaging of opposing effects. Majority men can be expected to be more concerned about prestige loss and to have learned more norms of racial intolerance; however, they should also suffer less economic deprivation. We conclude that the overall result of these disparate processes should be that majority men should disapprove of Negro neighbors more than minority men do.

However, racial–ethnic rank affects the other forms of intolerance only through its negative effect on economic deprivation. Therefore, we conclude that majority men should be more tolerant of all of these forms of deviant behavior than should minority men.

More years of education can be expected to have consistently negative effects through its several mediating variables. Education, by promoting more flexible and sophisticated habits of thought and by teaching norms of tolerance rather than intolerance, should consistently reduce a man's disapproval both of Negro neighbors and of the variety of forms of deviant behavior. For much the same reasons, growing up in a household of high status should also be expected to reduce all forms of intolerance.

In building up the hypothetical pattern of effects in Figure 11.2, we were thinking only of the net effects of the various rank variables concerned, uncontaminated by the effects of such additional variables as age, being raised in the South and/or in a small town, etc. Hence, the predicted effects presented in parentheses in Figure 11.1 are the effects these rank variables should have if these additional variables are in some way held constant. Since a number of such potentially confounding variables were indeed held constant in the analyses presented above, it is appropriate to compare the effects derived from Figure 11.2 with the summary of the effects that were actually observed. That is, comparing the symbols summarizing the ob-served net effects in Figure 11.1 with the (parenthesized) symbols represent-ing the derived hypothetical effects will give us some notion of how success-ful we have been in accounting for the observed effects with our post hoc model in Figure 11.2.[14]

The fit between the predicted and observed effects is fairly close, although clearly the model is not totally adequate. Almost all of the failures of the model are in predicting effects which did not in fact show up in the data. Only one result, the positive effect of class self-placement on punitiveness toward deviants, appeared which was not predicted by the model. The model was never so far off as to predict the wrong direction for any effect.

Although we cannot provide explanations for some of the departures from the predicted effects, three sorts of deviations appear to warrant some discussion. Clearly, the model does not accurately represent the role of a man's subjective sense of self-placement. This variable failed to have a predicted effect on disapproval of Negroes, but did increase punitiveness toward deviants, a nonpredicted effect. These results could possibly involve a status inconsistency effect. As we suggested in Chapter 5, inconsistency effects could show up as additive effects of opposed sign, which is the pattern that appears with respect to punitiveness toward deviants. For these particular variables, the argument would run that men whose self-ratings are higher than their objective social ranks should feel considerable concern about their prestige, possibly augmented by the frustration of interacting with other people who refuse to accord them the class standing which they claim. This form of stress might well lead to feelings of intolerance, but it is not at all clear why the result is to increase punitiveness toward deviants but not the other three forms of intolerance.

A second major failure of fit concerns the effects of social rank of origin: Out of eight predicted effects only two appeared, both of them weakly. Indeed, the model in Figure 11.2 would generate better predictions, on the

---

[14]The reader will remember that the effects discussed above are net after certain additional nonrank variables have been controlled, among them a measure of general satisfaction. To some extent, this might mask the effect of rank on intolerance through deprivation, since general satisfaction is a partial indicator of deprivation. However, as Chapter 6 shows, this measure of satisfaction is only weakly related to rank and so can be considered to tap deprivation only weakly, hence its inclusion as a control should not mask these effects very much.

whole, if the rank of origin variable were simply removed entirely. This could be justified, since some previous research (summarized in Erlanger 1974) shows only mild relationships between social class and patterns of child-rearing and these differences in child-rearing were a major reason for thinking that the rank of the household of origin would affect the mediating variables and through them the four forms of intolerance.

Thirdly, the mixture of effects on the disapproval of Negroes as neighbors suggests that the variable of being concerned about losing prestige could be fruitfully elaborated to specify the kind of loss the man is worried about. Contact with Negroes threatens most the prestige derived simply from a white skin; for this reason, the net effect of majority racial–ethnic rank is especially strong. Negro neighbors also threaten, in many people's minds, the prestige derived from living in an obviously wealthy neighborhood. This concern, usually appearing in the form of worries about "property values," probably falls most heavily on men of high income, thereby explaining the effect of that variable. (Of course, concern with property values could also be conceptualized as an instance of economic insecurity.) However, having Negroes as neighbors does not directly threaten that aspect of prestige which is derived from high occupation and therefore this rank variable has no net effect on this form of intolerance.

The generalization follows that social intimacy with low-ranked groups will be most resisted by men who stand high on some specific form of prestige which would be threatened by the contact. But forms of high rank not threatened by the contact will not affect that particular form of intolerance.

The effects on disapproval of Negroes as neighbors represent another instance of rank effects of opposed signs, as discussed in Chapter 5. Education reduces this form of intolerance, while income and high racial–ethnic rank increase it. We suggested in Chapter 5 that such patterns of effects could be interpreted as due to inconsistency or social mobility. In this case, for instance, the discrepancy hypothesis would be that men with incomes higher than warranted by their educations disapprove of Negro neighbors while those underpaid in relation to their educations tend to welcome them. Yet this interpretation in terms of a status inconsistency effect is counter to any plausible theory of such effects. Its mechanism should be relative deprivation or psychological incongruency. In the case of relative deprivation, underrewarded men would be expected to displace hostility. In the case of incongruity, the ambiguity of status discrepancy should be as great for the underrewarded as for the overrewarded. Neither of these predictions is met—intolerance of this kind is found among the overrewarded but not among the underrewarded. In this instance, then, it seems to be more reasonable to understand these opposed effects in terms of independent effects of different rank variables acting through different forms of mediating variables. An interpretation in terms of status discrepancy appears to be neither reasonable nor necessary.

We should also remind the reader that we found no evidence for hypotheses (see Bettelheim and Janowitz 1964:25–48) that the strains of mobility, particularly downward mobility, tend to generate intolerance. Neither intergenerational nor career mobility seems to contribute to an explanation of intolerance any better than an additive model of rank effects (see Jackson and Curtis 1972:707). Further, the net effects of father's occupation and of first occupation would be positive in an additive equation if downward mobility led to intolerance, but these effects, when they occasionally appear, are usually negative.

Several other possible explanations for the observed effects deserve brief mention. First, some sorts or levels of intolerance may affect social rank, in addition to rank effects on intolerance. Persons of higher rank may be more tolerant, in general, because those of more rigid minds are less likely to attain success in the U.S. educational system or are less likely to do well at some kinds of high-ranking jobs. Second, Hamilton (1972:442–444) has suggested that the negative link between education and intolerance may arise because tolerant parents are also likely to value education and therefore in addition to passing tolerant attitudes along to their children will also encourage and enable them to complete more years of school. Without over-time measures of intolerance and measures of parents' tolerance it is difficult to examine the validity of these arguments.

The negative rank–intolerance relationship might also occur because respondents of higher rank, perhaps especially ones of higher education, are more likely to recognize the intolerance questions as ones dealing with currently sensitive issues and hence to give socially desirable, that is, tolerant answers. Put another way, education doesn't really reduce bigotry, it merely allows one to avoid the appearance of being bigoted (see the discussion of education in Bettelheim and Janowitz 1964). But if this were true, the negative effects of education should surely be greatest for the most sensitive question, that dealing explicitly with Negroes. But the effects on this variable were not as large as on dogmatism and on punitiveness toward deviants. Of course, a social desirability response set could be responsible for masking an even greater positive association between rank and disapproval of Negro neighbors.

What are the implications of our results for Lipset's theory (1960:Chapter 4) of working-class authoritarianism? If we accept the findings as mainly reflecting true rank effects on the various forms of intolerance, they partially support the theory and partially do not. The major supporting finding is that most of the rank effects on intolerance are negative. Individuals lower in various types of rank tend to be less tolerant. Further, some of the forms of intolerance are among the stronger correlates of rank we have encountered in this study; *relative to other dependent variables*, differences in intolerance between the social ranks appear substantial.

To form a rough notion of just how much difference rank might make, we made a prediction of each intolerance score for two typical rank profiles: an upper-middle class man (a salaried manager with a college degree, making $18,000, identifying himself as upper-middle class, whose father was also a salaried manager and whose mother had 14 years of education) versus a working class man (an operative with 11 years of education, making $7000, identifying himself as working-class, whose father was also an operative and whose mother had 9 years of education). We assumed both men to have majority racial–ethnic rank. Using a rough average of the net effects of the rank variables in the cities (but excluding those variables summarized as having no effect in Figure 11.1), we predicted the difference between these two men in the four forms of intolerance.

In all cases, the predicted intolerance for the working-class man was higher. The differences were:

Form of intolerance	(1) Approximate difference (UMC–WC)	(2) Approximate standard deviation	Ratio: (1)/(2)
Disapproval of Negroes as neighbors	−.06	.82	−.07
Conventionalism	−.89	1.60	−.55
Dogmatism	−1.19	1.60	−.74
Punitiveness toward deviants	−8.42	12.20	−.69

The standard deviation of each variable is given to provide a criterion for judging the importance of a difference. Evidently, a typical working-class man would disapprove of Negro neighbors (due to rank differences alone) only slightly more than a typical upper-middle-class man—the difference amounts to less than 10% of the standard deviation in this variable. The differences in other forms of intolerance are more substantial, amounting to between half and three-quarters of a standard deviation. These differences cannot be attributed to such factors as being raised on a farm, or in a small town. Hamilton's thesis that such factors account for much of the class differences in intolerance (1972:455) may be true, but the above differences remain with such variables controlled.

Other facets of the findings call for modifications in Lipset's thesis. First, the small or absent effects of the parents' characteristics (along with the findings of Erlanger 1974) argue against the thesis that methods of child-rearing are responsible for class differences in tolerance. There appears to be an association between rank and tolerance, but child-rearing practices do not appear to be the reason for it. Second, in some instances rank variables had *positive* effects on intolerance, so that in our illustration above the differences between the upper-middle class and working class men were muted by the effects of income on disapproval of Negro neighbors and of self-placement on punitiveness. Finally, the results suggest that "intolerance" cannot be treated as a global concept, since different forms are not well correlated with each other and may be affected differently by different rank variables.

CONCLUSIONS AND IMPLICATIONS

In this chapter, we consider the community system of social inequality as a whole and the role that it plays in general in the lives of individuals. Previous chapters have considered the ways in which specific domains of attitude or behavior are affected by social rank; here we wish to focus on the pervasive role of social inequality, searching for generalizations about community stratification systems and their individual effects across many dependent variables. From this wider perspective we wish to give our conclusions with respect to the major questions of the study and draw out—at least tentatively—some of the implications of these conclusions for the workings of inequality in the U.S. today.

We will first take up the question of how social rank affects individual behavior. Then we will consider the contrasts between communities, differences both in the stratification systems of the communities and in how these systems act as contexts within which individuals adapt (in general) to their social ranks. Since our cities differed greatly in size, region, and other important characteristics, these contrasts should allow us to approach some conclusions on the question of whether American communities represent distinct systems of stratification or whether they represent local replications of stratification at the level of the society.

THE EFFECTS OF SOCIAL RANK

To understand the way in which social rank affects attitudes and behaviors, one must think of a number of rank dimensions each of which has its own net effect on each dependent variable. Our findings make it clear that behavior is not shaped by position on some general dimension of rank. It could have been that general social rank consisted of a given combination of rank measures—for example, occupation plus income plus twice education plus one-half mother's education. If this were true, as we explained in Chapter 5, the rank dimensions figuring most significantly in this general dimension should have the strongest effects and those contributing less to the general dimension should have lesser effects, and this relative ordering should hold consistently for each and every dependent variable which we considered (within any given community). The previous chapters have made it abundantly clear that this prediction fails: There is no single combination of ranks within each community that correctly states rank in general for that community. Hence, we reject a unidimensional model of rank effects in favor of a multidimensional model.[1]

Our analysis of these multidimensional effects next showed us that the separate rank dimensions had generally linear effects (at least with respect to the major dimensions of achieved rank), usually had independent (i.e., additive) effects, and tended to affect a given dependent variable in the same direction. This relatively simple pattern of effects tends to reject otherwise plausible hypotheses that the experiences of upward or downward mobility and/or of status inconsistency have substantial effects on various behaviors over and above the effects of social rank itself (although we have noted one or two exceptions to this general conclusion in the analysis of particular dependent variables).

This rejection is somewhat paradoxical, since such hypotheses grow naturally from a view of rank effects as multidimensional rather than uni-dimensional. Our evidence, however, indicates that these individual effects are either weak or extremely rare. It would seem that everyone in an uncrystallized community is subject to whatever strains and ambiguities (if any) are caused by high rates of mobility and status inconsistency.

Finally, it appears that even a theory of rank effects which allows a number of rank dimensions to separately influence a given dependent variable cannot account for very much of the variation in most dependent variables. Our regression analyses in the preceding chapters rarely yielded R^2's greater than .25. This is true in part because of measurement error in the dependent variables and the various rank dimensions and in part because many factors besides social rank affect our dependent variables. But the moderately low levels of explanation may also be due to the moderately high rates of social mobility and status inconsistency in our cities. As we argued in Chapter 1, such low levels of status rigidity should act in a variety

[1]In Chapter 2, we presented factor analysis results which suggest that rank dimensions might be considered to reflect a single general dimension. However, this reflects the way in which the various rank dimensions are related to one another. In their effects on various individual attitudes and behavior, the rank dimensions seem to act separately and not via some general dimension.

of ways to reduce the influence of rank upon behavior. It would appear that the special theoretic significance of status consistency and social inheritance lies in the status system itself rather than in the individual's reactions to these experiences. In the contemporary U.S., social rank may be more important in its pervasiveness—the number of different dependent variables which it influences—than in the strength with which it affects any one attitude or behavior.

Effects of Specific Rank Dimensions

We began with a search for potent or consistent rank variables by examining correlates of a list of 17 rank variables (Chapter 5). The number of independently effective rank characteristics was strikingly large. Seventeen indicators of social rank were used in the prediction of each dependent variable in our analyses in Chapter 5. It might be reasonable to expect that, with all the other ranks held constant, some forms of rank would not show any particular net effect on a given dependent variable in any of the six cities, or that some forms of rank would not affect any of the dependent variables. The analysis with all 17 rank dimensions, that is, should have been expected to wipe out the potential independent effects of some rank variables. This is not what happened. Each rank variable had some statistically significant net effect on some dependent variable in at least one of the cities.

This variability in the impact of different measures can even be seen in zero order correlations. Looking for the rank dimension which has the highest zero order correlation with a given dependent variable within a given city suggests that education is by far the most *frequent* single best indicator of rank. The next most frequent set would include majority racial–ethnic rank, occupation, and income. But all 17 variables received this honor with respect to some dependent variable in at least one of the cities.

Moreover, such relatively weak predictors as mother's education, friend's occupation, neighborhood rating, and so on, were retained in different detailed analyses in Chapters 6–12. This appeared to be an instance of community variation: The detailed definition of which ranks dominate the explanation of dependent variables, once the effects of occupation, education, income, and majority have been taken into account, varies somewhat among communities. Part of the reason for this is probably random fluctuation, but we believe that is by no means the whole story. Let us consider, for example, a measurement explanation for the finding.

The measurement issue is this: Measuring , for example, "father's occupation" may yield information which gives a better estimate of son's occupation or income. Among the men we characterized as physicians, some are successful and wealthy, while others are relatively unsuccessful and receive much lower income. It may be that the successful and/or wealthy physicians come from homes of higher social rank (see Perrucci 1961, for research showing this is true for engineers). In this particular sense, the variable we have called father's occupation should not be regarded as an origin rank, but rather labeled "greater precision in occupational (or income) measurement." In short, the apparent utility of multidimensional models could be due to the precise and accurate measurement of general rank that they afford. But our index of general rank yields equally precise and accurate single dimensional measurement, and yet it does not yield the same high levels of explained variance, so the phenomenon we are reporting here cannot have been mainly due to the associated improvement in measurement. Nonetheless, it would be wise to remember that in addition to its own unique effects, each added new measurement of rank doubtless picks up some of the effects of other rank variables with which it is associated.

In addition, however, the salience of a given rank depends somewhat on local conditions, for some dependent variables. The realm of informal social participation yields extreme examples of this fact. Still, the effects of the four principal present ranks were generally stronger and more consistent than were the rest.

In general, racial–ethnic rank, education, occupation, and income provided the strongest effects across cities and across dependent variables. Among them the most influential variable was education. In particular, these present rank characteristics had much stronger effects than those of the background characteristics, which we will now discuss.

The consequences of *background or origin ranks* are mostly (though not entirely) indirect. In many of the analyses in the previous chapters, no consistent effects were found for father's occupation, father's education, or mother's education. In the few instances in which one of these variables did have an effect, that effect was generally not very strong. This conclusion is borne out by a systematic search for direct effects of parental status among the dependent variables listed in Table 5.1. Effects of origin status appeared with some consistency across cities for only one-third of these dependent variables. The strengths of the origin betas were all from .05 to .10, while the strongest beta affecting a dependent variable was generally between .10 and .30. Hence, reliable background effects are relatively infrequent and, when they appear, relatively weak.[2]

[2]The relatively poor showing of origin rank effects may be ascribed to poor measurement of these variables. However, the issue can be argued in two opposite ways. First, one could argue that the measurement of the background ranks is poor and leads us to underestimate the effects of these variables. It is certainly true that the rates of missing data were higher for these variables and probably problems associated with memory were more severe. In such cases, actual effects of origin rank might disappear as random variation or might appear as effects of current ranks, such as occupation or income, which are correlated with origin status. That is, by the earlier argument current occupation could partly represent greater precision in the measurement of origin status. On the other hand, it could be argued that our results may *overestimate* the effects

At a very general level, the results could have been patterned in four ways, each way suggesting a general type of intepretation. First, there could have been background effects but no effects of current rank, indicating an ascribed status system of a kind that we need not discuss because such a result never obtained in this study. Second, there could be effects of current rank with no independent direct effects of origin rank, which is to be expected in an achieved status system (remembering the imperfect relationship among ranks). This proved more or less to be the modal finding in this study. Third, there could be independent effects of present and past rank in opposite directions, and, fourth, both types of effects could occur in the same direction.

Absent or weak effects do not mean, of course, that origin ranks are ineffective, but only that they affect dependent variables by virtue of their effects on current rank. Weak direct effects of early rank are what we should expect in a world in which a change in rank is accompanied by a change in the value of a given dependent variable. In this way, social mobility does affect the lives of individuals and preserves the relationship between one's level of rank and the attendant variable at a given point in time. For example, the absence of a direct effect of origin rank on domestic liberalism suggests that upwardly mobile sons become less liberal, thus bringing their political attitudes into line with their new ranks. This suggests that the influence of family socialization does not have the long-lasting subcultural effects suggested in the first chapter.

The interpretation of any direct effect of parental rank depends on whether the origin effect is in the same direction or the opposite direction as the effect of current rank. Effects of present and past rank which are opposite in direction could conceivably be attributed to a major historical change. Barring such a dramatic change, origin effects of opposite sign could be interpreted in at least two (somewhat related) ways. First, as we discussed in Chapter 5, effects of mobility *per se* might result in this pattern of findings. If the extent, for example, of prejudice varied with the extent to which one's occcupational level fell below that of his father, one would expect in a multiple regression to find intolerance positively related to father's occupation and negatively related to current occupation. Second, such a pattern could also represent a kind of family socialization in which expectations were set in the stratum of origin and later behavior depended on the extent which one's achieved ranks measured up to those expectations, as in our argument on dissatisfaction in Chapter 6.

A notable finding of this study is that the pattern of opposed effects of origin and current rank, although quite possible, plausible, and theoretically

---

of origin rank, since the measures of origin status reflect increased precision in measurement of current rank as well as origin rank itself. Hence, measurement error might have led to overestimates as well as underestimates of the effects of origin rank.

interesting, seldom occurred. When direct origin effects did appear they were most often found to operate in the same direction as effects of current rank. In fact, in the previous chapters and in the search for direct background effects on the set of dependent variables listed in Table 5.1, when origin effects did appear they were in the same direction as current ranks in every instance except one—the case of general satisfaction. In all other cases of reliable effects, the various forms of origin rank provide a small additional effect in the same direction as that of current rank.[3]

Such origin effects are also open to at least two interpretations: (a) Origin rank has permanent and independent effects, perhaps because of the tenacity of behaviors or attitudes learned as a child; and (b) social background acts as an additional independent social rank in the present time, implying that the social status of ancestors is an important current rank dimension.

Although we have interpreted most of the effects of origin in previous chapters as instances of continuing (although weak) effects from family socialization, our data cannot definitely rule out the interpretation that background ranks actually stand for a present and effective status characteristic. To solve this problem, future research will have to either examine status effects more carefully through time or attempt to obtain direct measures of the degree to which the person's current prestige is inflated or pulled down by common knowledge of his ancestry.

Ancestry should be a more effective current rank dimension in small towns, where one's background is probably more widely known than in medium-sized or large cities. Therefore, the fact that we found effects of origin rank consistently across the cities would tend to argue that the ancestry interpretation cannot be entirely correct. On the other hand, the frequent finding that origin rank had unusually large effects in one of our small towns (Safford), tends to suggest that ancestry may operate this way in some localities.

Racial–ethnic rank, although varying in local definition, is a powerful influence in most communities. This is hardly a surprise to a student of minority relations. Yet the analyses reported here go a step further than many empirical studies in showing that belonging to a majority racial–ethnic group has important effects on many dependent variables *independent* of the accompanying advantages in occupation, education, and income levels. Majority (versus minority) social rank, although ascribed like the status of one's origin household, differs from origin rank in having both indirect effects through the current achieved ranks and also substantial direct effects in its own right.

As a rank variable, racial–ethnic status seems to have effects roughly

[3]This pattern is one that might emerge if parental rank is really no more than an additionally precise measure of current rank. This is probably true to some extent, yet if origin ranks only represented additonal precision, we should have expected them to have small effects on almost all the dependent variables; but this did not turn out to be true.

comparable in strength and pervasiveness to those of income and occupation. However, we must immediately qualify by observing that the effects of achieved rank are comparatively consistent from one community to the next, while in our cities majority effects depend on the composition of the racial–ethnic groups, in particular, whether the minority is mainly composed of blacks or Mexican–Americans. For example, income has a remarkably consistent effect on general satisfaction, but majority status increased general satisfaction notably only in Indianapolis. In a sense, then, being black had an effect on general satisfaction like having low income, but being Mexican–American did not.

In its net effects on many dependent variables, racial–ethnic rank seemed to operate simply as another form of social rank. That is, minority rank affected political orientations, anomia, and most of the forms of intolerance in the same direction as did low income or low education. However, being black *increased* formal social participation and political participation, while other forms of low rank decreased these types of activity. In this instance, minority rank does not appear to simply reflect low status as much as the current cultural patterns of the group in question. In other words, the social rank of the racial or ethnic group does not appear to be as important here as historical circumstances, internal organization, group culture and traditions, political considerations and so on. The effects of majority or minority status on formal participation probably reflect more about the current cultural patterns of blacks versus whites than it does about the direct implications of high rank.

The theoretical issue of whether race–ethnicity should be treated as an independent rank dimension, although partly a matter of orientation, receives a substantially affirmative answer from the evidence in this study. Several forms of attitude or behavior can be better understood by taking racial–ethnic ranks into account and in most cases the effects of minority rank (direct or indirect) are in the same direction as effects of low rank on other dimensions.

However, unlike income, occupation and (possibly) education, racial–ethnic groups do not intrinsically stem from the division of labor or the distribution of consumer goods, but are defined by local and historical conditions. Thinking of one racial or ethnic group as high and another as low is not related to the operations of technology or the division of labor; in this way, these assignments of value are essentially arbitrary. The existence of a majority–minority rank distinction is not unusual, and seems to operate in much the same way as other systems of rank. Usually, then, the question will be not whether to include race–ethnicity as a rank dimension, but which groups (if any) have been assigned to minority status in the community in question. Our data show that such definitions produce a rank dimension which has effects often similar in form and usually equal in magnitude to those of achieved ranks such as income and occupation.

A major conclusion from this study is that the single most influential rank dimension is *education*. To begin with, education holds a central place in the process of status attainment, since it transmits most of the effects of origin rank and has itself relatively strong direct effects on later career achievement. Beyond this, education generally has stronger and more pervasive dependent variable effects than any other rank dimension. In our analyses most dependent variables that were affected by social rank at all were affected by education. Furthermore, with a few exceptions, the effect of education was as strong as and usually stronger than the effects of other rank dimensions.

How can we explain these strong, pervasive effects of education? We must remember that these effects are net of any effects of occupation, income, and other rank dimensions. Education certifies people for high ranking occupations. Education may also teach the attitudes, motives, and skills necessary to achieve success in formal organizations. But we are dealing here with effects of education with occupation and income controlled, so such explanations must be substantially ruled out and we must seek elsewhere to understand the impact of educational rank. We have speculated in previous chapters about what mediating factors might operate with respect to certain specific dependent variables. We want to suggest here, in more general terms, that the effects of education may not be due so much to any immediate prestige conferred by degree-holding, but rather due to differences in socialization.

In the first place, one notable effect of education may be to establish motives and norms and hence guide the person's preference toward certain types of attitude or behavior. In contrast, income and occupation (among a host of other factors such as family life cycle) set the actual conditions under which people try to implement their motives and preferences. We see education as an agency of socialization that transmits cultural prescriptions, that is, whereas actual outcomes depend substantially on personal resources, historical circumstance, and even weather.

In particular, education may play a central role because it teaches norms and values about social interaction and also teaches the communication skills necessary to participate in certain kinds of social relationships. Communications are critical in a large and complex society and access to the system of communication (both in sending and receiving messages of various types) is therefore a particularly important aspect of social stratification. For example, even in the age of television the printed word is a crucial means of status-relevant communication. The role of the opinion leader would appear to be one which uniquely combines written and verbal communication. By definition, the opinion leader is one who accepts communication from a variety of sources, many of them written, processes this input and passes on selected portions of it to numbers of other persons verbally. For such reasons, skills in communication and general levels of participation in the culture of the society are central in the operation of national or community-wide communication networks, and status-related social contact networks depend quite heavily on such communication.

The effects of *occupation* in our analyses were fairly pervasive, although usually it did not exercise the strongest net effect on our dependent variables. Certainly, significant portions of the zero-order correlations between occupation and the various dependent variables could be accounted for by the direct effects of education and income. Yet, a substantial number of rather moderate net effects of occupation remained after such other rank dimensions were controlled.

What we have called occupation in this study was actually the level of socioeconomic status of an occupation which is strongly related to the general standing or prestige of individual occupations. As one moves from low to high on this scale, a large number of characteristics of the occupation undoubtedly change. In addition to becoming more prestigious, occupations become cleaner, generally more desirable and involve greater exercise of authority. Although we have speculated in certain of the preceding chapters about which of these correlated attributes might actually be responsible for a given net effect of occupation on a given dependent variable, our data cannot definitely settle such questions.

The effects of *income* were only moderately pervasive and were not especially strong. For many dependent variables in the above analyses income had no direct net effect at all. When such effects did appear, they were usually not as strong as the net effects of other rank dimensions (the outstanding exception is the strong effect of income on the number of associational memberships).

In recent years, there has been some sociological discussion of the so-called embourgeoisment thesis; that is, the proposition that as the income of workers rises they will come to resemble the middle-class in general life style and especially in political attitudes (for a discussion and assessment, see Goldthorpe et al. 1969:1–29). Our results suggest that as a general proposition this is false: Increases in income will not affect many aspects of life style and the effects it will have will be muted.

These findings also have some implications for the arguments advanced by Jencks et al. in their book *Inequality* (1972). The major case of this book (pp. 253–265) is that the ties between income on the one hand and such rank dimensions as education and occupation on the other are so tenuous that equalizing a population with respect to education or occupation would do little to equalize the distribution of income. Therefore, Jencks argues that the most feasible way to equalize income is through direct political redistribution. Our data suggest that Jencks' general argument can be carried one step further: that the ties between income and many aspects of life style are so tenuous that equalization of income will produce very little change in many current patterns of behavior and attitudes. However, our findings presumably are most valid in the broad middle range of incomes and offer less guidance about the effects of lowering very high incomes or raising very low incomes.

Income, personal or family, may only be a moderately satisfactory proxy for the more fundamental variable of economic status or financial position, leading us to regard our results even more tentatively. It may well be that many attitudes and behaviors are adjusted less to the income received in a given year than to the financial position the person or the family is able to maintain or expects to maintain over the period of a lifetime. In the nineteenth century, this meant that capital was a more appropriate indicator of economic status than current income could ever be. Governmental policies (e.g., in social security and the financing of housing) and some increases in the reliability of work (even to the prospect of a guaranteed annual wage) make current American incomes a more adequate indicator of family economic status than capital assets. Still, the fundamental independent variable of interest may well be a family's long-term financial prospects, on which they can reasonably base their level of living.

The measures of income used in this study probably understate the relative effect of long-term economic status, both because educational skills and features of occupation are also involved in long-term financial prospects and because of problems in measuring income. On the first point, consider a physician and a carpenter both of whom make $20,000 in some one year. The physician's income may be low because he donated much of his time to unremunerative medical pursuits, because the local community experienced a severe depression and his patients were unable to pay, because he is a public health officer rather than in private practice, or simply because he deliberately devoted less time to his practice and more time to leisure activities. The carpenter, by the same token, may have had an unusually good year, being employed a great deal, working considerable overtime, holding moonlighting jobs, and so on. Still, the physician and his family can look forward to a stable high income for the rest of his productive life in a way the carpenter and his family probably cannot. Furthermore, the physician is likely to be able to increase his income substantially if the need should become pressing while the carpenter is not. In consequence, the contrasting economic status of these two people is represented in their occupations (or in their scores on occupational prestige), not in their incomes. A similar argument could easily be constructed for education. The potential of occupational roles and skills (including those more reputed than real) acquired through years in educational institutions plays much the same role as capital did for middle-class families during the nineteenth century. In consequence, some of the net effects of occupation and education should properly be allocated to long-term economic status.

Similarly, errors in the measurement of income, either due to inaccurate reporting or nonresponse, are probably greater than in the measurement of education or occupation. In consequence, some of the real effects of true income should contribute to the observed net effects of education and occupation (and majority racial–ethnic rank). Also, we ask about income in a single year, although income obviously varies systematically with age and also fluctuates yearly while race, occupation and education are far more stable. Thus the other rank measures are, among other things, better partial predictors of financial prospects than current income in some respects.

The suggestion that *all* the effects of education, occupation, and majority racial–ethnic rank could be attributed to economic status is, however, extremely implausible. If these variables were essentially only imperfect proxies for economic status, we would expect to find that they had essentially the same effects on each dependent variable as that of income itself. However, there are a number of variables which are affected by education but not by income. Also, we occasionally find the effects of income in a direction opposite to those of education, as in the analyses of general satisfaction and disapproval of Negroes as neighbors. It seems most likely that we should regard effects of education, occupation, etc., as essentially being due to the particular noneconomic qualities of those variables, but recognize that the effects of economic status are to some extent understated by the income effects taken by themselves.

Finally, *subjective rank* appeared to have moderately pervasive, although usually weak, effects. The effects of self-placement seem concentrated with respect to variables of formal and informal social participation, including political participation, although self-placement also exercised a positive effect on levels of general satisfaction.

We did *not* find in general that *objective* ranks had effects through their influence on self-placement, or that self-placement had direct effects as strong as those of *objective* rank. People's opinions of their general ranks, on the other hand, did, for some dependent variables, exert an influence on behavior over and above the effects of education, occupation, etc.[4]

Our closest approximation to a measure of class consciousness (the "businessmen agree" measure) behaved much the same way with respect to political attitudes. It is not simply that some individuals perceive common interests with others of their rank, while others do not (though this is true, as far as it goes), but that there are also individuals making interest-identifications not clearly indicated by their objective ranks. To a minor degree, then, there is a class-conscious status order not simply based on the

---

[4]It is also possible that class self-placement affects some dependent variables in part because it simply improves our precision in measuring income, occupation, education, etc. In instances where these objective ranks are measured with some error, the path from class self-placement to some dependent attitude or behavior may be overestimated because class-placement will partly reflect the variation in objective rank which is not perfectly represented by the measures of objective rank.

relations of production (insofar as those are indicated by our measures) that has political relevance.

Intervening Variables

In several previous analyses, we have attempted to identify the variables which mediate the effects of rank on the dependent attitudes or behavior. We suggested in Chapter 1 that two important intervening variables might be amount of felt deprivation and the rank level of close associates. Other possible intervening variables appropriate to particular analyses have been introduced in previous chapters.

Our attempt to explain the reasons for rank effects by introducing possible intervening variables has not been very successful. In particular, our measure of felt deprivation, the index of general satisfaction, was so weakly related to various dimensions of social rank as to suggest that it is an insignificant mediating variable. Similarly, occupational rank of friends, though included in all the 17-variable analyses, was seldom closely enough related to dependent variables (net of other rank effects) to qualify as an intervening variable. Rates of social participation and the perceptions of social stratification also failed to give any general interpretation of the major rank effects.

In certain of the preceding chapters, we have located some variables which do seem to play a mediating role, but with one or two exceptions these intervening variables only explain part of the effects of rank variables; even after controlling for the possible mediators substantial direct effects of social rank remained. We have speculated above about the basis for some of these empirically uninterpreted direct rank effects, but a major result of our analysis is to raise the problem of why certain rank dimensions do indeed influence certain dependent attitudes or behaviors. Our findings also raise, but do not answer, the question of why the various dimensions of social rank control substantial variation in some dependent variables and are only slightly related, if at all, to certain others.

Some General Implications

The pattern of rank effects which we have most commonly seen is that several dimensions each have a net direct effect in the same direction on a given dependent variable, while other rank dimensions either have no effects or, less frequently, have effects in the opposite direction. Only with respect to the dependent variable of anomia have we seen effects of income, occupation, education, and racial–ethnic rank all four present in most of the cities and all in the same direction. We usually find one or more potentially important rank effects to actually be zero with respect to any given dependent variable. For example, in most cities income has no effect on political party identification, while occupation has no effect on our measure of conventionalism.

This pattern has several implications. It suggests that accurate explanation of a given dependent variable must be pursued by taking the dimensions of social rank into account separately; that is, this commonly observed pattern confirms a multidimensional view of the impact of social rank. Further, it does not seem sensible to regard the various rank dimensions as simply several different forms of superiority and nothing more. If that were true, all the rank dimensions would affect any given dependent variable, and in the same direction. Thus it appears that there are several different kinds of reward.

When education affects some particular attitude or behavior strongly and income does not, while the reverse pattern holds for some other dependent variable, it suggests that income, education, and other rank dimensions carry different meanings in the system of inequality. For example, one primary meaning of income is the level of reward, while occupational and educational rank have somewhat more to do with positions in work and participation in culture. The occupational role system links individuals and families to the distribution of rewards in income, but it also describes the position of individuals in the social organization of work. Thus, it has a meaning based on social organization (e.g., independence, subordination, etc.), distinct from that of sheer level of reward. Similarly, one major meaning of education may be as an indicator of a level of cultural participation and therefore social access to other community members identified by extended socialization within the educational institution, over and above the economic stability which it may represent.

These "meanings" become important in trying to understand different patterns of rank effects. As a major example, consider the results for satisfaction and for anomia. Low income reduces satisfaction substantially, but the impact of education in reducing trust in a stable normative system is even stronger. Thus, the strongest effect of stratification in our communities was not *directly* economic, but rather a kind of institutional deprivation. Normative alienation, that is, is generated by other sorts of low rank in addition to low economic position, and it is normative alienation rather than dissatisfaction which characterizes the lower strata in these communities most strongly. Therefore, solving problems of income inequality would not remove the effects of institutional deprivation on normative alienation. The argument of Jencks et al. (1972:4–7), that being unable to afford a car in a society designed for car owners is a special kind of social punishment, can be extended to cultural participation as well: The barely literate in a highly literate society is especially cut off from participation in social life.

Our findings, then, support the orientation set forth in Chapter 1: Different rank dimensions may represent sufficiently different kinds of superiority and may affect individuals through different sets of intervening variables, so that their effects on a given dependent variable may take rather different forms. We should not be surprised, then, when one rank dimension affects a particular attitude or behavior and another does not. Several analyses above have carried this notion even further, suggesting that high (or low) rank on a given dimension may itself mean several different things, that is, may affect a dependent variable through a variety of intervening mechanisms. For example, education can mean increased information, increased scope of experience, more prestige or greater security, etc. Some of these aspects of a given kind of high rank represent status orderings (for example, prestige), while others represent effects relatively divorced from notions of superiority and inferiority (for example, amount of information).

The present study has mainly served to raise the question of how particular dimensions exercise their effects. We have done limited empirical investigations in some analyses, but in others have only speculated about which intervening variables might be operating. In particular, our orientation so far fails to explain one feature of the pattern of effects which we commonly observed, which is that the observed rank effects, when present, are generally all or almost all in the same direction. Given the great variety of things which high status on a given dimension might mean, and given the variation in these meanings from one rank dimension to another, this consistency in direction is mildly surprising.

Let us now trace the implications of our findings for the distribution of a given dependent variable throughout the community. For example, can we expect, given our observed patterns of effects, to find that one sector of society is markedly different in political party identification than another? Are strata in our communities likely to be polarized with respect to political attitudes, anomia, or other attitudes or behavior?

The distribution of a dependent variable through the structure of inequality depends on several things: the degree to which rank dimensions are correlated, the form of the relationships between rank dimensions and the dependent variable (for example, the linearity and additivity of these effects), the strength of the rank effects, and whether all the rank effects are in the same direction. Suppose that satisfaction or some other dependent variable were a multiplicative function of three rank variables and these rank dimensions took on a normal or slightly skewed unimodal distribution. Assuming that the rank effects were similar in direction and at least moderate in size, the distribution of satisfaction would be extremely skewed. Individuals low on any rank, that is, would be low in satisfaction while only those high on *all three* ranks would have great satisfaction. The most extreme case of such a model is one that involves nonlinearities also, so that satisfaction is given in substantial measure only to those holding very high ranks on all dimensions simultaneously, but is effectively withheld from everyone else.

Linear and additive models, on the other hand, imply that dissatisfaction (or some other dependent variable) due to low rank along one dimension can be "made up for" by high rank on another dimension, since the effects are independent (see Wilensky 1966a:132–133). However, if the rank dimensions are very highly correlated, few people will actually have their low rank on one dimension offset by high rank on another. If in addition the rank effects are all in the same direction and are substantial in strength, we would expect to find satisfaction varying greatly with one's social rank in the community, even though this substantial dispersion would be more or less continuous rather than polarizing the community into a relatively dissatisfied versus a relatively satisfied camp.

Any departure from this combination of simultaneous conditions would tend to make different rank levels more similar in their attitudes and behavior. That is, low correlations between the rank dimensions mean that substantial numbers will be able to balance low rank in one respect against high rank in another. Weak rank effects mean that a host of other factors more or less uncorrelated with rank tend to affect the dependent variable. If, in addition, some rank effects are positive while others are negative even individuals with all high or all low ranks will tend to have medium scores on the dependent variable. In our communities, rank dimensions tended to be correlated moderately at best, rank dimensions all together controlled at best moderate amounts of variance, and sometimes one rank dimension would exhibit effects (although weak) in a direction opposite to those of the other rank dimensions.

This pattern of effects implies that extreme values of whatever is caused by social rank will be rare, and large numbers of community members will exhibit similar, moderate values of such dependent variables, by virtue of *different* combinations of social rank (see Hodge 1970:183–184, 195). In particular, people high on a given rank dimension should not differ strikingly with respect to satisfaction, political orientations, or other dependent variables from people low on that dimension. Differences should even be moderate between people holding all high ranks versus people holding all low ranks.

Further, the patterns of rank effects varied considerably from one dependent variable to another. This involves yet another qualification of the notion of rank differences in attitude and behavior: Individuals different in education might well differ in anomia, but would tend to be more alike in their attitudes toward what we have called domestic liberalism. Hence, whatever rank differences may exist with respect to one attitude or behavior would not tend to be strongly reinforced by similarly distributed differences with respect to some other dependent variable.

Our results, then, tend to argue against any notion that differences in social rank tend to polarize contemporary American communities or produce clear and compelling differences in life style.

Finally, what do our findings imply for the view that American communities are structured as a hierarchy of more or less well-developed social classes which affect and organize behavior to a considerable degree? Is it accurate or helpful to talk about the "upper middle class" or the "working class" in describing either the structure of inequality or the way in which behavior is related to inequality?

Our results strongly suggest that contemporary Americans are individually influenced more by occupying ranks of varying kinds than by belonging to a social class defined by a general level of achievement or inheritance. We do not say this because of the generally moderate-to-low levels of variance explained by rank: Behavior could be organized by social classes while still being affected by a large number of other factors more or less unrelated to these classes. However, several other features of our data do tend to reject a class view of rank effects. If social classes were active agents in our community, we should expect to find one or more of five features in our data.

1. Organized and culturally distinct social classes imply substantial degrees of class crystallization and class inheritance. That is, the correlations among present rank variables and among present and origin rank variables should be relatively high. However, these correlations were actually moderate to low in all our communities.

2. If classes—rank-based interacting groups with relatively distinctive subcultures—do exist, some rank effects might well be nonadditive, that is, the effect of one rank would depend upon the value of others. If it is membership in a social class that causes a person to have some level of satisfaction or possess a given type of political orientation, then having some of the characteristics associated with the group will not produce the effect unless they occur with actual group membership itself. In the data, this would show up as a finding that, for example, having a white-collar occupation does not make a Republican unless the person has the proper school-inculcated culture to go with it, and being a college graduate won't produce a Republican unless one holds a job in management, but being a college-educated manager establishes a position in the upper middle class which makes one solidly Republican. However, our analyses in Chapter 5 established that rank effects almost always assume an additive form: The effect of one rank dimension is more or less independent of the value on other dimensions.

3. If class membership influenced individuals, we should expect roughly the same set of net rank effects to appear for the different dependent variables analyzed within a given community, namely the net effects which identify the composition of the class hierarchy. For example, if one's class position is heavily and equally influenced by occupation and education and to a somewhat lesser degree by residence, then if rank effects act via class

membership, we would expect to find that the coefficients of education and occupation would be equal with respect to every dependent variable affected by rank, and that the coefficient of residential rank should also always appear, but be smaller. We found, however, that the net coefficients for the rank variables varied considerably in order from dependent variable to dependent variable.

4. Our selection of general deprivation and interpersonal relations as intervening variables for the effects of rank was loosely based on a theory of class membership, in which class interests were thought to generate similarities which favored increased rates of interaction which in turn afforded the conditions for developing and maintaining relatively distinctive class subcultures. However, these selected variables did not turn out to have important intervening roles in the relationships between rank and the various dependent variables.

5. Finally, if social class membership is crucial to the effects of social rank, it might be expected that distinctions between social classes would be part of the general consciousness and these distinctions would be used to structure the social world. However, as the investigations in Chapter 4 made clear, we found considerable unconsciousness of class and little consensus on significant class distinctions or titles of classes.

Therefore, various features of the data tend to disconfirm the notion that social class of this kind is an important part of social reality in American communities and that class membership has an important influence on behavior and attitudes. We conclude that social rank is an important way in which communities are differentiated but that these various modes of rank differentiation have effects in and of themselves and not via incorporation into a well understood set of more or less discrete social classes.[5]

That interacting subgroups and associated distinctive subcultures associated with them exist under American conditions cannot be doubted by anyone who has experienced them. However, in this society in which crystallized and heritable social classes do not seem to exist, we begin to doubt the assumption, developed in Chapter 1, that group and culture formation are causal factors in rank-related individual behavior. On the contrary, under these conditions they may be purely expressive. High rank may result in deference and membership in the country club, respectability and a prominent pew on Sundays, and inside information along with cocktails at the mayor's table. But the dynamics of social stratification appear to depend on processes directly involved in individual rank dimen-

[5] It may be, as Lenski (1966:79–82) has suggested, that classes may arise along single rank dimensions, and these classes may involve consciousness, a sense of common interest, perception of a class enemy and intense communication within the class. If so, class conflict should be greatly mitigated or at least greatly confused by one's ability to hold membership in several classes based on several different dimensions of rank.

sions, and not on the social practices which grow up around people's tendency to express social status visibly. (A major exception to this statement in our data is that the effects of occupation on political party identification seem to depend on patterns of social interaction.) In general, rank-based social relations may be essentially derivative and without any significant causal role in our communities.

This does not indicate, of course, that classes could not form or if they did that they would not affect behavior and attitudes strongly in addition to the already present effects of rank differentiation. However, we do suggest that classes should not be expected to form in communities with as much status inconsistency, social mobility, and migration as the ones which we studied. In such settings, individuals are affected by multifarious aspects of rank rather than by membership in interacting culture-forming groups based on general rank. Contrasting social conditions might well be expected to yield different results. Where historic conditions drive similar people together in the name of a common interest, for example, we should expect class behavior in addition to, or perhaps instead of, multidimensional rank behavior.

DO SYSTEMS OF INEQUALITY DIFFER ACROSS COMMUNITIES?

The six-community design of this research was set up to compare communities which contrasted in ways that we thought might shape local systems of social stratification. The cities differed first in size and region, second in a number of known characteristics such as degree of industrialization, age distribution, and religious history and distribution, and third in a potentially infinite set of unknown and unmeasured characteristics. The question posed in this design was, do American communities represent distinct systems of stratification and contexts for the effects of social rank or do they represent local replications of the stratification of American society?

Community Differences in Stratification

In terms of distributions along the major rank dimensions, our communities differed markedly only with respect to racial–ethnic rank. Although the larger and more industrialized cities were somewhat higher than other cities in achieved characteristics such as income and occupation, the city distributions on the achieved dimensions were basically similar, probably because of the general economic requirements of a community division of labor and corresponding differences in power and influence. The existence of a local economy of course places no necessary limits on the shape of the racial–

ethnic distribution. The proportion of any given racial–ethnic group *could* conceivably vary all the way from 0% to 100% and the amount of actual variation, though less than that, is nonetheless substantial. Two of our communities had very few members of what we have called minority racial–ethnic groups and the composition of the minorities in the other four cities were quite different.

The processes of rank attainment were basically similar in our six communities. The effects of origin on early attainment and early attainment on later attainment varied little across communities, with two exceptions: There were some differences, unpatterned by region or size, in the determinination of income, and the handicaps imposed by minority rank appeared much more consistently in the two larger cities. The basic similarity across cities in process also appeared in the makeup of a principal component extracted from the relationships between all posssible pairs of rank dimensions. Nor did the communities differ in the rigidity of the stratification system: All cities exhibited similar, rather high, rates of social mobility and status inconsistency.

We should emphasize the exact meaning of this finding: The *present inhabitants* of each community exhibited, in their life histories, the same process of attainment as the present inhabitants of the other communities. This does not imply that economic conditions are identical in the different communities, but that after migration has sorted people out, communities consist of individuals who have been subject to the same attainment process. If the conditions for rank attainment differ markedly by community, these differences are felt in the selective moving and staying of individuals, rather than in producing populations whose aggregated work histories indicate different processes. For example, when the economic base of a community declines, the result a generation later is not a community of family heads whose educations were not appropriately converted into occupations or incomes, but rather an older population: The "excess" youths have moved to other communities. Hence, the processes exhibited by present populations appear to be more or less similar.

In some aspects of the perceptions of rank and attitudes about the rank system, the communities were similar; with respect to other aspects they differed somewhat. First of all, respondents tended to place themselves in a prelisted set of class titles in much the same way across communities, both in terms of the resulting frequency distribution and in terms of the way in which self-placement was affected by other rank dimensions. However, there were several respects in which the small towns tended to differ from the other cities. Class self-placement was determined less strongly (although in the same fashion) by objective ranks in the small towns. Working class respondents were less likely to see community dissensus in the small towns. And finally, the generally weak relationship between social rank and attributing legitimacy to the system of attaining success dropped to zero in the small towns, meaning that in this setting the disadvantaged were no more likely than the advantaged to attribute illegitimacy to the system. All these differences were more of degree than of kind.

Also, the statistical results are consistent with (but cannot prove) the proposition that self-placement is determined more by national than by local standards of ranking. That is, it does not appear that the poor attribute much higher status to themselves if they live in a relatively poor community.

In sum, our communities are surprisingly similar in many respects, especially those pertaining to the distribution on various dimensions of achieved rank, the processes for attaining achieved rank, and the processes determining subjective self-placement in a class category. It appears that even sharply different local conditions (size, region, industrial composition, etc.) do not produce sharply contrasting local systems of stratification. For example, stratification is not more rigid and success does not depend more on family background in the small towns. We will suggest below some of the reasons why local communities seem mainly to reflect national stratification patterns in these respects.

Some features of the local setting do appear, however, to have at least mild effects on some aspects of stratification. First, within limits, the distribution on occupation as well as income or education can differ across communities depending on the configuration of the local economy and the extent to which the local economy is totally self-contained. Second, substantial variations are possible with respect to racial–ethnic composition. Third, cleavages and conflict on the basis of rank may be somewhat more severe in the larger communities. In the cities, individuals of low achieved rank are more likely to place themselves in a relatively lower class category, and are more likely to deny legitimacy to the system and perceive political dissensus between businessmen and workers. Conflict between majority and minority also seems more likely, since in the large cities minority handicaps were larger and found at nearly every step of the process.

Finally, there are some trace suggestions in the data that local prestige may influence self-placement more in small towns than in larger cities. Perhaps objective rank explains less of the variance in small towns because local prestige is an important additional factor in those settings. Since our study included no direct measurement of local prestige, these must remain as strictly speculative notions. If local prestige is an important factor in small town stratification systems, it does not act to alter or disrupt the rank attainment processes found in other settings. These processes are found to be more or less similar from setting to setting. The importance of local prestige must be as an additional rank dimension affecting, possibly, perceived status and a variety of attitudes and behavior in addition to the effects of the variables measured in this study.

The Community as Context for Rank Effects: Form

The question of this section is whether rank dimensions affect individual behavior in different ways in different community settings. That is, do cities which differ in size or region or other characteristics act as different contexts for the effects of social rank? In the section on rank effects earlier in this chapter, we concentrated on those effects which tended to be found across most communities. In this section, however, we are especially interested in those rank effects which did *not* replicate across our six community samples.

Let us consider hypothetical extremes. The communities could have been so similar as to resemble six samples drawn from the same population. If so, the pattern of rank effects should have been very similar from community to community, differing only due to random fluctuation. The rank effects on anomia came close to this hypothetical extreme. At the other extreme, the direct effects of various social ranks would have to reverse, or otherwise vary wildly, from city to city, indicating no general regularities in rank effects. In fact, it would be impossible or the next thing to it to talk about rank effects at all, since every such discussion would have to be with reference to a specific community. In one city, poverty might produce dissatisfaction and anomia, while education reduced anomia, but in the next city in the sample we might see opposite patterns. Our results in Chapter 7 on the frequency of visiting relatives approximated this kind of result.

Our results for most other dependent variables fell between these two extremes: There was clear evidence that some rank effects occurred more or less consistently from community to community, accompanied by some cross-community fluctuations in the size of these replicable effects. Also, there were some relatively weak effects which fluctuated considerably from city to city. The variations across cities tended to occur within a moderate range. That is, we might observe standardized coefficients for education varying from about .25 to .10 or effects of, let us say, father's education varying from +.07 through 0 to −.07, but only very rarely would we find a very strong positive effect on a given rank dimension in one city and zero or a strong negative effect of that same dimension in other cities. It is this degree of replication that allowed us to reach the general conclusions on rank effects which were discussed above. For dependent variables strongly affected by social rank, the common effects across cities tended to swamp the variations between cities. Indeed, in many cases the between city variations were fragmentary and virtually uninterpretable. Our analyses of visiting preferences, political orientations, and the forms of intolerance tended to exhibit these consistencies coupled with minor variations. Our analysis of number of associational memberships provides a rare example of a variable powerfully affected by social rank but also exhibiting considerable variations in patterns of effects from community to community.

Cross-community variations in effects showed up principally with respect to those variables that were not powerfully affected by social rank. Our analysis of some aspects of informal and formal social participation tended to show this pattern. The additional variation explainable by taking cross-city differences into account ranged usually between 2% and 4%. Put differently, there were only infrequent instances where rank explained a considerable amount of variation in a given dependent variable within each city, coupled with substantial differences between cities in patterns of rank effects. In sum, the effects of social rank on individual behavior do tend to vary somewhat depending on the community context, but these variations are usually small relative to the replicable rank effects.

However, the findings fail to explain why the patterns vary the way they do from city to city. We had built size and regional differences into the sample, yet we almost never obtained clear differences in the form of rank effects by size or region. We had also expected that the shape of rank effects might vary depending on the social rigidity (for example, rates of mobility and status inconsistency) in the communities. This hypothesis also failed to work out, because the cities turned out to be more or less similar in their degrees of status rigidity.

The composition of the cities in terms of racial–ethnic status did have clear consequences for these effects. Columbus and Linton, with no measured minority exhibited no important racial–ethnic effects. In addition, for several dependent variables, we observed that racial–ethnic effects were stronger in Indianapolis than in the three Arizona cities, probably reflecting the fact that the minority in Indianapolis was composed almost entirely of blacks while in Arizona the minorities were either Mexican–American or Mexican–Americans combined with blacks. For some dependent variables (such as associational memberships) memberships in the different minorities had opposite consequences.

The effects of father's education, father's occupation and mother's education on many dependent variables tended to vary quite considerably across communities. In part, this was because these effects were relatively weak. However, with respect to some dependent variables the data suggested that the origin ranks had somewhat more effect in the small towns than in the medium or larger size cities. The effects of father's occupation seemed especially pronounced in the city of Safford.[6] We also had an occasional glimpse of a consistent regional effect; with respect to a few dependent variables such as the forms of formal social participation, the effects of occupation tended to be stronger in Indiana than in Arizona, while the

[6]In comparing the magnitude of the b's associated with various independent variables in the regressions of 25 dependent variables on 17 rank dimensions, the effects of father's occupation were strongest in Safford for a majority of these dependent variables.

effects of education tended to be stronger in Arizona. None of our analyses, however, have provided a clear reason for this regional effect which in any case only appeared in a few of our regressions.

Those dependent variables which were strongly affected by education tended to show relatively consistent patterns of effects from community to community. Since these tended to be attitudinal rather than behavioral variables, this may account in part for the greater consistency of effects on the attitudinal dependent variables. It would appear that in contemporary American society public education institutions promote greater cultural uniformity (within a given educational level) than do the institutions involved in the other rank systems (such as corporations, ethnic associations, etc.).

As an overall conclusion it appears that the effects of social rank on individual attitudes and behavior within a community are local variations on a basic societal theme. Although the community context does make some nonnegligible differences in the effects of social rank, these contemporary American communities do not represent fundamentally different conditions of life. The patterns of rank effects on individual behavior do, however, vary more from community to community than the patterns of effects of one rank dimension on another. The system of status attainment appears to be more constant across cities than the ways in which social ranks affect other aspects of life. Also, we do not imply that if one picks two communities he can necessarily expect similar multidimensional patterns of rank effects in both. In fact, two extreme communities may differ quite substantially from one another. But neither will differ too greatly from the pattern of the societal average.

The Community as Context for Rank Effects: Strength

Does social rank constrain behavior in general more in some communities than in others? In this section, we will investigate the strength with which social rank explains attitudes and behavior, regardless of whether the patterns of such rank effects are the same from community to community. Our original, tentative, hypotheses were that positions in the stratification system would be more constraining in Midwestern as compared to Southwestern cities, in small towns as compared to larger cities, and in those communities in which status rigidity was highest, that is, which exhibited lowest rates of social mobility and status inconsistency.

Such questions about the impact of rank in general can only be approached by comparing communities across a range of dependent variables. Our index of constraint is the proportion of variation in a given dependent variable explained by the seventeen rank variables within each of the cities.

We have seen in previous chapters some differences among cities with respect to certain dependent variables, for example, that the R^2's yielded by regressing intolerance measures on rank dimensions were generally higher in Arizona than in Indiana cities. In this analysis, we want to ask if any pattern of city differences shows up generally for a large number of dependent variables. From an initial set of 50 dependent variables, we chose the 30 variables for which the 17-variable prediction equation was significant at the .05 level in four or more of the six cities. The other 20 dependent variables were discarded on the grounds that they were essentially not influenced by social rank.

We begin, then, with 180 R^2's, representing the strength of association between a collection of rank variables on the one hand and 30 dependent variables on the other, within each of six cities. With respect to each dependent variable, we ranked the six cities by the size of their R^2's. Each city can be characterized by a distribution of its 30 ranks, by the mean rank of its 30 R^2's, and by the absolute mean of its R^2's. These data are shown in Table 12.1.

If the structure and process of inequality in a given community are clearly more constraining or coercive than in other communities, we would expect that community to have a relatively high mean R^2, but also that many of its 30 R^2's would rank first or second, yielding a mean rank somewhere between 1 and 2. To what extent do the results in Table 12.1 allow us to identify several communities as having highly constraining (or, conversely, relatively noncoercive) status systems?

The status system seems to constrain behavior somewhat more in Indianapolis and Safford and somewhat less in Linton and, especially, in

Table 12.1 *City Ranks by Amount of Variation Explained in 30 Dependent Variables by Dimensions of Social Rank*

Rank of R^2	Indianapolis	Columbus	Linton	Phoenix	Yuma	Safford	Total
1 (largest)	11[a]	5	3	0	3	8	30
2	3	7	7	2	6	5	30
3	4	5	2	4	7	8	30
4	4	5	1	7	8	5	30
5	4	6	12	4	1	3	30
6 (smallest)	4	2	5	13	5	1	30
Mean rank	3.0	3.2	3.9	4.7	3.4	2.8	
Mean R^2	.149	.144	.121	.108	.135	.156	

[a] To be read as follows: For 11 of the 30 dependent variables, the 17 rank dimensions explained more variance in Indianapolis than in the other five cities. Similarly, for three dependent variables the Indianapolis R^2 was second largest among the six city R^2's.

Phoenix, as revealed by the mean R^2's and the mean ranks of the R^2's in Table 12.1. Closer inspection of the data, however, indicates that these differences are not so strong nor so regular as to dispel a basic impression that the cities are much alike in the general impact of social status. In the first place, the mean R^2's vary only within a relatively restricted range, from about .11 to about .16. More importantly, the ordering of the cities with respect to the size of the R^2's varies considerably from dependent variable to dependent variable. Rank may have especially strong or weak effects on some given dependent variable in some given city, that is, but the ordering of the cities varies so much by dependent variable that there is no compelling general sense in which the effects of ranks are notably stronger in one city than another. As Table 12.1 makes clear, each city ranked in every possible position with respect to some dependent variable (except for Phoenix, which never yielded the highest R^2).

In this sense, there is little consistency or regularity that gives an authoritative meaning to the way in which cities are ranked according to the average R^2. The variability is so great as to call into question the notion that any city is notable for a strong or weak impact of social stratification in general. At best, we can see some mild city differences in central tendency, but these differences are relatively unstable and relatively weak.[7]

These results disconfirm all the hypotheses which we had tentatively advanced. In the first place, the irregularities in the data incline us not to take the average orders of the cities very seriously. But even in these tentative orderings no clear patterns emerge. Constraint increases with city size in Indiana, but decreases with city size in Arizona. Therefore, there is no clear effect either of size or of region, and we are not inclined to take the interaction of size by region very seriously given both the small number of cases and the lack of any theoretical explanation for such a result. Nor does our hypothesis that social rank exercises more constraint in communities with rigid status systems fare much better. To the limited degree that we were able in Chapter 3 to order the cities by rigidity, Indianapolis was the most rigid and Yuma was the least. Constraint does appear to be relatively high in Indianapolis, but not as high as it is in Safford, a less status-rigid community. And Yuma, the least rigid community, tends to have a middling position with respect to the degree of average status constraint. In sum, the ordering of the cities with respect to constraint of status on attitudes and behavior is far from regular across dependent variables, shows only mild differences between cities and does not appear to be due to city differences in size, region, or community rates of mobility and status inconsistency.

[7]Was this ordering due to the effect of a single rank dimension? The data indicate the answer is no. When we consider, for example, the regressions for the 11 dependent variables that yielded the highest R^2 in Indianapolis, we find that the set of 11 best predictors in these 11 regressions included 7 different rank dimensions.

Implications of the Results on Community Differences

The basic question we have been asking is whether a community level of social stratification is important or irrelevant in the U.S. today. We took the importance of a community level to mean that the characteristics of the community would have important effects on the patterns or processes of inequality in the community which in turn might influence the effects of social rank on individual behavior within the community.

American cities are undeniably different in many ways; we chose our cities deliberately to contrast strongly in size and region. They also turned out to differ in many other respects. We thought it plausible that differences in many of these community characteristics might well produce differences in social stratification and its workings in the city. First of all, we thought systems of community stratification must vary with community size, for several reasons (see Lasswell 1959; Fischer 1972). Small towns might well have less extended ranges in occupation and income. This might mean that the processes of rank attainment might be different in such places, and also that relative deprivation might be less extreme. In smaller communities, each person should possess more information about other people and therefore a person's present and past social ranks are likely to be widely known in detail. Informal social controls might also be more effective. These factors suggest that a small town resident should find it more difficult to attain a position "inappropriate" to his background or other current ranks. This greater rigidity might also be matched by greater social constraint in a small town, that is, insistence that people's styles of life match their social ranks.

We also expected that community differences in region might be crucial, partly because of regional economies and partly because of regional differences in subculture. It seemed possible that status differences would be more salient in the older regions of the country than in the others. Regional differences in the definition and salience of racial–ethnic rank also seemed potentially important. The extent to which racial–ethnic rank is related to status achievement might well vary from community to community because of the degree of prejudice and discrimination organized into the normative system of the region.

Community differences in economic base might also have important effects on stratification systems. The nature of the major economic activities in the community (the importance of manufacturing, for example) should affect the occupation and income distributions in the community. In addition, the prosperity of the community's economy should affect the degree of in-migration which in turn should be related to the extent of social mobility. Since our communities differed deliberately in size and region and turned out to differ substantially in economic activities and in rates of in-migration, as well as in many other respects, we were prepared to find that they differed substantially in their systems of social stratification.

What city differences we found, as summarized above, were not as striking as we might have expected. Indeed, the similarities between the communities were usually so marked as to lead us to think of the cities as local developments of a single underlying pattern, rather than as unique systems of stratification. Our results do not prove that various aspects of rank may not be manufactured within each community, nor that local conditions might not have some influence on social stratification. However, they do suggest that such local phenomena do not seriously alter the process of rank attainment nor the relationships between individual social ranks and individual social behavior.

The differences which we did observe between communities were not clearly patterned by either city size or region. Small towns usually did not differ in any predictable way from the other cities nor were Southwestern cities regularly different from Midwestern cities. We had also thought that stratification systems might operate differently in communities with high as opposed to low rates of mobility and status inconsistency, but this hypothesis was not supported either. (Although our test of this generalization was weak, since our communities did not turn out to differ greatly in these respects.) The only community characteristic which did seem effective was racial–ethnic composition, which, logically enough, did affect the way in which the minority–majority distinction influenced individual behavior within the cities. We concluded that the stratification system of each community seems mainly to be a particular embodiment of a national system of stratification. In most respects, it seems more reasonable to think of the communities as fluctuating around a central process which holds throughout the society, rather than as qualitatively different community systems.

Why are the regularities between communities more marked than the differences? Why should stratification at the level of the society–nation apparently dominate stratification at the community level? We seek here for society-wide processes strong enough to override important differences in local conditions.

Consider first the "rules" which state how much education is needed for a job, the kinds of job and job performance required for a certain salary, etc., in other words, the rules which translate rank on one dimension into the appropriate rank on another. For several reasons, these rules of translation may well be the same in all communities within this society. Some of these rules may reflect technological requirements of an occupation position which in any community must be met for the successful performance of that job. The culture of the society may also reinforce some of these rules or prescribe others, for example, that doctors require more education than bricklayers. Some rules of translation may take their place in the general culture because of the success of an occupational group in raising standards for entrance to reduce competition, increase prestige, and increase income.

The rules of translation will also tend to be similar throughout the country because they are often administered by business corporations or by labor unions which operate on a national level and hence bring more or less uniform rules into any community they enter. As more of the economy comes to be handled by these national bureaucracies, their standards and practices come to overshadow those of any local community.

Uniformities in the relationships between education, occupation and income (that is, in the process of rank attainment) may also be encouraged by the operation of national or regional labor markets. Such markets require both widespread communication and migration. Suppose, for example, that a given job in a particular community requires more education or pays less money than the same job elsewhere. If communication (through the mass media or by word of mouth from fellow employees or relatives) is easy and migration is feasible, individuals will seek that same job in that elsewhere. Under these conditions, that is, people who are locally disadvantaged have the right if not the duty to move to another locality where better opportunities exist. Thus, communication and the feasibility of out-migration should press local communities toward rules of translation as favorable (or as unfavorable) as they are elsewhere. This argument is underlined by the fact that a majority of the respondents in all six of our communities were in-migrants.

If migration were not present, each community would have to place in its local occupational structure all persons growing up there. If educational attainment rose while occupations were stable, some relatively well-educated people would have to take medium-prestige jobs, thus changing the education–occupation relationship. But if migration is possible, such persons seek appropriate employment anywhere in the region or in the nation. With the process of rank exchange thus not restricted to local environments, the same pattern of equilibration can appear at all places in the country; the market place for rank exchange thus becomes the whole nation rather than separate markets existing in each community. Communication and migration thus allow and encourage uniform processes of rank attainment throughout the society.

We might expect also that these same conditions would encourage or at least permit the styles of life of persons of the same rank levels to be rather similar regardless of where they happen to live. Uniform rank effects should also be encouraged if the societal system of distribution is efficient. If the same kinds of goods are available everywhere, then wealth can be converted into the same sorts of consumption in all communities. The distribution of information by the mass media naturally encourages and strengthens this unifying process. Indeed, the mass media are the major system of distribution for many ideas and attitudes, so that as individuals of somewhat different educational levels partake of somewhat different sorts of mass media information throughout the country, attitudinal differences between educational levels tend to become uniform nationwide. The end result is that not only are ranks translated into other ranks in a similar fashion across the society, but rank levels are also more or less uniformly translated into styles of life.

For these reasons, American communities tend to be similar rather than unique arenas for rank attainment and status diplay. If people, goods, and information flow more or less freely throughout the society and if the rules of rank translation are more or less uniform, then a picture emerges in which each community contributes its share of the population to the nation's labor force and draws from the national labor force workers for its local occupational structure, but only to a limited degree imposes special conditions on these processes. Hence, local communities, although perhaps unique in many respects, are in their stratification systems mainly local manifestations of a national pattern.

REFERENCES

Antunes, George and Charles M. Gaitz
   1975 "Ethnicity and participation: A study of Mexican Americans, blacks and whites."
        American Journal of Sociology 80:1192–1211.
Artz, Reta D., Richard F. Curtis, Dianne Timbers Fairbank, and Elton F. Jackson
   1971 "Community rank stratification: A factor analysis." *American Sociological Review*
        36:985–1002.
Babchuck, Nicholas and Alan Booth
   1969 "Voluntary association membership: A longitudinal analysis." *American Sociological
        Review* 34:31–45.
Babchuck, Nicholas and Ralph Thompson
   1962 "The voluntary associations of Negroes." *American Sociological Review* 27:647–
        655.
Benoit-Smullyan, Emile
   1944 "Status, status types and status interrelationships." *American Sociological Review*
        9:151–161.
Bettelheim, Bruno and Morris Janowitz
   1964 *Social Change and Prejudice.* New York: Free Press.
Blalock, Hubert M., Jr.
   1966 "The identification problem and theory building: The case of status inconsistency."
        American Sociological Review 31:52–61.
   1967a *Toward a Theory of Minority-Group Relations.* New York: Wiley.
   1967b "Causal inferences, closed populations, and measures of association." *American
        Political Science Review* 61:130–136.
   1968 "Theory building and causal inferences." Pp. 155–198 in H. M. Blalock, Jr. and A. B.
        Blalock (Eds.), *Methodology in Social Research.* New York: McGraw-Hill.
   1972 *Social Statistics.* Second edition. New York: McGraw-Hill.
   1975 "The confounding of measured and unmeasured variables: the case of social status."
        Sociological Methods and Research 3:355–383.
Blau, Peter M. and Otis Dudley Duncan
   1967 *The American Occupational Structure.* New York: Wiley.
Blum, Alan F.
   1964 "Social structure, social class, and participation in primary relationships." Pp. 195–
        207 in A. Shostak and W. Gomberg (Eds.), *Blue-Collar World: Studies of the Ameri-
        can Worker.* Englewood Cliffs, New Jersey: Prentice-Hall.

Bogardus, Emory S.
1956 "Racial distance changes in the United States." *Sociology and Social Research* 43:127–135.
1959 "Racial reactions by regions." *Sociology and Social Research* 4:286–290.
Borhek, J. T.
1965 "A theory of incongruent experience." *Pacific Sociological Review* 8:89–95.
Bradburn, Norman M. and David Caplovitz
1965 *Reports on Happiness.* Chicago: Aldine.
Burstein, Paul
1972 "Social structure and individual political participation in five countries." *American Journal of Sociology* 77:1087–1110.
Campbell, Angus
1971 White Attitudes Toward Black People. Ann Arbor, Michigan: Institute for Social Research.
Campbell, Angus, Philip Converse, Warren E. Miller, and Donald E. Stokes
1960 *The American Voter.* New York: Wiley.
Carr, Leslie G.
1971 "The Srole items and acquiescence." *American Sociological Review* 36:287–293.
Centers, Richard
1949 *The Psychology of Social Classes.* Princeton: The Princeton University Press.
Cohen, Albert K.
1955 *Delinquent Boys.* New York: Free Press.
Cohen, Jacob
1968 "Multiple regression as a general data-analytic system." *Psychological Bulletin* 70:426–443.
Coleman, James
1964 *Introduction to Mathematical Sociology.* New York: Free Press.
Coleman, Richard P. and Bernice L. Neugarten
1971 *Social Status in the City.* San Francisco: Jossey-Bass.
Converse, Philip E.
1964 "The nature of belief systems in mass publics." Pp. 206–261 in D. Apter (Ed.), *Ideology and Discontent.* New York: Free Press.
Collins, Randall
1971 "Functional and conflict theories of educational stratification." *American Sociological Review* 36:1002–1019.
Curtis, Richard F.
1963 "Differential association and the stratification of the urban community." *Social Forces* 42:68–77.
Curtis, Richard F., Dianne M. Timbers, and Elton F. Jackson
1967 "Prejudice and urban social participation." *American Journal of Sociology* 73:235–244.
Davis, Allison, Burleigh B. Gardner, and Mary R. Gardner
1941 Deep South: A Social Anthropological Study of Caste and Color. Chicago: University of Chicago Press.
Davis, James A.
1975 "Communism, conformity, cohorts and categories: American tolerance." *American Journal of Sociology* 81:491–513.
Dean, Dwight D.
1961 "Alienation: Its meaning and measurement." *American Sociological Review* 26:753–758.
Duncan, Beverly
1967 "Education and social background." *American Journal of Sociology* 72:363–372.
Duncan, Beverly and Otis Dudley Duncan

1968 "Minorities and the process of stratification." *American Sociological Review* 33:356–364.

Duncan, Otis Dudley
1961 "A socioeconomic index for all occupations." Pp. 109–138 in Albert J. Reiss, Jr. with Otis Dudley Duncan, Paul K. Hatt and Cecil C. North, *Occupations and Social Status.* New York: Free Press.
1966a "Methodological issues in the analysis of social mobility." Pp. 51–97 in N. J. Smelser and S. M. Lipset (Eds.), *Social Structure and Mobility in Economic Development.* Chicago: Aldine.
1966b "Path analysis: sociological examples." *American Journal of Sociology* 72:1–16.
1968 "Inheritance of poverty or inheritance of race?" Pp. 85–110 in D. P. Moynihan (Ed.), *On Understanding Poverty.* New York: Basic Books.
1975 *Introduction to Structural Equation Models.* New York: Academic Press.

Duncan, Otis Dudley, David L. Featherman, and Beverly Duncan
1972 *Socio-economic Background and Achievement.* New York: Seminar Press.

Durkheim, Emile
1897 *Suicide.* Translated by John A. Spaulding and George Simpson (1951). New York: Free Press.

Erbe, William
1964 "Social involvement and political activity." *American Sociological Review* 29:198–215.

Erlanger, Howard S.
1974 "Social class and corporal punishment in childrearing: a reassessment." *American Sociological Review* 39:68–85.

Fairbank, Dianne Timbers
1973 The Measurement and Interrelations of Components of Authoritarianism in Arizona and Indiana Communities. Ph.D. dissertation: University of Arizona.

Featherman, David
1971a "The socioeconomic achievement of white religio-ethnic subgroups: Social and psychological explanations." *American Sociological Review* 36:207–222.
1971b "A research note: a social structural model for the socio-economic career." *American Journal of Sociology* 77:293–304.

Fischer, Claude S.
1972 " 'Urbanism as a Way of Life': A review and an agenda." *Sociological Methods and Research* 1:187–242.

Form, William H.
1975 "The social construction of anomie: A four-nation study of industrial workers." *American Journal of Sociology* 80:1165–1191.

Form, William H. and Gregory P. Stone
1957 "Urbanism, anonymity, and status symbolism." *American Journal of Sociology* 62:504–514.

Freedman, Ronald, Amos H. Hawley, Werner S. Landecker, Gerhard E. Lenski, and Horace Miner
1956 *Principles of Sociology.* New York: Henry Holt.

Fuguitt, Glenn V. and Stanley Lieberson
1974 "Correlation of ratios or difference scores having common terms." Pp. 128–144 in Herbert L. Costner (Ed.), *Sociological Methodology 1973–1974.* San Francisco: Jossey-Bass.

Gabennesch, Howard
1972 "Authoritarianism as world view." *American Journal of Sociology* 77:857–875.

Giffin, Roscoe
1962 "Appalachian newcomers in Cincinnati." Pp. 79–84 in Thomas R. Ford (Ed.), *The Southern Appalachian Region.* Lexington: The University of Kentucky Press.

Goldthorpe, John H., David Lockwood, Frank Bechhofer, and Jennifer Platt
  1969 The Affluent Worker in the Class Structure. Cambridge: Cambridge University Press.
Goodman, L. A.
  1969 "How to ransack social mobility tables and other kinds of cross-classification tables."
        American Journal of Sociology 75:1–40.
Granovetter, Mark S.
  1973 "The strength of weak ties." American Journal of Sociology 73:1360–1380.
Greenblum, Joseph and Leonard I. Pearlin
  1953 'Vertical mobility and prejudice: A socio-psychological analysis." Pp. 480–490 in R.
        Bendix and S. M. Lipset (Eds.), Class, Status and Power. New York: Free Press.
Greer, Scott and Peter Orleans
  1962 "Mass society and parapolitical structure." American Sociological Review 27:634–
        646.
Gross, Neal
  1953 "Social class identification in the urban community." American Sociological Review
        18:398–403.
Guest, Avery M.
  1974 "Class consciousness and American political attitudes." Social Forces 52:496–510.
Hamilton, Richard F.
  1972 Class and Politics in the United States. New York: Wiley.
Hauser, Robert M. and Arthur S. Goldberger
  1971 "The treatment of unobservable variables in path analysis." Pp. 81–117 in H. L.
        Costner (Ed.), Sociological Methodology 1971. San Francisco: Jossey-Bass.
Hochbaum, Godfrey, John Darley, E. D. Monachesi, and Charles Bird
  1955 "Socioeconomic variables in a large city." American Journal of Sociology 61:31–38.
Hodge, Robert W.
  1970 "Social integration, psychological well-being, and their socioeconomic correlates."
        Pp. 182–206 in E. O. Laumann (ed.), Social Stratification: Research and Theory for
        the 1970's. Indianapolis: Bobbs-Merrill.
Hodge, Robert W. and Donald J. Treiman
  1966 "Occupational mobility and attitudes toward Negroes." American Sociological Re-
        view 31:93–102.
  1968a "Class identification in the United States." American Journal of Sociology 73:535–
        548.
  1968b "Social participation and social status." American Sociological Review 33:722–740.
Hollingshead, August B.
  1949 Elmtown's Youth: The Impact of Social Classes on Adolescents. New York: Wiley.
Hollingshead, August B. and Fredrick C. Redlich.
  1958 Social Class and Mental Illness: A Community Study. New York: Wiley.
Hope, Keith
  1975 "Models of status inconsistency and social mobility effects." American Sociological
        Review 40:322–343.
Hyman, Herbert and Charles R. Wright
  1971 "Trends in voluntary association memberships of American adults: Replication based
        on secondary analysis of national sample surveys." American Sociological Review
        36:191–206.
Institute for Social Research, University of Michigan
  1974 "Measuring the quality of life in America." Newsletter 2:3–6.
Jackman, Mary R. and Robert W. Jackman
  1973 "An interpretation of the relation between objective and subjective social status."
        American Sociological Review 38:569–582.
Jackson, Elton F. and Richard F. Curtis
  1968 "Conceptualization and measurement in the study of social stratification." Pp. 112–

149 in H. M. Blalock, Jr. and Ann B. Blalock (Eds.), *Methodology in Social Research.* New York: McGraw-Hill.

1972 "Effects of vertical mobility and status inconsistency: A body of negative evidence." *American Sociological Review* 37:701–713.

Jencks, Christopher, Marshall Smith, Henry Acland, Mary Jo Bane, David Cohen, Herbert Ginnis, Barbara Heyns, and Stephan Michelson
1972 *Inequality: A Reassessment of the Effect of Family and Schooling in America.* New York: Basic Books.

Kish, Leslie
1965 *Survey Sampling.* New York: John Wiley.

Klatzky, Sheila R.
1972 *Patterns of Contact with Relatives.* Washington, D.C.: American Sociological Association.

Kleiner, Robert J. and Seymour Parker
1963 "Goal-striving, social status, and mental disorder: A research review." *American Sociological Review* 28:189–203.

Knoke, David
1972 "A causal model for the political party preferences of American men." *American Sociological Review* 37:679–689.

Kohn, Melvin L. and Carmi Schooler
1969 "Class, occupation and orientation." *American Sociological Review* 34:659–678.

Land, Kenneth C.
1969 "Principles of path analysis." Pp. 3–37 in E. F. Borgatta and G. W. Bohrnstedt (Eds.), *Sociological Methodology 1969.* San Francisco: Jossey-Bass.

Landecker, Werner S.
1960a "Class crystallization and its urban pattern." *Social Research* 27:308–320.
1960b "Class boundaries." *American Sociological Review* 25:868–877.

Lane, Angela
1968 "Occupational mobility in six cities." *American Sociological Review* 33:740–749.

Lasswell, Thomas E.
1959 "Social class and size of community." *American Journal of Sociology* 64:505–508.

Laumann, Edward O.
1966 *Prestige and Association in an Urban Community: An Analysis of an Urban Stratification System.* Indianapolis: Bobbs-Merrill.
1973 *Bonds of Pluralism.* New York: Wiley-Interscience.

Lazarsfeld, Paul F.
1959 "Problems in methodology." Pp. 39–78 in R. K. Merton, L. Broom and L. S. Cottrell, Jr. (Eds.), *Sociology Today: Problems and Prospects.* New York: Basic Books.

Lenski, Gerhard
1954 "Status crystallization: A non-vertical dimension of social status." *American Sociological Review* 19:405–413.
1963 *The Religious Factor.* Revised edition. New York: Doubleday.
1966 *Power and Privilege: A Theory of Social Stratification.* New York: McGraw-Hill.

Lenski, Gerhard E. and John C. Leggett
1960 "Caste, class and deference in the research interview." *American Journal of Sociology* 65:463–467.

Lipset, Seymour M.
1959a "Democracy and working class authoritarianism." *American Sociological Review* 24:482–501.
1959b "Social stratification and right-wing extremism." *The British Journal of Sociology* 10:346–382.
1960 *Political Man: The Social Bases of Politics.* New York: Doubleday.

Mann, Michael
   1970   "The social cohesion of liberal democracy." *American Sociological Review*
          35:423–439.
Meier, Dorothy L. and Wendell Bell
   1959   "Anomia and differential access to the achievement of life goals." *American
          Sociological Review* 24:189–202.
Merton, Robert K.
   1957   "Continuities in the theory of social structure and anomie." Pp. 131–194 in Merton,
          Social Theory and Social Structure. Revised edition. Glencoe, Illinois: Free Press.
Meyer, John W. and Phillip E. Hammond
   1971   "Forms of status inconsistency." *American Journal of Sociology* 50:91–101.
Mills, C. Wright
   1956   *The Power Elite*. New York: Oxford University Press.
Morse, Nancy
   1953   *Satisfactions in the white collar job*. Survey Research Center: University of Michigan.
Mueller, Charles W.
   1974   "City effects on socioeconomic achievements: The case of large cities." *American
          Sociological Review* 39:652–657.
Mueller, Charles W. and Weldon T. Johnson
   1975   "Socio-economic status and religious participation." *American Sociological Review*
          40:785–800.
Muir, Donald and Eugene Weinstein
   1962   "The social debt: An investigation of lower-class and middle-class norms of social
          obligation." *American Sociological Review* 27:532–539.
Myrdal, Gunnar
   1944   *An American Dilemma*. New York: Harper.
Olsen, Marvin E.
   1970   "Social and political participation of Blacks." *American Sociological Review*
          35:682–697.
   1972   "Social participation and voting turnout: A multivariate analysis." *American
          Sociological Review* 27:317–333.
Orum, Anthony M.
   1966   "A reappraisal of the social and political participation of Negroes." *American Journal
          of Sociology* 72:32–46.
Otto, Luther B. and David L. Featherman
   1975   "Social structure and psychological antecedents of self-estrangement and powerless-
          ness." *American Sociological Review* 40:701–719.
Perrucci, Robert
   1961   "The significance of intra-occupational mobility: Some methodological and theoreti-
          cal notes, together with a case study of engineers." *American Sociological Review*
          26:874–883.
Ploch, Donald
   1968   "Status inconsistency: A method of measurement and substantive evaluation." Ph.D.
          dissertation: University of North Carolina.
Reiss, Albert J. *with* Otis Dudley Duncan, Paul K. Hatt and Cecil C. North
   1961   *Occupations and Social Status*. New York: Free Press.
Rokeach, Milton
   1960   *The Open and Closed Mind*. New York: Basic Books.
Rosen, Bernard C.
   1959   "Race, ethnicity, and the achievement syndrome." *American Sociological Review*
          24:47–60.
Ross, J. C. and R. H. Wheeler
   1971   Black Belonging. Westport, Conn.: Greenwood.

Schnore, Leo F.
1967 "Community." Pp. 82–150 in N. J. Smelser (Ed.), *Sociology: An Introduction*. New York: Wiley.

Schooler, Carmi
1972 "Social antecedents of adult psychological functioning." *American Journal of Sociology* 78:299–321.

Schuessler, Karl
1971 Analyzing Social Data: A Statistical Orientation. Boston: Houghton-Mifflin.

Secord, Paul F. and Carl W. Backman
1974 *Social Psychology*. Second edition. New York: McGraw-Hill.

Seeman, Melvin
1959 "On the meaning of alienation." *American Sociological Review* 24:783–791.
1975 "Alienation studies." Pp. 91–123 in A. Inkeles, J. Coleman and N. Smelser (Eds.), *Annual Review of Sociology, Vol. I*. Palo Alto, California: Annual Reviews Inc.

Sewell, William H., A. O. Haller, and George W. Ohlendorf
1970 "The educational and early occupational attainment process: Replication and revision." *American Sociological Review* 35:1014–1027.

Sewell, William H. and Robert M. Hauser
1975 *Education, Occupation, and Earnings: Achievements in the Early Career*. New York: Academic Press.

Silberstein, Fred B. and Melvin Seeman
1959 "Social mobility and prejudice." *American Journal of Sociology* 65:258–264.

Simpson, Richard L. and H. Max Miller
1963 "Social status and anomie." *Social Problems* 10:256–264.

Smith, David Horton
1975 "Voluntary action and voluntary groups." Pp. 247–270 in A. Inkeles, J. Coleman and N. Smelser (Eds.), *Annual Review of Sociology, Vol. I*. Palo Alto, California: Annual Reviews Inc.

Sorokin, Pitirim
1927 *Social Mobility*. New York: Harper and Brothers.

Srole, Leo
1956 "Social integration and certain corollaries: An exploratory study." *American Sociological Review* 21:709–716.

Stirling, Robert M.
1973 A Definition of Ultra-Conservative Ideology. Ph.D. dissertation: Indiana University.

Stouffer, Samuel A.
1955 *Communism, Conformity, and Civil Liberties: A Cross-Section of the Nation Speaks Its Mind*. New York: Doubleday.

Theil, Henri
1970 "On the estimation of relationships involving qualitative variables." *American Journal of Sociology* 76:103–154.

Treiman, Donald J.
1966 "Status discrepancy and prejudice." *American Journal of Sociology* 71:651–664.

Tully, Judy C., Elton F. Jackson, and Richard F. Curtis
1970 "Trends in occupational mobility in Indianapolis." *Social Forces* 49:186–200.

Veblen, Thorstein
1899 *The Theory of the Leisure Class*. New York: Macmillan.

Warner, W. Lloyd
1949 *Democracy in Jonesville: A Study of Quality and Inequality*. New York: Harper and Brothers.
1960 *Social Class in America*. New York: Harper and Row.

Warner, W. Lloyd and Paul S. Lunt
1941 *The Social Life of a Modern Community*. New Haven, Conn.: Yale University Press.

Weber, Max
  1925 "Class, status, party." Pp. 180–195 in H. H. Gerth and C. W. Mills (Translators and Eds.), *From Max Weber: Essays in Sociology* (1946). New York: Oxford University Press.
Whitt, Hugh P. and Hart Nelsen
  1975 "Residence, moral traditionalism and tolerance of atheists." *Social Forces* 54:328–340.
Whyte, William Foote
  1955 *Street Corner Society: The Social Structure of an Italian Slum.* Chicago: University of Chicago Press.
Wilensky, Harold L.
  1966a "Measures and effects of social mobility." Pp. 98–140 in N. J. Smelser and S. M. Lipset (Eds.), *Social Structure and Mobility in Economic Development.* Chicago: Aldine.
  1966b "Class, class consciousness and American workers." Pp. 12–44 in William Haber (Ed.), *Labor in a Changing America.* New York: Basic Books.
Williams, J. Allen, Nicholas Babchuck, and David R. Johnson
  1973 "Voluntary associations and minority status: A comparative analysis of Anglo, Black and Mexican Americans." *American Sociological Review* 38:637–646.
Williams, Robin M., Jr.
  1964 *Strangers Next Door: Ethnic Relations in American Communities.* Englewood Cliffs, N. J.: Prentice-Hall.
Wirth, Louis
  1938 "Urbanism as a way of life." *American Journal of Sociology* 44:3–24.
Woelfel, Joseph and Archibald O. Haller
  1971 "Significant others, the self-reflexive act and the attitude formation process." *American Sociological Review* 36:74–87.
Wright, Charles R. and Herbert H. Hyman
  1958 "Voluntary association memberships of American adults: Evidence from national sample surveys." *American Sociological Review* 23:284–294.
Young, Ruth and Olaf Larson
  1965 "The contribution of voluntary organizations to community structure." *American Journal of Sociology* 71:178–186.

Index

QUANTITATIVE STUDIES IN SOCIAL RELATIONS

Consulting Editor: Peter H. Rossi

UNIVERSITY OF MASSACHUSETTS
AMHERST, MASSACHUSETTS

Seymour Sudman, APPLIED SAMPLING

James D. Wright, THE DISSENT OF THE GOVERNED: *Alienation and Democracy in America*

Roland J. Liebert, DISINTEGRATION AND POLITICAL ACTION: *The Changing Functions of City Governments in America*

Walter Williams and Richard F. Elmore, SOCIAL PROGRAM IMPLEMENTATION

Edward O. Laumann and Franz U. Pappi, NETWORKS OF COLLECTIVE ACTION: *A Perspective on Community Influence Systems*

Eric Hanushek and John Jackson, STATISTICAL METHODS FOR SOCIAL SCIENTISTS

Richard F. Curtis and Elton F. Jackson, INEQUALITY IN AMERICAN COMMUNITIES

In Preparation

Richard A. Berk, Harold Brackman, and Selma Lesser, THE MEASURE OF JUSTICE: *An Empirical Study of Criminal Law Change*

Donald J. Treiman, OCCUPATIONAL PRESTIGE IN COMPARATIVE PERSPECTIVE